Discovering the Beauty of Wisdom

Embracing Mysticism through the Ancient Path of Greek Philosophy

Mindy Mandell

The Prometheus Trust

The Prometheus Trust
14 Tylers Way,
Sedbury, Chepstow,
Gloucestershire, NP16 7AB, UK

A registered charity, number 299648

www.prometheustrust.co.uk

Discovering the Beauty of Wisdom
Embracing Mysticism through the Ancient Path of Greek Philosophy

Mindy Mandell

ISBN 978 1 898910 725

British Library Cataloguing-in-Publication Data. A catalogue record for this book is available from the British Library.

Printed in the UK by 4edge Limited, Hockley

To Nori

Table of Contents
Abridged

Table of Contents

Expanded

Introduction

What does it mean to live as a mystic? Perhaps you've picked up this book because you are curious about this lifestyle, yet imagine that you could never embrace it for yourself. Would you even want to? Aren't mystics special people, born with a strong inner calling to live off the beaten path? They are not like you and me. They are a strange breed who stand apart from society, never having been plagued by the insecurities or fears that challenge the rest of us, or tempted by images of the so-called "good life" such as wealth, fame and romance.

I used to hold such beliefs about mystics, too. When I first discovered Plato's dialogues in the late 1990s, I enjoyed his presentation of Socrates who very much fits this stereotype of the wise mystic. Peeking into the mind of this ancient sage filled me with wonder and an odd sense of connection, even though my lifestyle was nothing like his.

I was inspired by the mental challenges Socrates presented me with, yet I had no idea back then the power his way of reasoning has. I found myself getting sucked deeper and deeper into the unknown, questioning beliefs I hadn't even realized I held—everything from the universal metaphysical questions about God and reality to the most personal and private questions about who I really am. I've come a long way, and the journey I'm traveling has me convinced that anybody can break free from the shackles of images and false beliefs that hold us back from knowing true freedom.

To be truly free is to know and experience the world through the healthy state of mind that flourishes when we know our true nature. Our essence is far beyond the bodies that house us. It is beautiful and divine, and to touch this truth and to know it firsthand brings an undeniable shift to our states of mind. Our changed perspective welcomes into our lives a clearer sense of purpose and meaning, and so we relate differently to nature, society, and everyone we come into contact with.

This transition from who we were at the start of our journey is a gradual one, and it may take many years to mature. Yet don't dispair, for the journey itself is one to be valued and enjoyed. Mysticism is a way of life—a lifestyle that may seem daunting at the onset when these ideas are new to you, but is actually exciting and enriching. It takes hard work, fortitude, and commitment, but embracing a mystic practice can be done.

There are many misunderstandings about what mysticism is. I opened this Introduction with a few of the misconceptions I used to hold. *Mysticism* comes from the Greek word *mystikos,* which refers to initiation into one of the pagan religions of the ancient Greek world, known collectively as Mystery schools. Outside of those schools, little was known even to their contemporaries as to what precisely was taught to these initiates. We also can look to other traditions such as Hinduism and Buddhism for further examples of mystic systems, although these too can be hard for a beginner to understand. With a wide range of teachings from system to system, and much of those teachings either cloaked in secrecy or difficult to penetrate, we are left with only vague images of people whose lifestyles seem peculiar to us. Their actions and their beliefs seem out of step with mainstream notions of common sense, and so there is a tendency to dismiss mystics and their systems of mysticism as irrational nonsense.

This is an image that I need to dispel up front. The approach to mysticism that I will focus on in this book is built on the supposition that as we cultivate understanding of the nature of Reality, we will gain a commensurate understanding of our relationship to the whole of which we are a part. This will become clearer as the book proceeds. At the root of this issue is the idea that the quest to know the nature of Reality is not separate from the quest to know ourselves. If those two quests are connected, then it follows that there must be a way in which they are connected, a means by which the nature of Reality is connected to our own essence.

Being connected implies further that each has a relationship with the other. Discovering what these relationships are and living in accordance with them is largely what defines a life of mysticism. Therefore, in contrast to common notions of mysticism as hazy thinking, I use this word to refer to a rational system of studying metaphysics—the study of the nature of Reality—and applying the insights of that study to our lives.

The hunger and drive needed to maintain this way of life wakes up little by little as we gain understanding of both the self-images we currently identify with and what we are beyond those images. Take it at your own pace; there's no hurry. And don't be discouraged if you need to take a break and return to your old ways of being from time to time. Old habits have a strong hold on us, and they take time to break down. In this book, we will look not only at ways to contemplate and internalize insights into Reality, but also at ways to understand the nature of false belief so as to break its hold on us.

Once our mystic practice ripens, we no longer compartmentalize our studies in mysticism from other areas of our lives—the outlook we gain through our practice is simply the way we see the world. Until that day comes for you, it is fine to take it just as far as you are willing to. Even if you never choose to immerse yourself completely in this way of life, you will find that you will benefit to the degree you are open to these ideas. Don't worry that you are too "ordinary" to take on a mystic practice; mysticism is accessible to everyone.

I doubt any of the kids who had known me in high school would have ever guessed I would take on the life of a mystic, or write a book that introduces this way of life to others. I was very much a typical teenager—self-conscious and insecure. Looking back, if I had to summarize in one sentence my life before I discovered mysticism, I would say: "I floated along." I learned very young, as most of us do, which roles to play to fit in. My parents divorced when I was a toddler, so I grew up with two separate families. I played one set of roles at Mom's house and another set at Dad's. At both homes, I knew which rules could be challenged and which ones couldn't, which topics of conversation were desirable, and even which sides of my sense of humor would be appreciated.

Starting grade school opened a whole new aspect of society to me and so I learned different roles to play to fit in there as well. By high school, though, all that role-playing left me exhausted. I recall many hours I spent lying across my bed, thinking that I was too young to be this tired.

I was often told that I was a smart girl, but I had nothing to show for it. Indeed, my grades were only mediocre. I wasn't athletic or musical, either, and I had no impressive hobbies or abilities. I saw nothing about myself that made me stand out as special, and so I kept floating along.

Like many other high school girls, I dreamed of having some talent that would make me the envy of my classmates, or I wished I were prettier or more outgoing. I had a love-hate relationship with the most popular kids at school. I desperately wanted to fit in. I knew how to talk and act in a way that would win me acceptance—I just had to go with the flow and bite my tongue when I disagreed with anyone. The problem was, no sooner was I accepted that I would resent the very people who believed my act. I didn't merely want to be popular—I wanted people to like *me*. I didn't want to play roles anymore, but what else was there?

We put great value on the activities we are involved in, and we largely define ourselves by the things that we do. Yet the only thing I did in high school that seemed to give my life definition was alternating between trying to live up to other people's expectations and resenting them for having any expectations of me in the first place. I quickly earned a reputation for being moody and argumentative.

A vague dissatisfaction settled in that I couldn't quite put my finger on. This was the late 1980s, when daytime talk shows were enjoying the height of their popularity and *communication* was the hot buzz word. Everybody around me seemed to be trumpeting the value of talking about my feelings and explaining this unhappiness I carried inside. This annoyed me immensely because I couldn't very well explain what I myself didn't understand. There were only so many ways to say, "I don't know what I want" and "I don't know why I'm unhappy!"

I went on to university, drifting much as I had in the earlier chapters of my life. Although I liked the image of being a strong, modern career woman, I didn't actually have any concrete career goals. Nothing I studied grabbed me or filled me with passion. By this time in my life, I was quite sure I was lazy, and I suspect that most of the people around me were convinced of this as well.

I graduated after five years with a degree in Journalism and a second major in Political Science. I had no desire to burst onto the job scene, though, so I hid out in graduate school. I emerged a year later with a Master of Arts in International Relations and a huge student loan debt—and I still had no idea what I wanted to do with my life.

A recruitment ad on a university notice board caught my eye. An English school in Japan was looking for native speakers to teach conversational English. I'd had classmates over the years who took such jobs in foreign countries. I was told that it was simple work, and it was generally seen as a break between university and "real life." That was perfect for a floater like me.

Japanese culture was so far removed from anything I had known in America that I could immerse myself in it and temporarily forget that I was drifting with no aim or direction. It took four years of life in Japan and a marriage proposal from a Japanese man for me to finally hit a crossroads. Did I want to make a life in Japan, or was I still holding onto the American dream of becoming Miss Independent Career Woman?

I got lots of conventional advice—make lists of the pros and cons of each life option, and so on—but it was one friend's observation that changed the course of my life. He told me, "Mindy, these two lifestyles are as different as two lifestyles can be. If you don't know which one fits you, then you don't know yourself—and that's the bigger problem."

His words penetrated me deeply. I felt down to the very core of my being that he was right. *I did not know myself.* This was what had plagued me even back in high school. I had been spending my life looking outside myself to define who I was. I thought happiness would come by having an active social life, falling in love, finding the right career, and eventually by building wealth and reputation. I thought happiness would be found in having the right lifestyle, the right interests and hobbies, and the right friends. I hadn't been able to figure out why I had been unhappy all those years because I was looking outside myself, and there was nothing in my external world I could point to as the problem.

My frustration at not understanding why I wasn't happy had developed into a general sense of anger at the world. I remember a woman in university once telling me I had no right to be so angry. "You turned out all right," she had told me. On the surface, I certainly had. I had friends, a loving family, and I was getting a university education. Yet her statement begs the question: what has to be going on in our lives for us to conclude that we have *not* turned out all right? Do we look only at our external world? If, for example, I have no criminal record or history of drug addiction, does this mean that I turned out all right? And if I did have such a background, would that necessarily mean that I *hadn't* turned out all right?

Too many of us live isolated lives. Everywhere I turn, I see people who are lonely, confused, and unhappy, but sure that life would be good if only they found the right job or the right lover. They tell themselves that all will be better once they move into their dream house or get that big promotion. This focus on external circumstances has even taken hold of some mainstream approaches to spirituality, with people believing that if they pray with enough vigor and sincerity, they can manifest their fantasy world and find the happiness they assume this will bring.

I used to be caught in that skewed emphasis on external circumstances too, but that talk with my friend many years ago in Japan brought me to see that my search had to turn toward the internal world of my own mind. Once I saw this, my interest in mysticism was born. My laziness vanished. I found something worth working towards.

I dabbled in Hinduism and Buddhism, but it was the ancient Greek Platonic tradition that grabbed me for its precision with language, its rigorous logic, and its attention to the healthy state of mind that is at the heart of what it really means to "turn out all right." Some twenty years later, I am still in Japan (happily married), and guided not by social goals or some company's business goals, but by the goals that are in line with a higher, truer vision of reality.

Throughout this book, I will present this vision through the lens of the Platonic tradition, which is also referred to as Platonism. This tradition actually extends both before and after the teachings of Plato. A long and prestigious Greek tradition already preceded Plato, but it is because of his dialogues that his name is most directly associated with this tradition. Plato was a teacher who drew from the wisdom of his predecessors to form a spiritual system that can guide us from a state of ignorance about the true nature of reality to direct knowledge of Reality itself and our place in the whole. He wound this system through his various dialogues, although he acknowledged in a private correspondence that his most profound insights were never written down.[1] The tenets of the metaphysics behind his system were often only hinted at and left for readers to work out for ourselves.

It was the later philosophers in this tradition who unpacked the metaphysics. Plato's dialogues, then, function as the root from which

---

[1] See his *Epistle VII*, 341c~d

these later mystics grew out. We can symbolize Plato's place in this tradition with a bow tie, representing the philosophers before Plato by one of the loops and the philosophers after him by the other. Plato, then, is like the knot in the center that holds the whole bow together.

Once I found Platonism, I never looked back. This is a tradition that is both deeply spiritual and also rigorous in its treatment of metaphysics. The language of pure metaphysics presents the study of the divine essence of Reality in terms that are not limited to any single religious tradition. The Platonists instead speak straight to the soul. It is not necessary to have studied any other religious tradition previously in order to dive into the writings of these philosophers.

However, if you are coming to this book from another religious tradition, you will likely find that there is great compatibility with Platonism. When the precision of this metaphysical language is applied to the teachings of other traditions, clarity results. In my experience, Muslims, Christians and Jews who engage with Platonism appreciate their own religious texts on a more profound level, Buddhists see deeper into the wisdom of the Buddha's teachings, and Hindus celebrate the beauty of the Sutras more fully. In the twenty years or so that I've been a student of Platonism, I've seen this time and time again among fellow students. We can all benefit to the degree that we are open to the way of thinking the Platonic tradition ushers in.

I want to introduce this beautiful tradition to a wider audience. Plato's approach to a spiritual life may seem odd at first to some people. Our modern societies tend to value activities and outward shows of spirituality over inner contemplation. We light candles and incense, we seek to know the self through dance, yoga, nature hikes, and charitable giving, and we pray or engage in other ritual activities. None of these methods are necessarily in conflict with Platonism, but none are required, either.

The Platonists instead invite us on a divine intellectual journey— 'intellectual' in a sense that goes beyond abstract thinking, for Reality itself is contemplative. Mind is our entryway into the metaphysical, or that which is beyond the physical realm. The Platonists entice us to use our minds to penetrate to our very essence, exploring the depths of that very exploration. Who or what is it that thinks? Who or what is it that is searching for its essence?

We quickly discover on our spiritual journey that the outward quest to know the nature of Reality and the inward quest to know ourselves are two sides of the same coin, for what we are in essence is no different from divine Mind. This means that the metaphysical study of realms of reality—or realms of mind—is also the study of our own states of mind. We will find that understanding and experiencing higher realms of reality manifests in our lives as healthier states of mind.

Unfortunately, Platonism is too often treated in universities as a purely academic subject. I see this as, at least in part, tied to the mistake of limiting the treatment of *intellect* to discursive thought. For Plato and the other philosophers in this tradition, however, the intellectual realms are divine. Reality is Mind itself; it is the underlying fabric of all that is.

Through Platonism, we can learn to develop inwardly and penetrate more deeply into the realms of Mind. This allows us to bring that awareness and the insights that follow from such awareness into our everyday world. Platonism, therefore, is a highly personal practice. Its function is not merely to challenge us on a theoretical level as if we were separate from our topic of study—we are transformed through our intellectual effort. For this reason, I take the perhaps uncommon position of using the words *mysticism* and *philosophy* interchangeably. This is because, like mysticism, true philosophy is an approach to life that challenges us to discover the highest reaches of human potential, allowing us to act in the world with integrity and effect goodness through our actions.

I've met many people over the years who were intrigued by the notion of such a spiritual system, but found Plato's dialogues difficult to penetrate. Plato seems to jump around from topic to topic in each dialogue, and while many people sense that there is an overall picture of reality that all these dialogues point to, it can be hard to see what that picture is. And then there are the later Platonists, some of whom will be introduced in Chapter 1. They can come across as enigmatic or highbrow before we understand what they are doing.

My aim with this book is to help those of you who are new to this tradition get started on this spiritual path, and to offer additional guidance to those already acquainted with the general structure. These teachings resonate with many readers because they speak to something within us that is beyond culture or opinion. I firmly believe that Platonism can be presented in plain English without watering down the mental rigor of its content.

While I do introduce quite a bit of the metaphysics of the Platonic tradition throughout this book, metaphysics is not my focus. I'm instead interested in exploring how these metaphysical teachings can inform a well-rounded spiritual practice. This book is intended to be used in conjunction with the core literature of the Platonic tradition, not in place of it. I'm taking for granted that anyone who picks up this book already has an interest in, and perhaps some familiarity with, Plato's dialogues and the metaphysics behind them. This book could also be of interest to anyone with a background in another mystic tradition that uses the mind to reach spiritual wisdom (such as Zen Buddhism or the Hindu path called Jnana Yoga).

While I encourage academics to pursue the mystical aspects of this tradition, I am writing for a more general audience. Therefore, I will not be surveying modern scholarship on this topic. I'm also skipping over such debates as whether humans are more than physical beings. I assume that anyone reading a book such as this one is already convinced, or at least open to, the possibility that we are.

Because this is not a scholarly work, I will also refrain from detailed discussions about the nuanced differences between one Platonic philosopher and the next. I will instead be offering a broad overview of the whole tradition that ties in various thinkers as appropriate. All is presented, of course, through my own understand of the teachings. Some readers will find points of contention; such are unavoidable in any book of this nature.

It is undoubtedly the dream of many authors to create the perfect spiritual guide: a crash-course in mysticism that will illuminate beginner and advanced students alike. But alas, that is just a fantasy. No book can act as a magic wand to instantly turn you into a sage, nor would that be a good thing. A book can open new avenues of thought to you, and can offer you guidance and direction, but you must do the work yourself.

While this task can feel overwhelming at times, it is also highly rewarding when it culminates in insights and growth. Also, let's not underestimate the satisfaction that comes from being able to look back and acknowledge your progress—and know that it was your own courage and hard work that brought you here. As with any meaningful undertaking, you will get out of this practice what you put into it.

My hope is to present the Platonic tradition in a way that is more accessible than is generally found in academic studies, making it easier to recognize the personal relevancy of these ideas. However, not all the teachings are easy. You might find that parts are a struggle, especially those parts that focus on metaphysics. That is okay. That struggle is also part of the journey. We need to learn how to work through our difficulties without getting frustrated or being too hard on ourselves. Work with what you can, and trust that clarity will come as your insights unfold.

We are not chasing an experience or seeking information that we can get just by reading a book. We are questioning what Truth is, holding each of the images in our souls under a microscope, so to speak, and testing if any of these images withstand scrutiny. Most of us spend years running down rabbit holes before tossing out what doesn't work, and clarifying and honing that which points us in the right direction.

Rather than aiming for the impossible goal of creating that magical book that is all things to all people, I instead hope to give you a trusted resource that you can come back to again and again as you grow, and as your own vision matures. I hope that each time you open this book's covers, you find, somewhere in these pages, what you need, wherever you are in your journey.

To Help You Navigate

I start the book with a few chapters that I have grouped under the heading *Surveying the Landscape*. These four chapters, as the heading implies, are intended to give an overview of the entire scope of the book. We will look at the philosophers whose thoughts have shaped the Platonic tradition. We will also see a road map of the journey outlined throughout this book and the ideal state of mind from which to approach it.

I have divided the bulk of the book into two broad categories: *Understanding* and *Knowing*. What I am calling *understanding* is the Greek *dianoia*. I am using the word *knowing* for *noesis*. These are states of mind that we experience as our practice advances. As Plato uses these two terms, *understanding* refers to a level of belief that is reached through reasoning, whereas *knowing* is rooted in direct experience of Reality itself. *Understanding* is our preparation for *knowing*, and *knowing* is the cultivation and deepening of what I will call throughout this book the wise state of mind. However, we need to do away with the misguided belief that wisdom is a state we reach in a flash and then suddenly we are transformed into sages or enigmatic gurus with supernatural gifts. It is more accurate to think of wisdom as a state of mind we grow into.

The second part of the book—*Understanding*—outlines the fundamental building blocks of the Platonic tradition. Here, we look at understanding in the sense of understanding theories and concepts and how we can apply them, to some degree, to our everyday lives. It is in the third part—*Knowing*— where we will give our skeleton flesh and bring it to life, as a different kind of understanding takes place in the realm of knowing. We will move beyond the understanding of concepts into the depths of direct experience of Reality (which I denote throughout the book with capitalization). It is also in this third section of the book that we will focus on developing a mature understanding of those direct experiences. As the book proceeds, we will also aim for a better grasp of what it means to *know* in the sense that the Platonists use this word.

Surveying the Landscape   We begin, then, with a general look at some of the main thinkers in this tradition. Chapter 1 will look not only at Plato himself, but also at some of the thinkers who influenced him, as well as a few of those who carried on the tradition after him. Chapter 2 takes a look at the general methodology that guides us. In Chapter 3, I will introduce the stages of our journey. This will include a closer look at the precise way in which I use terms such as *belief, understanding* and *knowing*. In looking at the stages of our journey, Chapter 3 will also discuss our overall goals in taking on a life of mystic philosophy.

Then, in Chapter 4, we will look at the ideal state of mind from which to approach this practice. It is not a lifestyle that appeals to everyone. A growing number of people are attracted to mysticism in theory, but embracing it as a way of life poses multiple obstacles. Chapter 4 surveys the attitude that must be cultivated to get the most out of these teachings. We will look at the four virtues—wisdom, fortitude, temperance and justice—in this light. The fullest flowering of these virtues is the mark of the truly wise person, such as the figure that Socrates represents throughout many of Plato's dialogues. We will see, however, that the development of these virtues is also in part the means by which we work towards this goal.

Understanding   Chapters 5 through 20 turn to specific methods of developing understanding. Chapter 5 will focus on the most beneficial approach to reading wisdom literature. The kind of understanding we seek is transformational; it requires more courage and brings more significant changes to our lives than the kind of understanding we gain by, for example, reading our computer's user manual. Chapter 5 will explain this more fully. Chapter 6 will build on this by adding a few study tools and techniques.

Because some readers may be coming to this book from other systems of thought, I will also include an overview of metaphysics as it is presented in the Platonic tradition. This overview is found in Chapters 7 through 13, including a chapter on the proper approach to reading mythology. All of this is presented mainly to give us a starting point—a common vocabulary and set of ideas.

Most books about the Platonic tradition begin and end with metaphysical theories about the nature of Reality. However, my intention is to focus on *how to use* these theories as the fundamental building blocks of a solid and meaningful spiritual practice. Platonism is a way of life that allows us to appreciate the mystery of our own divinity and to experience ourselves and the world around us as interconnected and rooted in beauty and goodness.

So with a basic grasp of metaphysics under our belts, we are ready to dive further into our practice. Our desire throughout our studies is not only to read metaphysics, but to internalize our insights. This is a lifelong process that unfolds gradually. Chapter 14 introduces contemplative exercises that Plato gave us to go beyond an abstract understanding of metaphysics.

When we try to immerse ourselves in ideas that differ greatly from our current views, the assumptions and beliefs through which we have become accustomed to see ourselves and the world will, of course, be challenged. This is true for all of us, whether we were raised in families hostile towards mysticism or ones open to it.

Dealing with these challenges on a personal level will be the focus of Chapters 15 and 16. We will find that throughout our journey, we must see through what is false before we can fully embrace Truth.

Chapters 17 and 18 will build on the fundamentals covered thus far by introducing energy building and meditative techniques to be used in conjunction with our reading and contemplations. Such practices are important for anybody daring to go beyond a conceptual level of understanding.

Chapter 19 will introduce Plato's famous dialectic. We will see that the aim of dialectic is far loftier than merely showing off our cleverness or playing word games with our friends. Dialectic is a means to touch Truth itself, unhindered by the assumptions that are currently blocking us from further insights.

We will wrap up the *Understanding* section with Chapter 20, which adds further contemplative methods to our practice. Reading can open us up to new ways of seeing the world, but it is only by internalizing the teachings we have read that we really shake things up and are able to see the deeper layers of assumptions that we hold.

Knowing   The remainder of the book will focus on what Plato calls *noesis*, for which I'm using the English word *knowing*. We are now ready to move beyond theories into direct experience of Reality and the understanding of such experience. As we've already seen in this Introduction, understanding at this later stage differs from understanding concepts alone (*dianoia*). It follows, then, that when we cross the threshold into knowing, our practice must alter to meet our new needs. It is a common error to think that the methods which worked in the past to build *dianoetic* understanding should simply be continued.

Chapters 21 and 22 will bring us to a discussion on wisdom. There is debate among Platonists as to whether peak experiences have any place in Plato's works or in the Platonic way of life. I will argue in Chapter 21 why they do. In Chapter 22, I will explore the states of mind of people who have integrated insights from direct peak experience into their own lives. Many people hold this state of mind as an ideal, yet few know what it truly is. Therefore, before discussing practices to take us beyond the state of mind we call understanding, we must address some expectations of where this leg of our journey will—and won't—lead us.

Chapters 23 and 24 will revisit the topic of metaphysics, building on what was discussed in the *Understanding* section of the book, and Chapters 25 and 26 focus on the various ways our practice changes at this more advanced stage of our studies. Our needs are different than they were in the early years of our practice, and so our approach must adjust accordingly to meet our current state of mind. Chapter 25 includes a more detailed look at dialectic. Chapter 26 returns to the task of reading as extended contemplation.

Chapters 27 and 28 will revisit the issue of false beliefs, where we will see that as our understanding of the nature of Reality matures, so too will our understanding of the web of false beliefs we have picked up from childhood. In Chapter 27, we will look at some common fears and obstacles that challenge us as we advance. Chapter 28 looks at some of the tools at our disposal in our efforts to understand ourselves both as spiritual beings and as individuals shaped by our families and our societies. This chapter focuses on internal dialogue, daydreams and dreams that come to us in sleep.

Finally, Chapters 29 and 30 bring us to the highest rewards of all our efforts. In Chapter 29, we will look at the role of silence as we mature spiritually, and the states of mind it initiates. Chapter 30 wraps up my presentation of Platonism by focusing on the Good itself, the first cause of all in our metaphysical system. These final chapters will focus on practices and considerations for the advanced student. They are at the end of the book because everything before them offers preparation for this stage. I therefore recommend reading the chapters in order rather than jumping to the end.

Acknowledgements

I would like to thank my fellow seekers who are Greek scholars and have generously shared their insights over the years with those of us whose knowledge of Greek is more limited. Throughout this book, all explanations of Greek terms come from these lessons, as I myself am not fluent in Greek. A special thanks to Barbara Stecker and David Coe, whose explanations of key Greek terms have been invaluable.

I would also like to thank Dr. John H Spencer for introducing me to Plato's thought all those years ago. It was he who steered me away from considering only academic interpretations and opened my mind to the deeper possibilities of where these works could lead me. While arduous periods are unavoidable in anyone's practice, the journey is always smoother if we set off on the right foot with the proper preparation. Thanks to John, I was blessed with the best possible preparation anyone could hope for.

I also wish to thank John, along with Andrea Blackie and Ayelet Baron, for their insightful editorial advice on an earlier draft of this manuscript. A special thank you goes to my sister, Marlene Tyner-Valencourt, for her helpful suggestions, as well. My heartfelt thanks to Tim and Averil Addey and everyone at Prometheus Trust for helping me bring this book to its current form and for affording me this opportunity to introduce my approach to Platonism to the world. This book is unquestionably better thanks to Tim's editorial advice and our many talks fleshing out metaphysical issues.

I further wish to thank my husband and children. I remain humbly grateful to them for tolerating my laptop on the kitchen table and paper scattered on the floor during the writing of this book. More importantly, I thank them for sharing with me this most amazing experience we call life. I feel blessed to be surrounded every day by their love and support.

Finally, this introduction would not be complete without a few words about the teacher with whom I have studied for about 20 years. Dr. Pierre Grimes is an American philosopher who was first introduced to the writings of Plato and Plotinus in 1948 while a college student in Maryland.[2] His thirst to dig deeper into this tradition took many twists and turns, and finally brought him to study comparative religions with Alan Watts in San Francisco. This fateful meeting awakened in him an appreciation for the profundity of Buddhism and its similarities to the Platonic tradition.

Grimes founded the Noetic Society in Huntington Beach, California in 1972 to pursue the philosophic study of the mind. In 1982, he met the Korean Zen master Chong-An (later given the name

---

[2] This biographical summary is drawn from Grimes and Uliana, *Philosophical Midwifery: A New Paradigm for Understanding Human Problems*, pp. 6~13.

Myo-Bong[3]). Together they founded the Opening Mind Academy in 1983 to bring together the Buddhist and Platonic traditions. That same year, Chong-An sealed Grimes as his Dharma Successor and gave him the name Hui-An.

While Grimes was not directly involved with the writing of this book, his guidance over the years has played a major role in my own evolution of thought. A few of his books are listed in the bibliography, including his principle work on pinpointing and uprooting false beliefs, *Philosophical Midwifery.* Wherever I hit the mark, surely I owe much to his guidance. To the degree that I diverge from truth, however, the error is purely my own. I am indebted to him not only in my crafting of this book but, more importantly, for steering me along a path that has greatly contributed to my own inner sense of peace.

A Few Notes on Translations and Citations

In choosing which translations of Platonic works to draw from, I quote Thomas Taylor exclusively for Plato's dialogues, except where noted. There are fewer translations of the philosophers in this tradition who followed Plato, and in some cases there is only one. When I stepped outside the Prometheus Trust's library, I have opted to go with popular translations, in part because the spiritual approach to this tradition is still a minority view. I want to demonstrate that the richness of this system comes through with almost any translation.

I also recognize that many readers may shy away from using lesser-known translations. It is natural for people new to the spiritual aspects of this tradition to be dubious of obscure translations and to trust established university presses instead. While I am sensitive to this, I would also like to offer the caveat that as our grasp of the topic matures, we are likely to question this bias.

A notable alternative to the academically rooted translations are those by a not well known but highly inspired translator and mystic named Juan Balboa.[4] I began using his translations back in 2012 and

---

[3] See *Ibid.,* pp. 12~13: Chong-An was later sealed as "the Patriarchal Dharma successor of Venerable Hye-Am, the 33rd patriarch from Lin Chi." It was at this time that he was given the name Myo-Bong.

[4] As of this printing, these translations are only available at www.lulu.com

now use them extensively. Even though he is rarely quoted in this book for the reasons given above, you can be sure that the clarity of his vision has helped me cultivate a clearer vision of my own. I would therefore be remiss not to acknowledge his contribution here.

Rather than repeating complete citations in every footnote, I have included a bibliography at the end of the book. I indicate references in footnotes as follows:

- For Plato's dialogues, the title of the dialogue and the Stephanus number along with the translator if not Thomas Taylor.

- For Damascius' *Problems and Solutions Concerning First Principles*, the page number.

- For Plotinus, the number reference to the Ennead and section number. I used the format X:x:10 to indicate ennead grouping:essay within that grouping:section within that essay. Also, I cited the translator if not Thomas Taylor.

- For Proclus' *Elements of Theology*, the proposition number and the translator if not Thomas Taylor.

- For *Proclus' Commentary on Plato's Parmenides*, the section number and page number.

- For Proclus' *Theology of Plato*, the book number and chapter number.

- For *The Commentaries of Proclus on the Timaeus of Plato*, the now standard Diehl's text numbering by book/page/line number.

- For other sources, I give the author, the title of the book and the page number.

Unless otherwise stated, all the quotes from Plato come out of the Thomas Taylor collection from the Prometheus Trust. These quotes have a few minor changes to accord with modern English, such as *every one* being changed to *everyone*. Also, there are two words in particular with which I feel that Taylor's word choice has become antiquated to the point of changing the meaning. He frequently translated the Greek word *phronesis* as *prudence*. This word used to mean *wisdom* but has evolved into something along the lines of *pragmatism* or *practicality*. I have therefore uniformly changed each of these instances to the more accurate modern word *wisdom* (or its grammatically appropriate cognate). The second word that I wish to note is *science*. Taylor used this word to mean knowledge in a broader sense than how we use this word today. Therefore, in most places where *science* is used for the Greek word *episteme*, I have included *knowledge* in brackets.

One final point is that of gender pronouns. Although the philosophers of this tradition had a more egalitarian view of women than was prevalent among their contemporaries, they did tend to use male pronouns. This is evident throughout the quotes in this book. As a woman, I fully appreciate how this may offend our modern sensibilities. I ask the reader, however, to allow these ancient writers some latitude. Otherwise, we risk throwing out the baby with the bathwater, and the baby these writings have nurtured and continue to nurture is a precious one.

Surveying the Landscape

Introduction

At first blush, Plato's dialogues seem an odd place to look for wisdom. After all, they are a product of a different time and culture. Things have changed dramatically from Plato's day. Some may argue that our busy lives, with our two income households and multiple car payments, have no connection to a time when people spent hours chatting in the marketplace about the meaning of *virtue*. We feel that with all of our advances in psychiatry and science, we understand ourselves and our universe better than the ancient Greeks did. It seems to follow, then, that while Plato may be interesting to read out of curiosity, these teachings are not applicable to contemporary life.

Actually, Plato most likely had heard similar arguments back in his day (minus the part about multiple car payments!). Even during Plato's lifetime, most people never thought to pin down a definition for concepts such as *virtue*. This, in part, is why Plato's teacher Socrates, and later Plato himself, faced strong opposition. The path Plato advocates in his dialogues would have led the students at his Academy far from the main road followed by their contemporaries, and it was a path that required inner strength and endurance to overcome its multitude of obstacles. Although Plato had a following during his lifetime, most people probably viewed these teachings, at best, as harmlessly irrelevant or mildly curious and, at worst, as dangerously misguided. It was this latter fear that led to Socrates' infamous trial and execution.

The same type of misunderstandings that confronted Socrates and Plato confront us today, and the same general obstacles faced by philosophers at Plato's Academy await us, as well. Plato, then, had to address these concerns in his dialogues, to show not only that philosophy is worthwhile, but that if humanity has any hope at all of overcoming war and treachery, it is through philosophy that our salvation will come. He did this in the form of dialogues, most but not all of them using Socrates as the main character.

What is the power that philosophy holds? Surely it must be more than its modern academic forms of quibbling over definitions or surveying what various thinkers wrote, for Socrates was willing to die for it. In fact, at his trial (where he probably had a pretty good idea of what the outcome would be) he announced to his judges that they would be wasting their time by ordering him to stop philosophizing:

> "I say that to talk every day about virtue and the other things about which you hear me talking and examining myself and others is the greatest good to man, and that the unexamined life is not worth living…"[1]

This bold assertion is as true today as it was 2,400 years ago. Socrates still stands as the quintessential example of the beauty that shines forth from the soul that has grown courageous and wise. He is an inspiring figure who reminds us of the greatness we all intuit is within us, and he is our trusted friend and guide as we inch toward manifesting that greatness within ourselves.

In the dialogue *Republic*, Plato likened us to prisoners in a cave, chained since childhood and living unaware of the reality beyond our self-imposed confines. He maintains that through philosophy, though, we can escape this cave of ignorance and emerge into the brightness of wisdom. Our journey begins by surveying the landscape. I will briefly introduce the ancient philosophers of this tradition. Then I will turn to the methodology that guides us, and the stages of our journey. Finally, I will survey what attitudes and temperament we must muster in order to meet the challenge. Are you ready? It is time to loosen the chains and look around.

---

[1] Plato, *The Apology of Socrates*, 38a, trans. Harold North Fowler

Chapter 1: Who are the Platonists?

"These few are, in my opinion, no other than those who philosophize rightly; and that I may be ranked in the number of these, I shall leave nothing unattempted, but exert myself in all possible ways."

Plato[1]

The Greek philosophic tradition is a rich one that spans almost 3,000 years. It has produced many great thinkers who shaped much of what we call Western civilization. Before we dive into the teachings of Platonism or consider its implications in our lives, let's take a look at who the Platonists were. I will focus on a handful of philosophers, those who are most directly relevant to my presentation of Platonism.

Plato and Socrates

Only a few details are known of Socrates' life. What information we have has been gleaned through the dialogues of two of his students: Plato, and a less philosophically inclined man named Xenophon.[2] Socrates was probably born around 470 BC, a fact we can only surmise from the date of his execution and his age at death. He was married to a much younger woman named Xanthippe, and they had three sons, "one now a lad; but the other two, boys"[3] at the time of Socrates' death, when he was around 70 years old. Although Plato offers little indication of Xanthippe's personality, Xenophon depicts her as a difficult and easily angered woman. He reports Socrates saying of her: "I'm quite sure that if I can put up with her, I shall find it easy to get on with any other human being."[4]

We also know through Plato that Socrates fought in at least one war,[5] but he rarely traveled otherwise. In the dialogue *Crito*, Plato writes of Socrates: "[Y]ou never left the city for any of the public

---

[1] Socrates in *Phaedo*, 69d

[2] See *Xenophon: Conversations of Socrates*.

[3] *Apology of Socrates* 34d

[4] Xenophon, *Conversations of Socrates*, p. 232. Quote from *The Dinner-Party*, 2.10

[5] See *Symposium*, 219e~221b. The character Alcibiades tells a story of fighting alongside Socrates in a battle in Potidaea. According to the translator W.R.M. Lamb, this battle took place in 432 BC. See his footnote 1 in *Charmides*.

spectacles except once, when you went to the Isthmian games, nor did you ever go elsewhere, except in your military expeditions."[6] Socrates was instead inclined to remain in his native Athens, where he dedicated his life to testing the wisdom of his fellow Athenians, looking for someone wiser than himself. He took up this task when the oracle at Delphi declared that nobody was wiser than Socrates.[7]

Xenophon reports that Socrates had lively conversations, which were both enjoyable and thought-provoking, with merchants and craftsmen in the marketplace. It was his questioning of those of high social status, as dramatized in Plato's dialogues, that ruffled many feathers. Famously, that ire culminated in his being brought to trial on charges of corrupting the youth and of not believing in the gods recognized by Athens. Socrates was found guilty of these crimes and sentenced to death by the drinking of poison, probably hemlock.[8]

Plato was 28 years old when, in 399 BC, Socrates was executed. This event undoubtedly had a powerful impact on Plato. He closes his account in *Phaedo* of that fateful day with these words:

> "This, Echecrates, was the end of our associate; a man, as it
> appears to me, the best of those whom we were acquainted
> with at that time, and, besides this, the wisest and [most] just."[9]

Plato was born in Athens, Greece[10] in 427 BC to a political family. By most accounts, his family was not wealthy but they did occupy a respectable position in society. Plato enjoyed a comfortable childhood and received a formal education. Although he had political aspirations in his youth, he ultimately chose to abandon the ways of his family and instead followed the inspiration of his teacher, Socrates.

After Socrates' death, Plato threw himself into his studies. Whatever political ambitions Plato might have harbored died with

---

[6] *Crito* 52b

[7] See *Apology of Socrates*, 21a.

[8] This trial is chronicled in the dialogue *Apology of Socrates*.

[9] *Phaedo*, 118a

[10] The most comprehensive biography of Plato I have ever read is an essay by Debra Nails called *The Life of Plato of Athens*. It can be found in Benson, *A Companion to Plato*. Much of this summary comes from that essay. I also drew from the Introductions of *Plato: The Collected Dialogues* and of the Loeb series, as well as the Cambridge Dictionary of Philosophy.

Socrates. He spent the next twelve years studying philosophy and traveling through Italy and Sicily. Then, in 387 BC, he returned to Athens where he founded his now legendary Academy just outside the city on property he privately owned. The Academy is believed to have begun as informal gatherings of like-minded friends but then quickly grew.[11]

Plato never charged students any fees to attend his Academy[12] and there were no classrooms as we are accustomed to in modern schools. Rather, the school consisted of a gymnasium and a large open space called a commodious where groups could gather for discussions. Little is known of what precisely Plato taught during his reign as headmaster.

As far as we know, Plato never married or had any children. He devoted his time to writing his dialogues (34 in total, although the authenticity of some dialogues is in question) and running the Academy. One notable caveat to this otherwise quiet life was his excursion to Syracuse around the age of 40, where he met the tyrant Dionysius I. This would have been either at the end of Plato's 12-year travels or soon after his return to Athens. Plato's directness and his unwillingness to bend to the will of the tyrant so angered Dionysius I that he sold Plato into slavery. Plato was soon freed by a wealthy friend, Anniceris of Cyrene, and he returned to Athens.[13] He remained as headmaster of the Academy until his death in or around 346 BC. Accounts of his age at death differ, but he was perhaps in his late seventies or as old as 81. His body was buried on the grounds at the Academy.[14]

Plato's nephew Speusippus took the reigns as the second headmaster. The Academy stayed open some 300 years in total. It finally closed in 86 BC, although it may have continued informally until the death of its final headmaster, Philo of Larissa, in 83 BC.[15]

---

[11] See Nails essay *The Life of Plato in Athens* in Benson, *A Companion to Plato*

[12] See Nails, *The People of Plato: A Prosopography of Plato and other Socratics*, p. 249.

[13] See Nails essay *The Life of Plato of Athens* in Benson, *A Companion to Plato.*

[14] See Nails, *The People of Plato: A Prosopography of Plato and other Socratics*, p. 249.

[15] See Lindberg, *The Beginnings of Western Science*, p. 69.

Standing on the Shoulders of a Giant

For hundreds of years after Plato's death, many inspired philosophers carried the torch that Plato had lit. They built on his system by drawing out the implications of his metaphysics and by expounding on its relevance to our lives. Throughout this book, I draw not only from Plato's dialogues and his *Epistles* (personal correspondences),[16] but also from what is commonly called the Neoplatonic canon as well.

Neoplatonism is a technical term used in academia to refer to later philosophers in this tradition. The philosopher considered to be the father of Neoplatonism is a man named Plotinus. His teachings, dating from around 220 CE, mark the start of the Neoplatonic period. Philosophers in this tradition who lived from around 80 CE until Plotinus' lifetime are called, aptly enough, Middle Platonists. Academia has no official name for those philosophers contemporary to Plato through 80 CE.

I personally find these labels misleading, as all these philosophers are contributors to the same tradition. I see the term Neoplatonism as an attempt by academia to strip Plato's dialogues of their spiritual aspect by separating these dialogues from the later thinkers in this tradition and the mysticism they are associated with. However, there is a continuity of thought from Plato through to the so-called Neoplatonists, although some differences do emerge from one philosopher to another. I have therefore chosen to collectively refer to all these philosophers as Platonists, and this tradition as the Platonic tradition in recognition of the central role of Plato's thought.

There are three of these later Platonists in particular whose works add a great richness to our own practices: Plotinus, Proclus and Damascius. These philosophers will come up repeatedly throughout this book, so I want to briefly introduce them here.

Plotinus

Plotinus is that mystic mentioned above who is widely known as the father of Neoplatonism. Plotinus' life is generally dated from 204

---

[16] There is some debate among academics as to the authenticity of these letters.

to 270 CE,[17] and his surviving writings were all composed in the last fifteen years of his life, at the bequest of his students. A student named Porphyry, who himself went on to some distinction as a philosopher, organized and published these writings in a series of essays—54 in all—grouped into six blocks of nine essays each. It is from this numbering system that these writings have come to be known as the *Enneads*—*ennead* in Greek means *group of nine*.

Plotinus masterfully combines logical reasoning with mystical vision and a poetic flair for words. He embodies the wise state of mind that Plato encourages in his dialogues. Reading his Enneads invites us to see ourselves and the divine cosmos we are a part of through the loftier lens of his vision. He inspires us to join him on his explorations and to bask in the radiance that we find through those searches.

Proclus

Another towering figure in the Platonic tradition is Proclus, who found his place in a revived Platonic Academy that opened in the early fifth century CE, perhaps around the year 410 CE.[18] The Platonic Academy, sometimes referred to by modern scholars as the Athenian School, was started by a Platonic philosopher named Plutarch of Athens (not to be confused with the first-century biographer Plutarch of Chaeronea). Plutarch of Athens led his Academy until his death in 431 CE. The aged Syrianus then took the helm, but he passed away soon after and was succeeded by his star pupil, Proclus. Proclus was the headmaster of the Platonic Academy from around 437 CE until his death in 485 CE.[19]

Proclus was born in Byzantium (modern-day Istanbul) and grew up in Lycia (on the southern coast of modern-day Turkey). His wealthy parents sent him to Egypt in his youth to study with sophists, but his life is reported to have taken a turn when the Greek goddess Rhea

---

[17] For the biographical details in this summary, I relied heavily on a more detailed account by Ahbel-Rappe in *Problems and Solutions Concerning First Principles*, p. xiv.

[18] For more on the Neoplatonic Athenian School, see Whittaker, *The Neoplatonists: A Study in the History of Hellenism*, pp. 155~156.

[19] See *Proclus' Commentary on Plato's Parmenides*, pp. xi~xiii.

appeared to him in a dream. She told him he should move to Athens to study philosophy.[20]

Proclus never chose to marry or have children, instead devoting all his time to spiritual and philosophical endeavors. He was a prolific author who systematically expounded the metaphysics that Plato had hinted at or hid in complex analogies. His writings are a great help to us both early in our practice when we are first mapping out the metaphysical landscape, and as our practice matures, when we are filling in the details.

In Proclus, we find a brilliant mind, at once visionary and scholarly. He was rigorous in his use of logic and reasoning, but he was also a mystic who spent hours each day engaged in spiritual rites connected not only to the Greek world but also those of the Egyptian and of the Arab world. As his biographer and student Marinus reports, "[O]ne maxim that this most god-fearing philosopher had always at hand and was always uttering was that a philosopher ought not to worship in the manner of a single city…but should be the common priest of the entire world."[21]

Being both scholarly and mystical may seem on the surface to be a contradiction, but fitting the two together is actually a major component of this tradition. The Platonic tradition does share many similarities with the scientific method, such as working from hypotheses and applying rigid logic to investigations. However, it does this while turning us towards the spiritual realms rather than keeping our focus on our physical world. Proclus' purpose was not to explore the question of whether or not there is a god; rather, he started from the highest experience of union with the Divine, and from there unfolded a complex system that brings a remarkable degree of understanding and intelligibility to that experience and to the cause of that experience.

Proclus' writings, then (and indeed this entire philosophic tradition), are built on two assumptions: (1) there is such a thing as

---

[20] Most of the biographical details in this summary come from Edwards (trans.), *Neoplatonic Saints: The Lives of Plotinus and Proclus by their Students*.

[21] *Ibid.*, p. 88.

Reality and (2) it is knowable.[22] These two assumptions would arguably be reasonable ones for anyone to make who knew Reality through firsthand experience, as Proclus presumably did. Students earlier in their practice treat these assumptions as hypotheses—these are theories we want to test and discover for ourselves. Proclus is a great resource for us to turn to in this endeavor.

Damascius

And then we come to Damascius, the final headmaster of the revived Platonic Academy. By the time of his tenure, pagan philosophy had come under attack by Christianity. Damascius oversaw the closing of the Academy in 529 CE when the Christian emperor Justinian banned the teachings of pagan philosophy from the country.[23] Damascius is believed to have fled to Egypt or northern Mesopotamia with a circle of like-minded philosophers.

Only a small number of his writings still exist. The work I mainly draw from is a cleverly crafted book titled *Problems and Solutions Concerning First Principles,* which is ideally suited for those with a fair level of competency in metaphysics, particularly Proclean metaphysics (the metaphysics offered by Proclus). In this book, Damascius does an impressive job of pulling the rug out from under those who think they have a firm footing in metaphysics but whose grasp is still only conceptual. He turns all our conceptual understandings upside down,

---

[22] On the assumption that Reality is knowable, consider for example this argument against the hypothesis that there is no first cause (from Proclus' Proposition 11 in *Elements of Theology):* "If, however, there is no cause of beings, there will neither be an order of things second and first,...of things generating and generated, and of agents and patients, nor will there be any science [knowledge/*episteme*] of beings. For the knowledge of cause is the work of science, and we are then said to know scientifically, when we know the causes of things.......And if the addition of causes is to infinity, and there is always again another cause prior to another, there will be no science [knowledge/*episteme*] of any being. For there is not a knowledge of anything infinite. But causes being unknown, neither will there be a knowledge of the things consequent to the causes."

[23] For a more in-depth biography, see "Introduction to the Life and Philosophy of Damascius" in Ahbel-Rappe, *Problems and Solutions Concerning First Principles,* pp. 3~10. Damascius had a colorful, eventful life that I do not have space to summarize here.

reducing us to utter confusion. In this way, he compels us to really dig into these teachings to their deeper significance and implications. He understood that looking up to Reality from a distance is not enough; we must *become* the object of our desire in order to truly know it.

The Shoulders on Which the Giant Stood

Before founding his own Academy and becoming quite possibly the world's most famous philosophy teacher, Plato was a student who was influenced not only by Socrates but also by a long tradition of mystic philosophy that already existed in pieces throughout the Western world. Plato's brilliance was in his ability to recognize expressions of truth as described in very different ways by the theologists and philosophers who preceded him, and then to present through his dialogues a spiritual system to guide us from ignorance to wisdom. It is this vision that has been inspiring readers for about 2,400 years and that, as you will soon discover for yourself, continues to inspire anyone open to its power.

The philosophic tradition in the Greek world was already well established by Plato's day. However, two philosophers in particular stand out as profound influences on Plato. One is Parmenides, who bears the name of Plato's dialogue on metaphysics. The other is Pythagoras, a mathematician, mystic, and philosopher. You may be surprised to discover that his credits go far beyond what we learned in school as the Pythagorean Theorem.[24]

Parmenides

Parmenides was born around 515 BC in the Italian-Greek colony of Elea in southern Italy.[25] His greatest and most lasting contribution to philosophy is his assertion of metaphysical monism, the doctrine that Reality is one. His most famous work is a poem called "On Nature," probably written between 470 BC and 460 BC. Only fragments still remain, but from them we can get a fairly clear notion of his vision of metaphysics.

---

[24] Tim Addey has kindly pointed out to me that nobody in antiquity makes the claim that the Pythagorean Theorem was indeed discovered by Pythagoras. Whether or not this theorem has been accurately credited to him is therefore unknown.

[25] See Wheelwright (ed.), *The Presocratics*, pp. 91~105.

He describes Reality as what is true and unchanging, and contrasts this from our realm of reality that is always in flux. For Parmenides, the way to Truth is by following the path toward what *is;* our ever-changing world is in the realm of opinion and is not what is truly real. There are strong echoes of this doctrine in Plato's metaphysics and in his famous allegory of the cave.

Pythagoras

Pythagoras was born around 580 BC on the Greek island of Samos in the Aegean Sea.[26] He studied in Egypt before starting his own school in the Italian city of Croton. His school and its teachings were heavily shrouded in secrecy. While mathematics and music are the topics most commonly associated with the Pythagorean school, there is great debate as to what precisely the curriculum was. His impact on Plato is not any single teaching in particular but rather the underlying hypothesis on which all of Pythagoras' teachings were formed: number is a divine language on which the entire cosmos is built. Mathematical axioms and theorems (and yes, this includes the Pythagorean Theorem!) are for us to discover, not for us to create. For Pythagoras, numbers were a doorway into the study of metaphysics and, as such, were the building blocks for a spiritual life.

Mythologists

Plato makes wide use of Greek mythology throughout his dialogues. He recognized meaning hidden within these fantastical stories which, on the surface, seem outlandish and in some cases even immoral. His references to Greek mythology come almost exclusively from three sources: Homer, Hesiod, and the books of Orpheus. Another influence on Plato was the Eleusian Mysteries.

Homer

Next to nothing is known of Homer, but he is widely believed to have been blind.[27] He committed his lengthy epic poems to memory rather than writing them down. The two epic poems credited to Homer are the *Iliad*, composed around 750 BC, and the *Odyssey*,

---

[26] See *Ibid.*, pp. 200~230

[27] This brief summary of Homer's life was taken from the Introduction to Fitzgerald (trans.), *The Iliad*.

composed around 700 BC. Memorizing epic poetry rather than presenting it in written form was not unusual in those days, as literacy was not yet widespread. These epic poems were part of an oral tradition and most likely were sung before an illiterate audience.

Hesiod

Hesiod, a contemporary of Homer, is another important influence on Plato.[28] He lived in a district in central Greece called Boeotia. His two works that we know of, *Theogony* and *Works and Days*, rivaled Homer's in religious and moral significance in the ancient Greek world. He presented a history of the Greek gods in his *Theogony*, a chronology which, to philosophers in the Platonic tradition, veiled many metaphysical insights. His *Works and Days* includes some mythology but focuses instead on the value of working hard and living a simple life.

Orphism

The books of Orpheus are the third source from which Plato referenced Greek mythology. Orpheus himself is actually a mythical figure, said on some accounts to be the son of Apollo and Calliope, the first of the Muses.[29] A number of theological poems written in the sixth century BC were credited to him, and these collectively came to be known as the books of Orpheus.[30] The Orphic poems focused on the same mythological stories that Homer and Hesiod did, but added to or changed the earlier versions, seeping them heavily in an evolving vision of metaphysics. These poems gave rise to spiritual teachers who performed initiations and rituals, and this spiritual system came to be known as Orphism.

Plato makes many references throughout his dialogues to the Orphic poems. He was critical, however, of some of the more popularized beliefs attached to these teachings that popped up in the mainstream society of his day. For example, he denounced the notion that people could escape divine judgment for their wrongdoings by offering sacrifices to the gods.[31] However, the influence of the Orphic

[28] See www.britannica.com for a full biography.
[29] Uzdavinys, *Orpheus and the Roots of Platonism*, p.38
[30] See the *Cambridge Dictionary of Philosophy*, p. 636
[31] See *Republic*, 364e~365a

teachings is unmistakable in his myths about the afterlife in such dialogues as *Republic, Gorgias,* and *Phaedo.*

The Mysteries

Pagan religions, such as Orphism, that relied heavily on rituals and initiation ceremonies, have come to be known as mystery schools. No, these schools were not precursors to Sir Arthur Conan Doyle or Agatha Christie; *mystery* here is in a twofold sense. On the surface, *mystery* is in the sense of being secret. Initiates were required to take a strict vow never to discuss what went on in these rites. Because of such vows, we have far more speculation than fact concerning the content of these rites. On a deeper level, *mystery* refers to the fact that these schools addressed that which lies beyond the commonly accepted range of human consciousness.

The Eleusian Mysteries were by far the most popular and widespread of the mysteries in the ancient Greek world, dating back to the seventh century BC.[32] Like Orphism, they had an impact on the Platonic tradition. Initiation ceremonies were celebrated yearly. They were started in the Greek city of Eleusis, and then they spread throughout the Greek, and later Roman, world.

The celebration originally consisted of a ten-day ceremony that only Greeks were allowed to participate in. Over time, a purification ritual was added for foreigners who wished to partake in the main ceremony. Eventually, every initiate—Greeks and non-Greeks alike—underwent both ceremonies. The purification ceremony came to be known as the Lesser Mysteries, while the main ceremony was called the Greater Mysteries. Over the centuries, many emperors and powerful social figures were initiated, the most famous perhaps being Marcus Aurelius in 176 CE.

The Eleusian Mysteries, whatever the actual rites might have been, were based on the long and winding mythological story of Demeter, goddess of the harvest, and her daughter Persephone. Persephone, also known in Greek mythology as Kore, was fathered by Zeus. The main gist of the story is that Zeus allowed his brother Pluto, king of the underworld, to take Persephone to Hades as his wife. Demeter was heartbroken and angry. She vowed not to allow another harvest

---

[32] For the details in this summary, I relied heavily on Wright, *The Eleusian Mysteries and Rites.*

until Zeus returned their daughter to her. When humanity was swept up in famine, Zeus relented and ordered Pluto to return Persephone. However, as the young woman was leaving, Pluto offered her four pomegranates, not telling her that eating anything would prevent her from being able to return to the world of the living. As a compromise, Zeus allowed her to remain with her mother for eight months of the year but ordered her to return to Pluto the other four months as his bride.

There are various interpretations of this story.[33] On the shallowest level, the sadness felt by Demeter, goddess of the harvest, during the four months her daughter is away each year explains the "death" of nature during the winter months. On a deeper level, though, Persephone became a symbol of the reincarnating soul, only she follows the cycle of death and rebirth without actually dying and therefore without losing her memory of the world she is passing from. She is someone who knows both worlds, who lives on earth but also, as queen of the underworld, knows the soul beyond its human existence.

As with modern-day symbolic rites and ceremonies, the Eleusian Mysteries carried both exoteric teachings that had widespread appeal, and esoteric teachings that were understood only by a smaller number of people. The popular lesson of these ceremonies hinged on that of reward and punishment in the afterlife, with many people believing that initiation would guarantee them a favorable passage to the next world. However, the more esoteric approach, referenced by Plato most notably in the dialogue *Meno*,[34] was that of the soul recalling its inherent wisdom.

In this regard, the lessons of the Eleusian Mysteries had much in common with the Hindu notion of karma, which has the commonplace reputation of being about reward and punishment. To serious students of Hinduism, however, the law of karma is far more subtle, and understanding its nuances is tied to understanding the nature of Reality and our place in the whole. Such, as well, were the lessons of Demeter and Persephone for Plato and the philosophers who followed him in the Platonic tradition.

---

[33] Those readers more comfortable with the metaphysics of this tradition might enjoy Proclus' metaphysically intense explication of this myth in his *Theology of Plato*, bk. 6, ch. 11.

[34] See *Meno* 81c.

Chapter 2: A Different Approach

"Do not the manner of expression, and the words, correspond with the character of the soul?"

Plato[1]

All of us who are drawn to mystical practice have our own unique story of how we got here. As children, some of us followed the outward practices of the religion we were raised in without questioning what any of it meant. Others were raised atheist or agnostic and never questioned those ideas. Whatever the particular set of beliefs we were raised with, our parents and other influential adults showed us their view of the way the world is. When we were small, maybe that was enough for us. At some point, though, something caused us to re-evaluate that view.

I grew up in a Jewish home where the Bible[2] was talked about and never doubted, but it was also never read. The hypocrisy of this fact did not occur to me until somewhere around high school. That was when I started asking questions about God and about justice: Why is there death and suffering? Why do bad things happen to good people? What happens to us after we die? I got many different answers to the same questions, yet everyone seemed to *know* that their answer was right. Even people who said that nobody knows these things seemed to *know* that the answers I was looking for were unknowable. How did they know? Why didn't I know?

I used to fluctuate between anger and jealousy when I was around such people. I was angry because so much of what I was being told felt wrong, yet I also was jealous of those who had the comfort of these beliefs because their lives seemed happier and simpler than mine. Why did I have to question everything? If only I could have accepted what other people believed, I could have fit in and I wouldn't have felt so alone.

---

[1] *Republic*, 400e

[2] What Judaism refers to as the Bible, or sometimes the Hebrew Bible, is what is known to Christians as the Old Testament. See Rabbi Joseph Telushkin, *Biblical Literacy*, p. 595.

As I got older, I discovered that I had nothing to be jealous of, because everyone around me had confusion, even if they hid it away. We are all searching for answers. We want to feel meaning in our lives, which can seem at times to chug along with no purpose and without any rhyme or reason. We want to make sense of humanity as a whole, and of all existence on earth. Why are we here? Are we just a random result of evolution?

As a child, I was introduced to Judaism as a way to tackle these questions. The focus in my family was on the outward behavior of the wise as ideals for us to aim for. Yet I never learned the commensurate state of mind of one who would naturally behave in these ways. My parents taught me to be considerate of others, but sometimes I felt selfish anyway. At times I was proud, even though I learned that I should be humble. Anger towards friends who hurt my feelings lingered even though I was taught to be forgiving. Christians I knew offered much the same sort of lessons in morality, but again with no "how-to" manual to go along with their advice.

The result of this flawed methodology is that too many of us who sincerely want to be good are invariably left feeling guilty, ashamed, and inadequate for not being able to—or not knowing how to—live up to these ideals. Are we bad people? Are we inherently flawed? We may at times counter these self-doubts by repressing our emotions and denying our true thoughts, or we conveniently overlook those religious teachings that don't fit our personal views.

This can lead to the belief that wisdom is something reserved for a special, select few. The conclusion is that we are too small and insignificant to ever expect to understand—let alone directly experience—anything as grand as the Divine. Faith is all we need, according to this point of view. To seek more or even to think it is possible is blasphemous. *After all,* the reasoning goes, *We're only human.*

My university years were tinged with cynicism. The idea that we were all just doing our best struck me as woefully insufficient. I gravitated in those days towards others who shared the agnostic point of view I had come to favor, and we took comfort in our conviction that we were above that religious "nonsense." Although I was too proud to admit it out loud, in my private thoughts I secretly knew that I was just stumbling along, with little aim or direction. I could see that the people closest to me were all stumbling along, too, whether they had some religious affiliation or not.

I suffered through bouts of anger at and resentment toward organized religions. I grew bitter at what I saw as their hypocrisy. I saw others around me take that bitterness even further, rebelling against religious systems by concluding that their ideals are unnatural. Laws and institutions such as marriage are only social conveniences, they came to believe. There is no such thing as justice or morality; we are only animals at heart, they would say, and it is human nature to try to get away with as much as we possibly can. Those who obey the law only do so because they are too weak to be able to get away with acting otherwise. Anyone who could do whatever they wanted with impunity would jump at the opportunity, they concluded. Wealth and power seem to raise some people above the law.

What's more, their argument continues, there are no absolutes in regards to justice—or any other virtue, for that matter. When we look at the people around us, we see the notion of justice being treated as something relative; when people get their way they call this "fair" and when they don't, they cry foul. With so much injustice in the world, it's easy to conclude that justice and morality aren't anything real.

Of course, not everyone who rejects organized religion goes to the extreme of also rejecting notions of justice and social order. Some of us instead merely grow indifferent to the notion of a creator or a spiritual realm. My own path meandered more into these meadows. This line of thinking is rooted in the belief that the Divine doesn't affect our lives anyway, so it doesn't matter whether or not there is a creator. The argument is that we don't need religious beliefs to feel compassion for other human beings or to live in a way that is moral and ethical. This theory, which is a central tenet of humanism, is widely embraced by atheists and agnostics who, for the most part, prove their point by being caring, law-abiding people.

There is a certain power to this argument—especially when we consider all the wars and atrocities committed throughout history in the name of God or some other divine being. I found it compelling for a while, but I was still nagged by the question of *why* compassion is good and ruthlessness is not. This question reaches beyond the pragmatic issues involved in the smooth running of societies. What is it about humans that compels us to care about other people? Why are we moved by news of mass deaths in terrorist attacks or natural disasters? Why do we love our children? I've heard the argument that the reason we care about one another is found in our biology. Yet, if this is true, then morality and love are nothing more than chemical reactions. I finally had to admit to myself that removing all spiritual dimensions from our physical world removed meaning as well.

Humanism has its appeal, but it doesn't answer (or even ask) the deeper question of what is behind intuitions and inclinations towards goodness. It reduces intangible values such as goodness, truth, compassion, and love to mere chemical reactions and the wiring of our brains. If that really is all they were, then there would be something insignificant about those inclinations. Our sense of connection to one another would, in a sense, be an illusion. We can't have it both ways; we can't explain away our connectedness and still call that connection meaningful.

If you are reading this book, however, you probably sense that there is *something* true about spirituality. Perhaps, like me, your gut tells you that it is not wrong for us to search for meaningfulness and happiness in our lives. There *are* such things as goodness and divine law, even if we don't fully understand them. Our connection to one another is more than merely for the survival of our species. This intuition in itself does not prove humanism wrong, but it is enough to send us on a search for answers that are more satisfying.

I've met many people over the years who have developed a love-hate relationship with their family's religion. There are also many who reject religious traditions altogether. Too often, this rejection is equated to a rejection of any form of God. Yet this too is unsatisfying; it is not God that is being rejected, only certain religious interpretations of God. How, then, can we approach questions of the Divine sincerely without falling into any of these erroneous ways of thinking?

There is a way. We can retain our doubts about the conclusions, but then focus on seeking out a system with a different methodology, one which guides us to the state of mind of the wise, so that we can decide for ourselves which conclusions are correct and which are not. Plato developed such a system, which I will introduce in the next chapter, and the philosophers that followed in his footsteps each contributed to the unfolding of this system. The framework offered by Plato is a rational one that values logic, but which also recognizes experiences beyond what is the accepted norm, extending into the realm of the spiritual. To some readers, parts may seem controversial. To others, this will be a refreshing breath of fresh air.

I don't know of any teacher throughout the history of philosophy quite like Plato. Ralph Waldo Emerson once wrote, "Plato is philosophy, and philosophy, Plato—at once the glory and the shame of mankind, since neither Saxon nor Roman have availed to add any idea to his categories. No wife, no children had he, and the thinkers of all civilized nations are his posterity and are tinged with his mind."[3] Plato's natural talent with words afforded him the ability to present through his dialogues the foundation for how a student can move from ignorance to wisdom. History has known many wise people, and Plato undoubtedly can be counted among them. Plato stands out from even this most dignified crowd, because he was an innovative teacher who gave to our Western culture a spiritual system that stands shoulder to shoulder with the giants of the East. It is this methodology that will provide the framework for this book.

One key to understanding the value of Plato's approach lies in recognizing the role of sacrifice in the pious person's life. Plato hints at his own perspective in *Republic*, when Socrates suggests that religious myths can only be understood by those who have attained some degree of wisdom. Socrates advises that people should only hear these myths after they have sacrificed "not a hog, but some great and wonderful sacrifice..."[4] This is often understood to mean that the sacrifice ought to be personally significant to the giver, such as farmers giving the best of their crops to the gods. The idea behind this is that the sincerity of this act makes the act sacred in the heart of the giver.

We can see this principle play out in our own lives. When I was a child, for example, elementary schools in my area held yearly canned food drives to help the needy. I imagine that many readers grew up with similar programs. How many of us only gave foods that our families would never have eaten anyway, such as canned spinach? They were easy to give away because we didn't really want them. Now don't get me wrong, it was fine to give these foods. Giving them was certainly better than giving nothing. However, if we are being honest with ourselves we have to admit that there was no heart in these donations.

---

[3] Plato, or The Philosopher, *The Essential Writings of Ralph Waldo Emerson*, p. 421.
[4] 378a

Conversely, giving away something that you like and want, such as a coat that you still wear, can be painful. However, it is precisely because of that personal difficulty that the giving becomes a source of satisfaction and perhaps even joy. Such it was in the ancient world as well, and because these givings were in the form of offerings to the gods, the act was raised to the level of feeling sacred. In fact, the word *sacrifice* literally means *to make sacred*. This is certainly a valid understanding of how the practice of sacrifice was effected in the ancient Greek world.

I would suggest, however, that Plato's meaning in the *Republic* goes even further than that. He made the statement about giving a "great and wonderful sacrifice" in the context of discussing mythology. He was suggesting that people needed to reach some degree of initiation into spiritual matters in order to see beyond the common understanding of mythology. As we will see later in this book, the Platonists saw the gods as only good and never evil. However, Greek mythology presents the gods (at least on the surface) as jealous, vengeful, hateful and full of lust. It takes a certain level of insight to recognize the metaphysical view of reality that these stories are actually pointing towards.

For Plato, it was not enough to kill an animal as an offering, or to offer the best of one's crops to the gods. These offerings were only made sacred in a symbolical way, and added nothing to anyone's understanding of the nature of Reality. In other words, these such ritual acts triggered no initiation into spiritual matters. A more meaningful alternative, Plato is suggesting in this passage, is that we make ourselves sacred, and we offer ourselves to our spiritual quest. This is a truer, more meaningful form of sacrifice. The Platonic philosopher Tim Addey suggests of this passage from the *Republic*: "I would say that the "great and wonderful" sacrifice to which he refers is none other than the sacrifice of the self in the quest for intellectual truth..."[5] This idea, however, begs two questions from modern Platonists: what does it mean to make ourselves sacred, and how do we give ourselves to our spiritual quest?

---

[5] Addey, *The Unfolding Wings*, p. 103. The word *intellectual* in this quote refers to the more profound divine sense of the word, not our colloquial notion of conceptual thinking.

The short answers (which will be explored in much greater detail throughout this book) is that we make ourselves sacred by making our souls as virtuous and godlike as is humanly possible,[6] and we give ourselves to our spiritual path through our aspiration to know truth. We must care more about knowing truth than about achieving any social measure of success, such as wealth or popularity.

In practice, this involves seeing through whatever ignorance we currently hold about ourselves and humanity's place in the whole. As we deepen our studies and meditations on truth, we find ourselves questioning and ultimately dropping images that are incompatible with our insights. While this is often empowering and exciting, it can also at times be a painful process.

To some degree, this is part of the natural process of growing up. We naturally outgrow childish states of mind as we get older. As we go into our teenage years, for example, we gain more independence and maturity and so we outgrow our adolescent images. In adulthood, most of us outgrow the drama from high school.

At some point, though, our growth seems to come to a halt. We might take on a psychological or spiritual practice that allows us to evolve within a certain mindset that we have already embraced and solidified for ourselves, but rarely do we challenge our most fundamental assumptions about ourselves or about the nature of Reality.

Platonists, however, recognize a further level of growth. Beyond what we might call emotional maturity or psychological maturity is an even higher goal: spiritual maturity. Within the context of this deeper spiritual growth, we do not place a high value on merely changing our outward behavior, such as stopping ourselves from gossiping or competing with our friends. These types of behavioral changes are difficult when the insights involved are only conceptual. We understand, for example, that we should not begrudge other people's successes, but the heart and the mind are often in conflict. The aim of those who follow the Platonic path is to change inwardly. When this

---

[6] This idea of making ourselves virtuous and godlike comes up often in Plato's dialogues. See for example, *Laws* 716c~d: "he amongst us that is temperate is dear to God, since he is like him, while he that is not temperate is unlike and at enmity,—as is also he who is unjust and so likewise with the rest [of the virtues], by parity of reasoning." (trans. R. G. Bury)

inward change occurs, behavioral changes follow as a natural expression of the person we are evolving into.

In the *Republic*, Plato shows that when our soul is guided by wisdom, our desires and attitudes naturally fall in line with what is good and healthy for the soul.[7] Spiritual maturity develops by nurturing an understanding of the nature of Reality and our place in the whole. These insights will eventually compel us to question our sense of individuality and what it means to be a human being. All of these changes necessarily precipitate a shift in how we relate to other people and what we deem most important in our lives.

Looking back to who I was at the start of my own spiritual journey, I see great changes. For example, I've increasingly lost interest in outward signs of success such as job status and wealth, and I feel a deeper connection to the people around me and to nature. These are not changes that I forced on myself or have embraced because they are ideals I've read about. They are natural outgrowths of contemplating metaphysics and letting its implications reverberate through all areas of my life.

There are no Ten Commandments or Eightfold Path in Plato's system because the focus in our practice is on understanding what it means to be wise[8]—developing the state of mind of one who naturally desires what is beneficial for the soul. Socrates was a good man, but not because he denied himself things he wanted. His wisdom and piety did not lie in his ability to repress selfish or greedy desires. Instead, his thoughts and desires naturally fell in line with

---

[7] This will be discussed in more detail in Chapter 4. In the *Republic*, see 586e~587a: "When then the whole soul is obedient to the philosophic part, and there is no sedition in it, then every part in other respects performs its proper business, and is just, and also reaps its own pleasures, and such as are the best, and as far as is possible the most true."

[8] Here I am referring to wisdom in the sense of human wisdom. See, for example, *Theatetus*, 176c~d: "Divinity is never in any respect unjust, but is most just. And there is not anything more similar to him, than a man when he becomes most just....For the knowledge of this is wisdom and true virtue..." However, Plato states in many places throughout his dialogues that wisdom, when we are being most precise, is the property of the gods. See for example, Phaedrus, 278d: "To call them wise, Phaedrus, appears to me to be a mighty appellation, and adapted to a god alone..."

wisdom, and that is the mark of a wise person and the goal of this practice.

This is in no way meant to imply that we never feel growing pains; of course we do. It can be quite painful to let go of the person we had thought ourselves to be. Conceptual insights are not sufficient for the depth of growth we are seeking. We will find as the book proceeds that false beliefs still affect us even after we see through them conceptually. It is in that gap between the conceptual insight and the actual dropping of the belief that we feel pain and need to exercise fortitude—but our fortitude is aimed at challenging our belief structure rather than at strengthening our willpower to resist temptation.

The first step on this journey is to make a commitment to ourselves to proceed with fortitude, sincerity, and integrity. The exploration of Reality is not an objective reasoning process that separates us from our own states of mind. Our beliefs and assumptions about ourselves are the very lens through which we reason. Therefore, our study of metaphysics is very much a study of ourselves.

Chapter 3: The Spiritual Journey

"[D]octrine extends as far as to the way and the progression to him. But the vision of him is now the work of one who is solicitous to perceive him."

Plotinus[1]

Plato's *Republic*

One of the most enduring of all of Plato's dialogues is the *Republic*. This dialogue is often mistaken in academic circles as a treatise primarily or even entirely about politics. While political matters are certainly an element of this dialogue, it would be more accurate to describe the *Republic* as the closest thing to a spiritual manual that Plato offered those outside his inner circle. It is here that he outlines the spiritual path that underlies all of his dialogues and his approach to philosophy. The framework and methods employed in the *Republic* have played an important role in my own development and will be referenced frequently throughout this book. A short tangent is therefore warranted here to introduce this dialogue to those who are not already familiar with it.

Plato's teacher Socrates is the main character of the *Republic*. In the dialogue, Socrates is presented a challenge:[2] he must prove that being just—and not merely projecting an image of justice—is good and desirable. To set up the challenge, he is given two hypothetical men. One is completely unjust in his heart but has the image of being just. As a result, he is well respected and enjoys power, status, and wealth. Because he can make expensive sacrifices to the gods, a place in heaven has been reserved for him.

The other man is the exact opposite. He is a simple and honest man, but has the reputation of being unjust. He therefore is shunned by society and suffers a whole myriad of punishment and pain. Needless to say, he is friendless, poor, and powerless. He is unable to pay alms to the gods and as a result, the depths of Tartarus await him after death. Despite all this, he clings to justice all his life.

The task for Socrates, then, is to show why being the just man is still better than being the unjust man, even though the consequences

---

[1] Ennead VI:ix:4

[2] The following is a summary of 358b~368c

appear to be negative for the just man. This presents Socrates with a curious difficulty, and it is one we must deal with in our own lives as well. The pictures painted of justice and injustice are the common views of each. Those descriptions carry with them many assumptions about human nature—humans are intrinsically greedy, lazy, selfish, power-hungry, and so on. Are these assumptions true?

Socrates doesn't think so, and so he can't start from the same place his friends had. Nor can he accept notions such as the gods absolving us of our sins in exchange for sacrifices and gifts. All of these images of justice carry with them assumptions about what it means to be human and about our place in the whole of reality. Therefore, Socrates has to unfold what justice really is before he can show that it is worth valuing in and of itself. He needs a technique to highlight justice in the soul. The method he chooses is described as follows:

> "Since, then, said I, I am not very expert, it seems proper to make the inquiry concerning this matter in such a manner as if it were ordered those who are not very sharp-sighted, to read small letters at a distance; and one should afterwards discover, that the same letters were written on something else in larger characters: it would appear eligible, I imagine, first to read these, and thus come to consider the lesser, if they happen to be the same.
>
> Perfectly right, said Adimantus. But what of this kind, Socrates, do you perceive in the inquiry concerning justice?
>
> I will tell you, said I. Do not we say there is justice in one man, and there is likewise justice in a whole state?
>
> It is certainly so, replied he.
>
> Is not a state a greater object than one man?
>
> Yes, said he.
>
> It is likely, then, that justice should be greater in what is greater, and be more easy to be understood: we shall first, then, if you incline, inquire what it is in states; and then, after the same manner, we shall consider it in each individual, contemplating the similitude of the greater in the idea of the lesser.
>
> You seem to me, said he, to be right."[3]

---

[3] *Republic,* 368d~369a

This excerpt shows us clearly that the *Republic* is about the soul; the city-state is used as a tool to help Socrates in his exploration. The entire dialogue is set up as an extended analogy of a city-state to the soul, and this requires the reader to frequently stop and consider the implications of what is being said about the city-state in regards to its analogue, the soul. We will take a closer look at the value and usefulness of analogies in Chapter 6.

The Divided Line

Justice, as we saw above, is the theme of the *Republic*. In order for Plato to clarify his vision of justice and its value in our lives, he has to lead us from our conventional notions of justice to one more in line with the nature of Reality. This means taking us on a spiritual journey. This journey is a lifelong one, not a quick checklist of "Things to Do." With that in mind, there are six stages in his presentation of this spiritual journey.[4] The first four are illustrated in his famous allegory of the cave. We will discuss this allegory, but first let's turn our attention to what has become known in academia as *the divided line*, which is introduced in the *Republic* as the basis for the allegory.[5]

The divided line looks something like this:[6]

	The visible realm		The Intelligible realm	
	Opinion		Knowing	
	A	B	C	D
Cognitive function:	Image-thinking	Belief	Under-standing	Knowledge/Pure Reason
Greek:	*eikasia*	*pistis*	*dianoia*	*noesis*

---

[4] Summarized at 536d~540c

[5] See 509d~511e

[6] This chart is adapted from *Great Dialogues of Plato*, trans. W.H.D. Rouse, p. 309.

As you can see in the chart above, Plato first divides our cognitive functions between the visible realm and what in Platonic metaphysics is called the Intelligible realm, or what we can more colloquially label *opinion* and *knowing*. He then divides these two sections into two parts each. This distributes the cognitive functions, or faculties of the mind, into four categories. The sections are not equal in size because the width of each section represents its degree of power. Image-thinking, for example, functions at a lower degree of power than does understanding. And we will see as the book progresses that power is commensurate with unity. What this means is that the more divided we are by images and conflicting beliefs, the less potent the power with which we relate to the world.

Some translators use the word *understanding* for section D. This could add a layer of confusion for those of you who have been defining *noesis* in this way. In this chapter, and throughout this book, I use the word *understanding* for *dianoia* and thereby limit it to a more narrow range of gnostic activity. Notice that belief and understanding are equal in width in the divided line. This signifies that they are equal in their degrees of power. We will look at why that is a bit later in this chapter, but the answer hinges on the fact that both belief and understanding are built on assumptions.

It is also important to recognize that we are not found solely within one of these categories on the divided line. A person with knowledge also holds beliefs, for example. Beliefs will always be a part of our lives and are not in and of themselves anything evil. They only become a problem when we hold false beliefs and we mistake them for facts or even wisdom.

Let's take a closer look at each of the sections. Sections A and B in the divided line cover the totality of the physical realm. Section A represents that most basic level of thought regarding whatever information our physical senses take in and whatever is going on around us. It is that ability to put together sense data from each of the five senses and to combine this with thought to reach a conclusion about what each thing is that we come into contact with, be it a book or a tree or a double-decker bus. Thomas Taylor refers to this as the phantasy power of the soul. He distinguishes it from unfiltered sense data: "sense is extended to externals, but the phantasy possesses knowledge inwardly."[7]

Section B represents the cognitive faculty called belief. Here we include the whole range of our beliefs, from those about Reality itself to politics, from human nature to our own self-image. Even though our goal is ultimately to gain knowledge of the nature of Reality, the cognitive faculty of belief is not inherently bad or something we ought to try to fully escape. All of the cognitive levels in the divided line have a place in human life; they are all good in their proper mode of existence. Not all beliefs are harmful. That said, the ways in which we see and interact with the world around us is very much shaped by our beliefs and expectations. Therefore, it is these beliefs that we must challenge and, if a belief is limiting and at odds with our true nature, we must discard it.

Recognizing what sections A and B represent is the relatively easy part. Seeing how they function, including how they affect one another, is where it gets tricky. At a basic level, the conclusions we draw in section A are the basis for the beliefs we form in section B. This is the rudimentary way in which we relate to and function in the world, and a necessary element in the survival of our species. You and I would never be here in this exploration of Platonism had our ancestors not been able to recognize dangers such as those posed by wild animals and freezing cold snow storms. Of course, some of the beliefs we form have to be debunked later, such as the belief that the Earth is flat. However, it was also due in part to observations such as ships seeming to fall off the face of the Earth when they sailed into the distance that such false beliefs opened themselves to questions in the first place.

This building up from one cognitive level to the next extends throughout the divided line. Much as image thinking helps inform our beliefs, so too our beliefs are the basis from which we seek understanding of the world around us and the whole of which we are a part. Further, as our understanding deepens, this becomes our launch pad, if you will, into direct knowledge of Reality.

---

[7] Taylor's introduction to *De Anima* in *Works of Aristotle, vol 6*. We will see later in this chapter that Taylor's use of the word *knowledge*, while perfectly fine in the context in which he uses it, is more casual than in the precise way Plato presents knowledge in section D of the divided line.

However, Plato shows us in his description of the divided line that this relationship of the lower influencing the higher is only one part of the story. There is also a relationship of the higher section influencing the section below it. For the sake of simplicity, let's stay for now with sections A and B. Plato describes the images of section A, image thinking, as "shadows, and in the next, reflections in water, and such as subsist in bodies which are dense, polished and bright…" He then describes section B, belief, as "the visible which this [section A] resembles…"[8]

In other words, our beliefs shape the way we perceive the world around us. Our knee-jerk reaction is to reject this idea because it goes against common notions. Of course we first perceive objects and situations as they really are and then form beliefs about them—or do we? Some aspects of image thinking are almost universally agreed upon, rooted in our shared recognition of the physical world. Yet even here, interpretations differ. What one person sees as an inviting ski slope another sees as a mountain daunting and steep. Where one person sees a crowded, dirty city another sees an exciting, bustling metropolis. What these examples point to is that rather than taking the time to form beliefs about everything our senses take in, our current beliefs shape the impressions our perceptions of the world make on our souls.

To better understand the significance of this relationship between image thinking and belief, Plato sets up an analogy between these two sections and the two halves of the divided line:

> "[Are you willing] that the same proportion, which the object of opinion [the visible realm] has to the object of knowledge [the Intelligible realm], the very same proportion has the resemblance [section A] to that of which it is the resemblance [section B]?[9]

What Plato is setting up here in this rather cumbersome sentence is a copy-model relationship throughout the divided line. Note here that by *copy* I do not mean an exact replica. Rather, each section is a diminution of power from the section above it. A simple example to illustrate this might be a painter looking at a vase of flowers and

---

[8] These two quotes are at 510a.
[9] *Ibid.*

painting that image onto a canvas. The final painting is not itself living flowers, but rather a copy that captures the appearance of its model, the vase of real flowers. Going back now to Plato's quote, we can summarize the analogy Plato set up like this:

An object of Opinion is to an object of Knowledge as Resemblance/ Copy is to its Model

Using the shorthand form for writing analogies, it would look like this:

object of opinion : object of knowledge :: resemblance/copy : model

This copy-model relationship reverberates throughout Platonic metaphysics. In regards to the divided line, this analogy allows us to contemplate the various relationships between the four cognitive functions. If the Intelligible realm is the model for the visible realm, just as belief is the model for image-thinking, then we can apply that same relationship throughout the divided line. Knowledge [section D] is the model for understanding [section C]. Understanding, in turn, is the model for belief [section B]. By implication, then, where we lack knowledge, our understanding and beliefs will reflect this in the form of distortions and errors in our thinking. Even where we have right opinion, our beliefs will have no anchor in reasoning to hold them down until we understand *why* they are right.[10] Without that anchor, we are susceptible to being swayed by charismatic arguments and chop-logic. We can even hold beliefs that are disconnected from our view of reality and beliefs that contradict one another.

To see all of this more clearly, let's take a wise individual, such as Socrates, to see how the divided line applies to him. Socrates is someone who presumably had gained the firsthand knowledge that comes from knowing the objects of knowledge in the Intelligible realm (more on that coming up). His understanding of Reality, then, would be a reflection of this knowledge. He would have examined conclusions that he had held before gaining direct knowledge and he

---

[10] This is a main theme of the dialogue *Meno*. See for example 98a: "For true opinions also, so long as they abide by us, are valuable goods, and procure for us all good things; but they are not disposed to abide with us a long time; for they soon slip away out of our souls, and become fugitives. Hence are they of small value to a man, until he has fastened and bound them down, by deducing them rationally from their cause."

would have dropped those that were faulty. Likewise, any false beliefs about Reality he had held before would have been examined and eventually eradicated with understanding, bringing his beliefs in line with his understanding. Furthermore, even his most basic thoughts at the level of image-thinking would have been reflections of his beliefs. Socrates is presented throughout Plato's dialogues as a man who walks happily through the streets of Athens, never judging others by their social status or lamenting his own modest lifestyle. Plato never went so far as to support the notion, embraced in some spiritual circles, that we can create matter or that we can manifest the objects of our dreams. However, he did recognize a sense in which we cognitively create the world around us.

As for those of us who fall short of Socrates' knowledge, we will tend to compensate for this deficiency by drawing on beliefs in order to build understanding of the world, of the self, and of Reality itself. Every one of us does this to some degree, myself included. This is the conventional mindset that we all bring with us the first time we are introduced to Plato's thought. This is the upward progression of the cognitive functions.

This upward progression can be misleading, though. Just as our senses can trick us into believing that the sun is only a tiny ball of light in the sky, so too our beliefs can trick us into thinking we have an understanding, and perhaps even knowledge, of the world that turns out to be false. Plato, therefore, suggests that we need to turn this around: belief is ideally rooted in understanding, not vice versa. We understand, for example, that our distance from the sun accounts for the sun's small appearance in the sky. This understanding shapes our belief into something more accurate than what our aggregate sense data alone conveys.

Those of us delving into a wisdom tradition, then, must go the next step on the divided line and root our understanding in knowledge. Other philosophical schools, those that fit under that umbrella of Relativism, conclude that the physical realm, whether they maintain that there is anything beyond it or not, is all that we are able to experience. They focus mainly on sections A and B. This opens the door for them to conclude that if all is in the realm of opinion, we are all entitled to believe whatever we want and who's to say who is right and who is wrong?

Mystic philosophers such as Plato, however, argue that it is possible to turn the soul towards that which is eternal and real and never changes. This points us towards the value of wisdom traditions. Before we have gained firsthand knowledge of our own, we can draw on the wisdom of sages who are able to guide us towards a healthier, more accurate understanding of truth. Doing so allows us to cultivate first understanding of Reality on a conceptual level and then, once that understanding matures and ripens, knowledge opens to us.

For Plato, only that which is real and eternal and never changes can be an object of knowledge. In metaphysics, we call this the Intelligible realm. In the *Pheadrus*, Plato writes of this realm: "For the colorless, formless, and intangible truly existing essence, with which all true knowledge is concerned, holds this region and is visible only to the mind, the pilot of the soul."[11] Our souls look to this realm of truly existing essence beyond what can be seen or touched. These are the only true objects of knowledge. The word *noesis*, or *knowing*, is used by Plato in this very strict sense.

The aim of our studies, then, is to see through our veil of beliefs so as to raise our state of mind into that higher realm, the realm of knowledge. The study of metaphysics makes up a large part of our efforts. However, we must also understand how the mind functions, and particularly how the beliefs that we are striving to overcome ever took root in the first place. Understanding is cultivated in part by seeing through what is false. It is not a process of adding to our collection of data "as if…inserting sight in blind eyes."[12]

The World Inside the Cave

The famous allegory of the cave depicts this first half of the divided line by opening with prisoners in a cave chained in such a way that they cannot turn their heads. They cannot see behind themselves, nor can they see each other. All that they can see, and all that they have been able to see since childhood, is the wall of the cave that is facing them. This wall is smooth and flat and therefore acts as a screen that displays shadows of the objects behind the prisoners and of the prisoners themselves.

[11] 247c, trans. Harold North Fowler
[12] *Republic,* 518c

There are two sources of light in the cave allegory. Sunlight can be seen at the wide mouth of the cave, which requires climbing up a steep incline to reach. The second source of light, a fire, is deep in the cave. This fire is behind the prisoners and therefore outside their line of vision. In front of the fire but behind the prisoners, people parade to and fro with utensils balanced on top of their heads. Some of these people speak, others do not. Their angle to the fire is such that shadows of the objects they are carrying are cast on the flat wall that is in front of the prisoners.

After describing this bizarre scene, Plato tells us that the prisoners take these shadows to be real. After all, this is the only reality they have known for most of their lives. They even attribute to the shadows the voices of the people walking behind them.

This strange world inside the cave represents our physical existence as it is experienced by the vast majority of people in the world. It is the realm of opinion in the divided line, sections A and B. Plato is perhaps most famous for this ontological representation of the world around us. His ontology, or study of reality,[13] can be broken down into various levels, each represented in the allegory.[14] Metaphysics will be explored in greater detail from Chapter 7. For our purposes here, Platonic metaphysics recognizes Mind itself, called the Intelligible realm, as ultimate reality. Reality unfolds through six realms, or levels, each more diffused and weakened from the previous, yet each perfectly good and right in its own proper power and degree of mindfulness. Three of these realms function in the cave and are reflections or diminutions of power modeled off the three higher realms that have their proper place outside the cave.

The images cast on the wall represent the physical forms around us, the realm of matter. This is the lowest metaphysical realm. It is the most passive of the realms, yet still mindful in the sense that it is able to receive reason-principles from the realms above. Analogous to this, the wall of the cave is able to receive the shadows cast by the utensils via the light of the fire.

The realm just above contains the reason principles of nature. These are the life force of reality as it manifests on the physical plane.

---

[13] The Greek word *ontos* means *to be* and *–ology* means *study of,* so ontology literally means *the study of being/existence.*

[14] I thank Tim Addey for our thought-provoking conversations on this topic that aided to the formation of this section.

In the cave allegory, then, these would be represented by the utensils being carried on the tops of people's heads. They cast their shadows on the wall, indicating the unfolding from their realm to the next. These utensils are made from natural sources such as stone and wood, yet they are called *utensils, implements, artificial* or *artifacts* (*skeuaston* in Greek). This is because realities in the cave are removed from ultimate Reality, represented in the allegory as the upper world.

While there is an unfolding from the realm of nature to the realm of materiality, it is ultimately the fire that gives these natural objects the power to cast their shadow. Ontologically, this fire represents the reason principles of soul, which get passed down to the physical world. The realm of soul is the link between what we might call, in remaining consistent with the imagery of this allegory, the upper and lower worlds. The realm of soul gets its mindfulness from above and is therefore not autonomous, yet it does exercise a certain degree of authority in the cave in the sense that it is the self-motive power of the lower realms.

The prisoners see the shadows cast by the fire and mistake them for reality. Analogously, our conventional mindset does not recognize the physical forms around us as receivers of vitality and intellect, but rather as the original sources of them. The insight into this fallacy is then the trigger that sets us free to discover the cause of our physical world—the shadows—and ultimately even the cause of the realm of soul. That higher search is what eventually brings us out of the cave.

Through the imagery of this allegory, we can contemplate how reality unfolds from the spiritual realm into this material world that many people insist is all that is real. This is a necessary and meaningful level of interpretation. However, the *Republic* is not really about metaphysics. I would suggest that rather than focusing on metaphysics *per se*, Plato is using metaphysics to describe the human experience. Remember, his aim in the *Republic* is to demonstrate justice in the soul and why it is of value in and of itself.

This requires us to add an epistemological[15] layer of analysis to our understanding of this allegory. Each element of the cave allegory can be matched to the cognitive functions on the divided line. Plato is not just showing the unfolding of reality to our material level. No, he is

---

[15] *Episteme* in Greek means *knowledge*. Therefore, epistemology is the study of knowledge or cognitive functions.

using this unfolding of reality to explain why we accept this lowest manifestation of reality as Reality itself and so accept interpretations of beauty, justice and goodness as though they were unquestionable truths. He has to show why so few of us dare to venture outside the cave even if our shackles are removed. In other words, we need to add to our analysis the power of belief.

The chained prisoners are said to name the shadows, believing them to be real.[16] They even assign to the shadows the voices of the people walking behind them carrying utensils on their heads. The echoes of these voices represent the spoken manifestation of the *logos,* truth as an intellectual reality that unfolds throughout the cosmos. The chained prisoners even argue with one another about the value and meaning of the various shadows, giving prizes and accolades to those who have what is deemed the best understanding of them.

And so the question arises as to how the fire, which represents the reason principles of soul, could cast shadows which are falsely interpreted. If each realm is true and good at its own proper power, then how could anything false enter into the unfolding of Reality? What Plato is showing us in this allegory is that false belief is able to enter into the cave because of the very nature of the unfolding of reality. In other words, the epistemological reading of this allegory is indelibly tied to the ontological one.

By giving us a bird's-eye view of all the levels of reality, Plato is showing us where the conventional mindset fits in, and then goes on to describe the subsequent stages of development. Opinion is recognized by Plato as the lowest functioning of the rational faculty of the soul. He defines *opinion* as the soul carrying on a discourse with itself.[17] The realm of opinion in the divided line is represented by the world inside the cave. To experience the realm of knowing and the increased power of its higher cognitive functions, we must climb the steep ascent out of the cave and emerge into the sunlight of the upper world.

The Stages of Our Journey

The first stage of our spiritual journey, then, is to break free of our chains. These are chains that have held us since childhood, not

---

[16] See *Republic,* 515b
[17] See *Theatetus,* 189e~190a and *Sophist,* 264a

since birth. Plato introduces the prisoners in this way: "Suppose them to have been in this cave from their childhood, with chains both on their legs and necks…"[18] It is in our formative childhood years, after all, when beliefs take root and shape our interpretations of ourselves and of our families and communities. In Plato's cave allegory, a prisoner who has been newly freed from his chains looks around the cave. He sees the bearers carrying objects on their heads and the fire that casts shadows on the wall. He gradually comes to understand that what he had taken for Reality and Truth were only images.

At the same time, he sees that the cave itself is real, even if the images he had once mistaken for truth are not. He now has the task of making sense of what this physical realm really is, as well as why he had been so mistaken about reality up to this point. Plato recognizes the physical realm to have, in its own right, a mode of reality which is good. He shows us through this allegory that all the cognitive functions—and indeed the whole progression of reality—is ultimately good. It is the natural order for falsehood to enter into the epistemological progression at the level of the physical realm.

A purely epistemological reading of this allegory, however, would limit us to a psychological study of states of mind. Many people around us recognize the role of belief in shaping us in our formative years, yet those people are not necessarily freed from their shackles. It is not enough to see only the role of belief; we must also see the metaphysics behind it. We need to recognize the interconnectedness of both the ontological and epistemological readings of this allegory to understand the shock and confusion of this ex-prisoner as he struggles to make sense of that first look around the cave. Plato asks: "what do you think he would say, if one should tell him that formerly he had seen trifles, but now, being somewhat nearer to reality, and turned toward what was more real, he saw with more rectitude…"[19]

It is easy to see with the ontological reading why he is "nearer to reality" once he turns around and sees behind himself. He realizes that the physical world that he had mistaken for ultimate reality is actually just the passive receiver of reason principles functioning beyond his previous understanding. We must combine this, however, with the epistemology of this newly freed prisoner. Another insight

---

[18] 514a~b.

[19] 515d

open to this ex-prisoner is that what he had accepted as truly good, beautiful and just were actually beliefs about goodness, beauty and justice formed through the shared experience of these shadows with others chained in the cave.

Recognizing the depths of our ignorance is vital to our growth, and this first step of our journey is one which Socrates was never so proud as to claim to be above. At his trial, he famously declared that in comparing himself to an Athenian politician respected for his wisdom, Socrates actually was the wiser in one small regard: "because I do not think that I know things which I do not know."[20]

It is not just reason principles in nature and material forms that function in the cave, but also the power of belief. While false beliefs have caused and will continue to cause humanity unquestionable pain and anguish, they are not evil when looked at in the totality of all the realms of reality. Our false beliefs point us towards what we need to see in order to learn and grow. If humanity had only reason principles to guide our cognitive functioning in the cave, we would never grow psychologically or spiritually. It is our curiosity that spurs our thoughts, and discoveries that contradict previously held beliefs that fuel further curiosity. Our newly freed prisoner did not question reality until discovering that his initial state was erroneous.

The approach we take to achieve this initial stage is twofold. Before the desire to know Truth can be awakened, we must first recognize the role that belief and imitation play in our lives. After all, why would anyone seek truth if they think they already know it?[21] In the analogy to the city-state, Plato calls these initial studies music.[22]

In contrast to our exploration of belief and imitation, the exploration of the nature of Reality is initiated through our readings

---

[20] *Apology*, 21d

[21] Compare *Symposium* 203e~204a: "None of the Gods philosophize, or desire to become wise; for they are so....Nor yet does philosophy, or the search of Wisdom, belong to the Ignorant. For on this very account is the condition of Ignorance so wretched, that notwithstanding she is neither fair, good, nor wise, yet she thinks she has no need of any kind of amendment or improvement. So that the ignorant, not imagining themselves in need, neither seek nor desire that which they think they want not."

[22] This will be discussed in Chapter 15.

and also our contemplations of Reality. We will see various practices in the *Understanding* section that are all geared towards these ends.

The second stage of the spiritual journey is to mature the contemplations of the studies of understanding into a unified whole. Our practice begins ripening when we see the interconnectedness of its various elements.[23] This is the road into the depths of understanding. Plato depicts this in his cave allegory by the long, arduous ascent to the mouth of the cave.[24] At this stage, the Intelligible realm is the object of our studies, but we don't yet see this realm directly. We are still hindered by assumptions that block our view. The ex-prisoner in Plato's allegory is guided by the light at the wide mouth of the cave, but doesn't yet know what the world outside actually looks like.

This is where most of us dwell when we ponder metaphysics. When we are functioning at the level of understanding—section C of the divided line—we rely on assumptions that are at the base of our discursive reasoning. These assumptions create limitations when we ponder more complex issues, such as whether or not we have a soul. Our childhood influences and upbringing, whether religious or not, have shaped our ideas about what words such as *soul* mean. We may question some of these assumptions, but others will slip by unnoticed. Built into this will be assumptions about time and space, which are very much limited by our experiences in physical form. This is why sections B and C of the divided line are equal in length, representing an equality of power.

When we talk about metaphysical Realities such as *Soul, Time, Truth,* or *Justice*, our minds are turned to the things themselves. However, we don't yet know these Realities firsthand; we have only an image of them based on our still-limited understanding. They are concepts to us. What's more, we don't know how to drop our assumptions (even though we understand in theory that we *should* drop them), and often don't recognize which assumptions we are making.

---

[23] For stage 2 in *Republic*, see 537c: "let those disciplines which in their youth [i.e., in the earliest stage of practice] they learned separately, be brought before them in one view, that they may see the alliance of disciplines with each other, and with the nature of real being."

[24] *Republic*, 516a

Let's look at an example. Many esoteric mystical writings describe time as circular rather than linear.[25] Some savvy students of spirituality may read these accounts and think that they have intimate knowledge beyond the average person's understanding. However, without having experienced this circularity of time firsthand, can any of us really say that we don't harbor *any* assumptions in the way we understand these esoteric teachings? Until we gain firsthand experience, there will always be presumptions coloring our understanding. Understanding, of course, admits of degrees. We aim to mature our studies over time to a clearer, more insightful vision. However, the sections of the divided line are incommensurate. There is a great leap between even the most mature understanding (Plato's ex-prisoner reaching the top of the steep ascent) and the shallowest degree of knowing (that first step out of the mouth of the cave).

Emerging into the sunlight after a lifetime of darkness presents new challenges, and this is **the third stage** of our journey.[26] Socrates says: "And after he had even come to the light, having his eyes filled with splendor, he would be able to see none of these things now called true."[27] This person, Socrates surmises, would first look at shadows and reflections before finally being able to see the upper world—the Intelligible realm—as it really is. It is here that we can survey the Intelligibles, the absolute Realities that are the only true objects of knowledge. Touching Reality itself, metaphorically represented in the *Republic* as looking to the sun itself, is the highest expression of the Intelligible realm and the peak of this third stage. "And, last of all, he may be able, I think, to perceive and contemplate the sun himself, not in water, nor resemblances of him, in a foreign seat, but himself by himself, in his own proper region."[28]

Advancing our practice once we step out into the upper world will be the focus of the *Knowing* section of this book. Most of us involved in this practice dabble with dialectic early on, but it is here that it shows its true strength. The successful dialectician is the one who,

---

[25] For example, in *Timaeus,* Plato wrote about "time imitating eternity, and circularly rolling itself according to number." 38b.

[26] *Republic,* 537d

[27] *Ibid.,* 516a

[28] *Ibid.,* 516b. See also 517c: "In the intelligible place, the idea of *the good* is the last object of vision, and is scarcely to be seen..."

"without the assistance of his eyes, or any other sense, is able to proceed with truth to being itself."[29]

True knowing is only achieved by directly touching the nature of Reality and then understanding that encounter. Plato writes that the philosopher:

> "comes into contact with the nature of everything which *is,* by that part of the soul whose office it is to come into contact with a thing of this kind. But it is the office of that part of the soul which is allied to real being; to which when this true lover of learning approaches, and is mingled with it, having generated intellect and truth, he will then have true knowledge, and truly live and be nourished…"[30]

Both the leap from understanding to knowing and also the exploration of that experience require the power of dialectic, ideally practiced with a teacher and also on one's own through our readings and in the form of contemplation.

The common image of dialectic is that of a battle of wits. However, this is far from the heights to which dialectic has the potential to take us. The challenge is to recognize the assumptions hidden in our conclusions so that we are able to jump beyond them. "But do you not call him skilled in dialectic, who apprehends the reason of the essence of each particular? And as for the man who is not able to give a reason to himself, and to another, so far as he is not able, so far will you not say he wants intelligence of the thing?"[31]

In this practice, assumptions are not treated as starting points that we build our arguments upon; they are steps from which the soul can climb, pushing its way to the beginning of all and grabbing hold of that region.[32] You might think of it as a climb backwards, because we need to question each assumption to see what foundation it is built on. We keep going backward, challenging our beliefs one by one until

---

[29] *Ibid.,* 537d

[30] *Ibid.,* 490b

[31] *Ibid.,* 534b. Plato goes on at 534c to state that the philosopher must also be able to give an account of the *Idea* of the Good. See also 533b: "[N]o other method can attempt to comprehend, in any orderly way, what each particular being is…"

[32] See *Ibid.,* 511b

all of the assumptions fall away and we are enveloped in Reality itself. The experience of Reality itself is what mystics often refer to as a peak experience.

This, however, is not the end of the journey. Once we have enjoyed the beauty of Reality, we must grasp whatever follows first from this vision. The contemplation continues as we struggle to understand what we have experienced. In this way, we are able to reach a conclusion without the use of the senses. We use only the absolute Realities, moving one to another, and ending in absolute Realities.[33] Understanding the experience of Reality itself, then, is a higher form of understanding than is the understanding of Reality as an object of theory alone.

Plato is stressing here that wisdom does not result from discursive thought alone or even from experience itself, but arises from an understanding of that experience. Wisdom is a state of mind, a rare one which springs from knowing the Reality behind the images that we hold. Knowing, much like understanding, admits of degrees. It can be cultivated and deepened. The more fully dialectic is used prior to an experience, the deeper the experience. After experience, it is by thoroughly examining the Reality we beheld that our state of mind is able to ripen further into deeper spiritual maturity. Even for the wise teacher, there is room for growth.

This distinction between understanding and knowing separates mystic systems from mainstream religions. Rabbis, priests, and sheiks are generally leaders who have studied religious texts and can discuss them with an air of authority coupled with some degree of what we might call worldly wisdom. Yet, for all this, they may not have gained the firsthand experience coveted by mystics. This is not to downplay the important role such wisdom plays in our societies; it can be of great value in the betterment of many people's lives. However, in clarifying the difference between understanding and knowing, it is imperative that we see this distinction.

Insights into the human heart, however beautiful they may be, are not always evidence of knowing in the strict sense that Plato uses this word. Oftentimes, those insights are rooted in assumptions about the nature of Reality that tie our identities to our current human

---

[33] See *Ibid.,* 511c.

incarnations. However, we are more than our bodies. We are even more than individuals who each have a soul. We therefore must look upward and directly behold the Reality that is our essence. Falling short of this, we are still living among the shadows in Plato's allegorical cave, sometimes acting on right opinion but other times missing the mark. For this reason, Platonism recognizes religious leaders whose experience falls short of true knowledge as having achieved right opinion at best, colored to some degree by false beliefs.

Some may doubt that knowledge as Plato presents it really is humanly possible to attain. Certainly, teachers from different traditions have points of contention. Even the wisest among teachers will disagree from time to time. This is partly due to varying degrees of vision. However, there is another dynamic to what is going on here. We ultimately bring our vision of Reality down to the physical level. We must interact with other people, most of whom do not share our insights. This means that we must learn how to recognize the various ways in which images of truth permeate all of human affairs, and to live amidst apparent relativity without losing sight of the unitary vision we beheld.

This is **the fourth stage** of the spiritual journey.[34] Socrates insists:

> "Everyone then must, in part, descend to the dwelling of the others, and accustom himself to behold obscure objects: for, when you are accustomed to them, you will infinitely better perceive things there, and will fully know the several images, what they are, and of what, from your having perceived the truth concerning things beautiful, and just, and good."[35]

This fourth stage is a reminder that wisdom is about cultivating a spiritually mature state of mind. It is a life-long process, not a one-time event. Our physical world is not ultimate reality, but it is also not an illusion. It is real in its own mode of being. The ex-prisoner returning to the cave knows the intelligible Realities and so recognizes their proper proliferations here. Recognizing this world as part of a greater whole and adjusting to a new way of relating to it are challenges we must face. This, of course, involves further metaphysical insights and applications.

---

[34] *Ibid.*, 539e

[35] *Ibid.*, 520c

Equally pressing, this ex-prisoner will also recognize false interpretations of beauty, justice and goodness. This is implied by Socrates' conclusion that such a person is better able to serve in public office, better than those who "fight with one another about shadows...."[36] It is only by understanding the nature of belief that we are able to answer the question as to why the prisoners fight about the shadows. We don't fight over metaphysical levels of reality. In fact, the prisoners don't even know there *are* metaphysical levels of reality. They think the shadows are all that is real.

No, what we fight over are interpretations of goodness, interpretations of beauty and interpretations of justice. We fight, for example, over whether the good life is one of wealth and privilege or one of service and devotion. Or maybe it's one of adventure. Then again, it could be one of learning and intellectual discussions. And so on. We equally have multiple images of beauty and of justice. All modern societies struggle, for example, with questions of how to keep citizens safe without impinging on their freedom. This could be seen as the clashing of different images of justice. And then there is the more cynical question that asks if there is one mode of justice for the wealthy and another for everybody else.

The wisest person, Plato tells us, is the one who recognizes both the true reflections of beauty, justice and goodness and also their false images. This person is a contrast both to those who fight over shadows and those who leave the cave but choose never to return. He states this in the language of the analogy that carries throughout the *Republic*, that of building a city-state. Political leaders in this analogy are the analogue for that aspect of the soul which guides us through our lives, ideally guiding us wisely:

> "[N]either those who are uninstructed and unacquainted with truth can ever sufficiently take care of the city; nor yet those who allow themselves to spend the whole of their time in learning. The former, because they have no one scope in life, aiming at which they ought to do whatever they do, both in private and in public; and the latter, because they are not willing to manage civil affairs, thinking that whilst they are yet alive, they inhabit the islands of the blessed."[37]

---

[36] *Ibid.,* 520d

[37] *Ibid.,* 519c

From here, Plato leaves his cave allegory behind, moving beyond anything that images can capture. While a growing number of people in modern society achieve some degree of wisdom, few reach its pinnacle. These few who reach the challenge of **the fifth stage** "are to be obliged, inclining the ray of their soul, to look towards that which imparts light to all things, and, when they have viewed *the good itself*, to use it as a paradigm…during the remainder of their life."[38] What he's alluding to here is moving beyond even the oft-described experience of beholding Reality itself, of knowing our essence to be no different from that of the essence of all. It is not enough to know Reality; we also must answer the question *Why?* Why does Reality exist? Not in the mechanical sense (that's more of a *how?* question) but in the sense of, *What's the point?* Without looking to the Good itself, which is that for the sake of which all things exist, we will never answer this question to our satisfaction.

This, Plato tells us, is at last the height of our practice. However, our journey is still not over. While we all have infinite room to grow and learn, the student who has integrated these highest insights is finally ready to take on the role of teacher. This is **the sixth stage**, and the integration process could potentially take many years. When at last we are ready, it is time to pay forward on one's own gains. Those few who mastered this sixth stage "educated others in the same manner still, and left such as resemble themselves…"[39]

This role of teacher is hinted at in the cave allegory yet never focused on. When Socrates introduces a prisoner first unchained and looking around the cave, he asks: "what do you think he would say, if one should tell him that formerly he had seen trifles…"[40] No information is given as to who this person is who aids the newly freed prisoner. Yet doesn't this person function as a teacher if he or she should assist by "pointing out to him each of the things passing along, should question him, and oblige him to tell what it was….And if he should oblige him to look to the light itself, would not he find pain in his eyes and shun it…?"[41] And so it is that this mysterious teacher is

---

[38] *Ibid.*, 540a (italics included)

[39] *Ibid.*, 540b

[40] *Ibid.*, 515d

[41] *Ibid.*, 515d~e

the one who leads our befuddled ex-prisoner to the steep ascent out of the cave.

Functioning as a teacher is, in effect, another return to the cave. What this highlights is that the ultimate goal of Platonism is not the peak experience. Rather, our aim is to live wisely in the material world, encouraging everyone around us to recognize their own wisdom and beauty.

The chapters that follow will take us through these stages. The six stages of our journey, then, can be summarized as follows:

1. Drop our chains and look around the cave.

Initiating understanding of the nature of Reality; recognizing the role that belief and imitation play in our lives.

2. Climb up the steep ascent to the mouth of the cave.

Maturing the contemplations of the studies of understanding into a unified whole.

3. Emerge into the sunlight.

Exploring the objects of knowledge dialectically, dropping assumptions as necessary. Culminates in exploring the peak experience of Reality itself "in its own proper region."

4. Return to the cave.

Integrating our insights, learning to live in the world as one who knows the true nature of Reality.

5. Rise to the Good.

Turning to the source of all that *is*.

6. Guide others.

Paying forward on our education.

Chapter 4: Starting Out

"[T]he beginning is more than the half, and…no one has sufficiently praised it when properly accomplished."

Plato[1]

Taking on the Challenge

Aside from going through the motions of celebrating holidays on the Jewish calendar, I grew up with no sense of spirituality in my life. I got my first taste of it in my late teens when a friend coerced me to join her for a weekly meeting of Michigan State University's yoga club. It was early on a Sunday morning. There were only about 10 of us together in one corner of a room large enough to easily hold four times as many people. A few brought their own yoga mats, and the rest of us borrowed one from the bubbly woman running the class.

I went into that session with only a vague image of what hatha yoga was. I mirrored the instructor as she guided us through various postures of Iyengar-style hatha yoga. I had no initial interest in Hinduism *per se*, but something about doing those poses gave me a peace of mind I had never known before. I was hooked on that first day and became a regular attendee. This earned me strange looks from friends and acquaintances who couldn't even imagine what a yoga club was. Back in those days, few people knew about things such as chakras and auras. Hatha yoga was not fashionable or common. It had a niche appeal, and those associated with such practices—and non-Biblical spiritual practices in general—were largely seen as strange or eccentric. This was a time when science was gaining its foothold as the religion of the educated. I too had this image to battle. Being young and self-conscious, I found myself trying to justify embracing something that most of the people I hung out with saw as weird or even crazy.

Much has changed since then. Hatha yoga classes (as well as kundalini yoga and many other forms of yoga) have become popular at health clubs and gyms. The internet is bustling with videos on how to balance and heal energy. There's been an explosion of self-help books on such topics as astral travel and how to talk to angels. Living spiritually is no longer for a few fringe loners and "weirdos"—it has

---

[1] *Laws*, 753e

become trendy. Being aware of ourselves as spiritual beings is seen as something positive rather than as something requiring justification.

These are positive changes for the most part. If you are looking to add an element of spirituality into your everyday life, you are living in the perfect age. Reading spiritual books and attending spiritually-focused retreats is now widely accepted and even encouraged. However, those of us who dare to go beyond this level of a spiritual life into that of the mystical will face the same social roadblocks that obstructed past generations. We, too, will be met with skepticism.

Before we go on, let me clarify the way in which I'm using the words *spirituality* and *mysticism*. The word *spirituality* can be a broad umbrella term that covers any belief in something beyond our physical world. To the degree that we embrace a metaphysical aspect of ourselves and incorporate it into our daily lives, we can be said to live spiritually. This is true whether we identify with an organized religious system or not.

I think of *mysticism*, in all of its forms, as the far end of the spirituality spectrum. It embraces the notion that divinity is not only an aspect of who we are, but is our true essence. Mysticism rejects the assumption that we are fundamentally physical beings but have a spiritual side as well. We don't *have* soul, mind, spiritual energy (or whichever other term you like to use);[2] we *are* these things. We are immortal and we reincarnate. Our physical body is something temporary that we change whenever it wears out.

The life of a mystic, therefore, goes beyond incorporating practices into our lives that help us get in touch with our spiritual side. We are learning to shift our identity from the person we are in this incarnation to the essence itself that underlies that identity and, perhaps we will discover, even underlies all that exists. It is an entire overhaul of our understanding of what reality is and how our physical realm fits into a grander cosmic whole.

Through hatha yoga, I was introduced to Hinduism, which offered me my first taste of mysticism. I also dabbled in Buddhism for a while. It wasn't until my late twenties, though, when a friend introduced me to Plato's writings, that my desire for a mystical life

---

[2] As you get deeper into metaphysics, you will discover that these terms are actually not interchangeable. For our purposes here, though, the distinction is not relevant.

fully awakened. I discovered in his dialogues, and in the writings of other Platonic philosophers, a doorway into understanding what I am and the nature of the reality of which we are all a part.

Clearly, there are many schools of philosophy that do not embrace mysticism, and not all mystics make philosophy their focus. Yet, philosophy at its best is the systematic contemplation of Reality, and mystics who seek the Divine through a path of contemplating and internalizing metaphysics are true philosophers. It was when I first recognized this that the words *mysticism* and *philosophy* became synonymous to me. Philosophy—the "love of wisdom"—is the love of knowing Reality.

When I made my first steps away from mainstream spiritual practices into mysticism, I faced various criticisms. I was told that I was too intense. Others thought I was conceited and judgmental to reject the best-seller spiritual books they embraced in favor of the writings of obscure mystics such as Proclus and Plotinus. Some saw the increasing amount of time I spent reading and meditating as dangerous, pulling me away from what they saw as a healthy, active social life. To others, my practice was impractical or downright strange. Fortunately, I also crossed paths with people whose interests were in line with my own. They shared stories of comparable experiences, and through them I came to realize that facing this kind of resistance was common.

Those readers who opt to take on the type of lifestyle outlined in this book will probably face at least some of this resistance. Friends or loved ones may ask, "What's wrong with the way *I* live? Why isn't it good enough for you?" These sorts of questions miss the mark; this way of life is not a condemnation of others. We all have beauty and goodness in us, as well as a fair amount of ignorance. I certainly see that in myself. No doubt, you see that in yourself, too. Embracing philosophy has nothing to do with passing judgment on others; it is a choice that we make for ourselves because we want to know our true nature and the nature of reality.

Diving into this lifestyle, though, will present us with many worthy challenges. Along the way, we will be forced to look at our own shortcomings with raw honesty. As we will see in the chapters to come, our practice explores not only the nature of truth and reality, but also the nature of ignorance. We must come to recognize the false images we picked up in childhood and how we ever came to believe them in the first place. This may be easy to accept in theory, but it can be extremely difficult in practice. We need to fight the understandable urge to deny our shortcomings or simply rationalize them away. There is also the common tendency to flip to the opposite extreme and glorify our darkness, as if we were proving our intellectual depth by wallowing in some sort of existentialist hell. Both extremes can prove tempting, but our goal demands that we stay on track.

We will find ourselves tearing down walls we have spent our whole lives building, walls that were constructed through beliefs learned in the formative years of our childhood and reinforced throughout our lives by their commensurate states of mind. There is certainly no room here to climb up on a pedestal and look down on others. When philosophy is properly undertaken, it does not feed our pride; it cultivates a healthy humility.

What will allow us to take on this challenge with no goal other than to be healthy? It could only be love for ourselves as divine essences, the recognition that the Delphic Oracle's challenge to *know thyself* is a challenge to know true freedom. This knowledge is worth more than the apparent comfort we might gain by avoiding the effort and difficulties of the path we have chosen. Living as a true philosopher, then, is an act of self-compassion.

Diving into this lifestyle heart and soul requires having the confidence to leave the pack behind, but also the humility to do so without being condescending. We must admit that we know nothing, and let wonder fuel our journey.[3] It is a rare combination of qualities that we need to cultivate and nurture, but it can be done. This is the state of mind of the true student. Even those of us working on our own without a teacher are students. We need the courage and openness to let truth guide our path and the flexibility to honor that guidance. It is in this spirit that I use the word *student* throughout this book.

Let's take a closer look at the ideal characteristics that allow us to approach our practice in the most productive way. Don't worry if you fall short of this ideal; we are all works in progress. It is natural to go through cycles of being intensely interested in philosophy and then falling out of it, only to be drawn back in somewhere down the road.

---

[3] This hallmark of Plato's thought was captured most concisely in the dialogue *Theatetus* at 155d: "[W]onder is very much the passion of a philosopher. For there is no other beginning of philosophy than this."

Over time, the periods of immersion tend to increase and the periods away tend to wane. This is largely because there are certain attitudes, which will be discussed below, that need to be developed. As these attitudes take root, they in turn support one another to further nurture a healthy state of mind.

There are four virtues that Plato singled out as those which must guide all philosophers: wisdom, fortitude, temperance, and justice. The fullest flowering of these virtues marks the state of mind of the wise man or woman, yet we will find that the development of these virtues is a vital element throughout all stages of our journey.

There are many misconceptions about the virtues. The virtues are not behaviors to be imitated, nor does being virtuous mean rejecting our emotions or denying having desires. The virtues, rather, are states of mind that gradually develop when we embrace Platonism as a lifelong companion. They are the fruits of our efforts as we as souls mature. A healthy state of mind is not something that passively happens to us in a mind-blowing instant of insight; it is a way of being that we actively grow into.

The four virtues come up in a number of Plato's dialogues, but it is in his dialogue the *Republic* that he presents detailed descriptions of all four of them consecutively.[4] I've adapted these descriptions below to show how the virtues can guide us to cultivate the ideal attitude regarding spiritual practice.

Wisdom

I will present a far more detailed discussion of wisdom in the third section of this book. What I will give now is a brief introduction to wisdom in the context of this current discussion.[5] Wisdom, in a nutshell, results when the soul is guided by that part of itself which knows the nature of Reality itself. A soul in contact with this knowledge of the nature of Reality knows how to best behave toward itself and toward others. That knowledge is awakened little by little when we turn our attention away from the physical, transient world and focus on the Intelligible, which is eternal and unchanging.

Here, and throughout this book, we are talking about wisdom in the sense of mastering the virtue of human wisdom. In *Protagoras*, for

---

[4] This is the focus of Book 4 of the *Republic*.
[5] This section is based on the *Republic*, 428b~429a

example, Socrates agrees that wisdom and knowledge are "the most powerful of all human affairs."[6] However, Socrates also states in various dialogues that human wisdom is only a shadow of divine wisdom, and that true wisdom is solely the property of the gods.[7] It is in this higher sense that we call ourselves philosophers, lovers of wisdom.

It is also important to clarify that compassion is not absent from the Platonic virtues; it is an element of wisdom. The dichotomy of the head versus the heart is a false dichotomy. Although Platonists tend to focus on good judgment as the manifestation of wisdom, it is with the understanding that compassion is the other side of that coin. Good judgment and compassion are indelibly linked; neither truly exists without the other. Being compassionate is about more than having sympathy for people; it implies good judgment. Without good judgment, what passes for compassion is just maudlin sentimentality.

At the same time, wise judgment also implies compassion. Without compassion, what passes for good judgment is just logical calculations. Being wise is more than merely being clever. Anyone who understands the nature of Reality, humanity's place in the whole, and our connection to one another naturally feels goodwill toward their fellow humans. A love springs up for all life on Earth and, for that matter, Earth itself and the universe we are all a part of. Socrates' life and death were shaped by compassion.[8] We can argue that Plato's was, as well. He forewent the power and social status of a life of politics to instead teach philosophy at his Academy, where he reportedly charged no money for the time he devoted to his students.

We will see with the other three virtues that they all hinge on wisdom. To the degree we know the nature of Reality, we will be able to master the other virtues. Therefore, the virtues admit of degrees.

---

[6] 352d

[7] See for example *Theatetus* 176c, *Apology of Socrates* 23a, and *Symposium* 204a

[8] At his trial, he explains that questioning people was something he was commanded to do by the gods (*Apology of Socrates,* 33c). He also expresses his belief that this calling is for the benefit of the Athenian people: "For be well assured that Divinity commands me thus to act. And I think that a greater good never happened to you in the city, than this my obedience to the will of Divinity. For I go about doing nothing else than persuading both the younger and older among you, neither to pay attention to the body, nor to riches, nor anything else prior to the soul…" (*Ibid.,* 30a) His famous analogy of himself to a gadfly arousing a sluggish horse follows at 30e.

They are not all-or-nothing but rather continually deepen into spiritual maturity.

Fortitude

What Plato calls *fortitude*, or *courage*,[9] is not the type of courage needed to bungee jump or to wrestle a tiger. Rather, this is a quality in the soul that allows nothing—neither pain nor pleasure—to deter us from plunging into the depths of our most profound questions about the nature of Reality or, once touching knowledge, from living in accordance with what we know to be true. There are many deterrents out there, some in the form of fears and others in the form of enjoyable distractions.

While nobody I have ever met has found contemplating metaphysics easy to do, it is more frightening for some than for others. Depending on our backgrounds, we may have grown up with a sense that evil is something real. Those raised with a belief in an evil entity such as the devil might fear probing beyond the physical realm. They may have become convinced that some things are best left unknown. I have met many religious people over the years who were afraid of mysticism for precisely this reason. Such a person is not likely even to get started on the mystical path.

However, Platonism recognizes that the Divine is only good.[10] The horrible ways people treat one another are born out of ignorance of our true nature, not powered by a supernatural evil force. As our practice develops, we cultivate an understanding about this goodness that is the mark of the Divine. Along with this understanding comes greater trust that no fearful supernatural force awaits us as we push forward, and that the negative qualities we perceive in ourselves are rooted in false beliefs. They are not our true nature, nor are they evidence of our being evil. This allows us to develop greater fortitude. Plato defines fortitude as a power rooted in this kind of understanding: "Such a power now, and perpetual preservation of right opinion, and such as is according to law, about things which are dreadful, and which are not, I call and constitute fortitude..."[11]

---

[9] This section is based on the *Republic*, 429a~430d
[10] See, for example, *Ibid.*, 379b
[11] *Ibid*, 430b

Before we go on, I want to pause for a moment to reiterate a point from the previous chapter about what Plato means by *understanding*. Initially, we may like an idea we read because it feels right. This is a starting point at best; we haven't yet gained wisdom or even understanding simply by reading an appealing argument. In fact, we've all undoubtedly read arguments that were appealing on the surface but then, upon further reflection, fell apart. As philosophers, we need to test our beliefs with reasoning and contemplation, first dealing with theories and eventually with direct experience of Reality.

Reasoning and contemplation of theories bring us to a state of mind that Plato calls understanding. Understanding is a type of belief, though, because it is rooted in assumptions that we are still in the process of testing. As students starting out, we don't actually *know* that the Divine is only good and not evil. We don't even know if Reality can truly be known. These are theories that our reasoning brought us to, and so we tentatively accept them. The person who rejects these conclusions would have no motivation to engage in a mystical practice such as Platonism. Those of us who do proceed do so because these conclusions appeal to us on a conceptual level and we want to understand them more deeply.

However, it is only through direct experience of Reality and the exploration of what we encounter in such experiences that we come to a state of mind we call *knowledge*. It is only through this process that we are able to confirm that Reality is indeed knowable and that the Divine is only good and never evil. Therefore, understanding differs from knowing and is a type of belief, but one that is quite unlike blind belief. We will find that our fortitude grows stronger as our understanding deepens, and even stronger yet once we cross into knowing.

Fears are not the only tests of our fortitude. Pleasures also have a way of testing our resolve and our capacity for proceeding courageously. We tend to want our pleasure to endure, and this gives birth to desire. As all of us undoubtedly know, desire can override our better judgment. If a desire to prolong or increase our pleasure grows, this can end up consuming all of our attention and energy at the expense of focusing on more meaningful matters. This is true not only for activities traditionally recognized as addictive, such as drugs, sex, gambling, and overindulging in food or drink, but in all areas of our lives. Even something as seemingly innocent as daydreaming can pull us off course from our higher goals.

In my experience, desires tend to be more of an obstacle in the early years of practice than our fears are. Perhaps this is because, early on, we haven't yet built up the energy or the one-pointed focus to stay immersed in our contemplations for extended periods of time. This was certainly true for me; I would grow tired of spiritual practice and need a break, or working on one of Plato's dialogues would be interesting until the phone rang, and then I would be off on a conversation with a friend. Of course, once we gain some direct experience, we realize that the ideas we are working with are more than merely theories. It is when we actually see and relate to the world as mystics that staying immersed in these thoughts is no longer tiring. Why would it be? It becomes just the way we see the world.

As for our fears, some of them will need to be addressed right away, such as the earlier example of belief in the devil. For the most part, though, I find that people in whom these types of fears are strong are not attracted to mysticism in the first place. Those of us who are attracted to it can usually placate the early manifestations of these fears with reason alone. Later on, though, when our practice gets more advanced, fear of the unknown can become a powerful obstacle to overcome. There is a more in-depth exploration about this issue in Chapter 27.

Fortitude is not only what allows us to pursue metaphysical questions in the first place, but it is also what preserves the understanding we have cultivated. It takes conviction to hold onto the conclusions our contemplations have brought us to because many of them differ from the beliefs we were raised on. Plato tells us that there is only one true danger on our path toward wisdom: accepting a falsehood about the nature of Reality.[12] We need to purge ourselves of our false beliefs. By doing so, truth will naturally shine forth, as right action flows naturally from right understanding.

This is why molding behavior to fit an ideal is neither necessary nor desirable, and why Platonists view sacrifice in its literal meaning of *to make sacred*. Devoting time to our practice may feel like a sacrifice in the colloquial sense if we still believe that a good life is rooted in such things as popularity and economic status. However, we will eagerly spend our time in practice once we realize that the best life is one spent in the pursuit of wisdom, as this makes us sacred. As mentioned in Chapter 2, sacrifice properly understood does not involve forcing

---

[12] See *Ibid.*, 382a

ourselves to avoid or give up the things we enjoy. We drop the attitudes and states of mind that we have outgrown and have come to recognize are not beneficial to us as spiritual beings. As our sense of who—or what—we are shifts, so too does our sense of what is beneficial and what lifestyle is best for us.

In this way, our spiritual practice brings about an entire modification to our states of mind that extends beyond our outward behavior. Sometimes people who have gained a theoretical understanding of the nature of Reality will talk in a way that is impressive on the surface; however, this is not the same as having the state of mind of one who is truly wise. What will that person do when faced with financial ruin or the sudden death of a loved one? Or how about a positive situation such as winning a large jackpot in the lottery? Powerful situations, whether seen as positive or as negative, trigger our knee-jerk reactions to the ways we perceive those events. If those perceptions are still rooted in beliefs about being a physical being limited in time and space, then all of our wise-sounding pontifications will be tossed out the window. Theoretical insights are one thing, but truly living with that wise state of mind is another.

To the degree that we achieve the goal of human wisdom, we need to protect what we have gained. This means being aware of our state of mind and noticing which triggers can cause it to deteriorate. Even small changes that may seem harmless make themselves at home in the soul little by little. Which activities pull you squarely into an unhealthy mindset? Does not getting your way make you angry? Or perhaps you sulk when you lose at some competition. Are you the type who can shrug off rejection, or do you take it personally? Everyone has a trigger (we each have many, in fact). Knowing yours and having the fortitude to acknowledge to yourself what is really going on as you experience emotional changes are crucial undertakings for anyone seeking psychical health (the health of the soul).

We must remember the one true danger to our spiritual growth, and therefore do our very best not to let falsehood into the soul and to toss it out wherever we do see it growing roots. Plato tells us that "the best mode of life consists in cultivating justice and the other virtues."[13] If we forget this, we can easily lose the resolve to protect

---

[13] *Gorgias,* 527e

the soul above all else. This steadfastness is what Plato means by fortitude.

Temperance

Alternative translations for *temperance*[14] include such words as *good sense, self-control,* and *sound-mindedness.* The Greek word is *sophrosunein.* This word has undoubtedly caused many translators sleepless nights because there is simply no perfect English translation. This makes it difficult to wrap our minds around what Plato is talking about here.

Even Plato, writing in Greek, seems to have had difficulty coming up with a short, concise definition of this word. Instead, he paints a word-picture of what it is, using words such as *concord, order,* and *harmony* to highlight these qualities of unity and peace within the soul. He intertwines these images with others such as *mastery* and *control* to further clarify that a soul at peace with itself and functioning as a unity is not a slave to any passion or false belief, but rather is master of itself.

For Plato, the desires that come with being in human form—eating, sexual gratification, and so on—are good, or at least not harmful, when not indulged to excess. They have their proper place in our lives, and so the notion of *measure* is also closely tied to temperance. A soul that is master of itself does not need to abstain from desires but rather is able to exercise self-control in the best sense of the word; it is in control of itself (as opposed to repressing desires and emotions, which is what we usually mean by *self-control*).

There are many misconceptions about Plato's notion of temperance, especially in regards to emotions, and so I think I need to take a step back to dispel those myths here. It is absolutely *not* a Socratic virtue to repress one's emotions or to somehow rise above them, whatever one imagines that to mean. For Plato, desires and emotions are a natural part of being human and so nothing to look down on or try to escape from. However, both are ideally guided by intuition, right opinion, and understanding. The temperate person will desire what is healthy for the soul and not desire what is unhealthy.

Socrates is Plato's consummate example of temperance, but this does not mean that Socrates' actions were carried out without emotion (which is a common interpretation that needs to be put to rest). Socrates, as presented in such dialogues as the *Apology of Socrates,*

---

[14] This section is based on *Republic,* 430d~432a

was a compassionate man who dedicated his life to the service of the people of Athens. This is hardly the behavior of a man who believes that emotions have no place in human life. It was love that guided him, both his love for his fellow Athenians and his love for the gods.

What is more relevant in understanding Socrates' temperance is that Socrates had his soul's eye always on true goodness and therefore was not torn between conflicting goals. Temperance, then, is closely tied to wisdom. Doing the right thing was, for Socrates, an effortless choice. This is the state of mind that gradually develops through our spiritual practice.

The popular image of having an angel on one shoulder and a devil on the other does not apply to the notion of temperance. A person who faces this all-too-understandable battle and chooses the angel is certainly worthy of being called good and also courageous. However, temperance at its fullest flowering involves no such battle. People with a temperate soul are decisive because they are not torn in multiple directions by conflicting desires. They are of one mind and, following the guidance of intuition, right opinion, understanding and knowledge, they are always attracted to what is healthy and good for the soul.

Justice

When we hear the word *justice*,[15] we often think of courts of law. Or we think of all the misery in the world, from wars to crime and poverty. In a more basic sense, the word triggers our notions of fairness in the ways we treat one another. However, the ways that images of justice manifest at social levels differ from what Plato is writing about.

Plato singles out three functions—or aspects—within the soul. These are not physical divisions, however, since the soul, of course, is not physical. First, there is the *logos*. This, we might say, is where wisdom can be accessed, both wisdom in its conventional forms as well as in its more spiritual aspects. It is the *logos* that is associated with the mental process of reasoning, thinking things through step by step. Yet the *logos* is also that aspect of us that is most closely tied to the Divine. It is that voice of intuition that comes to us when we gently turn inward and take the time to listen. That inner voice might inspire us to take a chance and go for it, or perhaps to step back from

---

[15] This section is based on the *Republic,* 432b~441e

doing something that very likely would have resulted in disaster. It is this aspect of the soul, therefore, which has the responsibility of guiding the soul as a whole.

The second aspect, the *thumos,* is what we might call the high-spirited part of the soul. This is the part of us that defends what we believe to be right and attacks anyone and anything that we deem an enemy. This could manifest in various ways, such as pride, self-righteousness, or an overly defensive personality. Ideally, though, the high-spirited aspect of the soul will function as a bodyguard of sorts for our love of wisdom. It safeguards the integrity of the soul as a whole. This second aspect of the soul is where fortitude makes its home.

The proper function of the high-spirited part is to be the bodyguard or watchdog of the soul. Too often it happens that people who gain wisdom later lose their way because the desire for wealth and popularity overwhelms them. This is something we all must guard against by never letting unhealthy desires wear down our fortitude and our capacity to protect our love of wisdom.

Being guided by the high-spirited aspect of the soul is another danger we must guard against. Such people might be too proud or argumentative, caring more about clever arguments than actually seeking truth; others are preachy and love to get up on their soapbox. Then there are those who value money and status over wisdom, and we can't forget the type who are courageous where only fools rush in.

Lastly, we have the aspect of the soul which is home to our appetites and desires, the *epithumia.* Acting on our every whim may seem on the surface to be the ultimate freedom. To Plato, though, it is precisely the opposite; no soul is more enslaved than the one ruled by desires, lacking the wisdom to determine which desires are healthy and which are not. In a healthy soul, desires flow naturally in accordance with wisdom. People who have achieved this high level of order and harmony within themselves will be drawn to what is healthy for the soul and repelled by what is unhealthy. This third aspect, therefore, is generally associated with temperance.

Looking to these three aspects within the soul, Plato recognized justice to be when each part is carrying on its own proper function. Ideally, wisdom should guide all of our thoughts and actions, our high-spirited part should guard whatever wisdom we've attained and encourage us to continue growing, and our desires should fall in line with what is healthy for the soul. Justice, then, describes all three aspects functioning together in their optimal balance and relationship. This is the mark of a healthy soul.

Interconnectedness[16]

The four virtues work closely together. Wisdom is the state of mind of those who know the nature of Reality and so know what is truly good. Staying focused on what is truly good requires the fortitude not to be sidetracked by fears or distracting pleasures. People who successfully maintain this focus on goodness will naturally be temperate; they desire only what is healthy for the soul, and their emotional reactions naturally reflect wisdom. The soul that enjoys this balance is in a state of justice.

Justice binds the soul together, so to speak, into an ordered unity. It is not only what maintains this order and unity, but also what allows this order and unity to take hold in the first place.[17] Temperance is the sober, composed state of mind that naturally awakens in the soul guided by wisdom. The temperate person does not chase every whim, but rather desires only what is healthy for the soul. We are acting justly whenever we conduct ourselves in a way that maintains this healthy condition and works along with it. It is wisdom that guides us in these activities. On the other hand, whatever tears our focus away from this healthy condition of the soul is called injustice, and the opinions which guide us to make such unhealthy choices are nothing other than ignorance of our own nature and of the nature of Reality. Fortitude, too, comes together with the other virtues in that it is a key factor that allows the other virtues to take hold—and then they, in turn, strengthen our resolve.

The virtues all merge into one within the soul. This becomes more apparent as our practice ripens and we are able to attain each of the four virtues to a deeper degree and to integrate them more fully. Early on, the virtues are the means by which our practice is able to unfold. Yet the virtues are also the goal of our practice. At their fullest

---

16 This section is based on *Ibid.*, 441c~444e

17 See *Ibid.*, 433b~c: "Besides those things we have already considered in the city, *viz.* temperance, fortitude, and wisdom; this, said I, seems to remain, which gives power to all these, both to have a being in the state, and, whilst they exist in it, to afford it safety; and we said too, that justice would be that which would remain, if we found the other three."

flowering, they merge into one and collectively describe the condition of soul and state of mind of someone who has traversed the entire journey outlined in Chapter 3. As the *Republic* focuses on justice, Socrates uses justice in this dialogue as the common thread running through all four virtues and tying them into a unity. He uses the word *justice* interchangeably with the word *virtue:*

> "Then again, to produce justice, is it not to establish all in the soul according to nature….Virtue then, it seems is a sort of health and beauty and good habit of the soul…"[18]

The Hindu concept of karma has become commonplace in Western thought and culture. Although the word *karma* is never used in any of Plato's writings, it is easy to see that this natural law of justice was very much recognized in the Platonic tradition. In fact, seeing how justice is developed by Plato may aid those who are having trouble getting past the simplistic notion that karma is about punishment and reward.

What Plato focused on is more of a cause and effect relationship between our thoughts and actions on the one hand, and their results on the other. Simply put, healthy things implant health and unhealthy things implant that which is unhealthy. We see this very clearly on the physical level: if we eat too much junk food, we get sick. Healthy foods, on the other hand, help us maintain a healthy body.

The same general rule applies to the soul. Virtue is the healthy food of the soul; vice is its junk-food diet. Therefore, unjust—or unvirtuous—states of mind implant disease in the soul, and just—or virtuous—ones implant health in the soul. This may be confusing for many people who are new to Platonism. We are used to talking about justice in terms of how we treat other people, not in terms of our own internal states of mind. For example, we turn to the courts to get justice for people who were wronged. We complain about the injustice of poverty. We teach our kids to treat their classmates fairly. This definition of justice compels many people to look at their unhealthy behavior and ask, "Why is it unjust? I'm not hurting anyone."

However, this is not at all what Plato means by justice. For this reason, discussions of justice and what is *good* or *bad/evil* should not be read through our conventional usage of these words. Rather,

---

[18] *Ibid.,* 444d~e

Platonism focuses on what is *healthy* or *unhealthy* for the soul. This way of thinking broadens our understanding of how beliefs and attitudes play out in our lives. For example, insecurities do not render a person evil in the conventional understanding of that word, but such beliefs are unhealthy in the sense that they cause unhealthy states of mind that manifest negative effects in our lives. Whenever we catch ourselves rationalizing that our unhealthy thoughts are not hurting anyone, we can counter that by recognizing that yes they are—we are ultimately hurting ourselves.

Adjusting our thinking in this way allows us to separate the beauty and integrity of the soul from the disease that afflicts it—namely, ignorance. By nurturing a healthy soul, we learn to live in a way that is truly happy. We cultivate understanding of our true nature and, if our practice takes us far enough, we ultimately reach a state of knowing.

In the practice of Platonism, developing a healthy state of mind will draw us to philosophy on an increasingly deeper, more intuitive level. We will be enthusiastic to jump in and do the work. These studies also require that we be persistent, because there will be stumbling blocks along the way. But as our states of mind ripen and our fortitude grows, we will become less likely to give up no matter how difficult the challenge.

There comes a point along the spiritual path at which turning back is a more precarious option, that point when it is clear that the everyday world is not ultimate reality. Before arriving at this insight, spiritual teachings can remain merely interesting theories to us. Even if the theories appeal to us, it is still possible to file them away and get back to what most people would call the "real world." Once the insight sinks in, though, we find ourselves in a whole different situation. To quit would mean to know that there is something artificial about our lifestyles but to pretend not to notice.

And so we must steadfastly push forward, combining all of the studies and practices that will be discussed in this book. We will dive into metaphysics, contemplating things in themselves separate from their physical manifestations. Meditation and contemplation will help us to internalize our insights so that they do not remain merely theoretical. All of these studies help us to cultivate the virtues outlined above, and in turn the gradual manifestation of these virtues further deepens our practice. The virtues, then, are both the aim of our efforts and the means by which we realize the coveted state of mind they usher in.

Understanding

Introduction

Plato's allegory of the cave, which we were introduced to in Chapter 3, has left a lasting impression on Western cultures. In that allegory, he compares us to prisoners chained in a cave since childhood, watching nothing but shadows on a wall and confusing the shadows for Reality. He then surmises what it might be like for one of those prisoners to break free from his shackles and make the painstaking journey up the steep ascent to the mouth of the cave.

It is time now to turn our focus to the ascent out of the metaphorical cave. At this early stage of our journey, our task is to muster the courage to stay fixed on the light coming through the opening at the end of this ascent. It is like our North Star that we must never lose sight of, no matter how afraid we are to leave behind all that is familiar or how arduous the climb may be.

The ingress into understanding Reality brings us closer to—but does not replace—knowing. We don't yet know what we will find in the upper world, but we are fortified by our conviction that we would rather know Truth than live with even the most pleasant of illusions.

This current section of the book, then, will lay the foundation for the last part. We have broken our shackles and are now beginning to explore the key directive that has confronted us all in this tradition: *know thyself.* These words—*gnothi sauton* in Greek—were inscribed on the ancient temple to the god Apollo in the city of Delphi. These words were a challenge to know ourselves not only as people existing in a certain time and place, but as divine essences that transcend this physical world, depicted through the cave we are leaving behind. If knowing ourselves requires stepping out into the upper world, then doesn't it follow that our true selves must be found there? And indeed, we may yet discover that experiencing the upper world is to know Reality and to know that we are in essence no different from that.

But let's not get ahead of ourselves.

Chapter 5: Transforming through Reading

"[T]here is a difference between the things one can be taught and those things one can only learn by removing the blocks to one's own seeing."

Dr. Pierre Grimes, Platonic philosopher[1]

Spiritual practices emphasizing physical activity, such as the various schools of yoga, have gained popularity throughout the Western world. And why shouldn't they? These practices relax us, they help us unwind from our hectic lifestyles, and we walk away from a yoga or tai chi session feeling refreshed. I have been doing yoga for years, and I have recommended it to many of my friends. What's more, I like that these sorts of practices have become commonplace. Compared to my university days, I see far more openness in recent years to the notion of opening blocked chakras or balancing spiritual energy.

However, what I think is still missing is a commensurate level of interest in the study of metaphysics that ought to rightfully accompany the physical side of such traditions. The emphasis on the effects of spiritual energy on the physical body has lent itself in Western cultures to a few common misunderstandings. One is that relaxation and mental balance is the whole point. This book will challenge you to push far beyond that.

Another common misunderstanding is that the goal of mysticism is to strengthen spiritual energy so as to initiate a peak experience. From this perspective, our sole goal is that electrifying moment when knower and known become one. This exhilarating image of divine union has lured many people to mystic practice, and I admit I found it enticing in the beginning, too.

The day-to-day reflection on metaphysics seemed dry and boring by comparison. I soon discovered, though, that this more sober aspect of the mystic's life is crucial. Platonists perhaps emphasize this even more than do our Eastern counterparts. One point that we will come back to again and again throughout this book is that wisdom is not an experience—it is a healthy state of mind that matures through the understanding of what we are beyond our physical bodies.

---

[1] *Philosophical Midwifery*, p. 10.

Peak experiences are our moments of touching things-in-themselves. As we gain peak experiences, these experiences certainly do become an important reference to help us wade through what is true versus all the myriad of faulty conclusions that we read in books and hear from various sources. Yet, our emphasis is always on understanding. Many people have had powerful experiences, but this in itself is not what it means to be wise. The mark of wisdom is understanding the nature of Reality and integrating that understanding into our lives.

Without such understanding, these experiences would just be something cool or weird—or perhaps even frightening—that happened. Some people have even dismissed such events as nothing more than a trick their brains had played on them. They struggle to figure out what happened because whatever it was, it was completely outside of anything in their everyday world. Therefore, as time diminishes the immediacy and intensity of the peak, they conclude that they were mistaken about its significance. They were caught up in the charisma of the teacher, they decide, or it was sleep deprivation or the drugs they had taken or the ritual they had participated in.

Don't get me wrong—energy building is certainly important. Without it, we are chained to our armchairs, so to speak, never venturing beyond theories. It is not wrong to work toward peak experiences; it's just that they must be seen in their proper context. We need a foundation and a framework that can reveal to us the meaning of those peak experiences. When we have that foundation and framework, we are able to recognize beauty and goodness within our experiences. Further, understanding is what opens us to even greater depths of that beauty.

It is actually misleading to talk about energy building versus understanding, as if the two were mutually exclusive. The kind of understanding we seek has a transformational power, and this means that we are purifying and heightening our spiritual energy through our studies. This kind of understanding is more than merely the addition of information; it is a state of mind that allows us greater participation in the divine realms of which we are a part.

As this participation increases, our studies take on a new direction. We can use our past insights into metaphysics to make sense of peak experiences. In turn, our growing understanding of those experiences informs our everyday lives. We gradually shed the falsely-imposed limitations we had put on ourselves and we settle into a clearer, truer vision of what it means to be human. All of this occurs not by chasing experience, but by nurturing a mature understanding of Reality and of our place in all that is.

This chapter therefore focuses on how to use wisdom literature and the words of sages to cultivate the special kind of understanding that will have this transformational effect. This is not a typical book on spirituality, in the sense that it does not focus on how to act wisely in our daily interactions. It puts forth no exercises, for example, in being more compassionate to others. Instead, Platonism turns our focus toward the cultivation of the state of mind of one who is wise, so that we can discover those wise conclusions for ourselves. Platonists are not less caring or compassionate than other mystics; rather, we value the impact of self-discovery. Having the insight for yourself is more meaningful than reading about someone else's insight in a book. Our journey, then, begins with an appreciation for the role of interpretation.

Interpretation

Wisdom literature, whether Platonic or that of another tradition, has a transformational quality that can actually raise our spiritual energy when we connect with and internalize the ideas we are contemplating. One way it does this is by exposing us to the vision it points us towards. This benefit is well known. The words of sages have a power that expands our minds and heals our souls. They open us to new ways of relating to the world, to each other, and even to ourselves.

There is another benefit of reading wisdom literature that is less understood: reading these books also highlights our current assumptions and difficulties. Let's assume for the sake of this discussion that we are dealing with true wisdom literature and not faulty philosophy. Invariably, something that we read will contradict our currently held beliefs. Sometimes this is no problem; either we like what we are reading or we are willing to see how the discussion unfolds, and so we keep going.

Other times, though, the assumptions we bring to our reading play such a powerful role that they interfere with our ability to understand what we are reading. I've identified four ways in which this plays itself out:

1. The passage contradicts our currently held beliefs, and so we reject it outright.

2. The passage makes no sense to us at all. I am not referring here to the kind of beliefs that refute what the author is writing about; I'm talking about assumptions that prevent us from even understanding what we are reading. This often leads to frustration and possibly even to concluding that we are not intelligent enough to understand these types of writings.

3. We think we understand the passage, but the meaning we walk away with is either partially or completely wrong.

4. We get the basic gist of the passage, but overlook or cannot grasp the details.

In all of these situations, the power of interpretation reveals itself. We all experience the world through our senses and our thoughts. It is natural to assume that our experiences are accurate reflections of what *is*. Yet, as Plato argues in Book 6 of his *Republic,* our experiences of the world are only our interpretations of the world, filtered through our limited states of mind.[2] Plato defines interpreting as either adding to or subtracting from what actually is: "Then he who attributes everything proper, will produce beautiful letters and images; but he who adds or takes away, will indeed produce letters and images, but such as are defective?" "Certainly."[3]

We carry our assumptions with us, rarely even noticing the power they hold over us. To give a simple example, imagine you are feeling unusually quiet one day. You may notice your coworkers each reacting differently to your change in behavior. The one who likes to take care of people worries that you're coming down with a cold. The "armchair psychiatrist" in the next cubicle is sure you must have had a fight with your significant other. And then there is your colleague who lacks self-confidence and wants to know why you're upset with him or her. The outgoing one thinks you are just being moody again, and the busy sales representatives brush past you without the slightest acknowledgement.

---

[2] *Republic*, 510a. This was discussed in Chapter 3.

[3] *Cratylus,* 431c

This example is easy to relate to because we all recognize that other people are interpreting our behavior, but how aware are we that we are doing the same thing to the people and situations around us? For our purposes here, it doesn't matter *which* response in the above example is the most accurate, or if none of them are. What we need to see is that every one of them is an interpretation. Most of these hypothetical interpretations add something to the equation, such as a sense of concern or worry. The person who doesn't even notice your change in behavior is subtracting from the situation by overlooking this change.

As we pay more attention to the role of interpretation in our lives, it becomes increasingly apparent that interpretations and assumptions play a significant role in shaping the way we see the world and the person we identify with as "me." This realization may even boil to a crisis. I went through an uncomfortable period in which I doubted that there was anything about myself that was real. I was just a bundle of learned thoughts and behavior, as was everyone around me. The people I was imitating were in turn only imitators themselves. It was as if, as Shakespeare wrote, "All the world's a stage/ And all the men and women merely players."[4] That was a surreal period in which all of my private actions and my interactions with others felt contrived and often dream-like.

Is anything real, or are these interpretations all we have? If we could peel away all the layers of belief and learned behavior, would there be anything left? Plato assures us that there would. That discovery is the high point of the noble quest to *know thyself*.[5] It is possible—and indeed natural—to act in the world with little to no interpretation. Such is the state of mind of the wise.[6] Our goal involves clearing away our prism of false beliefs so that Reality is able to shine through us with unified clarity. Most of us fragment this divine light into multiple pieces, displaying one image of goodness

---

[4] From *As You Like It* by William Shakespeare

[5] This goes beyond the mainstream spiritual quest to tear down insecurities so as to develop a more confident self-image. As beneficial as this is, a confident self-image is still an image and so the quest to *know thyself* has not yet been satisfied. The Self, as the term is used by mystics, has no qualities or distinguishing marks and so is prior to all images.

[6] Compare *Republic*, 396e

one minute and another the next. However, when we see clearly what *is*, our actions are spontaneous, guided by true virtue, goodness, and beauty.[7]

As a side note, the discomfort of not knowing the reality beyond all these interpretations can easily open the door to the various forms of relativism. Relativists can broadly be divided into two camps. Some believe that there is no Truth on which we base our opinions. Others acknowledge that Truth may very well exist, but they maintain that it is beyond the grasp of human knowledge. In both of these forms, the best we can hope to find is what is *true for me*. This theory is the foundation for a number of different philosophic movements, from empiricism to existentialism to humanism.

The relativist position, in all its variations, is riddled with problems. If everything you believe is *right* because it is *your truth*, then it follows that no behavior is immoral or unhealthy for the soul so long as you claim it to be right from your relative perspective. For our parts as spiritual students, if relativists are correct then we might as well throw all of our wisdom literature away, because there is no such thing as living wisely or living foolishly. I don't imagine that anyone reading a book such as this one buys into this conclusion, so I will leave the debates to the academics. This tangent is relevant to our discussion only to point out that this is not Plato's intent.

It is important to recognize how widespread a role interpretation plays in our lives, but it does not follow that there is no Reality being interpreted or that we can never know this Reality firsthand. In the study of metaphysics, we are challenged to see that there is such a thing as Reality, but it is nothing at all as we imagine it to be at the start of our studies. What this means for our practice is that no matter how open-minded we try to be, our assumptions about Truth and Reality are inevitably going to wreak havoc on our efforts to understand discussions and readings about what *is*.

---

[7] In *Republic* 484d, Plato tells us that philosophers who have beheld Reality have "knowledge of each particular being" and so carry "a clear paradigm in their soul" of this knowledge. Their goal, then, is in "looking up to the truest paradigm, and always referring themselves thither, and contemplating it in the most accurate manner possible to establish on earth just maxims of the beautiful and just and good."

Reading Just What is On the Page

Most approaches to metaphysics involve reading what the Buddha or Plato or some other sage taught about Reality. Competency is believed to be gained when a person can discuss these teachings in some detail. Certainly this is an important aspect of study—to expose ourselves to perspectives that challenge our conventional notions. These efforts, though, are too often taken up without an appreciation for the role of interpretation.

We bring an entire worldview with us everywhere we go. If you are like me, you probably have collected a number of spiritual books over the years. Have you ever returned to one that you hadn't read in a long time? It seems like a different book now, doesn't it? You have changed and grown since the first read-through, and so you bring something different to the narrative. Another interesting little experiment is to read a few pages of a book while in a period of self-doubt, and then to read the same pages while in a clearer, stronger state of mind. We discover that comprehension will be helped or impeded by our current state of mind.

This becomes especially obvious when reading perennial wisdom literature because of the profundity and difficulty of the content. Reading spiritual literature and grasping its meaning requires us to temporarily put our worldview aside and see only what is on the page. We need to go back to the basics and learn how to leave our baggage on the bookshelf.

Among the earliest teachings I received from Dr. Grimes involved reading "just what is on the page." Dr. Grimes likes to say that all he really does is teach people how to read. It's a rather modest statement on the surface, and obviously said tongue-in-cheek, yet it is also a lofty and profoundly meaningful task that he has chosen to focus on. When interpretation hinders our ability to do this seemingly simple task, we must be willing to turn inward and figure out why. What belief or beliefs are being challenged?

On the surface, putting our opinions aside smacks against our common ideas of what it means to read critically or intelligently. Our high school teachers encouraged us to share our opinions. How can we put our opinions on the back burner? It seems counter-intuitive. However, we can't very well form an opinion about what Plato or any other philosopher wrote until we understand the ideas being put forth. We have to understand what we read *and then* turn it inward to see what effect it has on us.

That is really all that is going on in this first stage. Nobody is saying that we must believe what we read or that philosophers in the Platonic tradition are above reproach. Before jumping to judgment, though, we must strive to put interpretations aside and not assume the author is saying one thing when it may very well be another.

Imagine for a moment that we were talking about Albert Einstein's special theory of relativity. How many of us would approach it from the perspective that the author is stupid and we are going to find flaws in his argument? Of course, if the theory is flawed, we want to recognize that. However, we go into the reading with the idea in mind that this man was a brilliant scientist and we want to understand the theory he had formed. More than that, we hope to walk away from the reading with a better understanding of the aspects of physics that his theory helps elucidate.

It is this kind of openness with which we ought to approach mystic studies. It is the same latitude we'd grant anyone whose views we respect. Very early in our practice, we tend to want to sample many different systems until we find one that resonates with us. And some of you are probably still on the fence regarding mysticism. This practice is helpful any time we want to understand some new idea, whether we are reading or listening. I especially have in mind, though, our approach to reading once we have recognized something meaningful in a spiritual system—be it the Platonic tradition or some other one—and we want to penetrate it more deeply.

When dealing with the writings of sages, the effort it takes to grasp even the basic meaning behind the words requires in itself a shift in state of mind. These writings challenge our current notions about the way things are, and this has a way of triggering our defensiveness and our insecurities. If we approach these readings with a belligerent desire to strike them down, we won't be able to engage them in the right spirit. Likewise to those who open a book assuming it will be too difficult for them to comprehend. Only an open, courageous soul willing to challenge itself will benefit from the effort.

Here we can clearly see the difference between being a skeptic in the colloquial sense and a Skeptic in the philosophic sense. The conventional notion of a skeptic is someone who approaches anything new with negativity and intense criticism. Such a person will struggle to read just what is on the page without passing any judgment. However, the Skeptics of ancient Greece strove to maintain a healthy level of doubt about everything—especially about their own doubt. They understood that it was their own assumptions that needed to be examined most critically.

Holding a Question

Suspending judgment and focusing on understanding precisely what is written is a crucial first step in the process of questioning our own assumptions. Our knee-jerk reaction to something new is often a judgment about what we *think* the author means. A more productive approach is to hold onto our questions. Doing this allows us to do three things: first, we can be on the lookout for the answer in the text. This gives our reading structure and hones our attention to what is most significant. Secondly, our questions can help us pinpoint which assumptions we need to explore.

Connected to this is the third benefit of holding onto questions: doing so wreaks havoc on our states of mind, inviting in confusion. This probably doesn't sound like a good thing, but it actually is. Whether this confusion awakens frustration, anger, irritability, or some other such reaction, it will reveal to us which self-images are hindering our ability to move forward. We all like closure, and so we tend to jump quickly to any convenient solution to our questions. This is natural; nobody enjoys being confused. But it is by having the courage to stay confused that we remain open to answers that are not merely convenient, but that lead us toward wisdom.

Working with an example should help clarify these points. Here's a paragraph from the *Republic* in which Socrates describes the motivations and intentions of those philosophers who had left Plato's proverbial cave of ignorance and seen Reality in what he likened to the "upper world:"

"For somehow, Adimantus, the man at least who really applies his dianoetic[8] part to true being has not leisure to look down to

---

[8] This is a reference to the reasoning part of the soul, described in Chapter 4 as the *logos*, the wisdom-loving part of the soul that rightfully leads the whole soul.

the little affairs of mankind, and, in fighting with them, to be filled with envy and ill-nature. On the contrary, beholding and contemplating such objects as are orderly, and always subsist in the same manner, such as neither injure nor are injured by each other, but are in all respects beautiful, and according to reason, these he imitates and resembles as far as possible; or, do you think it possible by any contrivance that a man should not imitate that, in convening with which he is filled with admiration?

It is impossible, replied he.

The philosopher then who converses with that which is decorous and divine, as far as is possible for man, becomes himself decorous and divine."[9]

This excerpt is fairly straight-forward. However, there is plenty of room for interpretation for anyone who has never experienced this state of mind firsthand. For example, were you offended by the phrase "little affairs of mankind?" It sounds condescending, doesn't it? We've all met some arrogant "philosopher" who talks this way, someone who stands aloof from regular working-class folks and sneers. I met many of them back in my university days. Did Socrates think philosophizing was the *only* worthwhile activity? Athenian society would have come to a screeching halt had everyone spent their days chatting. Working hard to provide for one's family is hardly a "little affair."

The problem with jumping to such conclusions is that a great number of assumptions are tied in to this criticism. Socrates didn't define in this paragraph which activities he was referring to with the phrase "little affairs of mankind." Bringing in our resentments toward someone who angered us in the past is hardly fair to Socrates. Socrates never suggested looking down on shopkeepers, carpenters, farmers, or any other members of society who kept the city running. He certainly never said that people who work for a living could not also think about philosophic issues.

In fact, Socrates had a reputation for engaging anyone who was willing to talk with him, from blacksmiths to powerful politicians. I

---

[9] *Republic*, 500c~d

suspect that he would have more readily assented to the claim that it is better to be a shopkeeper who philosophizes than to be a shopkeeper who doesn't, and so on all throughout society. The either/or dichotomy between philosophers and workers was neither stated nor implied.

The point of this example is to demonstrate that reading intelligently does not mean passing judgment and then defending our opinions (regardless of what our high school English teachers may have told us!). Rather, it means recognizing where we are jumping to conclusions and then allowing ourselves to become baffled. What are the "little affairs of mankind" anyway? Instead of assuming an answer, we can hang onto our question. We simply don't know from this passage alone what affairs Socrates had in mind.

With closer inspection of the example passage above, we will discover that there are a great many phrases which are open to interpretation. You might enjoy going back over it and seeing which questions jump out at you.

Here are a few examples:

- What does Plato mean by "true being?" And how is true being connected to "such objects as are orderly, and always subsist in the same manner?"

- How does a person go about imitating these eternal objects? Is it done through behavior? Thoughts? Words? Or is there some other way?

- What should we make of those curious phrases "as far as possible" and "as far as is possible for man?" Is there a limit to how far humans can know and be like the eternal objects?

This list is by no means exhaustive. Its purpose is to highlight that there is a great deal that is open to interpretation. A quick read might leave us thinking that we understood the passage just fine, yet we now see that we had assumed many things in order to reach that conclusion. To the degree that answers can be captured by words, the answers to these sample questions—as well as whatever list of additional questions you may have generated—can be found in a careful reading of the *Republic*. However, as with all great wisdom literature, we get out of it what we put into it. I've been reading

Plato's works for some 20 years and still see something new each time I open one of his dialogues.

In Western cultures, there is a tendency to associate having opinions with being an intelligent, thinking person. Therefore, being advised to withhold judgment is often interpreted as reading mindlessly. As I hope this example demonstrates, the intention of this method is quite the opposite. The close, critical reading required to generate the list of questions such as the one above proves far more insightful and beneficial than does the knee-jerk opinions and assumptions that marked the hypothetical reaction to the phrase "little affairs of mankind." Once this method is understood, it can be rewarding, and even fun.

I've met students of mysticism who come from traditions less focused on metaphysics. Some have complained that the approach described above is too impersonal. We must be in direct relationship with the Divine, they argue. That relationship can't be found by focusing on "reading just what is on the page." They don't see how this kind of reading could in itself be a large component of a spiritual system.

I understand where this objection is coming from, but—again—it ignores the role of interpretation. It is only after reaching an initial level of understanding of the teachings that we can even begin to apply them. This is easy to agree with in theory, but in practice a whole lot of criticism and touting of wisdom is going on by people who have read and/or heard the words of sages but misunderstood them.

More importantly, there is a deeper issue here. What often gets overlooked in these debates is the effect that tearing down false assumptions has on our souls. Platonic philosophers recognize thinking as far more than brain activity; it is a function of soul.[10] Reading just what is on the page and hearing just what the teacher is saying are practices that require us to identify those assumptions that make this task difficult. We are forced to examine our own view of the world and our view of ourselves, as was also exemplified by the

---

[10] As we saw in Chapter 4, wisdom is recognized as a virtue of the soul guided by its wisdom-loving aspect. On the tripartite soul, see *Republic*, 436b~441c

Skeptics. Ironically, then, reading in this "impersonal" way is the most personal approach one could take.

To some degree, the study of metaphysics is largely a process of tearing down false assumptions about Reality. From this perspective, there is actually nothing to study. There are no data or pieces of information to memorize or figure out or learn, because we already intrinsically know Truth. What could be more natural and inherent to our being than Reality? We are blinded, in a sense, by all of our interpretations. By tearing away what is false, we open ourselves to recognizing the brilliant luminosity of Truth that never is, has been, or will be separate from us. Plato suggests in the dialogue the *Cratylus* that the Greek word for human being, *anthropos,* comes from a phrase that means "contemplating what he beholds," for this is the quality that distinguishes humans from other animals.[11]

Because we as divine essences already know Truth, Plato tells us that learning is really nothing more than remembering:

> "The soul then being immortal, having been often born, having beheld the things which are here, the things which are in Hades, and all things, there is nothing of which she has not gained the knowledge. No wonder, therefore that she is able to recollect, with regard to virtue as well as to other things, what formerly she knew. For all things in nature being linked together in relationship, and the soul having heretofore known all things, nothing hinders but that any man, who has recalled to mind, or, according to the common phrase, who has learnt, one thing only, should of himself recover all his ancient knowledge, and find out again all the rest of things; if he has but courage, and faints not in the midst of his researches. For inquiry and learning is reminiscence all."[12]

Wisdom literature can function as a key that unlocks our remembrances of Truth. However, there is an inherent contradiction between what we truly are and the images we hold of ourselves. When these two views—the real and the false—collide, our ability to understand the full implications of the wisdom literature we are

---

[11] See the *Cratylus,* 399c. Damascius also makes reference to this definition in *Problems and Solutions,* p. 327

[12] *Meno,* 81c~d

reading is hindered. We hit a wall, so to speak. We then must explore why a certain passage is causing us trouble. What belief or beliefs is it challenging? Developing the fortitude to hold our questions and to examine how they affect us are fundamental elements in properly reading wisdom literature.

Chapter 6: Study Tools

"In general these analogies should not be taken as unimportant, especially if we believe Plato, who said that nothing else is so beneficial to the soul as what draws it from phenomena to being, freeing us from the former and making it easy for us to imagine immaterial nature with the help of these."

Proclus[1]

Analogy

Reading only what is on the page, as we saw in the last chapter, is a complex issue. It can be frustrating for people who excelled in traditional academic settings to discover that the type of understanding we are aiming for doesn't hinge on our IQs or our technical command of language. We do try to define words, but our goal is far more than definitions. We are seeking a vision that is beyond words. This means that indelibly tied to our efforts to minimize interpretation is a process of internalizing the teachings we are studying. One way to accomplish this is by using analogy as a tool to awaken the soul.

Plato and the philosophers that influenced him recognized that analogy is embedded into the order of the cosmos. The reality we experience in this physical realm has an analogous relationship to Reality itself. Such is the basis for Plato's famous allegory of the cave and the upper world.

This is the law of similitude,[2] which states that Reality unfolds through a series of realms. Each realm is, in essence, like its prior but with greater differentiation,[3] because of its distance from the One. The result is a likeness, or similitude, that connects the entire cosmos into a single unity. For Plato, and for the Pythagoreans before him, analogy is far more than merely a tool of logic; it is the divine bond that holds together the entire cosmos. This is not hyperbole, nor is it a metaphor. They did not *compare* analogy to a divine bond; they stated that it *is* the divine bond. This function is built into the very

---

[1] *Proclus' Commentary on Plato's Parmenides*, sec. 676, p. 59

[2] See also *The Elements of Theology*, props. 18~20 and 28~30

[3] In the metaphysical, not the physical, sense.

organization of the cosmos. Here is a quote from Plato's *Timeaus* which demonstrates this notion:

> "It is impossible for two things alone to cohere together without the intervention of a third; for a certain collective bond is necessary in the middle of the two. And that is the most beautiful of bonds which renders both itself and the natures which are bound remarkably one. But the most beautiful analogy naturally produces this effect."[4]

The study of metaphysics advances via analogies and possibilities. This can be a struggle for people raised in a culture that places a high value on data and proof. Understanding doesn't give us proof. This is disturbing to many people who had turned away from belief systems with the hopes that once they gained understanding, they would finally find certainty. Peak experiences are often sought with this same expectation that they will at last give us the proof we are hungry for, but even these fall short. How can we prove that what happened was not just reducible to brain activity? Technically, we can't even prove that we are awake right now; this could all be an elaborate dream.[5]

Analogy, being an inseparable element in the fabric of our universe, is our connection to understanding. Understanding functions as a kind of belief because it requires tentatively accepting assumptions that we haven't yet tested. We can't prove the conclusions we reach through our reasoning, nor do we know them to be true. For this reason, many people waver in their early studies or leave them all together. Those who honor that inner drive to keep going gain a stronger conviction as understanding deepens. It is belief, but it is not blind belief. It is reached through contemplation and reflection, by turning inward, and by challenging competing beliefs.

Plato recognized that the passive reading of a book was not sufficient to awaken understanding in the soul. I believe this is the reason he chose to focus the centerpiece of his dialogues, the *Republic*,

---

[4] *Timaeus*, 31b~c. Many translations use the word *proportion* instead of *analogy*. In modern English, we use the word *proportion* in reference to numbers, such as $2/3 = 4/6$. *Analogy* functions a bit differently in that we plug in words or concepts for the numbers and look for a likeness between them. However, both of these words—proportion and analogy—are the same word in Greek (*analogia*).

[5] Cf. *Theatetus*, 158c~d

on the development of spiritual understanding, and analogy plays a key role. The beauty of this dialogue is that figuring out how to read it is in itself an exercise in understanding.

Plato uses something we all are somewhat familiar with (the city-state) to help us better understand something that we know little to nothing about (the soul). Therefore, every statement about the city-state must be lined up against one about the soul. However, Plato doesn't always give us the statements about the soul; we must figure those out ourselves.

For example, Plato gives us rules such as that women of the guardian class are to be held in common by the men of the same class, and children are to be separated from their parents at birth and raised in common.[6] We have to ask ourselves what condition this is intended to produce. In such a community, bizarre as it may seem, nobody would be sure whose children were whose. Everyone of a certain age would be like a sibling or a parent or a child. The picture Plato paints is for the citizens to all function as one big family, sensing a common bond to one another and resolving problems without resorting to an *us vs them* mentality.

It doesn't matter if this outcome would be realistic if this society actually existed,[7] nor does it matter if your own family or the families around you function as smoothly as the fictional community does in the picture Plato paints. What is important is that this is a condition Plato is setting up as analogous to a condition of a healthy soul. As we must do throughout the *Republic*, we take his comments about the city-state and apply the same condition to the soul. In these examples, he set up the image of the city-state functioning as one unified whole. Now we must ask ourselves what would result from the soul functioning as a unified whole. The important thing to remember here is that this is not a political treatise; what Plato is actually focusing on is the soul.

Someone might object that if the healthy state of the soul that he advocates is ideal, it should result in an ideal society when magnified. After all, isn't that the point of the analogy in the first place? By this reasoning, the dialogue would read as *both* a political treatise *and* a spiritual guidebook. That sounds reasonable on the surface, but let's

---

[6] *Republic*, 457c~d

[7] Plato is not advocating that this society *should* exist

consider it more closely. Plato uses personifications to signify various functions or aspects of the soul, such as in the above example of children being raised by the entire community. However, in a real society, people are not reducible to this one aspect and nothing else. Each member of society is a whole person, and so we each contain all of these aspects within our own souls.

We each contain within ourselves the analogue of every class that he names in his fictitious society: the farmers, the shopkeepers, the soldiers, and so on. In other words, we can recognize within ourselves the aspects of the soul represented by each of these classes. Most importantly, we all have the potential to become *philosopher-kings* (or *queens*),[8] if we choose to make the effort. To divide the individual up into personified parts necessarily results in a city-state populated by overly simplified, two-dimensional cardboard cutouts of people. I do not advocate taking this city-state seriously. However, working out this analogy allows us to contemplate and learn about the soul.

Of course, Plato could have simply dumped the political analogy and stated directly, "This is what 'wisdom' is and this is how to get it." It would have been a much shorter and easier read! However, it also would have been easier to discard as wrong if it didn't fit our current assumptions about wisdom. Every day we read things that, when interpreted through our current beliefs and worldview, we quickly judge as right or wrong. We then tend to put that reading aside and never think about it again.

The straightforward approach would not have challenged us to wrestle with our currently held beliefs. By working through the analogy to the city-state, we are compelled to figure out precisely what Socrates is saying about the soul without dragging our own assumptions in and complicating matters. This is a difficult task that forces us to puzzle out what the nature of the soul really is.

This is where we start to internalize the dialogue and make it personal. We draw our own conclusions about the soul, and doing so necessarily has a stronger impact on us than merely being told, "This

---

[8] Plato recognized that women were just as capable as men were of attaining a state of wisdom. Cf. *Republic,* 540c~d: "And our governesses likewise, Glauco, said I. For do not suppose that I have spoken what I have said any more concerning the men than concerning the women,—such of them as are of a sufficient genius [nature]."

is what the soul is." Of course, we adjust and readjust our conclusions as our level of insight matures.

There are many places in the dialogue that allow for this level of reflection and contemplation. As an example, I picked a passage that I hope we can have some fun with. Most everyone I know who hasn't read Plato's works has at least heard of the *Republic* and knows one or two of Plato's "crazy" political ideas.[9] I'm often asked why Plato advocated censorship. This is one of those highly misunderstood aspects of the dialogue, resulting from taking the analogy literally.

Let's take a look at how Plato introduces this topic:

"And do you not know that the beginning of every work is of the greatest importance, especially to any one young and tender? For then truly, in the easiest manner, is formed and taken on the impression which one inclines to imprint on every individual.

It is entirely so.

Shall we then suffer the children to hear any kind of fables composed by any kind of persons; and to receive, for the most part, into their minds, opinions contrary to those we judge they ought to have when they are grown up?

We shall by no means suffer it.

First of all, then, we must preside over the fable-makers. And whatever beautiful fable they make must be chosen; and those that are otherwise must be rejected; and we shall persuade the nurses and mothers to tell the children such fables as shall be chosen; and to fashion their minds by fables, much more than their bodies by their hands."[10]

On the surface, this position comes across as oppressive and arrogant, does it not? It stirs up images of religious fundamentalists burning mounds of books in the name of moral rectitude. Who would want to raise their kids in this environment? I certainly wouldn't. From this perspective, it is easy to understand the

---

[9] Plato having crazy political ideas is a common notion, and not one I share. Actually, as stated earlier, the *Republic* is primarily a spiritual dialogue, not a political one.

[10] The *Republic*, 377b

widespread criticism Plato has received for his ideal city that is anything but ideal.[11]

However, something interesting might emerge if we look at this passage again, this time keeping in mind that this dialogue is actually about the soul. Notice that in the first line, Socrates is focusing on childhood, when we are "young and tender." Since the soul is immortal, it is never truly young. However, this could be a reference to the state our souls were in when we were children.[12] It could also be a reference to each of us when we are at the early stages of our spiritual journey (regardless of our body's age in years). And we will find that there is some overlap between these two interpretations, as our upbringing greatly affects our states of mind at those early stages.

We are surrounded by advice and words of wisdom both in our private spheres and by figures on the world stage. Through what prism do we judge true wisdom from conventional notions that sound good on the surface but are ultimately rooted in ignorance? At the early stages of our journey, we still hold many false beliefs instilled through our social conditioning, and these beliefs are highly influential. This holds true for all of us, regardless of which country we grew up in, our social class, and so on.

Imagine for a moment that one of your parents or guardians were reading over your shoulder right now. What might he or she say? While writing this paragraph, I could not only imagine my parents' words, but also hear their voices and visualize their body language. Could you? Those words make a strong impression, don't they? They convey a whole way of seeing and relating to the world.

Is this how you spend your time? Don't you have anything better to do?

Interesting idea. I wish I could believe in such things.

---

[11] Again, this is the common view of the *Republic*. However, Plato's focus is on the soul; he is not interested in created an actual political model. Even as an analogy, Plato made clear at 372e that he was creating not a healthy, ideal city but a luxurious one swelling to excess, so that he and his interlocutors might be able to see in it both justice and injustice.

[12] Cf. the *Parmenides*, 154c~155d, where Plato suggests that the circular motion of the soul means that we are growing both younger and older at the same time. We grow older in the sense that we age as time moves on, yet we are also becoming younger because reaching the end of one lifetime brings us to the start of the next incarnation.

None of this is scientifically proven, you know.

I don't know; there was none of this spiritual talk when I was a kid.

Whatever you imagined in the above exercise, those few words or gestures capture an entire worldview. Simply being aware of that view, though, is not enough to squelch it. We hear the voices throughout the day, occasionally praising us but more often judging or criticizing us. Common sense tells us that as our spiritual practice progresses, we will grow wiser and so these voices will be quieted. However, the opposite could happen. Wholeheartedly pursuing a meaningful goal— be it spiritual or otherwise—might cause these voices to grow in strength. This is because the insights we are gaining challenge self-images we currently hold.[13]

This becomes a formidable obstacle to overcome. If we, along with Socrates, wish to include philosopher-kings in our imaginary city-state—healthy, mature souls guided by the wisdom-loving part of the soul—we would have to imagine people who held as few erroneous worldviews as is possible. A person with a truly healthy soul would know Reality itself and would therefore be able to weed through the various commonly held opinions and beliefs to find which are compatible with that highest vision and which are not.

Let's go back to Plato's passage. Socrates asks, "Shall we then suffer the children to hear any kind of fables composed by any kind of persons; and to receive, for the most part, into their minds, opinions contrary to those we judge they ought to have when they are grown up?" Which opinions are desirable for the spiritually mature person to hold, and which ought to be rejected as we "grow up" through the stages of our journey?

As this chapter still has us focused on the early stages (and so we are still young, if you will), we need to be careful here not to superimpose our own opinions, or those taught by any particular religion or philosophy, onto this topic. We know Socrates was looking to build for us an image of someone who is wise.[14] We can therefore safely assume that whatever these desirable opinions are, they are the ones the wise person holds. Since we ourselves are seeking this same state of mind, we can apply these questions to

---

[13] This topic will be discussed in Chapter 16.

[14] That is, wise in terms of mastering the virtues outlined in Chapter 4, including wisdom.

ourselves to better see the answers in a general sense (without adding our own specific beliefs).

We may disagree as to which points of view block us from recognizing true wisdom, but if we are honest with ourselves we will see that we do hold views that function this way. We each need to strip ourselves of those views which are incompatible with our highest goals. We must mature the rational part of our souls so as to be able to evaluate "fables" wisely. This will allow us to weed out true wisdom from conventional wisdom that is ultimately faulty.

Mature judgment such as this develops over time and with tremendous effort and courage. For the moment, therefore, let's sidestep this endeavor by imagining a hypothetical person who never held false views in the first place, or who managed to get through childhood with as few of them as is humanly possible. How would this be achieved? This person would have to have been raised by wise parents, I suppose, and surrounded only by others who also were either wise or held right opinions. To create such a hypothetical person, it's understandable why Plato chose to censor the "fable-makers."

When we recognize the *Republic* as a spiritual text cloaked in analogy, a very different message reveals itself than what initially appeared on the surface. Plato was not truly against poets (a term used in ancient times to refer to all artists of literature and music). He quotes Homer extensively throughout his dialogues and, of course, his own dialogues would themselves fall into the category of poetry. He writes in the dialogue *Io*: "For a poet is a thing light, and volatile, and sacred…"[15] In the *Symposium*, he writes:

> "For those there are who are more prolific in their souls than in their bodies; and are full of the seeds of such an offspring as it peculiarly belongs to the human soul to conceive and to generate. And what offspring is this, but wisdom and every other virtue? Those who generate most, and who are parents of the most numerous progeny in this way, are the poets, and such artists of other kinds as are said to have been the inventors of their respective arts."[16]

---

[15] 534b

[16] 209a

In contrast, the poets in the *Republic* are the analogue to the people who influence us both in our private lives and on the world stage, and their artistic writings are analogous to their beliefs, many of which have either left us with or reinforce a false self-image and a false image of the way things are. We must "banish" these false images from our souls on our journey toward wisdom. Of course, banishing this metaphorical notion of poetry from our fictitious city-state is not the same as saying that there is no place for poetry in our actual "republics," our souls. Art, and indeed all creative endeavors, are a great way to explore our current questions and to express our current insights. In fact, the insights Greek philosophy has fostered have been inspiring artists for centuries.

For example, the outflow of art and literature that is the mark of the European Renaissance got a major boost in the fifteenth century when the Italian priest and scholar Marsilio Ficino fused his two loves: Christianity and Platonism.[17] He translated all of Plato's dialogues as well as a number of the later Platonic works from Greek into Latin. Ficino also translated the *Aesclepius* and most of the *Corpus Hermeticum*, which make up the core texts of the Hermetic tradition. Although the *Corpus Hermeticum,* a collection of fifteen treatises, has been credited to Egyptian roots, the Renaissance historian Frances Yates describes it as having been written "by various unknown authors, all probably Greek, and they contain popular Greek philosophy of the period, a mixture of Platonism and Stoicism, combined with some Jewish and probably some Persian influences."[18]

Plato and the philosophers who followed him have been influential to many other artistic and spiritual movements as well, including thirteenth century Kabbalah[19] and the Transcendental movement in nineteenth century America. And we haven't even looked at the creative influence Plato's works have had on the natural sciences.[20]

---

[17] A beautiful introduction to Ficino and his work can be found in Yates, *Giordano Bruno and the Hermetic Tradition,* pp. 13~18.

[18]*Ibid.,* p. 3 Ficino used the title of the first treatise in the *Corpus Hermeticum, Pimander,* as his title for his entire translation.

[19] See Matt's Introduction in his book *The Essential Kabbalah: The Heart of Jewish Mysticism.*

[20] Two excellent sources on this connection between the natural sciences and Plato are Wilbur's *Quantum Questions* and Spencer's *The Eternal Law.* Both books are listed in the bibliography at the end of this book.

So, with this long tangent behind us, let's also put behind us the erroneous belief that Plato is an enemy of art and poetry. The *Republic*, rather than being a stuffy treatise on politics and social organization, is a challenge to see beyond appearances to the true nature of Reality. Analogous to this dichotomy between appearance and reality in our everyday lives, Plato played with that same dichotomy throughout the *Republic*. It takes work to extract the true meaning from the layers of appearance along the surface.

It is well worth the effort to make the attempt, though, because we will only see as far into the text as our vision allows us to see. Puzzling through the more obtuse passages, such as this one on censorship, and piecing various passages together will challenge our vision and compel us farther along. Working with analogy, therefore, is in itself an exercise in understanding.

Memorization

Many of Plato's dialogues include a character who had memorized an entire discussion between Socrates and an interlocutor. The dialogue, then, is a reiteration of that long-distant talk. The *Symposium*, for example, is designed in this way. Consider this exchange at the opening of the dialogue:

> " Do you then give me an account of it yourself...But first, said he, tell me, were you yourself one of the company? It appears plainly, said I, indeed, that your author by no means gave you an exact account of the circumstances of that conversation, if you suppose it passed so lately as to admit a possibility of my being of the company....[I]t is not yet three (years) since I first became a follower of Socrates, and began as I have continued ever since, daily to observe and study all his sayings and actions. Before that time, running about here and there, wherever chance led me, and fancying myself all the while well employed, no mortal was in so wretched a condition as I..."[21]

In this passage, Plato presents his readers with a technique to clear interpretation from our reading. He introduces us to this character whose practice, it seems, consists mainly in studying Socrates and his words. This man has committed entire conversations to memory,

---

[21] 172b~173a

even conversations that had taken place many years earlier. We have to ask ourselves: what is the value in this?

It often happens that something we read makes sense to us at the time we read it, but later we have difficulty piecing the argument back together. This is because when we try to commit an argument or line of reasoning to memory, we find that the points we understand are easier to recall than the points that we don't. Therefore, trying to recall what we read is a good way to find where our confusion lies. Plato showed a recognition of this phenomenon in the *Timaeus*, where, in regards to poets who traveled from place to place reciting poetry, he writes this:

> "[A]s these kind of men are studious of imitation, they easily
> and in the best manner express things in which they have been
> educated; while, on the contrary, whatever is foreign from their
> education they imitate with difficulty in actions, and with still
> more difficulty in words."[22]

The effort to commit part or all of a reading to memory tends to awaken an inner dialogue in which we imagine the questions or objections the people around us would have. What is really going on here, of course, is that we are highlighting our own questions. Therefore, before going on to the next section of whatever we are reading, it is a good idea to test our basic understanding. We need to keep in mind, though, that summarizing arguments is an early stage of our growth. From here, we are ready to go on to practices that allow us to contemplate more deeply.

Pencil Yourself In

This next tool is not actually a study technique *per se*. It's more about the aspiration we bring to our practice and the decision to dedicate time to it. Most of us have busy, active lives. Whether we spend our days in a classroom, an office or at home, it can be hard to find time to dive into the practices outlined in this book. We have the best of intentions, but it's easy to get caught up in tasks that need to get done and deadlines that need to be met.

Finding like-minded people to study and talk with can be helpful. With the advent of the internet, building such a network has gotten

---

[22] 19d

much easier than it used to be. Still, if your situation is anything like mine, you will find that away from the cyber world, you are surrounded by family and friends who are perhaps supportive of your spiritual practice but don't necessarily share your interests. This makes it hard to stay motivated.

I recommend keeping a journal. This allows you to keep track of the puzzles you are working through. It also allows you to gauge your progress. When you are working by yourself, it is easy to feel like you are spinning your wheels. I find this to be especially true when I am caught up in self-doubt or some other such unhealthy state of mind. However, hitting another block is actually a sign of progress. It means that I've advanced enough to confront another limiting self-image. It was by looking back at old journal notes that this pattern became obvious to me.

It is also important to convey to the people in your immediate circle that these spiritual activities are meaningful to you. Even friends who are supportive of your spiritual practice in general might downplay the importance of those elements of your practice that they themselves don't value. A friend from yoga class, for example, might see you reading Plato and wonder, *Why can't you go out to lunch? You're just reading a book.* However, you are not *just* reading a book; you are challenging long-held assumptions and purifying the soul. You are on a journey to remember the wisdom that is our birthright.

The first step on that journey is to love yourself enough to put aside time for personal growth. This means making a schedule. Designate time during the week for reading and contemplation, for meditation, and for yoga or dance or some other energy-focused technique.

Once you have a schedule, it is crucial to stick to it. It helps to set yourself realistic goals. If a 10-minute meditation is a struggle, don't aim for half an hour. Don't schedule reading every single day if you know in your heart you won't do it. Instead, be honest about how much you are currently willing to do and then exert will power when needed to stay on schedule.

Aspiration is the key to spiritual growth. You recognize value in this lifestyle, so treat it like something that matters. Don't relegate your practice to stuff you squeeze into spare moments when there is nothing good on TV. Spiritual practice is an act of compassion for yourself. Your practice begins when you are ready to commit to a practice schedule. So have enough self-compassion to pencil yourself in.

It's All Greek to Me

Of course, no survey of reading the Platonic canon would be complete without mentioning the study of the Greek language. Learning to read Greek requires a commitment of tremendous time and effort if you are to gain enough proficiency for the undertaking to prove fruitful. However, making this commitment carries many benefits. Anyone who has ever studied a foreign language knows that it is a doorway into another culture. The shift in perspective is of great value. Another benefit is that of side-stepping the potential for meaning to be lost or changed in translation. Even the best of translators will alter the connotation of words from time to time.

In all fairness to translators (to whom I am greatly and humbly indebted), the writings of mystics are particularly difficult. Proficiency in Greek is not enough to successfully translate these writings accurately, for one must also grasp the meaning to capture the proper nuance. This is always the challenge any translator faces, but becomes most precarious when dealing with philosophers who are pushing the limits of language to try to reach beyond our normal mental boundaries into the ineffable. The writings of the 3rd-century philosopher Plotinus are reputed to be among the most confusing. The translator Stephen MacKenna acknowledged being in over his head with Plotinus: "I'm in agony over the Sixth, and not the difficulter parts, 'tis all too difficult for me and I wish I were dead..."[23]

One caveat I must add is that there is a danger in putting too high a significance on the native Greek over secondary languages. It is a mistake to believe that reading Greek equates to seeing beyond concepts. Our goal ultimately is to leave *all* language behind. Since we are looking at the Greek language now, we can turn to a Greek word to help us better understand this point. We were introduced to the word *logos* as the wisdom-loving aspect of the soul. This word has a wide range of meanings, but is often translated as *word* or *reason*.

---

[23] *Collected Writings of Plotinus*, p. xi

The Gospel of John, originally written in Greek, opens with the sentence: "In the beginning was the Word, and the Word was with God, and the Word was God."[24] The Greek term translated here as *Word* is *Logos*. We can easily see from this example that *logos* extends far beyond our usual notions of words or logical reasoning. It is something more akin to Truth as a reality intellectual in nature. To make this definition even more precise, we can think of *logos* as the unfolding of Truth throughout the cosmos, extending to us through the wisdom-loving aspect of the soul most akin to divine Truth. As our practice advances and we are able to participate in higher realms of reality, we are equally able to participate in higher degrees of Truth through the *logos*.

In our approach to philosophy, we use logic as a tool, but we do more than follow logic and reasoned arguments; we follow the *logos*. All of our discursive thoughts and discussions use words that represent Reality or some aspect of it. It is the Reality beyond the words that we ultimately have our eye on, not merely concepts about it. We try to give metaphysical functions and Realities their proper name, not because we value names *per se*, but because we value the Truth that the names point us towards. Plato tackles this topic most comprehensively in the dialogue the *Cratylus*.

I've met students who insist that learning Greek is essential to any serious study of Platonism. I would counter that while it certainly has clear merits and I would never discourage the effort, it is possible to penetrate the teachings by comparing various English translations and with awareness of certain key Greek terms. The study of Greek is most meaningful to us in regards to words that do not translate well, such as *logos*. Seeing more deeply into the ways such words were understood by their original audience is a valuable method of moving beyond static images that tend to result from our familiarity with English. Studying such words also takes us beyond the academic interpretations of the Platonic canon and opens us to its deeper meaning.

We can see this more clearly by looking at an example. We were introduced in the section on analogies to the law of similitude, which postulates Reality unfolding through various realms each similar to its prior but with a diminution of power. In our later discussion of

---

[24] This translation comes from The King James Study Bible, p. 1604.

mythology,[25] we will see a quote from the *Timaeus* that describes Reality itself as the paradigm, or model, for the physical universe. Plato writes:

> "(the physical universe) is fabricated according to that which is comprehensible by reason and intelligence…"[26]

The Greek word he used for *reason* is *logos,* and the Greek word for *intelligence* is *phronesis.* We just looked at the word *logos,* the unfolding of Truth throughout the cosmos, which indicates the power in accurate words and reasoning in our efforts to discover Truth. *Phronesis* is another key Greek term that comes up often. It is the power in the soul that turns the whole soul from the physical realm to that of Reality itself.

Now let's go back to the quote above, plugging in the Greek words we just learned:

> "(The physical universe) is fabricated according to that which is comprehensible by *logos* and *phronesis*…"

Plato is telling us that the paradigm towards which the creator of the physical universe looks can be comprehended by following the *logos* to find Truth itself and through the soul's ability to turn toward Reality. We opened Chapter 5 by comparing mystic systems that focus on building energy to ones such as Platonism that focus on developing understanding. We saw that the transformational quality of the kind of understanding we are building made this dichotomy moot. Developing understanding naturally results in building spiritual energy. That is *phronesis,* and such is the result of following the *logos.*

Knowing just these two Greek words has brought greater profundity to this quote than what you had probably imagined from the English words *reason* and *intelligence.* Studying Greek (or at least the Greek words for key metaphysical terms) could be a valuable tool. In itself, the study of Greek is not the goal, but this step away from one's native language could be a meaningful step toward the wordless.

---

[25] Chapter 13

[26] 29a

Chapter 7: Search for Causes

"[W]e then think we know anything when we know the causes and the first principles of it."

Proclus[1]

Before we go further in our discussion of how to practice Platonism, let's look at a few basics of this metaphysical system. A general framework will be presented here and in the next few chapters. As the book proceeds, I will elaborate and build on these basics. I hope the tools discussed in the last two chapters—reading just what is on the page, holding onto questions, memorization —will be helpful to those readers new to this study.

Aside from a few personal correspondences, all of the writings we have of Plato's are in the form of dialogues. The main character in most of these writings is Plato's teacher, Socrates. Socrates never wrote any of his teachings down,[2] and so we cannot compare Plato's presentation of him to the historical man. However, the Socrates that we know, thanks to Plato, was a charismatic man with a quick wit and a keen gift for rational dialogue. More than that, he was a man of great virtue who valued nothing more than truth, someone worthy of inspiring greatness in readers the world over for 2,400 years.

The Search for Causes

According to Plato, the young Socrates started his life of philosophizing with a simple recognition: to understand what anything is, he had to discover its cause.[3] This is a very important insight, but one that might not seem obvious until it is pointed out. Our first reaction to wanting to understand something is generally to

---

[1] *The Theology of Plato*, bk. 2 ch. 2

[2] There is one possible exception to this. In the dialogue *Phaedo*, Socrates is in jail awaiting execution. He tells his friends that he felt compelled by dreams to write. (60d~61b) If there ever were actual writings by the historical Socrates, they unfortunately have not survived.

[3] Phaedo, from 96a. This same idea can be found throughout the Platonic canon. Here's an example from Proclus, *Elements of Theology*, prop. 11: "we are then said to know scientifically, when we know the cause of things."

study the thing itself and how it functions. This approach makes sense when dealing with things such as staplers and computers.

However, in understanding the world around us, we find many instances in which we cannot fully understand what a thing is without looking to its cause. This approach has guided our natural sciences for centuries. This is how we study our natural world. Take earthquakes, for example. Anyone who has experienced an earthquake can describe the experience, and certainly there would also be value in studying the event itself. In order to truly understand what happened, though, we have to look to its cause. We understand what an earthquake is because we know that it is caused by two tectonic plates in the earth rubbing together. To understand earthquakes more fully, we can research what causes the plates to rub together, and then what causes *that* situation to occur. Scientific research tends to move backward, looking to causes and then to what caused that cause.

We do the same in other areas of life as well. For example, one issue which is still under debate is the question of whether or not addictions are biological in root. A similar dispute is ongoing regarding what are commonly referred to as mood disorders— depression, for example. These are controversial issues, and well beyond the scope of this book, but there is one thing we can all agree on: we all intuit that we will better understand what the thing is by knowing its cause. Those who point to a gene to explain the cause of addictions have one notion of what addiction is, while those who point to belief systems or to blocked chakras have different notions. What is important for our discussion here is to see that knowing the cause allows us to reach more accurate definitions. As in the previous example of earthquakes, we can describe the behavior associated with addiction or with various mood disorders without knowing their cause, but we have no hope of understanding what these things really are without undertaking that deeper study.

Looking for causes helps us bring a greater sense of understanding to all areas of our lives, and this is one of the reasons science enjoys its revered position among educated people. Superstitions are generally debunked by pointing out the lack of a cause-effect relationship.[4] When there is a thunderstorm, we no longer worry that

---

[4] Although, strictly speaking, nobody has ever seen a cause functioning as a cause. We only see the effects. The cause-effect relationship is one that we intuit.

the gods are angry. We understand what thunder and lightning are because we understand their causes. Similarly, by the time we reach adulthood few of us still believe that we will suffer bad luck if we break a mirror or if a black cat crosses our path. We understand that these actions cannot be the cause of future bad luck.

There is a common notion that this scientific approach of linking cause and effect makes spirituality obsolete. The examples above of thunderstorms and superstitions might fall into this category. However, Plato approached metaphysics in much the same way that scientists study the natural world. In fact, I would argue that Plato carried logic to its natural conclusion by asking what the cause is of this physical universe, whereas many scientists seem quite satisfied to ignore that fundamental question. By the physical universe, I am not referring just to our Milky Way or our solar system. Galaxies come and go, suns burn out, and new solar systems evolve, but throughout all of these changes, all of it collectively remains bound together as one physical universe.

Whatever the cause is, it must be found outside the physical universe itself. After all, we are now considering the physical universe as the effect; the cause must come before it. A cause, in general, can be thought of as the conditions that make it possible for the effect to happen. Say I am reaching for one of my multiple notes scribbled on a piece of scrap paper and, in my haste, I knock my cup of coffee off the table. The cup didn't fall until the conditions for that effect were in place. The cup had to be pushed off the edge of the table in order for gravity to bring it crashing down, and the cup hitting the floor set up the conditions for the puddle waiting for me to wipe it up.

This is a simple example, dealing with events that exist in time. When we get into metaphysics, though, we have to stretch our way of thinking about causes. Throughout this book, I will often refer to one metaphysical reality being *before* or *prior to* another, but I do not mean this in the sense of linear time; rather, it is in the sense of essence and power. It can be hard to wrap our minds around this notion, but *prior to* in the metaphysical sense means that something is the condition for something else to be, or to *come into being*. Whatever the cause is of the physical universe, it set the conditions for the existence of the physical universe and must therefore be outside of it—much like my pushing the coffee cup is outside of the effect of its falling to the floor.

The concept of power is important in understanding metaphysical causes. A metaphysical cause is always greater than its effect. This idea can be difficult to grasp because we can think of many examples in our physical world that are to the contrary. We can talk, for example, about a child growing up to be stronger and wiser than his or her parents. However, in the context of this example both the child and the parents are functioning in, and so elements of, the same realm of reality. They are both physical beings.

When we get into metaphysics, though, we are looking at the issue of one realm of reality unfolding a subsequent realm of reality. Whatever caused our physical universe must have been powerful enough to give it the power it needed to exist and to function. An effect cannot contain its own cause.[5] That would be like a child conceiving itself and being born without the aid of any parent. As we saw above, causes are the conditions that make it possible for the effect to happen. Our physical universe could not have created itself any more than a baby could create him- or herself.

This brings us back to the young Socrates who was in search of causes. In the dialogue the *Phaedo,* Socrates tells his friend Cebes:

> "When I was a young man, Cebes, I was in a wonderful manner desirous of that wisdom which they call a history of nature: for it appeared to me to be a very superb affair to know the causes of each particular, on what account each is generated, why it perishes, and why it exists."[6]

It wasn't long before the search drew him beyond the natural world. Where this search eventually took him was to what is known to modern university students as the theory of Forms. The example used in the *Phaedo* is Beauty:

---

[5] Compare to Proclus' prop. 7 in his *Elements of Theology:* "Everything productive of another is more excellent than the nature of the thing produced." To summarize the rest of this proposition, if causes were equal to their effects, all beings would be equal and so we could not account for the differences that exist between realms of being. Further, causes cannot be inferior to their products because, as Proclus explains in this proposition, "But if it imparts essence to the thing produced, it will also supply it with essential power."

[6] 96a~b

"[I]f any one tells me why a certain thing is beautiful and assigns as a reason, either its possessing a florid colour, or figure, or something else of this kind, I bid farewell to other hypotheses (for in all others I find myself disturbed); but this I retain with myself, simply, unartificially, and perhaps foolishly, that nothing else causes it to be beautiful, than either the presence, or communion, or in whatever manner the operations may take place, of the beautiful itself."[7]

This was Socrates' modest way of rejecting sensory explanations of cause, for the senses can hardly be trusted. All such explanations are in the realm of opinion. What one person calls a beautiful color, another calls ugly. And where a color is called beautiful, the question of beauty arises again. What makes it beautiful?

Something awakens inside of us when we perceive a thing as beautiful. Socrates recognized that there is no point debating which things in this sensory realm of opinions and relativity are beautiful. Instead, he looked for the cause of that recognition itself. While we each may choose different objects to identify as being beautiful, we do all recognize this thing we call beauty. It touches something within us because through perceived beauty, our souls are stirred to recall Beauty itself.

This may seem like a stretch to our modern, agnostic ways of thinking. Perhaps some of us would prefer to point to a physical cause, such as one found in the brain. It is certainly fine to explore such theories, but since the brain is part of our physical world, we will eventually be forced to ask what caused *that* cause (what caused the physical brain itself)?

Let's back up and look at this issue again from another angle. Anything that exists must have a cause.[8] Since our physical universe exists, it too must have a cause. Even if scientists find conclusive proof pointing to some first physical cause of the current configuration of our galaxy—such as the Big Bang theory's

---

[7] 100d, parentheses included

[8] See *Timaeus*, 28a: "But whatever is generated is necessarily generated from a certain cause." This same idea is echoed in *Philebus* at 26e. As we will see as this chapter progresses, the search for causes will eventually bring us even to the cause of existence itself. Because whatever is the cause of existence must be prior to it, this cause cannot technically be said to exist and therefore needn't have a cause of its own. This notion of a First Cause is central to Platonism and so will be treated at length.

speculation that all began with one infinitesimally small particle—we still would have to ask what caused that physical cause. What caused the first particle to exist, what caused it to explode, and so on? We could speculate about past configurations of the physical universe *ad infinitum*. But to find the cause of the physical universe as a whole, our search would necessarily take us beyond the realm of physics and into metaphysics.

Regardless of how many galaxies rise and fall, the physical universe is perpetual, meaning that it exists throughout all time.[9] Let's take a look at why this must be. Where there is time, there is movement. Time, after all, is a kind of motion. Plato even defines time as "a moveable image of eternity."[10] In Platonic metaphysics, we use the words *becoming* and *generation* to refer to things in our physical universe that come and go. Such things are always in flux and exist in time. All physical things fall into this category. Everything physical is moving in time and therefore ages. *Being*, on the other hand, is used to talk about that which is eternal (in the sense of being beyond time) and never changes.

However, we can equally say that where there is physical movement, there must be time. To those who might be scratching their heads at this, I challenge you to scratch your head without any time passing. Can't do it, can you? This is because physical movement requires time. Okay, now let's put it all together: anything that exists in time moves and all physical movement requires time. Therefore, the two—time and physical movement—are inseparable. Add to this the fact that the universe must have a cause (because anything that exists must have a cause), and that the physical universe as a whole is constantly in flux. Because it is always moving, it has been, is, and always will be in time. What all of this points to is that time and the physical universe were created together.[11] If the physical universe

---

[9] In Platonic writings, the word *perpetual* is commonly used to describe existing throughout all time, whereas the word *eternal* is used to describe the whole beyond time.

[10] *Timaeus*, 37d. The passage goes on to read: "and thus, while he was adorning and distributing the universe, he at the same time formed an eternal image flowing according to number, of eternity abiding in one; and which receives from us the appellation of time."

[11] In *Timaeus* 37e Plato writes: "[H]e fabricated the generation of days and nights, and months and years, which had no subsistence prior to the universe, but which together with it rose into existence. And all these, indeed, are the proper parts of time."

were ever to stop, so would time.[12] Hence the conclusion that the physical universe is perpetual in the sense of existing throughout all time.

Since it is perpetual, our search for causes must move us away from thinking of cause in the temporal sense and instead look for conditions outside of time. Its cause must be non-physical and even more powerful than the infinite expanse of physical matter that spreads beyond our imagination's grasp. This non-physical cause, whatever it might be, must be of greater power than the result, for it gave to the result all that the result is. Therefore, the cause of the physical universe must be greater than the physical universe itself. This ever-changing realm in which things constantly come into and go out of existence points to a never-changing cause: Existence itself. In other words, our reasoning will eventually bring us to a realm of absolute Realities from which the temporal draws its very existence.

Here's another way to look at it: we see that there is function and order in nature. Were there not, a palm tree might grow from a pumpkin seed or a puppy might give birth to a full-grown lion. We know such events would be preposterous because seeds and eggs have specific functions, and nature proceeds according to order.

Where there is function and order, there is intelligence. You might argue that the order of things could be coincidence, that it is random. However, anyone who appreciates the intricate beauty and order of nature, and recognizes this order even at the subatomic level, must admit that this is highly unlikely. This point is open to debate among scientists, but I find this ironic; the natural sciences can only exist and advance because there is an order to be studied and upon which to develop hypotheses and theories. Order cannot be built on a foundation of randomness.

Someone may argue that the order of the physical universe is a *de facto* reality and therefore not evidence of any sort of intelligible cause. To this, Plato could reply that even if we were to imagine the universe having a completely different configuration with different laws of physics, biology, chemistry and so on, it would all still have to fit together perfectly—if it existed. In other words, the very *de facto* reality of either this universe or a different, hypothetical, one implies

---

[12] This hypothetical could only occur if the cause of the universe, the conditions for its existence, were to cease functioning as a cause. As we will soon see, this is impossible.

perfection when considered as a unified whole. Any configuration of the physical universe would be beautiful and worthy of awe, and that order and beauty would point to a cause that is intelligible.

Intelligence can be seen in this and other ways as well. Function requires not merely order, but also intention and purpose. A smartphone functions beautifully not only because of the precise order of its parts. We cannot overlook the fact that the choice of parts and the order in which they are placed are guided by intention and an eye toward function by the designers. Intention and function point to a plan, which points to some form of intelligence.

Intelligence in the universe presupposes existence. This one seems obvious enough. After all, how could something that *isn't* have intelligence? The existence of this intelligence must be eternal, in the sense of being beyond time. We can say this because this existence is a condition for this physical universe, and therefore must be prior to it—and therefore prior to time.

Whatever is prior to time must also be prior to physical movement, since, as we have seen, physical movement and time are inseparable. Therefore, whatever the cause of the physical universe is, it must be immoveable.[13] And so, once again, we reach the conclusion that our physical universe has a cause that is eternal and never changes. This realm of reality is the realm of the absolute Realities, or what is commonly referred to in academia as the realm of Forms. Sometimes they are called Ideas. Both of these terms—Forms and Ideas—can be misleading. They have no physical form, nor are they concepts or thoughts.

Throughout this book, I will use the term *absolute Realities* instead, because that is a more accurate description of what they are—they are not potentialities or images of anything more real than themselves. Sometimes we talk about the absolute Realities in the plural form, but we can also refer to them collectively as an undifferentiated (unseparated and without divisions) unity. As an undifferentiated unity, they are Reality, or Being itself.

The philosopher Proclus defined the absolute Realities in this way:

---

[13] A great deal has been written on the Intelligible as the unmoved mover, Soul as the self-moved, and Physical Body as the externally moved. See for example Proclus' *Elements of Theology*, props. 14~20 and his *Theology of Plato*, bk. 1, ch. 13. See also Plato's *Phaedrus*, 245d~e.

"[T]he Idea in the truest sense is an incorporeal cause, transcending its participants, a motionless Being, exclusively and really a model, intelligible to souls through images, and intelligising causally the existents modeled upon it."[14]

With the word *model,* some readers may imagine static, lifeless archetypes. However, the absolute Realities are quite different than that. Conventional thinking assigns reality to what is manifested physically. Prior to manifestation, we say that things exist only in potential. A house that exists in my head is less real than the one that is built of bricks and mortar. From this conventional perspective, it is easy to see why academia has gripped onto the word Ideas, and how a person can make the error of imagining that Ideas are merely cosmic blueprints.

However, Plato turns it all upside down (or perhaps we'd be better to say that he turns it right side up). The Beings or absolute Realities are what are most real. Being progresses through various realms, weakening in its potency as it unfolds, until finally reaching our physical realm.[15] What most of us consider to be reality, Plato recognizes as only the shadows of reality that parade on the wall of his allegorical cave.

All of the absolute Realities can be said to have a three-fold quality: first, they are beings, meaning that they always exist. Second, the absolute Realities are vital, in that they exert some sort of power. They are not merely abstractions. Finally, they exercise an intellectual activity. They relate a certain nature or quality that is their character. Beautiful things are beautiful because of Beauty itself; just things are just because of Justice itself, and so on.

It is this realm of absolute Realities that the philosopher longs to explore. However, in order to understand this realm of absolute Realities, we must in turn understand *its* cause, if it has one. Is this realm of absolute Realities the First Cause of all? Plato says no, for nothing can exist without unity.[16] Unity is a condition for all existence.

---

[14] *Proclus' Commentary on Plato's Parmenides*, sec. 935, p. 288.

[15] This will be described in more detail in Chapter 10.

[16] This comes up at many places throughout Plato's dialogues. For example, *Parmenides*, 166b (italics included): "[F]or no particular of these will have any existence, nor will others appear to be, *if The One is not*....If we should, therefore, summarily say, that *if The One is not, nothing is*, will not our assertion be right?"

There is unity to our bodies. Each part, from our lifeless hair to our beating hearts, also has its own individual unity. When the unity dissolves, the thing ceases to exist as what it had been. The page that you are reading right now came from a tree. That tree no longer exists as a tree; it has lost the unity of a tree. When this page disintegrates, it will lose its unity as paper.

Move away from the physical realm, and still you will find that unity is the condition for existence. Even order and intelligence themselves presuppose unity. A thought exists as a unit. Single thoughts come together to form concepts and theories. These clusters of thoughts also function each as a unity.

The highest unity that exists is *the One that is*.[17] It has many names in the Platonic tradition. In the *Republic,* Plato calls this the Idea of the Good.[18] *Idea* here is in the sense of the Ideas or the absolute Realities that were discussed above. Damascus, the final headmaster of the fifth-century Platonic Academy, called this Unitary Being or the Unified.[19]

Proclus calls its highest expression One-Being[20] because it is the One that *is* and Being that is one.[21] Plato also uses this term in his dialogue on metaphysics called the *Parmenides,* where he describes the One-Being in this way: "neither does *being* desert The One, nor The One, *being*: but these two always subsist, equalized through all things."[22] This is the fountain of Being from which all that is and all that comes into and out of existence flows.

---

[17] See *Parmenides* 142d and 143a

[18] *Republic,* 508e

[19] See for example *Problems and Solutions Concerning First Principles,* p. 132: "Unitary Being is all things in the One that is established prior to Being, and that is, in its rank before Being, could also be considered as the Unified…"

[20] Distinctions between the One-Being and the Idea of the Good will be made as the book progresses.

[21] See for example *The Theology of Plato,* bk. 1, ch. 10: "In short, being which subsists according to, or is characterized by *The One,* proceeds indeed from the unity prior to being, but generates the whole divine genus….And though all the conclusions harmonize to all the progressions of *the one being,* or of being characterized by *The One…*" (Italics included.) See also Proclus' *Elements of Theology,* prop. 2: "Everything which participates of *The One* is both one and not one."

[22] 144e, italics included

Chapter 8: Beyond Existence

"[A]s it appears, The One neither is one nor is, if it be proper to believe in reasoning of this kind."

Plato[1]

The Cause of Existence

So far, the search for causes has brought us from the physical, or natural, realm to the metaphysical; from the realm of becoming to that of being. Finally, it culminates in the highest unity of being, what I'll call the One-Being.

Some mystical systems stop here with the One-Being, recognizing it as the pinnacle from which existence can go no higher. The One-Being is the fountain of all that *is*. If there is anything prior to what *is*, it follows that it cannot be experienced in any way. After all, how can we experience anything that doesn't exist? For that matter, how can there even *be* anything prior to what *is*? In other words, if it's prior to existence itself, then it must not exist!

Yet, strange though it may seem at first, the Greeks' search for causes is not yet complete. Plato makes the case that even this unity must have a cause. To illustrate this point, imagine that you are walking through a park and you smell the strong scent of jasmine. If you recognize the scent, you will know that the flower (or something that smells like it) must be nearby. The scent does not exist by itself.

The scent flows from the flower without the flower actively doing anything to create it. Of course, there is something happening within the flower at the chemical or organic level to explain the emission of scent. Any analogy drawn from the physical realm will never be a perfect example of divine functions, which surpass the laws of physical nature. However, we can draw from the physical realm to help us in our efforts to make sense of divine functions. The flow of scent from a flower happens quite naturally without any visible effort from the flower. In this sense, this analogy can help us visualize the One-Being as the fountain of existence that overflows from the One without the One actively doing anything to create it.

---

[1] *Parmenides*, 142a

Why must there be a One prior to union? The word *union* means a joining of two or more things into one. Indeed, the One-Being is a union of *one* and *being*. It is the One that *is* and Being that is one, as we saw in the previous chapter. It is a union of two (called a *dyad* or *duad* in Greek). Yet, how can there be a two without first having a one? For what is two if not *two ones?*

Some readers may balk at this point. They may believe that one and two are just numbers invented for our convenience. They are counting tools, not Realities in this higher sense. Plotinus anticipated this objection and argues that this cannot be so: "But if The One is nothing more than the energy of the soul attempting to number, The One will have no existence in things themselves. Reason however has said, that whatever loses The One, loses entirely at the same time its existence."[2] A mere counting tool does not have that power.

Prior to any union, therefore, there must be a pure One. In metaphysical terms, we would say that One is the condition for any union, and since the One-Being—the fountain from which all existence flows—is the first union, the One is the condition for all existence.

Platonism recognizes that the One-Being must have conditions that allow it to be. These conditions, however, are beyond existence. Technically, then, we cannot say that they *are* (that they exist in some way). Yet, being the conditions for all existence, we can hardly say that they *are not*.

Let's go back to our jasmine analogy for a moment. The scent of the flowers indicates to us that the flower (or something that smells like jasmine) must be nearby. However, the scent and the flower are two different things. The scent is not the flower and the flower is not the scent. Plato makes this clear in the *Republic*, where he refers to the Idea of the Good as "the offspring of the good." Socrates in this dialogue says that he cannot talk about the Good itself, as that is beyond all knowledge. The best he can offer his interlocutors is a discussion about this offspring.[3]

When we try to reason about the One itself, we quickly discover that our efforts to reason are strained, for we are trying to grasp what is beyond the grasp of all thought. Being is something that we can talk

---

[2] Ennead VI:ix:2

[3] See *Republic* 504e~506e

about. This is precisely because it is *something*. Being is a many. It has attributes, which I am calling the absolute Realities. We also see in Being vitality and intelligence. There are many things we can say about it (some of which can be found in the chapters ahead).

Not so with the One. The One is beyond all things. In a sense, it is *no thing*. There are no attributes we can assign to it. We cannot say it has intelligence, that it is alive, or even that it has being. As just discussed, we cannot accurately say that it *is* One, because that implies that it has Being.

Nor can we say that it lacks any of these things. It is none of these things in the sense of being greater than any of them; rather, it is the cause of all things. As such, it is none of the things that it is the cause of. Plotinus tells us:

> "For the nature of The One being generative of all things, is not any one of them. Neither, therefore, is it a certain thing, nor a quality, nor a quantity, nor intellect, nor soul, nor that which is moved, nor again that which stands still. Nor is it in place, nor in time; but is by itself uniform, or rather without form, being prior to all form, to motion and to permanency. For these subsist about being which also cause it to be multitudinous."[4]

Indeed, there is nothing we can say about the One that will be accurate. Even calling it the One is not precise, nor is the term First Principle. On this point Proclus wrote:

> "[W]hatever you may say of it, you will speak as of a *certain thing;* and you will speak indeed *about* it, but you will not speak *it*. For speaking of the things of which it is the cause, we are unable to say, or to apprehend through intelligence what it is."[5]

Damascius carries this argument even further:

> "We are not saying that it is only unknowable, so that it is some one thing, which then has a nature that is unknowable, but rather that it is not even something that is, nor is it One, nor is it all things, nor is it the principle of all things, nor is it beyond

---

[4] Ennead VI:ix:3, trans. Elmer O'Brien.

[5] *The Theology of Plato*, bk. 2, ch. 8. Italics included. Plotinus wrote something strikingly similar in Ennead V:iii:14: "We are able indeed to say something of it, but we do not speak *it*. Nor have we either any knowledge, or intellectual perception of it."

all things; we simply have no way to predicate anything of it at all."[6]

In fact, we cannot even say that we can say nothing about it, for this is still saying something about it! It is beyond all thought, beyond all experience, and therefore beyond all words. Damascius warns us: "[H]ow can we say it is completely unknowable? And if we know, at least in this respect it is knowable, namely, insofar as it is unknowable, it is known as unknowable."[7]

Anything that exists must have a cause, but that reasoning does not follow for what is prior to existence. While the complexity of the Platonic metaphysical system does make further distinctions beyond existence (these will be covered in Chapter 9), the One itself is completely transcendent, stretching beyond division, beyond ranking and beyond all differentiation. We therefore can make no further distinctions between cause and effect. In this sense, we can think of the One as the Uncaused. We have finally reached the First Cause of all.

Naming the Unnamable

This "uncaused" is that which is beyond all definition and explanation. Yet, as we got a taste of in the last section, a great deal of effort has been devoted to explaining its very inexplicability. What I would like to focus on now are two names that we give to this unnamable.

In the *Parmenides*, Plato calls the First Cause *the One*.[8] In the *Republic*, he calls it *the Good*. Why two names for that which is beyond any name at all? Proclus explains it in this way:

> "In the *Republic* indeed he calls it The Good.... But in the *Parmenides*, he denominates such a principle as this The One... of these names, the one is the image of the progression of the whole of things, but the other of their conversion."[9]

---

[6] *Problems and Solutions Concerning First Principles*, p. 75. Damascius used the term Ineffable rather than the One.

[7] *Ibid.*, p. 74.

[8] An alternative translation of this is One Self. The significance of this distinction will be discussed later in this chapter.

[9] *The Theology of Plato*, bk. 2, ch. 6.

The First Cause is itself beyond all experience, but we can see its effects. Two key words here from Proclus' quote are *progression* and *conversion*. Let's first look at *progression*. *Progression* refers to the unfolding of the cosmos from the One-Being, from the most unified manifestation of being, to this physical realm. To illustrate this, we can use a triangle to represent all that *is*.

unified Being

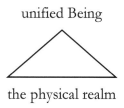

the physical realm

At the top is a pure unity. From this pure unity, Reality unfolds through various realms. As Reality progresses from one realm to the next, it becomes increasingly differentiated (i.e., Reality becomes less unified). At the base of our triangle diagram, we can put our physical realm. The unnamable First Cause is the cause of all of these realms and its unfolding. In other words, the First Cause is the condition that allows Reality and all its progressions to exist.

When we call the First Cause by the name the Good, we are not saying that it truly is good (since we cannot say anything about it at all). Rather, we are indicating that this ineffable cause is the cause of the goodness that allows the entire cosmos to unfold. As we saw in the last chapter, there is order and function in nature, and therefore also intelligibility. Indeed, as we get deeper into our studies of metaphysics, we find that order and function extend beyond the physical realm to the metaphysical. The Good is said to be the condition that allows this providential order and goodness to unfold. As Being proceeds from the Good, subsequent realms of being receive a lesser power of unity, yet each is perfectly what it is.

Conversion—more commonly translated as *reversion*[10]—refers to the return of all that *is* to its cause. In regards to the human soul, this return to our essence is central to the spiritual quest. This upward

[10] Throughout this book, I use the more common translation *reversion*. In addition to being the more common choice among translators, there is also the issue of the word *conversion* having a different meaning in Christianity. The last thing I would ever want to do is add unnecessary confusion to an already challenging topic.

journey (not only for the human soul but for all that *is* throughout all the realms of reality) is also guided by providence. The law of providence essentially states that we each participate in divine goodness to the degree that we are able. We are able to participate in this goodness more fully by bringing unity to the soul.[11] Therefore, all spiritual paths are largely a series of methods to strengthen and unify the soul and point it toward truth by cutting away what is fragmentary and extraneous—namely, ignorance. Thus, the name *the One* is generally used when referring to this unification that results from our spiritual efforts and then eventually initiates our reversion to our true essence.

This connection that Proclus makes between goodness and unification—equating the Good and the One—can be traced back to Plato, although he never stated it specifically as a metaphysical principle. Consider this definition of good and evil given in the *Republic*:

> "Is there not something, said I, which you call good, and something which you call evil?... That which destroys and corrupts everything is the evil, and what preserves and profits it is the good."[12]

So whatever holds things together in unity is good, and that which dissolves things is bad or evil. This is in a precise sense, of course. Death is bad for the physical body, but it is not bad for the whole of existence, because death is a natural part of the cycle of life. And of course this definition of Plato's does not imply that a gang of bank robbers are doing something good because they function together as a unit. The goodness that keeps them together is their ability to trust one another. If that honor among thieves breaks down, so does their union. Either way, though, the states of their souls and the moral implications of their actions are another issue altogether.

How these definitions can be applied to the soul will perhaps become clearer by considering them in terms of Plato's discussion of

---

[11] See, for example, *Commentaries of Proclus on the Timaeus of Plato Part 1*, p. 350: "Not only, therefore, must providence be defined to be that which converts all things to the first, but also to be that the energy of which extends to all things, and which adorns all things according to one union."

[12] 608e

justice in the soul.[13] Plato states that the person who has succeeded in cultivating justice in the soul has "become of many an entire *one.*" Such a person will "call that action just and handsome, which always sustains and promotes this habit; and to call the knowledge which presides over this action, wisdom."[14]

He states of justice and injustice that "as these are in the body, so are the others in the soul…Virtue, then, it seems, is a sort of health and beauty, and good habit of the soul; and vice the disease, and deformity, and infirmity."[15]

It might be a helpful reminder at this point that while reading Plato's dialogues or any of the works of Platonists, *good* and *evil* are used in the sense discussed here. Our largely Judeo-Christian society brings a whole different set of baggage to these terms. Conventional notions of sin have no place in Platonic thought. While it is understandable to interpret Platonic writings through our colloquial lens, doing so adds layers of meaning that were never intended. It is more accurate to read *good*[16] as *healthy* and *evil* or *bad* as *unhealthy.*

Proclus explains the principle of equating goodness with unification clearly and concisely in proposition 13 of his *Elements of Theology*: "Every good has the power of uniting its participants, and every union is good; and the Good is the same with the One."

This proposition further explicates the connection between unification and goodness:

"For if the Good is preservative of all beings, (on which account also it is desirable to all things) but that which is preservative and connective of the essence of everything, is the One; for all things are preserved by the One, and dispersion removes everything from essence;—if this be the case, the Good will cause those things to which it is present, to be one, and will connect and contain them according to union. And if

---

[13] See Chapter 4.

[14] Both of these quotes are from the *Republic*, 443e

[15] *Ibid.*, 444c and e. See also 457b: "For that ever was and will be deemed a noble saying, That what is profitable [beneficial] is beautiful and what is hurtful is base."

[16] That is, *good* as an adjective. *Good* as a noun is, of course, another name for *The One.*

the One is collective and connective of beings, it will perfect everything by its presence. Hence, therefore, it is good to all things to be united. If, however, union is of itself good, and good has the power of uniting, the simply good, and the simply one are the same, uniting and at the same time benefiting beings."

From this proposition, we see the basis of all mystic practice. Our contemplations and our meditations are all efforts to bring unification to the soul. Dialectic, also, is an element of our mystic practice in that it is a precise method of contemplation that counters the dispersal effect false beliefs have on the soul.

Proclus concludes thus:

"Hence it is that things which in some fashion have fallen away from their good are at the same stroke deprived of participation of unity; and in like manner things which have lost their portion in unity, being infected with division, are deprived of their good. Goodness, then, is unification, and unification goodness; the Good is one, and the One is primal good."

Personalizing the One/the Good

How academic-sounding all of this is! It makes for some interesting theoretical discussions, but what does any of it have to do with me? I used to wonder this often. Perhaps you've wondered it, too. The Good has a healthy aspect to it, which I suppose personalizes it to some degree, but it is admittedly hard to feel warm and fuzzy about the One.

Other systems talk of the Self—this we can relate to more easily. We can talk about *myself* and *yourself* and *themselves*. It feels personal, so we can readily foresee a connection between ourselves and the Self, even if we don't yet know what precisely that connection is. You might be wondering why none of the quotes from the Platonic canon bring in the notion of the Self. (And if you weren't, I bet you are now!)

Actually, this notion of selfhood that is central to other mystic traditions is an integral part of Platonism as well. What is commonly translated into English as *the One itself* is the Greek *enos autou,* which would literally translate to *One Self,* or, in other words, the Self as the pure One.

I suspect that this translation has been resisted among English-language translators because Platonism has been under the domain of academia for many years.[17] There is no place for the Self in a system that does not value direct experience and that is purported to be rational only in the sense of valuing logic. Plato did value logic in the search for truth, and so in that sense, we can call his system rational. More importantly, though, his system is rational in the sense of recognizing that Reality itself is rational—a divine intellectual cosmos that is rooted in order and intelligence. As Plotinus puts it, the entire cosmos is eternally in contemplation.[18]

When translators do carry the notion of selfhood into their English versions, a remarkable parallel to other mystic systems emerges. It is beyond the scope of this book to delve into such a comparison; however, as this book unfolds I will point out areas in which this distinction is significant. Here's one example from Thomas Taylor's translation of Plato's *Alcibiades I:*

"By what means might it be found what is the very self of everything? For so, we might perhaps find what we ourselves are; but so long as we continue in the dark as to that point, it will be no way possible to know ourselves."[19]

Another quick example is this statement of Plotinus' about the One as translated by Stephen MacKenna and B. S. Page: "He is what He is, the first self, transcendently The Self."[20] Indeed, the inscription at the temple to Apollo in Delphi, *know thyself,* would make no sense if what we discover ourselves to be in the highest experience were not the presence of the Self.

---

[17] A notable exception to this is the translator Juan F. Balboa. As of this writing, his translations are available through the self-publishing website Lulu.

[18] This is the focus of Ennead III:viii—On Contemplation

[19] *Alcibiades I,* 129a

[20] Ennead VI:viii:14, trans. MacKenna, Stephen and B. S. Page

Chapter 9: Super-Essentials

"And in short, every divine nature is that which it is said to be, on account of this light, and is through it united to the cause of all beings."

Proclus[1]

We've now got some of the basics under our belts. Up to this point, the metaphysical structure we've been looking at has been fairly simple: there are realms[2] of being, peaking in unified Being, or the One-Being. Prior to this is the ineffable cause of Being itself. Now it is time to fill in some of the gaps. The philosophers who followed Plato contributed to this tradition by openly exploring the metaphysics that Plato had hinted at in his dialogues and by drawing out the basic metaphysics we've discussed so far into greater detail and clarity.

The level of detail in the next few chapters can seem overwhelming at first, but the nuances of this system add depth and texture to our contemplations once we grow familiar with them. I'll be the first to admit that at times metaphysics can seem a hellish and confusing study. However, that needn't be the case. We must keep in mind that the study of metaphysics is not an objective task that is academic in nature and without any connection to us. Quite to the contrary, metaphysics is the language of Reality; it gives us the tools to contemplate and discuss what we are in essence and what the nature of Reality is. Once we see this, our studies become fascinating and fun. So take a deep breathe, and here we go.

The Bound and the Infinite

The basic scheme we've seen thus far depicts Reality as something of an overflow from the One itself, with the One-Being as the

---

[1] *The Theology of Plato* bk. 2, ch. 4.

[2] The word *grade* is also sometimes used here. It could be the preferable term when we wish to stress that the difference between levels of unfoldment is being explored as a quality or a power. *Realm* has a spatial aspect to it that adds a layer of confusion for some people. We must remember that we are not referring to physical locations. However, *realm* is used more frequently in the literature and so for the ease of the student still learning the metaphysical layout, I chose to stick with convention.

highest, most unified expression of Reality. Now it is time to add a few more landmarks to our metaphysical map. We will start with what are called *super-essentials*. This term refers to that which is prior to the One-Being. *Super* here means *beyond* and *essential* refers to Essence or Being.

No survey of Platonic metaphysics would be complete without looking at the super-essential dyad (union of two), the bound and the infinite.[3] We will take a closer look at the bound and the infinite in Chapter 24, but I'll briefly introduce them here.

Why do we even need to talk of super-essentials? What role do they play? The One itself is so utterly transcendent that we can say nothing about it nor attribute any activity to it. We cannot even call it *one* since it is beyond unity. The same is true when we use the name *the Good*. It is beyond goodness, beyond providence, beyond any description. Yet we also see this ineffable as somehow being the cause of providential goodness and indeed the cause of all of existence. Therefore, we need a way to understand the One/Good as the cause of providence and as the first cause. The One as the cause of providence will be covered in the next section.

First, though, let's look at the bound and the infinite as the extension of the One as the first cause. This dyad was introduced by Plato in the *Philebus*: "God, we said, has exhibited *the infinite*, and also *the bound* of beings."[4] Socrates demonstrates in this dialogue that these two elements, mingled by the One (expressed as *God* in the above quote), are the cause of all being.

Proclus picks up this theme in his *Theology of Plato:*

"Hence there is a certain one prior to being, which gives subsistence to being, and is primarily the cause of it; since that which is prior to it [i.e., the One itself] is beyond union, and is a cause without habitude [relation] with respect to all things, and imparticipable, being exempt from all things."[5]

---

[3] In English translations of Platonic writings, other names commonly used for the bound are *limit* and *finite*. Other names for the infinite are *unlimited* and *infinity*.

[4] 23c

[5] *The Theology of Plato*, bk. 3, ch. 3, brackets added. The word *imparticipable* will be introduced in the next few pages. It means to be transcendent and not entering into the chain of subsequents of which it is the cause.

The value of distinguishing the bound and the infinite among super-essentials is to offer us the means to ponder more deeply the most profound creation, that of the One-Being. Although the One is beyond all attributes and qualities, it must be the cause of unity in the universe and also must be the source of infinite power. The bound denotes that which binds all into a unity. The infinite is the bound's infinite power.

Onenesses: Henads

In addition to the super-essential dyad, we also need to look at the henads. That metaphysical region prior to the Intelligible has suddenly gotten crowded! We were introduced to the law of similitude in Chapter 6, which Proclus summarizes in proposition 29 of his *Elements of Theology:* "Every progression is effected through a similitude of secondary to first natures." In the coming chapters, we will see that this principle runs through the whole progression of reality. Proclus saw this law functioning even prior to Reality itself. While the One, most properly stated, is incommensurate with anything that flows from it, in another sense we can say that its first emanation must be most akin to itself. What is more akin to the One than Oneness?

> "It is necessary...since there is one unity the principle of the whole of things, and from which every hyparxis derives its subsistence, that this unity should produce from itself, prior to other things, a multitude characterized by unity...."[6]

The image we were previously introduced to of the One-Being overflowing from the One is now getting more complicated. Before giving subsistence to Being, the One emanates the super-essential dyad and the unities. The Greek word *henad* is used to denote these unities. *Henad* means *oneness*, and the henads are many onenesses that are not quite aspects of the One (since the One has no aspects) but are not separate from the One, either. They are an emanation of the One, yet even collectively, they fall short of the One's majesty.[7]

---

[6] *Ibid.*, bk. 3, ch. 1. The word *hyparxis* refers to the highest flowering of a given metaphysical term.
[7] See *Elements of Theology*, prop. 133, which ends with this concise statement: "For all the hyparxes of the Gods, are not together equal to the One, so great a transcendency is the first God allotted with respect to the multitude of the Gods."

These henads are the many gods that have been personified by mythology, but which hold a real and meaningful place in the metaphysical understanding of Reality. In the words of Proclus, "every god is a henad, every henad is a god."[8] There is a forgivable resistance among modern Platonists to referring to the henads as gods. I myself have struggled with the desire to distance myself from polytheism and all the stereotypes attached to it. The fear is that if I accept this idea, next I'll be sacrificing goats!

However, it is also problematic to view the henads as no more than static concepts of onenesses. They are the supervital and superintellectual principals of all life and intellect that actively function throughout the universe, both at the physical and at the metaphysical levels. It is these functions that have lent themselves to mythological personification. However, whether you are interested in these mythological stories or not, the forces themselves are a key element of Platonic metaphysics.

Plato's writings are brimming with references to the gods. Socrates is presented as a highly spiritual man, a follower of the god Apollo.[9] At his trial in which he was accused, among other things, of not believing in the same gods recognized by Athens, Socrates replied: "This however is far from being the case: for I believe that there are gods more than any one of my accusers…"[10]

Making sense of the henads has no doubt caused Platonic philosophers over the centuries great headaches. One way to comprehend the henads is to see them as the power of providence. Providence, as we have seen, is the goodness that flows from the Good itself through the whole procession of reality, and it is the divine goodness that calls us home. This image is a far cry from how common conceptions of Greek mythology have characterized the gods. I therefore urge you to put your preconceived notions of the gods aside, as these images will make this metaphysical exploration exponentially harder. In fact, understanding the metaphysics behind the gods will give us a wiser, more sober way to read mythology, and a better appreciation of how these mythological stories truly function.

---

[8] *Ibid.*, prop. 114, trans. E. R. Dodds

[9] *Phaedo*, 85b

[10] *Apology*, 35d

For now, though, let's return to metaphysics. If the bound and the infinite are the extension of the One into existence, then the One as the cause of providence is captured in the notion of the gods.[11] Since the One is also the Good, each of these henads or *onenesses* is also a *goodness*. Proclus tells us: "if we wish to explore what it is which makes a god,…we shall find it is nothing else than goodness."[12] Through the gods, divine providence flows through all the realms of reality.

Each god is marked by a characteristic activity, which it carries into the realms of existence. Whereas the One itself completely transcends its creations, the gods transcend their subsequents but in another sense are participable, meaning that they enter into the causal chain of reality that extends their particular characteristic.[13] Every henad is participated by some essence.[14] In this way, the gods can also be understood as the immanence of the One itself. Through the gods, the One's unity and providential goodness is carried through and functions throughout all that *is*. As super-essential onenesses, the gods are called henads. But as unities participated by essence, the gods are called realities.

The gods provide the measure and order of all that exists:

> "All beings, and all the distributions of beings, extend as far in their progressions, as the orders of the Gods. For the Gods produce beings in conjunction with themselves, nor is anything able to subsist, and to receive measure and order external to the Gods. For all things are perfected through their power, and are arranged and measured by the Gods."[15]

What this demonstrates is that providence is not only functioning in the world around us, but can also be recognized in the very existence and the unfolding of all that *is*.

---

[11] See *The Elements of Theology*, prop. 120: "[A] providential energy is primarily in the Gods."

[12] *Commentaries of Proclus on the Timaeus of Plato* I, 360, 27.

[13] See for example, *The Elements of Theology*, prop. 141: "Every providence of the Gods is twofold, one indeed being exempt from the natures for which it provides, but the other being co-arranged with them."

[14] *Ibid.*, prop. 135

[15] *Ibid.*, prop. 144

Chapter 10: Realms of Reality

"This triad, therefore, is the fountain and cause of all things; and from it all the life, and all the progression of the Gods, and the genera superior to us, and of mortal animals subsist."

Proclus[1]

We are now ready to extend down from the super-essentials to the realms of reality. I'm going to focus on two philosophers in particular: Plotinus and Proclus. First, let's look at Plotinus.

Plotinus

Plotinus created a three-pronged scheme of levels, or hypostases.[2] In metaphysics, the word *hypostasis* refers to an essential nature or an underlying reality. We can roughly think of the word *hypostasis* as the essential nature of a realm, except we must keep in mind that *realm* is only used to refer to grades of being. The One prior to existence is not a realm. We do, however, call it the **first hypostasis.** This first hypostasis is the first cause of all, the transcendent One. It creates without any movement on its own part, as we discussed with the jasmine analogy.

Plotinus calls the **second hypostasis** either Intellect or the Intelligible. Beings, or absolute Realities, in this hypostasis can be known by divine Intellect. In fact, the absolute Realities here are the only true objects of knowledge, as we saw in our discussion of the cave allegory. It is the unified Intelligible that is Reality itself, and reality weakens in potency as it unfolds into increasingly differentiated realms. We will see this hierarchy become significantly more complex when we move from Plotinus to Proclus. Plotinus chooses the name *Intelligible* when he's stressing this highest, most unified aspect of the

---

[1] *The Theology of Plato*, bk. 3, ch. 22

[2] This can be found in greater detail in ennead V:i—*The Three Primal Hypostases.*

second hypostasis, whereas he chooses the name *Intellect* when his focus is on its ability to know itself.

Another name for the Intelligible is Being, since this is Reality itself, or what truly *is*. For Plotinus, the complete unity of Being and Intellect is the highest expression of the second hypostasis:

> "For both these are consubsistent, and never desert each other. But being two, this one thing is at once intellect; and is being, intellective, and intelligible. It is intellect indeed, so far as it is intellective; but being, so far as it is intelligible."[3]

As we have seen with our jasmine analogy, Being is more of an overflow or radiation of the first than a creation in the usual sense of that word, for the One has no parts and therefore cannot be said to move or act. Being overflows from the One without the One actively doing anything to cause this overflow, much as scent emits from a flower without the flower actively doing anything to cause the fragrance to flow out. An analogy that Plotinus likes to employ is that of light radiating from the sun:

> "We must conceive a surrounding splendor, proceeding indeed from this cause, but from it in a permanent state, like a light from the sun shining, and as it were running round it, and being generated from it, the cause itself always abiding in the same immoveable condition."[4]

The **third hypostasis** for Plotinus is that of Soul. Soul is the link between the Intelligible and the mundane. That aspect of soul which can participate in the second hypostasis he calls the higher soul.[5] He also recognizes an aspect of the human soul more closely tied to the mundane, or physical, realm. It is via this mundane aspect of soul that divine intelligence extends into the physical realm, but humans also enjoy the higher soul, through which we as divine, intellectual beings are able to rise up and discover our true nature. Very much in line with Plato's treatment of temperance as the desires falling in line with wisdom, Plotinus too sees this more mundane aspect of soul naturally

---

[3] Ennead V:i:4

[4] Ennead V:i:6

[5] See for example Ennead 4:4:18 for a discussion of these two aspects of souls.

following the higher soul. The less attached the higher soul is to the second hypostasis, however, the more the mundane aspect of soul loses its direction.[6]

Proclus

Proclus, who lived around 200 years after Plotinus, laid out far more metaphysical detail. We can use Plotinus' basic structure to help us outline what Proclus did. When more distinctions are made, deeper exploration is possible. It is helpful to keep in mind that the distinctions made in any metaphysical scheme, Platonic or otherwise, do not necessarily denote actual separations in reality. This issue takes on greater urgency to the advanced student and so will be covered in more detail in Chapter 23.

The Proclean metaphysical structure is complex and confusing, but it offers the student a profound degree of insight when pondered as extended contemplations. This structure gets confusing very quickly, so I'm going to present a simplified version of it here. As we go on, we will add nuances to our mental sketch.

The First Hypostasis

Proclus leaves the One/Good itself (what Plotinus calls the first hypostasis) as the first cause. The One/Good itself, as we've seen, completely transcends its subsequents such that nothing can be said about it and nothing is coordinate with it. This does not mean, however, that the loquacious Proclus became uncharacteristically reticent in his treatment of first principles. The details he adds can itself fill an entire book. The previous chapter on super-essentials is an overview of the metaphysical structure beyond Being.

The Second Hypostasis

Proclus divides Plotinus' second hypostasis, Intellect or the Intelligible, into three parts. To make matters even more confusing for the reader new to Proclus' approach, Proclus uses both of these

---

[6] See also Ennead I:ii. The division of soul into a higher and lower is very much reminiscent of Plato's depiction of the two winged horses in his analogy to the soul in the *Phaedrus,* from 246a.

terms—Intellect and Intelligible—in naming these parts. In accordance with the Chaldean Oracles, a 2nd century CE mystery tradition that highly influenced the later Platonists, Proclus organizes his metaphysics at all levels into triads.

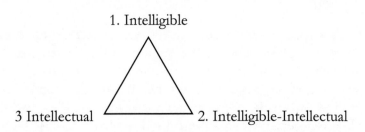

At the hyparxis, or peak, of this triad is the Intelligible realm (see diagram above). The word *hyparxis* refers to the fullest flowering of any being in its proper station among the realms of reality.

In Proclus' Intelligible realm, much like in Plotinus', reality is in its most unified state. This is not a pure One, as the first hypostasis is. Rather, it is a state in which the Beings, or absolute Realities, are completely unified.

The third position of any metaphysical triad is called the extremity. The extremity of Proclus' divine triad is the Intellectual realm. Whereas the absolute Realities are unified in the Intelligible, they are differentiated here. Yet the absolute Realities are not truly separate from one another; collectively, they are Mind, or Intellect. In the *Timaeus,* Plato writes that Mind looks upward to the Intelligible as a paradigm, and then creates the physical universe in accordance with that divine model.[7] This is metaphorical, of course; Plato is giving us a poetic description of creation.

Proclus puts a realm between the Intelligible and the Intellectual realms as a means to connect them. Fittingly, he calls this

---

[7] See *Timaeus*, 29a~b: "Again: this is to be considered concerning him, I mean, according to what paradigm extending himself, he fabricated the world...But it is perfectly evident that he regarded an eternal paradigm. For the world is the most beautiful of generated natures, and its artificer the best of causes. But, being thus generated, it is fabricated according to that which is comprehensible by reason and intelligence, and which subsists in an abiding sameness of being."

intermediary realm the "Intelligible-Intellectual realm." He sees this intermediary realm as being inhabited by intellectual gods primarily, but holding a higher rank than those of the third realm: "[T]hey intellectually perceive the gods prior to them, but are objects of intellection to the gods posterior to them."[8]

Now that we have this basic triadic structure, the next step is to appreciate the interconnectedness of these three realms. Here is where things get confusing, as we are dealing with realms beyond the laws of our physical universe. Time and space do not apply. Each realm has both a transcendent and an immanent aspect to it. This means that as immanent, we can talk about each of these realms as a whole world in its own right filled with gods. Yet, as transcendent, there is a sense in which the three Intelligibles are also exempt from and beyond their respective worlds.

As transcendent, they are unities called *monads*. These unities are often called *principles* because they transcend the multiplied aspect of their respective realm and are the conditions that allow that realm to unfold. Intellect, for example, is the third of these monads. This monad is the exempt principle from which the Intellectual realm, in all of its breadth and detail, unfolds.

Sometimes Proclus treats these three realms separately, one flowing from the next. When he does so, he discusses them with great detail and breadth.[9] Each of these realms is a separate world. Collectively, however, they are the monads of the Intelligible. This is something that our linear thought processes have great difficulty grasping. We have to think of the Intelligibles as the first of the three worlds and also, simultaneously, as the monads of each of these three realms. As monads, they are each the united essence of all that their respective realm contains.

---

[8] *The Theology of Plato*, bk. 4 ch. 1

[9] To give you some sense of this breadth, Proclus focuses on the Intellectual realm in book 5 of his *Theology of Plato*. This book is nearly 100 pages long.

The Intelligible—three separate worlds that are collectively one:

"For the intelligible triads, with reference indeed to the highest union and which is exempt from all things, are triads; but with reference to the divided essence of triads, they are monads, unfolding into light from themselves total triads."[10]

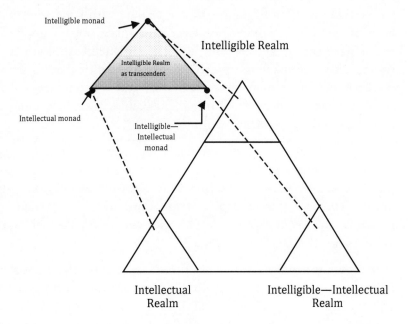

Taking the three monads Intelligible, Intelligible-Intellectual, and Intellect, we have a triad much akin to what Plotinus calls the second hypostasis. This triad is transcendent from all that it creates, eternal and unmoving both in its essence and in its activity. It creates by its very being, analogous to the 'overflow' of the One. The monad of this monadic triad is the One-Being.

The Third Hypostasis

From the Intellectual realm (the extremity of the divine triad described above), reality continues to unfold. Following the Intellectual realm is what Proclus calls the Supermundane realm, or the realm of soul. This level of reality is also discussed with more

---

[10] *The Theology of Plato*, bk. 4 ch. 1.

metaphysical precision by Proclus than it is by Plotinus. Both philosophers, however, agree that it is here that we've found the link between the Intelligible and the physical.

The Supermundane realm is analogous to the Intelligible in that these gods are exempt and uncoordinated with the physical world. For this reason, Proclus sometimes refers to them as the Ruling Gods and calls them principles in relation to the physical world. The realm of Soul looks upward to its cause, yet in a sense is a principle in its own right, being self-motive and filling the physical realm with vitality and intellect.[11] This is very much in line with Plato's description in the *Phaedrus* of the soul as self-motive and the principle of motion in the physical world.[12]

Outside the cave, both the essence and the activity of the higher realms are eternal and unmoving. The soul, however, has an eternal essence but its activity is in time. What this means is that even though our essence is immortal and tied to the divine intellectual realms above, our energies are focused on this physical, temporal world. As souls, the realm of Mind is one that we can participate in but do not possess. This is consistent with Plato, who describes this phenomenon in this way:

> "When it [the soul] firmly adheres to that which truth and real being enlighten, then it understands and knows it, and *appears to* possess intellect: but when it adheres to that which is blended with darkness, which is generated, and which perishes, it is then conversant with opinion, its vision becomes blunted, it wanders from one opinion to another, and resembles one without intellect."[13]

As our practice matures, we come to discover that we are not the physical bodies we have been identifying with. We gradually recognize ourselves as divine intellectual essences. This is the aspect of the human soul that Plotinus calls the higher soul. In Proclean terminology, this is called the rational soul. As divine essences, we are

---

[11] See for example *The Theology of Plato*, bk. 6, chs. 1 and 2.

[12] 245c~e. Consider also the allegory of the cave in the *Republic*, where Plato represents this self-motive aspect of the realm of Soul by the fire in the cave. It is by the power of this fire that the objects being carried are able to cast their shadows on the wall, which is analogous to the physical realm.

[13] *Republic*, 508d, italics added.

immortal; only the earthly vehicle we call the body is born and perishes. As we are intellectual in nature, it is our birthright to participate in the realm of Intellect, or Mind.

Again, it is only through the realm of Mind that we can "see" true objects of knowledge. Most of us tap into this higher realm from time to time; we may call it intuition or gut feelings. One of the aims of our spiritual practice is to participate more fully and intentionally in the Intellectual realm. However, our goal as Platonists is not only to tap into this realm, but to use that connection to contemplate the objects of knowledge.

The realm of Soul is followed by that of Nature. You might call this the life force of the physical world. Whereas the rational soul is in the Supermundane realm, the realm of nature is the cause of the lower soul, or what Proclus calls the irrational soul. This is the aspect of the soul that acts on basic instinct. It is also the life force of non-rational life forms such as animals, insects and plants. It's energies, called natural reason principles, are not separate from the physical forms they vitalize. This realm is called Liberated because while its energies are tied to matter, its essence is not.

There is one further realm, called the Mundane realm. This is the realm of materiality, distinguished from the world of Nature in that both its energies and its essence are tied to the physical world. This realm is the passive receiver of Soul's and Nature's life forces. We must be careful, though, not to assume it devoid of life or intellect. For Platonists, all of reality is intellectual in nature. That includes even the Mundane realm. "Every divine intelligence exercises intellection *qua* intelligence, but providence *qua* god...For deity extends even to those things which the distinctive character of intelligence cannot reach. Even things devoid of intelligence have appetition of providential care and seek to receive some portion of good..."[14] Intellect and vitality can be found in the Mundane realm in the sense that this realm is able, to some degree, to receive psychical and natural reason principles.

In the dialogue *Timaeus*, Plato calls matter "the receptacle, and as it were nurse, of all generation."[15] A tree, for example, is mundane in the sense of having a physical form yet also is part of nature and so

---

[14] *The Elements of Theology*, prop. 134. *Qua* comes from Latin and means *as*.
[15] 49b

gets its vitality from the forces of nature. Humans, of course, enjoy life and intelligence as rational souls yet also are part of the physical world. We participate in all three of the lower realms, and are capable of participating in the higher realms as well. Our bodies *appear* to be self-motive because of the life and intelligence of the soul, yet body is only a passive receiver of these forces. Once the soul abandons its vehicle, that body ceases to live.[16] The Liberated realm is something of a link connecting Soul to the physical world, much as the Intelligible-Intellectual realm is the link connecting the Intelligible to Intellect.

Most of us live our lives focused predominantly, if not solely, on the natural and mundane realms. We identify with the person we know ourselves to be in this incarnation, and so our understanding of what it means to be souls is influenced by the assumptions that this identification with the physical body carries. The more we challenge these assumptions, however, the more open we become to the full potential of humanity.

The basic metaphysical structure, then, is as follows:

One
Intelligible
Intelligible-Intellectual
Intellectual
Supermundane
Liberated
Mundane

The highest term in each realm is called the *hyparxis*. This term is linked to the *extremity*, or lowest term, of the preceding realm.[17] In this way, there is an uninterrupted flow of reality from the most unified and divine all the way down to our physical realm.

---

[16] This notion of soul being the life force for the body is very much in line with Plato's own teachings. See for example Plato's discussion of what the soul is and how it functions in the *Phaedrus* from 245c.

[17] See *The Elements of Theology*, prop. 147: "In any divine rank the highest term is assimilated to the last term of the supra-jacent rank."

Chapter 11: Bite-Sized Pieces

"And everywhere indeed, there is a triad in each of the sections, but in conjunction with an appropriate peculiarity."

Proclus[1]

Dividing the Realms into Triads

The realms discussed in the last chapter are perhaps explored in the greatest depth by Proclus. His *Theology of Plato* runs systematically from the One itself through all the realms of reality.[2] This is where our simple structure really gets complex. To help our linear-thinking minds grasp the profundity of the divine functions that Proclus describes, he makes use of triads.

Proclus identifies three aspects to each realm: Being, Life, and Intellect. These aspects run throughout the entire cosmos, but let's start by looking only at the Intelligible realm. The Intelligible is Being primarily. In other words, it truly *is*. Being has a vitality to it that allows it to unfold into subsequent realms. Therefore, it is also called Life. This vitality, as we've already discussed in a number of places, is marked by intelligence. Therefore, the Intelligible is also Intellect.

Proclus sees a natural order in these three aspects—Being, Life, and Intellect. Whatever includes the widest range of participants is closest (in the metaphysical sense) to the One, of which all beings participate.[3] A thing must be alive to have intellect; dead things don't

---

[1] *The Theology of Plato*, bk. 4, ch. 3

[2] Thomas Taylor added a seventh book to his translation of *The Theology of Plato*. He pieced together the sections on the Mundane realm from other writings of Proclus'. There is some controversy as to whether there had ever been such a book which has subsequently been lost, or whether Proclus had ended his *Theology* with the Liberated gods. See Taylor's note on p. 47 of his translation of *The Theology of Plato*.

[3] See *The Elements of Theology*. Prop. 25 includes: "The more complete is the cause of more, in proportion to the degree of its completeness: for the most complete participates the Good more fully; that is, it is nearer to the Good...that is, it is the cause of more." Also, props. 60 and 126:

> Prop. 60: "Whatever principle is the cause of a greater number of effects is superior to that which has a power limited to fewer objects and which gives rise to parts of those existences constituted by the other as wholes.."
>
> Prop. 126: "A god is more universal as he is nearer to the One, more specific in proportion to his remoteness from it."

think. However, living things might lack intellect. Therefore, Life is more inclusive than Intellect and so we say that it precedes Intellect.[4] By the same reasoning, we can see that a thing might exist but not be alive, whereas all living things exist. Therefore, Being precedes Life.

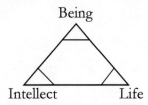

Being

Intellect   Life

Proclus therefore describes the Intelligible realm as a triad, with Being at the top, or hyparxis (see diagram above). Intelligible Life has the middle station, and Intelligible Intellect has the third. Subsequent realms can be divided into analogous triads. However, while the Intelligible realm is marked by the unity of being, the Intelligible-Intellectual realm is marked by the movement of life. The Intellectual realm is marked by the intellectual act of returning to its source to know itself. And if this is not confusing enough, Proclus further complicates the structure by dividing each of these triads into three further triads of being, life and intellect.

The lower three realms (the Supermundane, the Liberated and the Mundane) are seen as reflections of the higher three. These lower realms also follow the principle that realms closer to the One are the causes of more. However, at the lower end of the metaphysical chain, this results in an inversion of sorts. Causes nearer to the One are greater in power due to that proximity. Therefore, they extend farther.[5]

---

[4] It helps to keep in mind here that in metaphysics, the terms *precede* and *prior to* are not used in the sense of location or time. They refer to something being a condition for its subsequents.

[5] See Proclus, *Elements of Theology*, prop. 70. Also, props. 57, 59, 62:

Prop. 70: "Everything which is more total among principal causes, illuminates participants, prior to partial natures, and when these fail, still continues to impart its illuminations."

Prop. 57: "Every cause both energizes prior to the thing caused, and gives subsistence to a greater number of effects posterior to it."

Prop. 59: "Everything which is essentially simple is either better or worse than composite natures."

Prop. 62: "Every multitude which is nearer to The One is less in quantity than things more remote from it, but is greater in power."

The realm of soul, or the Supermundane realm, is a reflection of the Intellectual realm. It is as rational souls that we can participate in the realm of Mind. The Liberated realm (the realm of nature) is a reflection of the Intelligible-Intellectual realm and so is marked by Life. The Mundane realm of matter is so far removed from the One as to be the passive recipient of both Intellect and Life. It is marked by Being, which in its reflection is *becoming* or *generation*. Every realm is additionally marked by the uniting power of the One that allows all existent things to exist. These three lower realms, like the higher realms they are reflections of, are discussed triadically by Proclus.

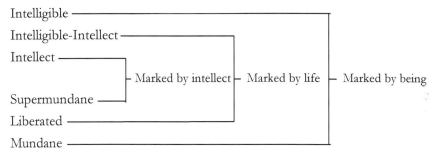

You may be wondering at this point why Proclus gave us all these triads—each realm is a triad, and each of these triads is made up of triads. What is the point? Did he actually see reality as chopped up into triangles or some such three-pronged configuration? The answer to that, I believe, is both *yes* and *not quite*. All these triads allow us to make detailed explorations of divine functions. The organizational charts that we draw are simply aids that help us see more deeply into the tapestry, if you will, of reality and its unfolding.

Distinctions can be made, and these distinctions are real and point to absolute Realities that proceed through all the realms of reality. Yet, in our efforts to see all the detailed nuances of each realm, we must be careful not to fall into the error of treating these distinctions as actual divisions that can be separated one from another. This will be discussed more fully in Chapter 23. The value of making these distinctions is that they allow for much greater depth of understanding than would be possible by trying to grasp these complexities as an undifferentiated whole.

As Easy as 1, 2, 3: The Triad as Abiding, Proceeding, & Reverting

Let's take a look at how this structure can help us better understand triads. Using this structure, we can start to grasp the notion of an unmovable and transcendent aspect of each realm that unfolds the very realm that it transcends.[6] This is a difficult concept to wrap our thoughts around, and so to guide students toward a vision of this dynamic, Proclus uses the triadic relationship of abide-proceed-revert. This relationship has become central to the Platonic metaphysical system.[7]

We will unpack this triadic relationship in steps. First, let's look at the hyparxis, or highest term of each triad. The hyparxis of each triad, the term analogous to Being, is said to abide in itself. In other words, it is at rest. At each level of being, this is the aspect of it that simply *is*—the aspect marked by Being, and therefore the triad at its fullest and realest. Yet, to be a divine power implies overflowing into generation.[8] The abiding term of each triad, being most fully what that triad is, produces posterior terms without any outward activity. Similarly to the One itself, it generates without motion and without diminishing its own power. We can turn to Plotinus to help us understand this difficult point:

> "But if something comes into being within an entity which in no way looks outside itself...that entity must be the source of the new thing: stable in its own identity, it produces, but the product is that of an unchanged being: the producer is

---

[6] For example, see *The Elements of Theology*, prop. 26: "Every productive cause produces the next and all subsequent principles while itself remaining steadfast."

[7] Damascus, for example, used this same structure throughout his *Problems and Solutions Concerning First Principles*.

[8] See *The Elements of Theology*, prop. 25: "Whatever is complete proceeds to generate those things which it is capable of producing, imitating in its turn the one originative principle of the universe....For that principle because of its own goodness is by a unitary act constitutive of all that is: for the Good being identical with the One, action which has the form of Goodness is identical with unitary action. In like manner the principles consequent upon it are impelled because of their proper completeness to generate further principles inferior to their own being." As we will see as the discussion the triad continues, creation is a common feature that runs through all aspects of the divine realms.

unchangeably the intellectual object, the producer is produced as the Intellectual Act."[9]

The hyparxis term remains unchanged. Furthermore—and this is where it gets confusing—its creations abide transcendently in their source while simultaneously falling away. These creations share a likeness with their cause, and it is this likeness that keeps them abiding in their cause. Were they to move away completely, they would have no sympathy with or similarity to their cause. Yet, there is always a diminution of power and unity at each stage of creation. To the degree, then, that these products differ from their cause, they move away: "Everything which is produced from a certain thing without a medium, abides in its producing cause, and proceeds from it....So far, therefore, as that which is produced has something which is the same with the producing cause, it abides in it; but so far as it is different, it proceeds from it."[10]

This procession is expressed as the middle term of each triad. This middle term is also creative. Analogous to Life, motion is introduced in this term. In metaphysics, *life* does not mean breathing. Obviously, divine functions don't breathe the way animals do. Life is motion. It is the Life of each triad, then, that proceeds away from the hyparxis. Generation, therefore, is implied by this term. As such, goddesses (indicative of the concept of fertility or generative power) generally hold the middle rank of each triad in Greek mythology. However, generation at this stage is not through child-bearing but through the power to proceed toward differentiation. Because of the significance of this power to the unfolding of subsequent realms of being, this second term signifies not only life, but also power.[11]

The third term in each triad is the intellect that is said to revert back to its hyparxis. In so doing, it knows itself, and so knower and known become one. The entire triad becomes unified in that act. Reversion holds a special role in metaphysics. It is always an intellectual act because, at each level of reality, it involves intellect turning to look at itself. The result, which is instantaneous and outside of time, is a knowing that is also a creative act. To the degree

---

[9] Ennead V:iv:2, trans. MacKenna, Stephen and B. S. Page
[10] *The Elements of Theology*, prop. 30
[11] Cf. *The Theology of Plato*, bk. 4, ch. 1: "And being indeed is characterized according to a divine hyparxis; but life according to power; and intellect according to intelligible intellect."

that intellect sees its own cause, it knows it and knows itself to be no different from it in essence.[12] However, there is another aspect to this dynamic; as the intellect of each triad looks to its cause, the creation that results is the unfolding of the next realm of reality.

As with all creation in the divine realms, this unfolding is not a one-time action; it has no beginning and no end. We talk of abiding, proceeding, and reverting as if they occur in stages. However, that is only for the convenience of our linear thought processes. It would be more accurate to say that these functions are going on all the time, and so creation is occurring every moment for all of eternity.

Further, these three aspects are all present in each rank of the triad. Abiding is a triad of the three, but is marked by the aspect of abiding. As such, it is the most unified of its triad, holding the other two aspects within its bounds, so to speak. In the second rank, proceeding is the most prominent aspect, and so the second triad is marked by a flow (or procession) from unity toward differentiation. Finally, in the third triad, differentiation is most prominent—a level of differentiation proper for that station in the realms of reality. The intellect of the Intelligible realm, for example, is less differentiated than the intellect of the Intellectual realm. This is because realms closer to the One are more unified. However, the intellect of the Intelligible realm is still differentiated.

This (the intellect of the Intelligible realm) is the home of the Ideas, or absolute Realities. From the perspective of the realms above them, they are differentiated. Yet as an Intelligible monad, they are a singular All, the paradigm of the cosmos which Plato calls "Animal itself."[13] This name denotes the paradigm of the cosmos being vital and intellectual. The absolute Realities there are united and participate in one another, yet due to the introduction of differentiation, each can be distinguished. To illustrate this, Proclus offers the image of a light shining through air.[14] The air and the light mingle together, yet each is clearly distinguished. The air is not light, and the light is not air. This example is of course not perfect because air and light have physical properties, but this imagery gives some notion of how the absolute Realities can be both unified and differentiated. This differentiation is what allows Intellect to revert to its cause.

---

[12] *Ibid.*, bk. 5, ch. 5: "Hence every intellect, by intellectually perceiving itself, intellectually perceives likewise all the natures prior to itself."

[13] See *Timaeus*, 30c. The Greek word is *autozoon*.

[14] See *Proclus' Commentary on Plato's Parmenides*, sec. 756, p. 125.

Chapter 12: Participation, Part 1

"We must therefore refrain from regarding defining concepts or attributes as identical with Ideas that exist in themselves..."

Proclus[1]

The division of Reality into realms creates what might possibly be the most troubling puzzle to the Platonists: how do the absolute Realities in the Intelligible realm give their qualities to the lower realms? Or, to put it another way, how do the lower realms participate in the higher? For example, how do beautiful things get their beauty from absolute Beauty? What does it mean to say that small things participate in absolute Smallness and equal things participate in absolute Equality? Our search for causes brought us to this conclusion, but it's a whole different challenge to wrap our thoughts around the question, *How?*

Plato shows us that even Socrates struggled with this issue. In his youth Socrates supported the notion that things in the physical realm have correlates among the absolute Realities that they participate in. We learn of his early position in the dialogue the *Parmenides,* which takes place when Socrates was a young man new to philosophy. Parmenides was an elderly and well respected philosopher visiting from Elea, an Italian-Greek colony in the southern part of modern-day Italy. In that dialogue, Socrates expresses the confusion that all of us undoubtedly feel when we first stumble into the conundrum created by the notion of participation.

Of course, the young Socrates has no difficulty talking about things in our physical world being both big and small, one and many, and so on. I am big in comparison to a baby but small next to a sumo wrestler. I am one person but have many body parts. We can all easily make many such statements about opposites. To Socrates, such talk is obvious, and therefore a waste of time. Talking about opposites in the Intelligible realms, though, is a different matter.

"But if anyone should, in the first place, distribute the forms of things, concerning which I have just been speaking, separating

[1] *Proclus' Commentary on Plato's Parmenides,* sec. 730, p. 107

them essentially apart from each other, such as *similitude* and *dissimilitude, multitude* and *The One,* and the rest of this kind, and should afterwards show himself able to mingle and separate them in themselves, I should be astonished…in a wonderful manner."[2]

From here, Parmenides begins a long discussion with Socrates that runs through all the main difficulties that arise from Socrates' desire to separate and mingle the absolute Realities. I'll summarize a few of them here. The first question to explore is which things in our physical world have a corresponding Reality in the Intelligible Intellect. Here Parmenides is treating the Forms, or Ideas,[3] as archetypes of sorts. In other words, he is presenting the Idea as something separate and distinct from the things in the physical world that participate in them.

This series of arguments takes me back to a philosophy 101 class I took my sophomore year at university. The Ideas or Forms were likened to blueprints in the sky, only without any physical aspect. They were more like what we might call intellectual blueprints, archetypes, or universals. These universals, according to the professor, explain why we recognize trees of many different shapes and sizes as all fitting within the class of *tree,* for example. Students asked if there were blueprints for *car.* How about *computer?* Needless to say, none of us found this theory persuasive. I remember wondering back in those days why Plato was held in such high regard.

Parmenides doesn't go quite this far into the absurd, but he probably sensed that Socrates was thinking of these Realities as some sort of intellectual entity, each distinct from one another. Socrates confidently agrees that there are Ideas for the just, the good, and the beautiful. He is less confident about the elements water, fire, air, and earth, however, and he is even more troubled by physical things such as mud and hair.

The question then arises of *how* physical things can participate in the Intelligible. Does the Idea touch all things at once, the way daytime does? Or perhaps it is like the sail of a ship, one part covering

---

[2] 129e, italics included.

[3] I'm purposely using Idea instead of absolute Reality here to be consistent with the content of this passage. Young Socrates treats them in this section as something along the lines of higher conceptions.

one thing and another part covering another. If this were true, then the Ideas would be divisible. We could cut them up into parts, and Plato seems to be having fun showing all the ridiculousness that would follow from that. Yet without any participation, the Intelligible would know only its own realm and we would know only the physical world. A chasm would exist reminiscent of those brought forth in existentialist arguments.

By far, though, the most troubling challenge to young Socrates' notion of participation is delivered in the form of an argument that has become known in academia as the Third-Man Argument. The reasoning basically goes like this:[4] When you look around you, you see many things that appear to you as great. Athletes, musicians, brain surgeons, people of all walks of life exhibit talents and skills that are great. Mountain ranges and oceans are great. The order in Nature's food chain—the interconnection of species to their natural habitats is awesome to ponder. It is nothing short of great. We have many notions of greatness. If we were to group all of these examples of greatness together, we could then envision one mega-conception of Greatness itself in which all of these examples of greatness participate. This is something along the lines of my former professor's notion of intellectual blueprints in the sky.

However, we then have to ask where this conception of Greatness itself got *its* greatness from. And so we end up adding Greatness itself to our collection of great things, and must therefore imagine another, greater Greatness itself that encompasses this larger grouping. Following this reasoning, we can go on forever adding one more Greatness itself to our collection. We call this an infinite regress.

We opened our discussion of metaphysics with the simple recognition that we ultimately know a thing by knowing its cause, yet an infinite regress implies that we will never reach a first cause. The Third-Man Argument, if sound, implies that Ideas cannot be known, and therefore Reality cannot be known. The resulting challenge, then, to Socrates—and by extension, to us as well—is no small matter.

Plato, in his usual fashion, gives us what we need to unfold the answer, but then leaves the work to us. The entire dialectical exploration that makes up the bulk of the *Parmenides* can be seen as

---

[4] The argument can be found in *Parmenides* from 132a.

his answer to Socrates' difficulties. By looking at the One (or the One Self) at each realm of reality, Parmenides shows its flow from a transcendent principle exempt from the whole, to its functions as an immanent cause that enters into the procession at various levels. Continuing downward to the level of matter, it is participant only, a passive receiver of form, vitality and energy.

Before getting to that long explication, though, Parmenides drops a few hints in his comments to Socrates. Let's look at one of them now. Parmenides asks: "Do you see, Oh Socrates, how great a doubt arises, if anyone defines forms as having an essential subsistence by themselves?"[5] The implication here, stressing the *if,* is that these problems follow from assuming the Forms or Ideas to be separate from one another and from the things that participate in them. If you think of the Forms or Ideas as distinct, then all these problems and more will pile up at your doorstep. But what other possibility is there? This is the puzzle we must carry with us, the question we hold onto in the backs of our minds, as we dive into the canon literature in search of a clearer vision of Reality. We must throw away the simplistic model that the young Socrates had assumed in the first part of the *Parmenides* and see what emerges in its absence.

---

[5] 133a.

Chapter 13: Greek Mythology

"[T]he world is throughout filled with deity; and on this account is according to the whole of itself the image of the intelligible Gods."

Proclus[1]

Our desire to break the basic order of the cosmos into bite-size pieces results in the complexities of most metaphysical structures. However, this is unavoidable and not to be dreaded. Systems without these complexities leave room for greater misunderstanding. This is because our conventional ways of thinking don't allow us to grasp all that *is* as one unified whole. We can understand the concept of a unified whole, but in order to explore it in depth, we have to first cut it up into parts that we must later allow to dissolve back into a unity.

To talk about the One itself that is beyond having parts, beyond even having existence, is infinitely more difficult. We realize that nothing we say about the One will be accurate, yet talk about it we must. We try to understand what it is the cause of by examining its effects in the Intelligible realm (Plotinus' second hypostasis). In this way, we can talk about it being the cause of certain qualities or realities. It is the cause of providential Goodness, divine Beauty, and so on. We know these qualities as absolute Realities, as the only true objects of knowledge. Their hyparxes, however, are prior to Being. Their highest expression is in the bosom of the One. These are the providential forces that are known in metaphysics as henads, or onenesses. In ancient times, these entities were personified, and the Greek gods as they are commonly known were thus born.

Modern students struggle greatly with these mythological gods. What should we do with them? We can't possibly take seriously the notion that Zeus and Hera are sitting on thrones, ruling over Mt. Olympus. What place could these ancient relics have in a modern spiritual practice? The dilemma is solved when we recognize that the Greek gods are not objects of belief. The proper approach to them, even in ancient times, has been to use them as tools to gain deeper understanding of the divine functions of the henads.

---

[1] *The Theology of Plato*, bk. 7, ch. 1

Any time a different function is being explored, a different name is given to it.[2] As the creator of our physical universe, God is Zeus. Zeus is known metaphysically as Intellect or Mind, and thus we see that the universe is essentially intellectual. His wife Hera represents pure creative power. In general, goddesses tend to represent the power of generation and proliferation. It is a complex system that I cannot do justice here, and would require a book in itself.

As proliferations of reality, the gods are absolute Realities that unfold goodness, being, life, and intellect throughout the cosmos. A number of these gods, then, are said to have a counterpart at various levels of reality, but to have their hyparxis, or highest peak, in the One. The counterpart in subsequent realms of reality denotes that god's downward progression in the cosmos. For example, Aphrodite is the goddess who personifies Beauty. She is a goddess because her hyparxis is said to be in the One, beyond existence. Yet we can also talk about Aphrodite as an absolute Reality in the Intelligible realm. Aphrodite then has her counterpart in the later realms as well. We can talk about Supermundane Aphrodite, Mundane Aphrodite and so on.

When we are reading the works of philosophers such as Proclus, who employs the gods in his explanations, we have to be careful to keep clear in our thoughts all the various differentiations of Zeus and Aphrodite and so on. Carrying the same name throughout the various realms signifies that the same function carries throughout as well. Our task, then, is to understand how that function manifests at each realm of reality.

Proclus explains the flow of providence as it unfolds from its most divine root all the way down to our physical realm: "The gods are present alike to all things; not all things, however, are present alike to the gods, but each order has a share in their presence proportioned to its station and capacity…"[3]

For those of you interested in going beyond this book to the ancient philosophers themselves, my advice is not to skip over sections that refer to mythological gods. The gods were used as instructional tools. As personified characters, they are fictions and not meant to be blindly embraced in a simplistic, literal fashion. However,

---

[2] Consider Damascius, *Problems and Solutions Concerning First Principles,* p. 415: "in reality, polymorph god is the differentiated aspect of the intelligible world." In other words, the gods are onenesses of the absolute Realities.

[3] *The Elements of Theology,* prop. 142

the divine functions they represent are absolutely real. The task is to see how the gods function with one another, because those relationships are analogous to the functioning of divine forces. Without the gods, the study of metaphysics is flat and lifeless; we can map out the structure on a dinner napkin while waiting for our entree. It only comes to life and becomes meaningful when we "see" how the various forces interact. In this regard, the gods are not fictions at all.

The stories on the surface are preposterous, but they point to the profound dynamics of our cosmos. For example, Cronus is the name given to the abiding hyparxis of the Intellectual triad. The Roman equivalent of Cronus is Saturn (see diagram below).[4] As the hyparxis, he is the *being* of Intellect in the sense that every triad can be understood as Being, Life, and Intellect. In other words, the hyparxis is analogous to Being. He is the most unified aspect of the Intellectual triad. His wife Rhea[5] is the middle term, the term analogous to Life. She is the generative principle that proceeds. Zeus, or Jupiter in Roman mythology, is the *intellect* of the Intellectual triad, the third or reverting term in that triad. He is said to revert back to his father, bringing intelligibility to himself by knowing not only himself but also his causes.[6]

The Intellectual Realm

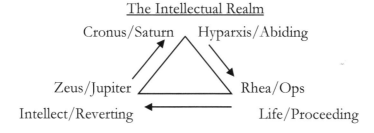

Cronus/Saturn   Hyparxis/Abiding

Zeus/Jupiter   Rhea/Ops

Intellect/Reverting   Life/Proceeding

---

[4] When reading Platonic works translated by Thomas Taylor, it is helpful to keep the Roman equivalents in mind, as Taylor generally (although not always) used these instead of the Greek names. Therefore, I will indicate these differences as they arise throughout this section.

[5] In Roman theology, her name is Ops. Thomas Taylor makes an exception by referring to her by the Greek name Rhea instead.

[6] *The Theology of Plato*, bk. 5, ch. 5: "Jupiter therefore, being at the same time intellectual and intelligible, intellectually perceives and comprehends himself, and binds the intelligible in himself. But binding this in himself, he is said to bind the intelligible prior to himself, and to comprehend it on all sides. For entering into himself, he proceeds into the intelligible prior to himself, and by the intelligible which is in himself, intellectually perceives that which is prior to himself. And thus the intelligible is not external to intellect."

We saw in the previous section that reversion is always a creative act. In the case of Zeus reverting to his father, the creative act is the unfolding of the next realm of reality, that of the junior gods most directly related to the physical realm.[7] Through Cronus, Zeus knows the Intelligible Realities and uses them as a paradigm on which to model this physical realm. There is a likeness that runs through all the realms,[8] and the relationship between the Intelligible and our physical realm is that of model to copy. As Plato explains in the *Timaeus*:

> "But it is perfectly evident that he regarded an eternal paradigm. For the world is the most beautiful of generated natures, and its artificer the best of causes. But, being thus generated, it is fabricated according to that which is comprehensible by reason [*logos*] and intelligence [*phronesis*], and which subsists in an abiding sameness of being. And from hence it is perfectly necessary that this world should be the resemblance of something."[9]

We may also recall that abiding and proceeding are creative as well, and that they take place simultaneously with reverting. Therefore, all the while that Intellect is proceeding into generation through Zeus and the power of Rhea, it is also abiding in itself, transcending its eternal overflow, as represented by Zeus' father, Cronus. All three of these gods are intellectual. Cronus, as the hyparxis of the Intellectual triad, is the personification of Intellect as a whole, prior to differentiation. Therefore, it is said that he knows all that he creates and holds in his bounds. As Proclus states, "a bond is the comprehension of the things that are bound."[10]

Proclus says of this abiding principle:

> "For king Saturn [Cronus] is intellect, and the supplier of all intellectual life; but he is an intellect exempt from co-ordination with sensibles, immaterial and separate, and converted to himself. He likewise converts his progeny and after producing them into light again embosoms and firmly establishes them in himself."[11]

---

[7] *Timaeus*, 41a~42e
[8] This is the law of similitude, introduced in Chapter 6.
[9] *Ibid.*, 29a~b. This same quote was used in part in the discussion of the Greek language in Chapter 6.
[10] *The Theology of Plato*, bk. 5, ch. 5.
[11] *Ibid.*, endnote on p. 674. Brackets added.

How is this relationship represented mythologically? In *Theogony*, Hesiod tells the story of Cronus eating all of his children as soon as they were born—all of them, that is, except for the youngest. His wife Rhea hid Zeus away from him so that the baby would not be eaten. Rhea represents that aspect of Intellect that proceeds away from the unified and abiding hyparxis of the triad, Cronus. Upon reaching adulthood, Zeus returned to confront his father. He castrated him, as Cronus had done to his own father, Ouranos.[12] Zeus then cut open his father's stomach and freed his siblings, who became the junior gods who help Zeus craft the physical universe. Zeus' actions represent reversion to the hyparxis, resulting in the further unfolding of reality.

Plotinus, much like Proclus, recognized lessons about the nature of reality expressed through this myth:

> "This intellect [Cronus], therefore, which deserves the appellation of the most pure intellect, and which is the genus of intelligibles, originates from no other source than the first principle. And being now generated, it generates together with itself beings, all the beauty of ideas, and all the intelligible gods. Being, likewise, full of the things which it generates, and as it were absorbing its progeny, it again contains them in itself, and does not suffer them to fall into matter, nor to be nourished by Rhea, as the mysteries and the fables about the gods obscurely indicate. For they say that Saturn the most wise god was born prior to Jupiter, and that he again contains the things which he generates, in himself, so far as he is full, and an intellect characterized by purity."[13]

Incidentally, castration signifies an important concept in Greek mythology. The notion that all being emerges from the One as its first cause is central to this system. The physical proliferation of galaxies and solar systems can potentially extend infinitely, but collectively they form only one realm. This physical realm is a copy, so to speak,

---

[12] He is often denominated Heaven in the Platonic canon, and he is the mythological representation of Intelligible-Intellectual Life.

[13] Ennead V:i:7

modeled off of the Intellect of the Intelligible realm. The Intelligible realm is only one, as is the Intellectual realm.[14]

In the *Timeaus,* Plato writes:

"Do we therefore rightly conclude that there is but one universe; or is it more right to assert that there are many and infinite? But indeed there can be but one, if it be only admitted that it is fabricated according to an exemplar. For that which comprehends all intelligible animals whatever can never be the second to any other. For another animal again would be required about these two, of which they would be parts; and it would be more proper to assert that the universe is assimilated to this comprehending third, rather than to the other two. That the world, therefore, from its being singular or alone, might be similar to all-perfect animal—on this account the artificer neither produced two nor infinite worlds; but heaven, or the universe, was generated and will be one and only begotten."[15]

In line with this, Zeus—the personification of that divine force which creates the physical universe—is fabled to be a generative god who frequently plants his seed, signifying the greater differentiation at the later realms of reality and also that materiality is the receiver of reason principles. However, his father Cronus and his grandfather Ouranos, who both are immediate causes to realms divine and incorporeal, have both been castrated.[16] Technically, the symbolism of castration is inaccurate because the creation process is not a one-time incident that finishes; it is an eternal process of creating. However, the stark and brutal imagery of this myth provides an unforgettable reminder that the divine cosmos is one.

On the surface, such stories are ridiculous. They certainly don't present the gods as models of good family values. Perhaps in times of

---

[14] Cf. *The Elements of Theology,* prop. 22: "Everything which exists primarily and principally in each order is one, and is neither two, nor more than two, but is only begotten."

[15] 31a~b, trans. Benjamin Jowett

[16] Cf. *The Theology of Plato,* bk. 5, ch. 6: "Saturn however is the only one of the gods who is said both to receive and give the royal dignity with a certain necessity, and as it were violence, cutting off the genitals of his father, and being himself castrated by the mighty Jupiter."

less widespread literacy, these myths functioned as memory aids.[17] As the example above demonstrates, the more outlandish the story, the easier it is to remember. However, for the modern reader coming newly to this tradition, these myths are downright perplexing.

To tell you the truth, in my early years of study, I got more benefit from the explications of the myths than from the myths themselves. Over time, though, the nuances of the myths have added layers to my understanding that would be hard to gain otherwise. They allow for insights that go beyond words. I find that the further I go in my studies, the more useful the myths become to me. The stories of the gods are tools of exploration and as such, rich sources for contemplation.

As our understanding of metaphysics deepens, so too will our understanding of the gods. We will develop greater insights into the ways that each functions. Greek myths evolved and changed over the ages, and today there are various versions of many of the stories. There is no heresy in rejecting some of these versions and embracing others. No fiery hell awaits the non-believer. As mythological figures, the gods and their stories are springboards into contemplation, not images to hold fast to.

It is a mistake to think that we are expected to believe, for example, that the Intelligible is one or that the cosmos is a copy modeled off of the Intelligible, simply because that is the mythological story. The point is to explore the metaphysics behind the story, to understand why the story unfolds the way it does. Our ultimate aim is to reach beyond all images—both of ourselves and of the Intelligible.

---

[17] As in the example of castration above, even the most violent of activities is symbolical of divine functions. Another, more peaceful, example is offered by Proclus in his Manuscript Scholia *On the Cratylus*, an excerpt of which is included in *The Theology of Plato*, p. 682, italics included: "Ocean is said to have married Tethys, and Jupiter Juno [Hera]…as establishing a communion with her, conformably to the generation of subordinate natures. For an according co-arrangement of the Gods, and a connascent co-operation in their productions, is called by theologists *marriage.*"

Chapter 14: Turning the Soul

"What now, Glauco, may that discipline of the soul be, which draws her from that which is generated towards being itself?"

Plato[1]

The moment of insight is instantaneous; it's a jump outside of time. However, it generally takes years to nurture a mature state of mind that will prove to be a healthy framework from which to understand insights and incorporate them into our lives. As we saw back in Chapter 5, our assumptions need to be challenged. When an assumption is overturned, we may need some time to adjust to living with the new outlook that emerges. The implications have to be absorbed before we can claim to have gained understanding. This is a kind of understanding that will alter our state of mind. This means that students of metaphysics must break away from traditional educational methods that limit understanding to how well one can summarize what had been studied. This deviation from the traditional definition of understanding presents a potential obstacle.

One reason I was drawn to Platonism in the first place is that I enjoy the mental challenge it offers. If this description fits you as well, then be aware: embracing the metaphysics of the Platonic tradition is not enough to be a mystic. Rejecting incompatible philosophic views, such as the various forms of relativism, is only half the battle. It is not enough to get the student out of the university; we also must get the university out of the student. That is to say, it is not just the *subject* of study that is different, but also the *methods* of study.

Plato recognized this. In addition to writing the *Republic* as an exercise in itself, he also included specific contemplations to pursue. In keeping with his extended analogy of the soul to the city-state, he calls these practices by names such as arithmetic, geometry, and astronomy. However, when we peel away the analogy, we find practices geared to turn our souls upward in higher contemplations.[2]

---

[1] Socrates in the *Republic*, 521d

[2] On these studies being symbolic of philosophic endeavors, support in addition to the *Republic* can be found in the *Philebus,* 56D: "Must we not say of this, that the arithmetic of the multitude is of one sort, and that the arithmetic of those who apply themselves to philosophy is of another

All of these contemplations are precursors to the study of dialectic. Let's take a look at what these practices really are.

Plato's Studies to Build Understanding

Arithmetic: The Study of "the One in Itself"

Plato calls arithmetic[3] one of the most difficult studies to tackle, but he is not referring here to our usual notions of adding and subtracting. He explains that we tend to get caught up in our sensory perceptions of the world. For example, we relate to the objects around us in terms of how they look (big, small, thick, thin), how they feel (smooth, rough, cool, warm), and so on through all five physical senses. Sometimes our senses even report opposite qualities about the same object, such as our pointer finger being long when compared to our pinky but short when compared to our middle finger. In these ways, we associate many qualities with one single object.

However, even though we see "manyness" all around us, everything also has a oneness to it. This book is one book, for example. Even when we break a book down into parts—chapters, pages, paragraphs, etc.—each part is one part. Each page is one page. Tear a page into tiny pieces, and each piece is still a one.

Plato tells us that recognizing the oneness inherent in all things—despite our senses reporting manyness—compels the soul to puzzle over what really *is*. What is this oneness that is inherent in all things? Just to be clear, the question here is not what one quality is, such as the quality of heaviness or the quality of lightness. Nor is it what one thing is, such as one box which felt light when I first picked it up but seemed heavy after I had carried it for an hour. The question, rather,

---

sort?/What is the difference by which the one may be distinguished from the other?/The difference between them, O Protarchus, is far from being inconsiderable. For the multitude in numbering, number by unequal ones put together; as two armies of unequal force; two oxen of equal size....But the students in philosophy would not understand what a man meant, who in numbering, made any difference between some and other of the ones which composed the number." In other words, the students in philosophy look to numbers-in-themselves rather than to physical things which can be counted. A discussion of "philosophical geometry" follows at 57a.

[3] Plato's discussion of Arithmetic can be found in the *Republic* at 523b~526c

is what that oneness itself is which is inherent in all these examples of one *something*.

We saw in Chapter 8 that the One itself is the condition for all reality. However, Plato doesn't want us to merely take his word for it; this is something that we must discover for ourselves. Can anything exist without that quality of oneness? And if we can recognize that quality in everything around us, then what is one itself?

This contemplation, challenging though it may be, is the first step in turning the soul away from the ever-changing physical realm. This physical realm, because it is constantly changing, is described as always *becoming*. In other words, it never simply *is*. Contemplating the oneness inherent in all things forces the soul to instead focus on that which is eternal, real, and never changing. Plato says that the philosopher must learn this "for the attaining to real being, emerging from generation [becoming], or he can never become a reasoner."[4]

Geometry: The Contemplation of *Ousia*

Plato does not approach geometry[5] in the way that our grade schools generally do. Geometry as presented in the *Republic* is far more than the branch of mathematics that studies points, lines, and angles. Reversion is the name we gave that activity of the soul that loops back to see its own cause. This is an intellectual activity, and our souls are of the same essence as that of Mind itself, or what we usually refer to in metaphysics as Intellect. Our souls can experience reversion and know the Mind that is our immediate source.

Before we go on, we need to review our metaphysical scheme just a little bit. The first three realms of reality—the Intelligible, the Intelligible-Intellectual, and the Intellectual—function together as a monadic triad and are collectively called the Intelligible or Intellect. Plotinus called this the second hypostasis. From here comes the Supermundane level of soul, which functions as a mediator between the Intelligible and the physical realms. *Nous* is the Greek word for Intellect and so is used to describe both that entire upper world collectively and the intellect as it functions within those upper realms.

---

[4] 525b

[5] Plato's discussion of Geometry can be found in the *Republic* at 526c~528c

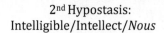

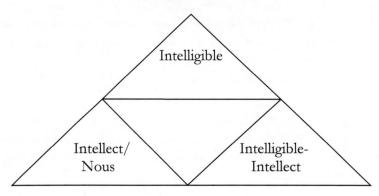

Nous as the third of the Intelligible triads is what the soul first encounters on its journey back to its source. As such, it is our entryway, so to speak, into the Intelligible.

As a metaphysical scheme, this all has the tendency to get dry and confusing. However, the experience of *nous* is one that most of us have experienced at some point in our lives. We touch *nous* when engaging in an activity we particularly excel at, be it sports or business or the arts. It is often described as being in "the zone." While in this state of mind, we are confident, graceful, and capable. I am not alluding here to the superficially cocky state of mind that competitiveness can trigger, but the one resulting from being completely one with the activity one is pursuing. This state of mind leaves no room for condescension. From this state of mind, we exude all the qualities of justice as they were described back in Chapter 4.

We generally associate being "in the zone" with Olympic athletes and professional musicians, but it exhibits itself in even the most mundane of activities, such as typing. My step-mother worked as a legal secretary for many years. One of her impressive skills was that she could type 138 words per minute. It was amazing just to watch her, the way her hands would fly over the keyboard. Obviously, she was moving too fast to be able to think about each letter as she was typing it. She was operating on some other plane, and anyone watching her could see it in her body language. Her shoulders never slumped. She never fidgeted in her seat. There was no smile or sadness on her face, just one-pointed focus.

This state of mind is not the same as that of the wise philosopher, but it is an experience of Mind that is meaningful and beautiful in its own right. To better understand what is happening when we get into "the zone," I'm going to introduce another Greek word here. The word is *ousia*. Like *nous,* the Greek word *ousia* is used in more than one sense. *Ousia* is often translated as *essence*. As the highest term of a triad, it is the essence of that triad. This is the term that abides in itself, a unity of everything that the triad is. Yet, we need to be careful not to evoke a static image. Being everything the triad is means that it is vivific and intellectual, and therefore it is creative and dynamic. This is a very different image from what usually accompanies the word *abide*.

Ousia further signifies the circular motion of reversion, as well as the dynamic power that results from reversion. What this means is that *ousia* is the ability for *being* to know itself. That, after all, is the significance of reversion. Further, this activity is going on throughout all the realms of *being*. You might think of *ousia* as '*being* in action.' It is in this dynamic sense that I want to look at *ousia* now.

The philosopher Parmenides, who made such an impression on Plato that Plato named his most profound dialogue on metaphysics after him, concluded about Reality: "Thought and being are the same."[6] This is because *ousia* is an intellectual activity that is inherent in existence. We talk of the realms as triads of being-life-intellect, and each of these triads is, in turn, its own triad. Yet we also saw that the three triads of each realm are not truly separate. *Ousia* is the term used to describe the three triads functioning together. This is different from *ousia* as the highest term, which is being-life-intellect as a unity. What I'm referring to here is a level of *ousia* that combines this unity with the progression of the second triad and the reversion of the third. This higher unity is the essence of the triad, or what it truly is.

Ousia: the essence of the triad as a whole

Intellect + Life + Being

---

[6] Wheelwright (ed.), *The Presocratics,* p. 98.

Each realm of reality is dynamic and intellectual, marked by the cyclical motion of *ousia*. It is the pinnacle of this intellectual power, Intelligible *ousia,* which is described as the nature of ultimate Reality. In the dialogue the *Symposium,* Plato calls the experience of this pinnacle, Beauty itself.[7] To know Intelligible *ousia* is to know that it is the source of all the beauty in the cosmos.

The real object of study in what Plato is calling geometry, then, is this intellectual power. To know this power is to know pure knowledge.[8] Plato tells us that essence, or *ousia,* has depth. What this means is that this power, this dynamic, can be experienced deeply or in a shallow way. It admits of degrees. The experience of *ousia* that we know through everyday activities such as sports and dancing is generally a shallower experience and more remote from the One than that known by the advanced mystic.

Because the words Mind and Intellect are used in multiple ways in the Platonic canon, as we read these ancient sages we must always ask ourselves in which way these terms are being used. I opened this section by introducing two ways: we can call the third of the intelligible realms by the name Intellect, and we can also talk about all the intelligible realms of reality collectively as Mind or as intellectual in nature. This is because Mind, or Intellect, is the nature of *ousia,* as in Parmenides' insight that thought and being are the same. It is in this highest sense that mystics conclude about the experience of Reality that all is Mind. Plotinus tells us: "If...it is being, it is also intellect, and if it is intellect it is being. And intellectual perception is simultaneous with existence."[9]

We all have the capability to know Reality, or Mind. The word *phronesis* was briefly introduced during the discussion of the Greek language. This is the Greek word Plato uses to describe this aptitude of the soul to know Reality. However, the usefulness of this ability is determined by what it is focused on.

You might think of *phronesis* as the eye of the soul. When this eye is turned downward, its focus is on the physical world. People in this condition, if their soul's eye is sharp, may excel at securing money and

---

[7] The description of Beauty itself in the *Symposium* begins at 211a.

[8] Cf. 526a: "it [geometry] seems to compel the soul to employ intelligence itself in the perception of truth itself."

[9] Ennead V:vi:6.

power and other such measures of status, which are really useless (and sometimes even harmful) to the health of the soul. Regardless of how charismatic and ingenious they may be, if the eye of the soul is focused downward, they are living oblivious to their true nature.

On the other hand, when this eye is turned toward that which is eternal, it recognizes and remembers eternal, real, and never-changing things. It is when we have succeeded in turning the eye of our souls upward that we are able to live in accordance with the knowledge of our true natures. It is through this power in the soul called *phronesis*, then, that our souls come to participate in the highest reaches of the divine realms.

It is also through *phronesis* that we experience the Intelligible in greater degrees. The more we turn our souls, the more our souls "see" and behold. The deepening of this vision is a vital element to the maturing of our souls. We therefore must understand this process and then let it guide all of our contemplations.

Solid Geometry: How to Contemplate

Plato's treatment of solid geometry[10] has nothing to do with three-dimensional figures and everything to do with the question of how to contemplate. The third of Plato's studies is not a contemplation in itself, but instruction on approaching the student-teacher relationship in the right state of mind. The difficulty of all of these studies requires that a teacher be found, initially either a living guide or one we only know through books. Both types of teachers are hard to find, but to Plato finding a teacher is indispensable for success: "those who do investigate them want a leader, without which they cannot discover them."[11]

To further complicate matters, though, most people wouldn't submit to the teachings even if they did find a teacher. This is because the teachings often seem counter-intuitive on the surface. We, as students, are still very much immersed in the assumptions about reality that we learned growing up, and we are even more certain that we already know ourselves. What can be more intimate to me than

---

[10] Plato's discussion of Solid Geometry can be found in the *Republic* at 528b~d

[11] *Ibid.*, 528b

myself—and therefore the Self? It is impossible to throw these assumptions away simply because somebody told us to—and that would be foolish, anyway!

We must learn to touch the internal wisdom which we all, with practice, can learn to access. However, it can even be difficult to trust that inner guide, especially when its guidance pulls us away from what everyone around us believes. What ultimately keeps us from quitting, Plato tells us, is that intuitive sense that this study has value. Plato calls this its *grace*, or in some translations, *charm*.

This study of Plato's is very much in line with the previous discussions on starting out and reading without interpretation. As we are building our connection to our inner guide, we must cultivate a special kind of trust in our teachers, be they living teachers we interact with or the teachers we only know through books. We must have enough respect for our teachers' wisdom to be willing to suspend our own doubts. We must be humble enough to consider that our teachers are more in touch with wisdom then we ourselves are. Therefore, instead of summarily rejecting any advice or teaching that sounds wrong on the surface, we ought to question and investigate the matter.

This means not assuming the teacher is wrong, but also not assuming the teacher is right, either. Doing so would amount to relinquishing our own judgment in favor of someone else's, and wisdom can never be cultivated in that way. What's more, assuming the teacher is right implies simply memorizing someone else's words and pretending that they are reflections of our own soul. Where's the value in that?

Instead, we must puzzle our difficulties out for ourselves. If the answer is not one we can conclude quickly, then we put it on the back burner while our studies continue. This is another example of holding a question to see how it affects us.

Astronomy: The Five Genera of Being

Plato shows little interest here[12] in studying the patterns of astral bodies in the sky: "if a man undertakes to learn anything of sensible

---

[12] Plato's discussion of Astronomy can be found in the *Republic* at 528e~530c.

objects, whether he gape upwards, or bellow downwards, never shall I say that he learns; for I aver he has no knowledge of these things, nor shall I say his soul looks upwards, but downwards even though he should learn lying on his back, either at land or at sea."[13] Plato has a much loftier object of study in mind for astronomy. "I, on the other hand," his Socrates tells us, "am not able to conceive, that any other discipline can make the soul look upwards, but that which respects being, and that which is invisible..."[14]

The study of being, which is the focus of what Plato is here calling astronomy, compels us to consider the five principles evident in all that *is* and, ultimately, in the experience of Being itself. These principles are motion, stillness, essence, sameness, and difference.[15] In all accounts of this experience, regardless of when or where it occurred, mystics recount circular *movement*, yet there is at the same time a *stillness* that pervades throughout. This experience has a powerful *essence* to it; it is absolutely clear to the person experiencing it that this is real and not a hallucination. It is, in fact, the realest experience possible. Because there is movement and the experience admits of degrees, there is *difference*. At the same time, Being itself is always the *same* regardless of who has the experience and when or where it occurs. Another translation for *same* is *Self*, and this brings us to consider the profound insight reported in all accounts of this experience that "I am That." These five principles participate in one another; they are all in all. In fact, they are the fundamental absolute Realities that every absolute Reality participates in. They are at the root of creation, and so are the principles that underlie all that *is*.

At this early stage of our practice, most of us we don't yet know this experience firsthand. Yet, contemplating these principles awakens the natural intelligence of the soul. It inspires the investigation of the beautiful experience described above as well as that of the Good or the One, which is the condition for its existence. This study, therefore, is closely linked to the study that Plato calls geometry—the

---

[13] *Ibid.*, 529b~c

[14] *Ibid.*, 529b

[15] For more on the five genera of being, see the *Sophist,* from 254a. Another translation for *Same* is *Self.* Contemplating the role of selfhood in, and therefore identity to, the highest experience adds a further layer of profundity.

contemplation of *ousia*, which is the natural motion of the soul and of Being itself.

Harmony: The Study of the Beautiful and the Good

Plato calls harmony a counterpart to astronomy.[16] From our conventional understanding of these two areas of study, we would be hard-pressed to find any similarities between them at all, let alone rank them as counterparts to one another. Yet Plato writes: "As the eyes, said I [Socrates], seem to be fitted to astronomy, so the ears seem to be fitted to harmonious lation. And these seem to be sister sciences [studies] to one another..."[17] He then goes on to tie the study of harmony to the school of Pythagoras, whom we were introduced to in Chapter 1. The Pythagorean school was shrouded in mystery and so little is known of it. However, one thing that is clear is that mathematics was used as a doorway into the realm of Mind.

For Plato, both astronomy and harmony are studies of Beauty— astronomy through the five genera of Being, and harmony through the study of numbers-in-themselves. He calls the study of harmony "profitable...in the search of the beautiful and good, but if pursued in another manner it is unprofitable."[18]

This differs from the way our grade schools teach mathematics. I have an older brother who is an electrical engineer. In high school, he always got high marks in math but struggled in literature classes. He has often told me that he likes the certainty of math. One plus one is always two. In math classes, it was clear what the correct answer was and what the teacher expected of him. There were no shades of gray. Literature, on the other hand, opened the door to subjectivity and uncertainty.

Many people drawn to math share my brother's penchant for logical clarity. However, as we've already seen, numbers are built on a foundation of mystery. The first of Plato's studies is to explore what *one* is. Remember what Plotinus wrote about the number one? "But if The One is nothing more than the energy of the soul attempting to number, The One will have no existence in things themselves. Reason

---

[16] Plato's discussion of Harmony can be found in the *Republic* at 530d~531d.
[17] *Ibid.,* 530d, brackets added.
[18] *Ibid.,* 531c

however has said, that whatever loses The One, loses entirely at the same time its existence."[19]

The certainty appreciated by those drawn to mathematics is the result of numbers being symbols for divine order. Those willing to consider numbers as more than a human invention can seek the reality that numbers symbolize. Plato tells us: "For no one discipline belonging to youth possesses such a mighty power...as the study of numbers."[20] Many students with a fondness for numbers find great satisfaction in this aspect of study. Euclid's *Elements* is a highly-cited addition to the core canon of literature. Another valuable source is Thomas Taylor's *Theoretic Arithmetic of the Pythagoreans*.

Putting the Studies Together

These contemplations stir the soul by kindling a spark of desire that had been lying dormant. The deeper we go in our investigation, the more questions we uncover. We discover that some of the assumptions we had been making are wrong, and this can lead to insights that deepen or even alter our understanding. Over the years, I've changed and adjusted my understanding of all the terms introduced in these studies, from the One to Being, from *ousia* to *phronesis*. As my understanding gains depth and detail, it also gains texture—the object of study has become real to me. I've come to realize that contemplating metaphysics is far more than catnip for the brain; it is a means of exploring what truly *is*. This opens me to levels of insight that go far beyond merely the conceptual level.

Through these contemplations, we can bring our souls more in sync with the motion of Reality itself, with the hope of eventually opening ourselves to union with the object of our desire. In the *Timaeus*, Plato writes:

> "Divinity bestowed sight on us for this purpose, that on surveying the circulations of intellect in the heavens we may properly employ the revolutions of our *dianoetic* part, which are allied to their circulations; and may recall the tumultuous

---

[19] Ennead VI:ix:2. Originally quoted in Chapter 8.

[20] *Laws*, 747b

motions of our discursive energies to the orderly processions of their intellectual periods."[21]

Perhaps you can already see some overlap among all of the studies outlined in this chapter and those from earlier in the book. Plato's studies and the attitude that ideally accompanies them will enhance our ability to read without interpretation and so see more deeply into our readings. In turn, getting more out of our reading will contribute to our efforts to tackle Plato's five studies. Reading in Greek can also enhance our practice of reading without interpretation by forcing us to puzzle over words that we would otherwise quickly pass over. Working with analogies is another form of contemplation, as is mathematics. Memorization is a powerful tool to test our comprehension. Therefore, none of these techniques and contemplations are separate.

These practices are not done linearly, but all together. If you choose to dive into these practices, their interconnectedness will increasingly reveal itself. You are now advancing into stage two of the spiritual journey, maturing the contemplations of the studies of understanding into a unified whole. In the cave allegory, you are like the ex-prisoner who is making that steep ascent out of the cave. This introduces a more mature stage of growth once the truth of this interconnectedness becomes your everyday experience.

---

[21] 47c

Chapter 15: False Beliefs

"And is not the assimilating one's self to another, either in voice or figure, the imitating him to whom one assimilates himself?"

Plato[1]

Between Two Worlds

Anyone embarking on a life of mysticism will, at some point, have to battle the challenge of pulling away from mainstream society. This, we will find, functions at multiple levels. On the surface, there are obvious differences between the life of a mystic and one that embraces mainstream society. The popular culture around us seeps into every area of our lives, from our job goals, to our notions of how to spend our free time, to every nuance of our self-image. Even those readers who were raised in a community with mystic teachings all around them are likely to find themselves feeling as though they have one foot in two different worlds, so different are our modern cultures from the world as seen through the eyes of mysticism.

For most of us living in a Western society, the worldview that we were raised on is markedly different from the one we are opening ourselves to now. In my case, I grew up with religion completely compartmentalized from the goals of everyday life. Of course I learned to value kindness and being an honest person, but I also picked up the mainstream culture of valuing popularity and social status. I didn't spend my teenage years thinking about what it means to be a good person or what wisdom is. In my daydreams, I was popular, beautiful, funny and the life of the party. Like most of the kids around me, I thought a good life meant having lots of friends, getting a high-status job and living in a big house in an upscale neighborhood.

To be clear, it is not wrong or bad to have wealth or popularity or status. These are simply not goals that the mystic holds in high value or aims for. It is fine to have them; it is fine not to. Happiness and a good life are not dependent on such things. Our spiritual practice will force us to question mainstream values, and this is true even for those of us who never thought of ourselves as particularly vain or greedy or

---

[1] *Republic*, 393c

status conscious. What we are moving towards is more complex an issue than that; it is a whole different way of relating to the human experience.

This divide between the world we are leaving and the one we are embracing is more than just on the surface. This chapter will take a look at the Platonic approach to states of mind as a general study. In the next chapter, we will focus on the subtle mental challenges to our practice that might be easy to overlook if a spotlight were not shone on them. There are attitudes and beliefs tied to our old ways of being, a whole complex web of self-images that has the potential to spring up and block our progress. We played certain roles in our family, at school, and with our friends. This molded our self-image and our assumptions about the way things are. These assumptions still affect us, often without our awareness of this fact, and can interfere with our focus and our contemplations.

Up to this point, we have dealt with the Platonic tradition only from the perspective of the study of Reality. We've seen that our objective is to turn the eye of the soul towards Truth, and to aim for that goal with all of our attention and all of our might. It was in this regard that we explored the four virtues—fortitude, temperance, wisdom and justice. We've seen that developing these virtues aids us in our growth, and in turn our efforts gradually blossom into a wiser, healthier and more virtuous state of mind.

It may not seem on the surface that the study of false beliefs has any role in the Platonic tradition. Indeed, Plato is not generally associated with such a study. However, Plato recognized that understanding ignorance is a key element in the quest to understand wisdom. He maintained that "all ignorance is involuntary,"[2] meaning that nobody would choose to hold false opinions if they knew them to be false. The study of ignorance, therefore, is prominent in his dialogue on understanding, the *Republic*.

He writes:

"[T]o cheat the soul concerning realities, and to be so cheated, and to be ignorant, and there to have obtained and to keep a

---

[2] *Sophist*, 230a

cheat, is what everyone would least of all choose; and a cheat in the soul is what they most especially hate."[3]

To hold false beliefs about Reality is the worst kind of cheat, for we hold these false beliefs in the soul and let their deforming effects seep first into our thoughts and feelings and then into our words and actions:

"But this, as I was now saying, might most justly be called a true cheat;—ignorance in the soul of the cheated person: since a cheat in words is but a kind of imitation of what the soul feels; and an image afterwards arising, and not altogether a pure cheat."[4]

We all have this ignorance in the soul to some degree, and our own precise web of ignorance is something we want to understand to the best of our ability. This may seem like psychology and therefore unrelated to Platonism, but we will soon see that this is very much a part of the philosophic life. To see why, let's start by taking a closer look at states of mind as a general study.

In Plato's *Republic*, the functioning of the mind at the level of belief is understood by exploring the role of *imitation*. Imitation plays a vital role in our states of mind, and it largely explains why it is that we see the world—and ourselves—through a veil of interpretation.

The Role of Imitation

Imitation[5] is the word Plato uses to describe conforming our thoughts and actions to the patterns which influenced us growing up. We watched our parents, siblings, teachers, and everyone around us and we learned from them, often without even realizing it. Not only their words but also their actions, behavior, and attitudes all had an effect on us. We combined the information we got from these various sources, and this to a large degree created the lens through which we see the world.

"Or have you not observed that imitations, if from earliest youth they be continued onwards for a long time, are

---

[3] *Republic*, 382b

[4] *Ibid.*, 382c

[5] The discussion of imitation in the *Republic* begins at 392d. The Greek word for *imitation* is *mimeiseos*.

established in the manners and natural temper, both with reference to the body and voice, and likewise the *dianoetic* power?"[6]

Have you ever felt that you were turning into your mother or your father? Sometimes I feel as though I am channeling my mother's energy. I feel her in my tone of voice, in my hand gestures, in the way I slump my shoulders when I'm tired or press my lips together when I'm angry. These are moments of recognition that imitation is still a part of me.

My parents are supportive and have always encouraged what they see as best for my siblings and me through their practical-minded advice. Having grown up with such a strong value placed on being practical, my early years in the Platonic tradition involved a struggle. I had to battle that little voice inside my head that asked, "What's the point of reading Plato? This won't advance my career." And as I read pages upon pages of obtuse metaphysics, there was a part of me that was intrigued and excited, but another part that balked and exclaimed, "This is all nonsense! Show me the physical proof."

What this example highlights is that it is possible to hold incompatible beliefs at the same time. My interest in Plato sprang out of a longing to understand myself and the nature of Reality. Whenever I read one of Plato's dialogues, I felt I was on the threshold of finding the answers I had been searching for, or at least that I was on the right track. Conceptually, I understood that without a sense of meaning, the practical life was, well, meaningless—and what would be practical about living *that* way?

On one level, I rejected this whole way of thinking that I had been raised with. Yet the voices were still in my head, forcing me into arguments with myself. Why? Because there was a part of me that believed things my own reasoning had rejected. A part of me was acting out learned behavior. That is imitation.

We may be tempted to try imitating the behavior of a spiritual teacher with the idea that doing so is what it means to live wisely. After all, if our thoughts and actions are imitations, what better role models can we find? However, imitation always functions through a

---

[6] *Ibid.*, 395d. The Greek word *dianoetic* refers to the power of the rational soul.

veil of beliefs. It is one thing to hold the wise as ideal models to learn from, but quite another to believe that attaining some success at this imitation is in itself sufficient.[7]

To the degree that we are acting from belief, we are separated from truth. Without knowing truth, the best we can do is to imitate what we *believe* is the state of mind of one who is wise. However, this is a difficult state of mind to comprehend. There will invariably be misunderstandings that can only be cleared away with genuine insight. Also, deeply-ingrained false beliefs will undoubtedly rear their heads from time to time. Periods of intense pleasure or pain will trigger our old patterns of thought and behavior.

For these reasons, the wise state of mind is not fully open to imitation. Wisdom cannot be truly known until it is attained for oneself, and this is the goal that is most desirable. After all, is it enough to merely hear about wisdom, or to imagine what it might feel like to be wise? Don't you want to know that state of mind for yourself?

Character

State of mind is, to some degree, volatile. Getting fired from a job will put us in a much more somber state of mind than, say, falling in love. Yet we also have seen that our structure of beliefs will greatly affect the way we interpret and react to events such as getting fired and falling in love. States of mind form a complex web that is affected by—and in turn affects—our interactions in the world.

Our character is far more stable than our state of mind. It is the culmination of all our beliefs, behaviors, and attitudes.[8] As such, it can be quite difficult to change. To illustrate the formation of our character, Plato sets up four general character types—matched to the governmental constitutions he calls timocracy (government marked by a love of honor), oligarchy (rule by a small group of people),

---

[7] From the *Republic* 392d, Plato contrasts imitation from what he calls narration—speaking through one's own voice without imitating anyone else. He concludes at 396c: "there is a certain kind of speech, and of narration, in which he who is truly a good and worthy man expresses himself when it is necessary for him to say anything...."

[8] See *Republic,* 400d-e

democracy, and tyranny—and paints in broad strokes the influences that shape them.[9] There is also a fifth constitution, the aristocratic,[10] whose analogue is the philosopher freed from the familial and social influences that imprison the others.

Plato offers an example of a boy whose father was wise but whose mother hungered for wealth and status. The boy's father appealed to the rational part of his soul, his mother to the appetitive, or desiring, part. The boy is pulled in both directions, and by society as well, until at last "he is brought to a mean between the two, and delivers up the government within himself to a middle power, that which is fond of contention and irascible, and so he becomes a haughty and ambitious man."[11] In this way, the boy is shaped by his parents' incompatible values and by his society as a whole. The compromise is struck among all these competing values and his own intuitive sense of what is good and right.

Plato's answer to overcoming the compromises we have made is by studying our own states of mind and learning to recognize the beliefs that have molded them. In the analogy to the city-state, the study of states of mind is called music and the building of spiritual energy is called gymnastics. "What, then, is the education?...gymnastic for the body and music for the mind?"[12] This was later stated more accurately:

> "[S]ome God, as appears, has given men two arts, those of music and gymnastic, in reference to the irascible and the philosophic temper; not for the soul and body, otherwise than

---

[9] This illustration is the subject of books 8 and 9 in the *Republic*. See 544c~545b for the methodology that guides these two books. It is helpful to keep in mind that these types of government are set up as analogies to the soul. Plato was not advocating any actual form of government over another. And in practice, of course, none of these forms of government function quite as they do in theory. The intention, as is true throughout the *Republic*, is to see what Plato writes about each form of government and then apply that to the soul.

[10] Literally, rule by the best. This definition, of course, does not necessarily apply to actual aristocracies as they currently function, or perhaps ever have.

[11] *Ibid.*, 550b

[12] *Ibid.*, 376e

as a by-work, but for that other purpose, that those two tempers may be adapted to one another…"[13]

The building of spiritual energy will be covered later. For now, our focus will be on the value of music.[14] As we come to better understand ourselves and how it is that we have embraced the beliefs that we hold, we will also come to better understand others.

In the *Republic*, Plato writes:

"[W]e shall never become musicians, either we ourselves, or those guardians we say we are to educate, before we understand the images of temperance, fortitude, liberality, and magnificence, and the other sister virtues; and, on the other hand again, the contraries of these, which are everywhere to be met with; and observe them wheresoever they are, both the virtues themselves, and the images of them, and despise them neither in small nor in great instances; but let us believe that this belongs to the same art and study." [15]

In practice, we come to recognize that we have all been conditioned by the same general methods, and that such conditioning was to some degree unavoidable and necessary. With this recognition, our character will naturally soften to one that is magnanimous and graceful. We will find ourselves more understanding of other people's points of view and less harsh in our judgments of their shortcomings. I find that this is true in my own life. Situations that used to cause friction have become easier to smooth out; I am less likely to act from pride and more patient in seeking common ground and engaging in discussion.

What Plato is pointing out here is that cultivating an understanding of metaphysics must be accompanied by a commensurate understanding of the human condition. Plato recognized that developing healthy states of mind is vital to our growth. Ideally, we gain these healthy states in childhood. Recall the discussion in Chapter 6 about censorship. Plato made the case that it is best for children to grow up hearing stories rooted in truth. He warns of the young children: "whatever opinions he receives at such an age are

[13] *Ibid.*, 411e~412a
[14] See also *Ibid.*, 401c~402c.
[15] *Ibid.*, 402c

with difficulty washed away, and are generally immoveable."[16] What is the ideal solution to this? "[W]e should endeavor that what they are first to hear be composed in the most handsome manner for exciting them to virtue."[17] In other words, avoid teaching false opinions in the first place.

What about those of us whose first stories were not those of "the most handsome manner?" Are we doomed to ignorance if our childhood fell short of Plato's ideal? No, this idea is flawed on multiple levels. I don't think this is at all what Plato was suggesting. If it were, there would have been no point in him taking the time to write dialogues or open his Academy. Further, it is overly simplistic to think that the hurdle over false beliefs will be easy for those students raised on teachings in line with Plato's and insurmountable for the rest of us. The issue of beliefs is far more nuanced than merely the acceptance or rejection of Platonic metaphysics. It involves the people who raised us and our relationships with them, with other caregivers and with the world at large.

In general, our beliefs about the way things are and our own self-image subtly affects all of our behavior. This is true not only for you and I but also for the adults who raised us. It is largely in the interactions that we had with the adults who influenced us in our formative years that we developed, for better or worse, our own self-image. And it is in these self-images that we will find the beliefs that block us as our spiritual practice challenges us to question not only metaphysical theories but also the implications of those theories in our day-to-day lives. There will be more on this in the next chapter.

We all need to attack that complex web of beliefs that we formed in childhood. Few of us had that ideal childhood that Plato advocates in the *Republic*. Plato must have realized this because he names the study of states of mind, including understanding the role imitation plays in our own states of mind, among the studies we need to incorporate on our path toward wisdom. We need to revisit our beliefs from childhood, to question the assumptions about ourselves and about the nature of Reality that we have carried with us into adulthood.

---

[16] 378e. The words "with difficulty" and "generally" imply that undoing the damage is possible, even if rare.

[17] *Ibid.*

Taking on this task introduces us to the language of Mind. Through that process, we come to know Mind's providential function. In this way, we accustom ourselves to the divine realm through direct participation in it.

Some people prefer to talk of "the Divine" as something cryptic and other-worldly. Perhaps they feel that shrouding Mind in mystery leaves its profundity intact, and so they insist on holding it at arm's length. However, the truth is quite the opposite. Leaving questions unexplored only adds a sense of profundity when that profundity is smoke and mirrors. It is when intelligibility and light is brought to our contact and understanding of Mind that we truly begin to appreciate its depths and beauty. Far from losing its allure, we are drawn to its beauty and power the more fully we participate in it. Therefore, studying our states of mind is not a tangent away from philosophy; it is philosophy in action.

It is through metaphysics that we seek to know the nature of Reality. It is through studying our states of mind that we seek to better understand our own natures. Ultimately, these two searches reveal themselves to be two sides of the same coin, for our true nature is, in essence, no different from that of Reality itself. Dialectic is the common factor that runs through both of these searches. It is by the use of precise questioning that we look for our assumptions, both about Reality itself and about our own self-image.

As small children, everything is new to us. We struggle to make sense of the way the world functions and the way the people around us behave. What makes people angry? What makes them laugh? What is okay to ignore and what is an issue of concern? With an openness and innocence that perhaps only a child possesses, we accept the behavior of the adults around us on face value. Without analysis or critique, this becomes our sense of what is "normal." We draw conclusions from these interactions, and these conclusions weave the fabric of our interpretation of reality.

As we get older, we have conceptual insights that counter many of these conclusions; we modify the outlook we held as small children as we continue to grow and learn. Yet below these conceptual insights and beliefs, those earliest childhood conclusions are still functioning. We don't always realize they are there, but we act on them all the same. How these beliefs manifest precisely will differ from person to person. One person might get defensive in a situation in which he knows he needn't do so. Another might conceptualize a wise response to something that nevertheless triggers sadness or jealousy or anger.

There is a tendency to want to dismiss this type of emotional reaction as irrational behavior, to conclude that emotions themselves are irrational. We've all heard the accusation, "You're too emotional," haven't we? Yet, what we come to recognize by studying our own states of mind is that even these seemingly irrational emotional reactions are logical; they follow logically from the beliefs we hold at the deepest level.

Beliefs that reflect a false view of reality compel us to act in ways that are unwise. While the culmination of our beliefs and actions define our current character, they do not define our essence. We are all, in essence, beautiful, pure, and good. After all, our essence is divine. As such, we all have the ability to grow wise in this lifetime—although when we look at how much hate and suffering there is in the world, we must conclude that some of our fellow humans are farther from wisdom than others. Still, the potential is always there.

We often hear the gaining of wisdom described as a kind of awakening or an opening of one's eyes. To Plato, however, the dwellers in the cave are just as wide-eyed as their wiser brothers and sisters in the upper world. The spiritual path from ignorance to wisdom is not one of opening our eyes. Rather, it is a process of turning the eye of the soul from its downward focus on the physical realm upward to the cause of this physical realm.[18]

Consider this exchange in the *Republic:*

"Or have you not observed of those who are said to be wicked, yet wise, how sharply the little soul sees, and how acutely it comprehends everything to which it is turned, as having no contemptible sight, but compelled to be subservient to wickedness; so that the more acutely it sees, so much the more productive is it of wickedness?

Entirely so, replied he.

But, however, said I, with reference to this part of such a genius [nature]; if, immediately from childhood, it should be stripped

---

[18] This ties in with discussions of the Greek word *phronesis.*

of everything allied to generation, as leaden weights, and of all those pleasures and lusts which relate to feastings and suchlike, which turn the sight of the soul to things downwards; from all these, if the soul, being freed, should turn itself towards truth, the very same principle in the same men would most acutely see those things as it now does these to which it is turned."[19]

It is this turning of the eye of the soul that is our desire, and this quest requires great effort and courage. Along the way, we will meet with various challenges. These challenges have been mythologized since ancient times as heroic battles against multi-headed monsters and the like. The actual battle, though, is against the ignorance that embraces the downward focus of the soul's eye and keeps us in chains.

This ignorance plays out in our daydreams, in the thoughts that pop into our heads throughout the day, and through the voices that judge and ridicule us. It plays out in our nighttime dreams, as well. Our souls are intellectual in nature, and the realm of Soul is the spiritual realm that links us to the Intelligible. This spiritual realm is constantly communicating with us, showing us what we need to explore in order to know ourselves better and bring our souls to a healthy state.

In the dialogue the *Symposium,* Plato writes: "For divinity is not mingled with man; but by means of that middle nature is carried on all converse and communication between the gods and mortals, whether in sleep or waking."[20]

There is a popular notion that these spiritual guides exist for the purpose of helping us attain wealth and status. This idea has been around for a long time, but in its modern form has come to be known as the *Law of Attraction.* The basic idea of this "law" is that we shape our own future through our thoughts, emotions, and actions. We therefore can manifest our earthly desires by directing our prayers, and all of our spiritual efforts, toward that aim. While Plato's teachings certainly support the dominance of the realms of Mind over the physical realm, they do not take this to the extreme of advocating antirealism—the belief that the physical world is something we

---

[19] 519a~b, brackets added.

[20] 203a

create.[21] Platonism recognizes the physical realm to have a mode of reality in its own right. The physical realm is not ultimate reality, but neither is it an illusion.

Further, the goals of this modern movement, to manifest our desires, is only compatible with Plato's teachings if the desire we wish to manifest is the attainment of wisdom.[22] The intermediaries in the spiritual realm are our providential teachers, not our servants. They do not exist to fulfill our every whim; their role is to help us learn what is truly desirable for our health as spiritual beings.

We can think of this issue in terms of the divine law of providence. Participating in the Intelligible to the degree that we are able is a double-edged sword. On the one hand, it means that we can participate at infinite depths so long as we keep pursuing growth with sincerity, courage, and integrity. However, we must also be aware that "to the degree we are able" implies that we set our own ceiling.

To the degree that we hold false beliefs about ourselves, Reality itself, and the interaction of the two, we also hinder and distort participation in the Intelligible. Limiting our contact with spiritual intermediaries to the pursuit of comfort and pleasure means never enjoying their highest gift: the means to know our true nature and what is truly good, beautiful, and virtuous. Without this knowledge, we are chasing mere images, hoping that if our prayers are answered our lives will feel meaningful and happy. Yet how often do we ask ourselves if the things we desire are actually worth desiring?

Consider this insight by the title character in *The Second Alcibiades*:

"But what I am thinking of is, how many evils are brought on men by ignorance; since to this it seems owing that we labour to procure for ourselves the greatest mischiefs…And yet no man would imagine that to be his own case; and everyone supposes himself sufficiently knowing to pray for things the most advantageous to himself, and to avoid praying for things

---

[21] See Spencer, *The Eternal Law* for an in-depth comparison between realism and antirealism.

[22] This notion can be found either implicitly or explicitly throughout Plato's dialogues. It is addressed extensively throughout the *Laws*. Also, the dialogue *The Second Alcibiades* focuses exclusively on this theme. I add as a caveat that there is some dispute among scholars as to this latter dialogue's authenticity.

the most mischievous: for to pray for these things would in reality be like a curse, and not a prayer."[23]

When the eye of the soul is focused on this physical world, we do not see the beauty of the Intelligible as it really is; we see only an interpretation of it as seen through our current assumptions. As a result, well-intentioned people who think of themselves as spiritual risk spending their time chasing concerns that are actually distractions from a genuinely spiritual life. Plato writes: "we ought not to pray, nor endeavour that all things may be conformable to our wish, but that our will rather may be obedient to our wisdom; and that…each of us ought to pray for, and endeavour to obtain, the possession of intellect."[24]

The law of providence allows for more nuances than merely dividing us into good and bad. Simply put, we each seek what we deem to be good, and we conform to that model. In the *Theatetus*, Plato writes of those who never turn the eye of the soul upward: "They therefore pay the penalty for this by living a life that conforms to the pattern they resemble…"[25]

To clarify, let's look at wealth as an example. Wealth is not in itself anything bad, but it can be misused. It can distract us from what is truly meaningful. This is equally true for the wealthy person passing life away in pleasure-seeking and for the poor person complaining constantly about the injustice of being among the have-nots. Further, a lack of wealth can just as easily be misused, inflating one's pride and feeding the false belief that living modestly is proof of one's wisdom.

However, when the eye of the soul is turned upward, it sees Beauty, Justice, and Goodness. It therefore recognizes its expressions here in the physical realm, as well as imitations of these Realities. Turning the soul's eye upward does not mean that we see no value in this physical realm. Quite the opposite occurs: we better appreciate what is truly meaningful in our daily lives, because we know the absolute Realities of which meaningful aspects of this world are manifestations.

---

[23] 143b

[24] *Laws*, 687e.

[25] 177a, trans. Harold North Fowler

Chapter 16: Road Blocks

"[L]et us in a quiet manner...again consider, not morosely, but examining ourselves in reality, what the nature is of these appearances within us."

Plato[1]

Personal Obstacles

There is quite possibly nothing more frustrating to those of us who read spiritual literature than to have our studies interrupted and our concentration high-jacked by seemingly random thoughts. It has happened to me often. I'm reading the same obtuse paragraph for the third time, trying to focus, and then my thoughts wander to some trivial event that occurred back in high school. For the few minutes I'm sucked into that memory, it feels incredibly real. Then I pop out with a jolt. There may be a second or two of confusion as my state of mind shifts back to my current, adult one. I chide myself for letting my thoughts wander. *What am I doing?* Perhaps I return my attention to my reading, stubbornly fighting my lack of concentration; perhaps I give up for the day.

What happened? Depending on who you ask, you may be told that it is *maya* (a Sanskrit term that means *illusion*), or *mind junk*, or the result of having a "monkey mind" that swings from thought to thought. Many teachers recommend developing greater discipline to counter this problem. This approach is not entirely without merit; some degree of discipline is certainly essential. However, this advice ignores the question of why *that* particular thought popped in my head at *that* particular moment. It treats these interruptions as purely random and as being of no value in and of themselves; they are nothing more than mental trash to be swept away.

However, those of us who become attuned to our own states of mind will quickly recognize that there are no random thoughts.[2]

---

[1] *Theaetetus*, 155a

[2] On the study of false beliefs and how they affect our daily lives, I am indebted to the work of Dr. Pierre Grimes. Much of this section is informed by his insights, including the discussion on uprooting our own false beliefs. He has a number of publications on this topic, a few of which can be found in the bibliography. I encourage those who are seeking a more detailed discussion on this topic to consult those references.

Certainly, we are all familiar with the experience I opened this section with, or one similar to it. Many of us have had difficulty focusing during meditations, too. There are some aspects of these such experiences that are universal and can be generalized. Yet, the thoughts that interrupt me are unique to me, just as yours are unique to you. They involve specific memories, or they are daydreams that are built out of certain images that the daydreamer reacts strongly to, be they positive or negative.

Maybe someone cut in front of me at the bank the other day and today my daydreams carry the same theme. Or perhaps in a daydream I find myself upstaging someone who dismissed me as hopeless back in high school. These may be situations many readers can relate to, but the specific details of my daydreams will differ from anyone else's. The story unfolds through my own state of mind, and the events in my life function as the settings in which I play out my own inner drama. You might say it has a personal signature on it.

In one sense, philosophy is the study of states of mind. Ignorance is a state of mind; so is wisdom. Our progress from one to the other, and deepening our wisdom once that threshold is crossed, is all a shifting of states of mind. To demonstrate this, let's look at an actual example from my own experience.

This incident took place in the spring of 2012.[3] I had been working on building my intuitive connection to divine Mind.[4] The intention behind this effort was to prove to myself that my practice was ripening. I had the tendency at the time to downplay my own efforts and growth.

Recall again the divine law of providence: the goodness of the gods flows through all the realms of reality, and we each participate in this goodness to the degree that we are able. The inner dialogue I was cultivating had the initial effect of building my self-confidence by confirming that my practice was indeed maturing. I was participating in divine goodness to a higher degree than I ever had before.

However, over time my connection with Mind deepened such that the wisdom of the answers flowing through me tossed me into

---

[3] The account here is based on my private journal notes and on memory.

[4] This involved nurturing an inner dialogue with divine Mind. Techniques for doing this will be discussed in Chapter 27.

confusion. I refused to accept that my practice had ripened enough for me to access such wisdom. I felt that I was in the presence of greatness, and that somehow it was arrogant of me to think that I belonged there. I found it a challenge to call it providence rather than grace, even though I knew it was. Grace, as it is commonly understood, implies that I received a gift I had nothing to do with. It was God's mercy and love, and had nothing to do with the efforts I had made over the years. Even in my private thoughts, I couldn't take credit for anything I had done. When I tried, I imagined self-righteous critics putting me in my place for my insolence.

In just this quick summary of the scenario, a number of different states of mind have already surfaced. Connecting to our intuition requires a spiritually mature state of mind. The doubts that sabotage our success are blocks to this growth, and those are states of mind that must be understood in order to be overcome. The imagined judgment that I was being arrogant marks yet another state of mind, one that gave my doubt the reinforcement it needed to appear valid and so keep its hold on me.

Let's break away from this example for a moment to look at what was really going on here. Blocks spring up whenever we seek a personally meaningful goal.[5] This is true for all of us, whether we are spiritually minded or not. Psychological blocks will challenge us whenever we dare to reach beyond our familiar sense of self-identity, such as aiming for a high-status job promotion, working towards athletic achievements, or taking steps to overcome shyness. For our purposes, we are going to focus on unhealthy states of mind that manifest when we are advancing in our efforts to discover our true nature.

False beliefs that shape our self-identity carry with them certain states of mind, ones that we still identify with. However, these states of mind (whatever they may be) are inconsistent with the healthier state of mind that we are working towards in our studies. As long as we can continue growing without challenging these beliefs, we will do so and the beliefs will cause us only mild inconveniences. They do not

---

[5] Cf. Grimes and Uliana, *Philosophical Midwifery*, p.2: "The more personally significant and meaningful the goal one pursues the more visible the pathologos [the name Dr. Grimes gave to debilitating false beliefs related to self-image] will become."

manifest into full-blown blocks until we reach that critical point when we can advance no further without rejecting this belief about ourselves and about the nature of Reality. We've reached a crossroads and must make a choice: drop the belief and evolve beyond its limitations, or conclude that the belief underlying our current block is true, and therefore knowledge is either a fairy tale or out of our reach.

In the case of my example, I found myself denying that I could achieve the goal I had been working towards for more than a decade. This was not due to the metaphysical questions involving grace and providence. I had already seen clearly, both in my studies and in my daily life, the role of providence in the divine order of the cosmos. It is not at all uncommon, though, to act in a way that is counter to our conceptual insights, as I had done in this example.

The problem was that my growth had surpassed my expectations. It surpassed an image of myself that I was only faintly aware of even holding. I was the perpetual student who knew nothing and did not claim to have any profound insights. As long as I could grow without challenging that self-image, I remained in that role. However, when my growth pointed to the possibility of graduating beyond being "just a student," the block was triggered and the crossroads was reached.

Those of us who take on the challenge of psychical growth discover over time that we hit against limiting self-images, and there are patterns to these interrupting states of mind. Situations come and go, but the states of mind appear again and again. What we need to do is distinguish what those states of mind are and which assumptions underlie them. These assumptions, when all pieced together, comprise our view of ourselves and of the world.

You may recall that I hit this block when I started a practice of turning questions inward and letting the answers manifest from within. Precise methods for this practice I was engaged in will be covered in Chapter 29. For now, let's focus on the difficulties I experienced in accepting that I could access wisdom. The clearer the response to my questions, the stronger my urge became to downplay my efforts and successes. I undercut my own confidence until it finally boiled to a crisis.

Such crossroads have compelled many to give up their studies altogether. However, once the state of mind in question has been explored and understood, it dissolves. With its dissolution, its formidableness dissolves as well. We see right through that mask, and marvel that it ever succeeded in exerting such a powerful hold on us in the first place. With this new level of clarity, we can return to our practice with even greater confidence and strength than we had before the unhealthy state of mind got in our way.

I explore a block by isolating the state of mind in question, be it one of restlessness or anger and so on.[6] Some states of mind are harder to identify, such as a vague uneasiness. I do my best, though, to put it into words, however hazy the state of mind may be. Then, once I've identified the state of mind in question, it is time to probe my memories. I trace back through my life to various times I've experienced the same state of mind. Remember, situations change but states of mind repeat over and over. The state of mind that I am exploring is always one I identify with strongly and know well. I will not only recall it mentally, but also feel the state of mind wash over my whole body.

Ideally, I want to trace my memories all the way back to the first time I ever experienced this state of mind. That was the moment I picked up a certain self-image that had since become second nature to me. As innocent children, we accepted some conclusion without any analysis. Through our meditations on the past, though, we can revisit that childhood incident and see it through adult eyes.

In the case of my above example, I traced my sense of being the perpetual student to an incident that occurred when I was eight years old. A relative told me that she greatly admired an Orthodox Jewish family she knew. I asked her why she didn't live that way herself. It was too hard, she told me. Her tone of voice confirmed that this was an unquestionable fact, and there was no further discussion about it. In that moment, I understood that we weren't the kind of people who did great things; we were ordinary. It was unrealistic to aim higher or to want more. I reached this conclusion with the innocence that perhaps only a child possesses. This wasn't seen as a judgment of anyone's abilities; it was just the way things were. Times in the past

---

[6] What I present here is a brief over-view of my basic process, which I've adapted from the work of Grimes. For a more detailed presentation of his procedure, please refer to Grimes and Uliana, *Philosophical Midwifery* or Grimes, *Unblocking: Removing Blocks to Understanding*. Both books can be found in the bibliography at the end of this book.

when I had heard family members say they couldn't do this or that finally made sense to me.

As you can see from this example, the events themselves tend to be mundane and therefore easy to forget. Yet the conclusion we, as small children, walked away with remains with us. Because it had never been subjected to reflection or analysis, there had been no opportunity to reject it. We embrace the conclusion and then forget the events surrounding that learning. It becomes one of our assumptions about ourselves. Seeing the world through that false belief becomes so natural that we don't even suspect that the distorting assumption is present. We integrate it at such a deep level that it becomes the way we *feel*, even if as adults our reasoning tells us this is wrong. We find ourselves sabotaging our own happiness, but baffled as to why we do it.

Recognizing our family's culture is perhaps enough to shed some light on the blocks we hit. I had big dreams when I was a child, as every young person does. Depending on the week, I wanted to be a world-famous novelist or maybe an investigative reporter who traveled the world. The caregivers in my life were all more pragmatic than that. They were enthusiastic about and supportive of my academic successes, but dismissed my more ambitious goals as impractical. In this way, they tempered my expectations.

Obviously, the state of mind I had entered before hitting my block was a more exalted one than someone with tempered ambitions would expect to encounter. However, this insight itself is not enough to stop the false belief from being triggered. It is also not enough to distinguish what exactly about that family culture was still affecting me as an adult. Further digging was necessary, and that is why I needed to recall that memory from when I was eight years old.

It has become commonplace in popular TV shows to feature psychiatrists or criminal profilers who connect someone's adult behavior to his or her childhood. In this way, we as TV viewers have become savvy in this area. We quickly connect, for example, someone's violent behavior to their upbringing in a similarly violent environment. We know that belittling a child will foster insecurities. Such examples demonstrate the connection between our behavior and the environment we grew up in.

The problem is, many people recognize these environmental factors in their own lives yet do not know how to change. Simply telling ourselves that we are good won't erase our insecurities. Reciting reasons to practice compassion will not end anger. Positive affirmations are simply not enough, and we can't talk ourselves out of unhealthy states of mind. You can plant beautiful flowers in your garden, but weeds will still spring up if their deepest roots have not been severed. What is worse, those beautiful flowers cannot grow strong roots themselves if the garden is overrun with weeds.

Trying to embrace positive beliefs on their own will not bring us meaningful success, because that practice will not show us the debilitating false belief that is compelling us to fail. There is more we have to see. It is not enough to recognize that these beliefs are present; we need to see precisely *how* we came to believe these falsehoods in the first place. This, simply put, is cause and effect. We are seeking to understand the causes of this self-image we identify with, much as we seek to understand the cause of our essence in our study of metaphysics.

Our explorations of blocks involve surfacing memories that have long been buried, and this has the potential to be temporarily disturbing. Working with another person is especially advisable for people who have experienced traumatic events such as abuse or who are currently prone to radical mood swings. That said, we needn't worry we are treading into dangerous waters by moving forward with this process on our own.

There is a fear that probing our own hearts will unlock some dark, sinister power. We suspect that our ugliest fantasies, the ones we would never admit in public, are evidence of having an evil nature. What's more, our insecurities grip us so strongly that we are convinced they point to inherent flaws in the depths of our being. These assumptions about sin and inherent flaws are false and are themselves hurdles that need to be explored and cleared. Our practice will confirm this once we've gained a bit of experience. We will see firsthand that false beliefs are at the root of our destructive patterns, not sin or intrinsic imperfections. These beliefs are not innate; they are learned behavior. Anything learned can be unlearned.

It is common early in our practice to be embarrassed by, and perhaps even ashamed of, some of the beliefs that we surface. This is normal, and it will pass. Over time, we see for ourselves that those beliefs do not define us. When they lose their power, they naturally fall away. Our identification gradually shifts from the masks we had picked up in childhood to the essence underneath. We are good and wise in essence, and this practice goes a long way in helping us manifest those natural qualities in our everyday lives.

Depending on the complex web of self-images we currently carry, some of us may be able to jump right over our hurdles quickly. Others will find the exploration of false beliefs to be a prominent feature in our practice, at least for a time. That's fine, if it is. The important thing is not to get so caught up in the study of false beliefs that we lose sight of our vision of Truth. The value of being aware of why our minds wander and why we hit blocks is that we can recognize whichever false belief is getting in our way, and we can tear it down. This is far healthier than merely depending on will power to bypass the falsities. We don't want to leave these false beliefs in the soul, for "everyone is most afraid of possessing a cheat there."[7]

Yes, This Will Be on the Test…

Once we've explored a block, we need to test our new insights. Otherwise, we risk allowing our energy to fall back into old, familiar patterns. We must go back to pursuing the goal we were working towards at the time the block initially stopped us. Can we move forward? If not, there is more to look at. Once we have sufficiently uncovered and uprooted this layer of the block, it will no longer pose an obstacle to us.

We may also find ourselves challenged by the uncertainty left in the wake of living without a long-held belief. I have found myself trying to fall into a familiar daydream, simply out of habit. However, once the basis of that daydream disappears, the daydream's appeal does as well. Faced with the absence of my usual thoughts, my knee-jerk reaction has been to ask myself, *What am I supposed to think about instead?*

It sounds crazy, but it's common. We oftentimes feel naked and uncertain without those familiar states of mind to fall back into. Fortunately for us, divine Mind has a way of offering us further lessons if we have the courage to venture into that great unknown.

---

[7] *Republic*, 382a

In this way, the graceful and courageous character discussed in the previous chapter continues to flower. Discovering our own web of beliefs allows us to become more forgiving and patient with other people's as well. We better appreciate that, just as these unhealthy states of mind are not who we are in essence, nor are they who other people are, either.

Being aware of our states of mind, when done in conjunction with the other practices discussed in this book, helps us manifest the benefits of our spiritual insights in our lives. It allows our understanding of ourselves and of reality to mature. It then helps us over that difficult bridge between understanding and knowing, and finally, it aids us along the rarely traveled road of the wise.

Understanding Our Past

Awareness of our states of mind brings us to a state of well-being that parallels the deeper spiritual journey. We gain an ever-greater understanding of how false beliefs take root. This kind of seeing brings an understanding of reality at the psychological level which is analogous to (but not the same as) the knowledge gained through the highest vision of Reality itself. Therefore, understanding our past brings a commensurate level of wisdom, which manifests as maturity and growth.

To the degree we see our past clearly and understand how its forces have shaped us, we can be said to "turn from darkness to light"[8] in regards to our past. This is not the same as knowing Reality itself, but it is a level of clarity that opens our lives to tremendous peace and beauty. By itself, studying our states of mind can help us rid ourselves of destructive patterns, and so make wiser choices. As part of a spiritual practice aimed at wisdom, it can help us remove whatever blocks us as we seek to know the true Justice, Beauty, and Goodness of which our loved ones and society have shown us images.

---

[8] *Republic,* 518c

Chapter 17: Energy Building

"[H]e who is careful in forming his body aright should at the same time unite with this the motions of the soul, employing music and all philosophy; if he is to be rendered such a one as can be justly called beautiful, and at the same time truly good."

Plato[1]

Unifying and Strengthening

Platonic philosophy as it is taught in modern universities is a sterile, empty shadow of the true richness this tradition holds. The ancient philosophers did contemplate metaphysics, science and mathematics, but those explorations were parts of a well-rounded practice that likely included such elements as meditation, ritual, and physical practices aimed at strengthening and purifying spiritual energy. Little information remains of these earlier practices, but we do have a few hints. Throughout Plato's dialogues are numerous references to physical endeavors highly valued in Greek society, from running to javelin throwing to dancing.[2]

Another hint might come from an unexpected source. The ancient Greek playwright Aristophanes pokes fun at Socrates in a play called *The Clouds*. Ironically, this comedian who clearly did not appreciate spiritual practice allows us a rare peek into aspects of Socrates' teachings other than those found in Plato's dialogues:

"The door opens, revealing the interior of the Thoughtery, in which the DISCIPLES OF SOCRATES are seen in various postures of meditation and study; they are pale and emaciated creatures.

Strepsiades :Ah! By Heracles! What country are those animals from?

Disciple: Why, what are you astonished at? What do you think they resemble?

Strepsiades: The captives of Pylos. But why do they look so fixedly on the ground?

---

[1] *Timaeus*, 88c

[2] See for example *Laws*, 795~6

Disciple: They are seeking for what is below the ground.

Strepsiades: Ah! They're looking for onions. Do not give yourselves so much trouble; I know where there are some, fine big ones. But what are those fellows doing, bent all double?

Disciple: They are sounding the abysses of Tartarus.

Strepsiades: And what are their arses looking at in the heavens?

Disciple: They are studying astronomy on their own account."[3]

From this humorous jab at the way spiritual practitioners appear to the lay person, we recognize a description of sitting meditation as well as some sort of practice involving poses, perhaps along the lines of hatha yoga. Indeed, these are both meaningful elements of any genuine spiritual practice.

Because we do not know the precise methods used by Socrates or at Plato's Academy, we find ourselves borrowing from other systems and modifying for our own use. This chapter and the next focus on the importance of building spiritual energy so as to reinforce the process of purification and the preparation for separation of the soul from the body, this separation being an element of peak experiences. These methods are most effective when they are made routine elements of everyday life, running concurrent with all the other areas of our spiritual life.

Platonists recognize that the essence of all, *ousia*, is intellectual. *Ousia* is the intellectual act of Mind turning to look at itself and knowing itself to be beautiful, good, and just. The highest expression of *ousia* is what we often call Essence itself. We can also call it Reality itself. It is because of the intellectual nature of Reality that we focus on using our minds as our main tool to experience and to know Mind. Whereas modern doctors and scientists tend to rank the physical brain as more significant than the mind, Platonists recognize our minds as our means to connect with and know the Intelligible. The physical body—including the brain—is merely the instrument that we use in our current incarnation.

In this chapter, we will look at how energy-building practices adapted from other schools of mysticism can supplement our main

---

[3] The Internet Classics Archive:
http://classics.mit.edu/Aristophanes/clouds.html

approach. Many Eastern systems recognize our intellectual essence as a kind of energy. This is the level of Soul in the Platonic metaphysical structure. Soul mediates between Mind and the physical realm. Eastern systems such as Tai Chi and hatha yoga focus on this energy, mainly (but not exclusively) as it correlates with the physical level. From this platform, they teach physical poses, chants, and meditations aimed at moving this energy. The intention is to clear energy blocks and smooth out imbalances.

On the surface, this may seem a far cry from what the Platonic tradition sets out to do. However, Plato hinted in various passages throughout his dialogues at the need for this attention to spiritual energy. The most notable example, perhaps, is in the *Republic* when, in his extended analogy to the city-state, Socrates introduces the study of gymnastics.[4]

In Athens at that time, gymnastics referred to such activities as wrestling and boxing, both of which were taught in an area of Athens' gymnasiums called the *palaestra*.[5] However, Plato makes it clear that he does not view these sports simply as athletic training for the body: "[T]hey who propose to teach music and gymnastic, propose these things, not, for what some imagine, to cure the body by the one, and the soul by the other....They seem, said I, to propose them both chiefly on the soul's account."[6]

In particular, Plato saw what he was calling gymnastics as a means to strengthen the high-spirited aspect of the soul.[7] This builds the courage and will power necessary to advance our spiritual practice. Indeed, the study of states of mind, referred to as music in the *Republic* and discussed previously, is very much intertwined with meditation and other forms of energy movement:

"Whoever then shall in the most handsome manner mingle gymnastic with music, and have these in the justest measure in

---

[4] The study of gymnastics in the *Republic* can be found from 410b.

[5] See for example: *Laws* 796a~c and 814d, *Charmides* 153a, *Lysis* 204a

[6] *Republic*, 410c

[7] See *Ibid.*, 410b: "And he will perform his exercises, and his labours, rather looking to the irascible part of his nature, and exciting it by labour, than to [gain] strength..."

his soul, him we shall most properly call the most completely musical, and of the best harmony…"[8]

The recognition of the connection between physical movement and spiritual energy is significant to spiritual practice. Athletic movement alone can build strength and agility. However, it is by bringing our focus and concentration to our movements that the actions become meaningful to the soul, and spiritual maturity is aided.

Indeed, this theme of intertwining our external actions in the world with the inner world of our minds is one that runs throughout the *Republic* and, as our spiritual practice deepens, we will better appreciate has direct application to our lives. In the *Republic*, this theme peaks with a declaration by Socrates that is too often understood only in terms of the political discussion on the surface of this spiritual dialogue:

> "Unless either philosophers, said I, govern in cities, or those who are at present called kings and governors philosophise genuinely and sufficiently, and these two, the political power and philosophy, unite in one…there shall be no end, Glauco, to the miseries of cities, nor yet, as I imagine, to those of the human race…"[9]

At the simplest level, we can understand this quote as pointing out the obvious observation that the world would be a more peaceful and loving place if world leaders were wise role models and actors in world affairs. However, there is a deeper level at which we can all apply this same basic premise to our lives.

Plato's ideal was not the philosopher who retreats from society, lost in the internal world of the mind.[10] Nor was it the sophist or the public servant who acts from good intentions but whose education falls short of truth. Rather, it is the union of action and healthy thought that culminates in the true manifestation of wisdom. In the exemplar of Socrates, we find a man whose insights guided his actions

---

[8] *Ibid.*, 411e~412a. See also the *Timaeus*, 89b: "And hence, of all the purgations and concretions of the body, that is the best which subsists through gymnastic."

[9] *Republic*, 473d

[10] At *Ibid.*, 519c, he describes such people as "thinking that whilst they are yet alive, they inhabit the islands of the blessed."

in the world and his reactions to whatever was going on around him. In turn, he relished his interactions with others as a means to spur further internal debate and exploration, both for himself and for his interlocutors.

This relationship between the external world in which we interact and the internal world of our minds is fundamental to all areas of our lives. Our growth risks developing lopsidedly if we undervalue either of these areas—the internal or the external worlds. As our practice deepens, we increasingly find that the challenge is to be in the world in a way that honors the insights we have gained, exerting the courage that Socrates showed when he faced harsh criticism and social rejection—and in his case, ultimately death.

In regards to what Plato calls gymnastics, it is important that we maintain awareness of the interconnection between our thoughts and our movement, whether we choose an activity traditional to the ancient Greeks, such as dancing or wrestling, or we opt for the methods of another spiritual system. Students of Platonism can find many different systems to be beneficial sources of this form of gymnastics. Hatha yoga and Tai Chi are perhaps the most common in the Western world. However, I encourage you to try many different practices to find what best suits your personality and lifestyle. And of course, there is nothing to stop you from borrowing from more than one system.

I personally enjoy kundalini yoga. Because it is the system I am currently most familiar with, I will refer to it throughout this section as an example of the compatibility of other systems to Platonism and of how to adapt their techniques to the Platonic tradition. Kundalini yoga teaches that there is a channel up the center of the spine, called *susumna* in Sanskrit, through which spiritual energy flows smoothly in one who is awake. Blocks in this flow manifest as the various false beliefs we hold about ourselves and about the nature of reality. Platonists, of course, would argue that this is backwards; it is the various false beliefs we hold about ourselves and the nature of reality that manifest as blocks.

Kundalini is a Sanskrit word that is often translated as the energy that runs up *susumna* during a peak experience. Hints of these such energy flows can perhaps be found in some of Plato's myths, most

212 Discovering the Beauty of Wisdom

notably in the *Timaeus*.[11] In the classic kundalini yoga text *The Serpent Power*, author Arthur Avalon explains the phenomenon in this way:

> "*Kundala* means coiled. The power is the Goddess Kundalini, or that which is coiled; for Her form is that of a coiled and sleeping serpent in the lowest bodily center, at the base of the spinal column, until by the means described She is aroused in that yoga which is named after her."[12]

The yogi master T.K.B. Desikachar defines it differently; he calls it an obstacle to this divine intellectual energy, not the energy itself.[13] The energy itself, in the form associated with bodies, is called *prana* in Sanskrit:

> "What is to enter the *susumna* [the channel up the center of the spine] at some state or other through your yoga practice is…not the kundalini itself, but simply *prana*…A snake killed while lying in a curled position unfolds and stretches out, the muscles no longer able to keep it coiled. It is said that when the fire in the body, *agni*, has killed the snake, the *kundalini* unrolls and the passage is open to the flow of *prana*. This does not happen overnight. Even when parts of the *kundalini* are destroyed, it remains capable of blocking *susumna* for a long time."[14]

If we recognize the above Sanskrit terms as metaphors for divine functions, then a great compatibility awakens between Platonism and kundalini yoga. The snake we must kill is made up of ignorance about ourselves and, by extension, about the nature of reality. As in the above quote, we see in our own practice that even when parts of this fiction are torn down—when some false beliefs have been identified and cleared away—our vision is still limited. Both understanding and knowing admit of degrees.

---

[11] See 77b~78a

[12] Avalon, *The Serpent Power*, p. 1

[13] Desikachar, *The Heart of Yoga*, p. 138. He cites the ancient Hindu source the *Yoga Yajnavalkya* for this understanding of *kundalini*. Arthur Avalon also, in his book *The Serpent Power*, acknowledges that some works refer to this spiritual path by the name Bhuta-suddhi. He defines this Sanskrit term as "the purification of the Elements of the body" (p. 1)

[14] *Ibid.*

The more common image of kundalini as the energy that must be awakened and strengthened is also compatible with Platonic thought. In fact, I see the two descriptions as connected, because unifying our energy and strengthening it are not two separate practices, distinct from one another. A basic premise of Platonic metaphysics is that that which is more unified is also more potent.[15] Monads (indivisible unities) precede triads, the unified comes before the manifold, and all multiplicity proceeds from the first cause of all, the One.

This basic premise of metaphysics has its application in our daily practice, as well. Plato recognized belief, understanding, and knowing to be faculties of the soul that operate at differing energies.[16] The function, therefore, of contemplating metaphysics is far more than merely mental exercises. We are raising our energy so as to allow us to function at the heightened power of knowing. This is an important aspect of the process of turning the eye of the soul upward and sharpening insight and vision.

The prisoners chained in Plato's cave are limited to the faculty of belief. Their states of mind are hindered by an endless sea of imitations that sap their potency[17] and create the ceiling of conventionality that limits their vision (and this holds true regardless of how intelligent they are). Remember the boy in the *Republic* whose father was wise but whose mother hungered for status and wealth?[18] His affections were torn in multiple directions. The compromise he made arose from a sympathy for incompatible views. Our practice teaches us, over time, to unify our fragmented states of mind into one that is potent and unified, pointed toward truth rather than diluted by an endless sea of opinions.[19]

---

[15] Cf. *The Elements of Theology*, props. 61 and 62.

[16] See *Republic*, 477b~c

[17] Cf. *Ibid.*, 394e~395a

[18] See Chapter 15. Also, *Republic*, 549c~550b

[19] Consider this statement of Plato's at *Ibid.*, 545d, shrouded in the analogy to the city-state: "Or is not this plain, that every republic changes, by means of that part which possesses the magistracies, when in this itself there arises sedition; but whilst this agrees with itself though the state be extremely small, it is impossible to be changed?"

Plato calls our practice one of purification[20] for precisely this reason. As we purify ourselves of ignorance, our sense of self becomes more unified. We are less splintered between conflicting self-images. Our goal, then, is very much in line with the goal of kundalini yoga. Removing blocks to allow for the unhindered flow of the soul's energy is central to both systems. The difference is that for Platonists, our focus is on blocks as false beliefs in the soul rather than as energy blocks. Yogis treat false beliefs as the result of energy blocks; we treat false beliefs as the cause of them. Energy movement practices such as those described in this chapter, then, aid our main approach rather than comprise it.

Using energy-focused techniques speeds up the process of strengthening and unifying energy. Kundalini yoga, for example, consists largely of various meditations and physical poses designed to open energy blocks and balance the flow of spiritual energy. If you are doing kundalini yoga for these purposes rather than for physical exercise, your attention should be on mentally following the breath and on the flow of *prana,* as directed for each yoga pose and meditation. Physical movement guides the flow of energy and, in turn, our one-pointed focus informs our movements.

The goal of all of the techniques presented in this book is to nurture a healthy state of mind, one that is strong and unified. However, the process of purification can be an uncomfortable one. It is a myth that energy-focused techniques such as yoga will always leave us feeling balanced and happy. When done correctly, blocks will be stimulated. This can sometimes feel like a step backward when unhealthy states of mind manifest. Some days, you may feel agitated, and other days angry or dejected. When this happens, it's helpful to remember that these states of mind are indelibly tied to false beliefs that can be surfaced, understood and cleared away.

Targeting blocks in the body where the tension of a belief manifests helps stir memories and emotions tied to that belief. I like to ask myself what memories are tied to that energy block, and then sit with quiet attention to see what thoughts manifest. I can often clear the energy simply by meditating on it and giving the energy time to work itself out. This is the common approach in most energy-

---

[20] Use of the word *purification* [*katharsis*] can be found in the *Phaedo* at 67c and in the *Sophist* at 230d, as well as scattered throughout the *Laws*.

based systems. When this is successful, it helps to imagine the blocked energy lifting out of the body through the top of the head.

However, if the memory tied to that blocked energy has not been sufficiently understood, the clarity that follows an energy-focused practice is only temporary. Practices such as those of kundalini yoga help energy blocks open. This is not enough, though. If the beliefs at the root of the blocks are not challenged and seen through, the energy will simply return to its former, unhealthy alignment. However, once the beliefs tied to that blocked energy have been effectively explored, the beliefs lose their power and the block dissolves. Whatever practice we undertake to move energy should ideally include clearing away false beliefs.

Rituals

In the Platonic tradition, reading is in itself a form of ritual. This practice is undertaken with the goals of stimulating spiritual energy and of turning the soul away from the physical realm towards the realms of the divine. Reading is ideally carried out with one-pointed focus that raises it beyond a mere study technique to the level of meditation.

When we read mystic literature in the way it was intended to be read as outlined in Chapter 5, we approach it with more than just our discursive thoughts. We engage it with our whole soul, letting the words penetrate through us and fill us with their intellectual illumination. This illumination is the *logos,* truth as an intellectual reality.[21]

Ritual practices such as chanting, incantations, and praying to divinity through material items such as paintings and statues also have a place in a Platonist's spiritual practice. The aim of such rituals is to cultivate a sense of closeness to the Intelligible. Ritual is a means to raise our energy and turn our thoughts upwards, away from mundane concerns. Ritual does this by recognizing the sacred in the realm of materiality. Because Platonists recognize that soul reaches into the realm of materiality to the degree bodies are able to receive it, a case

---

[21] See Chapter 6 for more on the Greek word *logos.*

can be made that statues built in honor of gods are to some degree appropriate receptacles.[22]

Anyone doubting the compatibility of rituals with an intellectual approach to spiritual practice ought to consider these words of Proclus': "For the wish to pray is a desire of conversion to the gods. And this desire itself conducts the desiring soul, and conjoins it to divinity, which is the first work of prayer."[23] For Platonists wishing to incorporate ritual into their practice, the Platonic philosopher Iamblichus wrote a treatise called *On the Mysteries* which could prove inspirational. It is largely a defense of ritual practice as a catalyst for divine inspiration. He tells us that "in all things the image of good exhibits a similitude of divinity…"[24] Iamblichus is an important figure in the development of Platonic thought, and was a rigorous dialectician. As such, ritual did not replace the basic approach of this tradition; instead, it was used to enhance and deepen the other means of development.[25]

---

[22] On this topic, see for example Plotinus' ennead IV:iii:11.

[23] Proclus, *Commentaries of Proclus on the Timaeus of Plato* I, 221, 21.

[24] *On the Mysteries*, p. 188.

[25] This summary of Iamblichus was adapted from Edwards (trans.), *Neoplatonic Saints,* from p. xxxix.

Chapter 18: Meditation

"The quiet of intellect, however, is not mental alienation, but is the tranquil energy of intellect, withdrawing itself from other things…"

Plotinus[1]

While most every spiritual system does include some form of meditation, this practice is treated differently from system to system. Some make it central, others peripheral. We saw in the last chapter, in the discussion of ritual practices, that Platonists treat reading as a form of meditation in its own right.

Formal sitting meditation, however, is not discussed in any of the Platonic literature. When we close our books, our focus is instead on contemplation. For Platonists, contemplation goes far beyond discursive thoughts. When we meditate, we hold a particular question or image. Contemplation, in contrast, is one-pointed absorption into that question or image. In other words, meditation at its best peaks in contemplation. We will see more about contemplation in the next chapter. Here, I would like to focus on meditation.

Formal sitting meditation can be a meaningful bridge into contemplation. Learning to meditate and doing so on a daily basis holds numerous benefits for students new to this aspect of Platonism. Many of these benefits are practical ones, from stress relief to encouraging a healthier, happier approach to life.

While these benefits are certainly worthwhile, meditation in the context of the Platonic system is fundamentally preparation for entering into union with the most profound realms of Mind. It helps us to focus and to tune out all the external activity of our fast-paced, high-tech modern lifestyles. Through meditation, we learn to quiet the mind and to reduce our need for constant external stimulation. As we work towards higher states of mind, meditation also functions as an aid to all areas of our practice, thus helping us both to build understanding and also to integrate our insights into our everyday lives. As such, it is vital to learn effective meditation techniques and to incorporate them into our practice as early as possible. If you don't already meditate on a regular basis, today is an excellent day to start.

---

[1] Ennead V:iii:7

Preliminary Considerations

Here are a few basics for those new to meditation:

Posture

You may wish to sit cross-legged or in a *sayza* position,[2] but using these traditional meditation postures is not necessary. A comfortable chair will be just fine. I have scoliosis, which can be a serious condition but in my case causes me only periodic back pain. It's a condition in which the spine is curved in either a C or, as in my case, something of an S shape. Most days I feel fine, but I do get back pain when I sit for extended periods. I've found that propping myself up on pillows helps. On more painful days, I find it best to meditate lying down. When I meditate lying on my back, I plant my feet flat on the floor and allow my knees to protrude upward. This gives me enough discomfort to keep me alert while simultaneously allowing my spine to rest. Whichever posture you choose, the key is to find the proper balance between being comfortable enough so as not to be distracted by aches and pains, yet not so comfortable that you fall asleep.

A second consideration which is equally important is that you keep your spine straight. Again, you want to find a middle ground here. Your back should be long and straight with your shoulders back, but not so taut that your muscles tighten. From a seated position, I find it helpful to prepare by rotating my shoulders in a circle. While taking a long, slow inhalation, I move my shoulders forward and then up. On the exhale, I move them back and then down. Another deep inhalation and exhalation releases any remaining tension in the upper torso. If you feel particularly tense, you may wish to take a few more slow, deep breaths to relax.

A third consideration in regards to posture is where to put your hands. Following the example of Buddhism, you can place your open hands with palms facing up in your lap. The left hand rests on top of the right and the thumb tips lightly touch. Another popular posture is to rest your hands on your knees with palms facing down. You may wish to curl the tip of the index finger under the thumb, forming a circle with these two fingers. Allowing all ten fingers to hang loose is

---

[2] Sitting on the heals with the calves under the thighs.

also fine. Those lying on their backs will probably find it most comfortable to let the arms lay gently at their sides. As with other aspects of posture, this is largely a matter of personal preference. What is important here is that you find a posture that you can hold without tensing your arms or shoulders.

Time

It is important to find a block of time in which you will not be interrupted. Your meditation time need not be long; 10 minutes is a good amount of time to start with. Those who find this too challenging may choose to cut the initial time down to five minutes. Once you grow familiar with the techniques, you can extend your sitting time. The amount of time is less important than your commitment to stay in meditation the entire length of time that you have decided on. Think of your meditation schedule as a promise to yourself; if you let yourself quit early, you will create that expectation and want to quit early again. Conversely, if you close that back door, you will train yourself not to keep knocking.

Attitude

Meditating well requires more than merely putting in the time. You have to be committed to approaching your meditations with the right attitude. Beginners often battle boredom, sleepiness, and restlessness. We all exert will-power in the beginning and force ourselves to endure the hell of feeling seconds creep by one hour at a time (or so it feels). We fight the urge to stretch our legs, drift off to sleep, let ourselves get lost in an exciting daydream, or simply open our eyes and check the clock one more time.

However, all of this will change as soon as we recall one basic tenet of Platonism: our practice is not built around molding our behavior to fit some ideal.[3] Yet this is precisely what we are trying to do when we *force* ourselves to meditate. Instead, we must keep in mind that our beliefs shape our state of mind and our attitudes, which contributes to our character. All of this is reflected in our behavior.[4] Therefore, instead of martyring ourselves on the meditation cushion or beating

---

[3] This was initially discussed in Chapter 2.
[4] See Chapter 15.

ourselves up for our dismal track record, a more useful approach is to explore the unhealthy states of mind that hinder our ability to meditate with comfort and ease. This directs us to the false beliefs that underlie those states of mind.

An initial cleansing of beliefs that manifest as anxiety, restlessness, and impatience is often a pre-requisite to entering healthier states of mind. The practices I recommend for beginners were all chosen with this concept in mind. While these practices are ideal for those new to meditation, they are also ones that we all tend to return to from time to time as needed throughout our lives.

Keeping a Meditation Journal

Because meditation plays an important role in our cleansing process, it is a good idea to meditate with a notebook close by. We try to focus our thoughts during our sittings, but the mind is bound to wander from time to time. Memories may surface, or we may imagine someone we know commenting on our activities. Sometimes an entirely imaginary scenario pops into our heads, involving people we don't even know.

One thing our practice reveals to us is that there are no random thoughts; there is a reason a particular thought pops into our heads at a particular moment. We are being shown which states of mind we need to examine. This is where the notebook comes in. During a single meditation session, our thoughts may jump from a recent memory, to the voice of our inner critic, to an old pop song we haven't heard in years, to a seemingly-unrelated daydream. On the surface, these thoughts may seem unconnected. It is only when we line them up that a common theme emerges that strings them all together. These themes are clues as to which false beliefs and self-images are being stirred by our meditation efforts. For this reason, it is important for our meditation notes to be as thorough as possible; something we initially deem insignificant might be the key that unlocks a crucial insight later on.

One difficulty all meditators need to tackle is deciding when to write our notes. If our attention is keen and we can wait until after our designated session, this is ideal. There may be very little mental wandering, and so jotting notes in mid-session would break our concentration. However, there will always be days when our thoughts are running wild. We can't possibly remember every thought our minds jump to, and trying to do so would only make meditation more difficult. On these days, I find that it helps to jot down a quick note and then get back to focusing on my meditation. Doing so helps quiet the mind. Once the meditation is complete, I return to my notes and fill in more details.

There is some degree of trial and error involved in deciding when it is best to break for note-taking and when it is not. We are each different, and our ability to focus will fluctuate day-to-day. Therefore, there is not a one-size-fits-all answer. The key is to be honest with ourselves. Are you writing because you don't want to forget something, or are you using the notes as an excuse to take a break because meditating is difficult?

The beauty, but also the challenge, of our practice is that success doesn't hinge on convincing anyone else of anything. No professor is grading us, and impressing our friends brings us no closer to our actual goals. There is no point in rationalizing or putting on airs. We only get out of our practice what we put into it, so we might as well put honesty, sincerity, and integrity into it. When we do, problems such as this one have a way of working themselves out, and growth is inevitable.

Meditation Techniques

Following the Breath

One of the most common techniques recommended to beginners is to breathe long and slow through the nose, focusing the attention on the movement of the breath. For this meditation, we want to follow the breath in through the nose, feel it filling the lungs, and then follow it back up and out through the nostrils. The goal is to keep this pattern going for the entire meditation period.

There are multiple variations of this technique. One common variation is to focus on the sensation of coolness around the nose as you inhale and the sensation of heat as you exhale. Another approach is to breathe as described above, but to focus your attention on a point just below the navel. To keep mental commentary at bay, it helps to follow the natural expansion of the lower torso during inhalation and its natural contraction during exhalation.

Counting Breaths

This is a variation on the above meditation. Breaths are long and slow as described above. On your first inhalation, think "one." On your first exhalation, think "one." Your second inhalation is "two," and your second exhalation is "two." Count up to 10 and then start over. Returning to one helps keep the mind focused in the present; otherwise, our counting has the tendency to become mechanical and lack mindfulness.

This meditation, along with any other you may try, has the potential to trigger frustration when our concentration falters. Staying calm, though, and not letting ourselves get annoyed is key to doing these meditations well. If you catch yourself going beyond 10 (and everyone invariably does at some point), don't worry about it. Simply return your attention to your counting and go back to one.

Watching Numbers

Grimes recommends another variation on this fundamental meditation. This one combines the basic attention training we've already been introduced to with an introduction to *koan* practice. *Koans* are Buddhist riddles intended to ready the mind for the leap beyond linear thinking. An example of a common *koan* is, "If a tree falls in the woods and nobody is there to hear it, does it make a sound?"

In this meditation, we count the breaths as described previously. However, we also ask ourselves on each inhalation, *Where did the number come from?* As we exhale, we ask ourselves, *Where did it go?* Try to really watch the numbers as they form and as they disappear. Where are they coming from? Are they merely products of brain activity? Are they in the soul? Are they from some place beyond soul? When you are thinking "four," does three still exist? If so, where is it? Can you see where the numbers go?

This is a *koan*; logical answers will not satisfy the questions. If fact, the questions themselves make no sense from our logical, practical mindsets. And yet, there you are watching numbers form and disappear. Once you gain some familiarity with this technique, you can deepen it further by asking what is watching the numbers. When searching for the watcher, is "the watcher" different from whatever is searching for it? This line of questioning opens a whole new level of exploration.

This meditation, albeit strange at first, can be a powerful tool to pique our curiosity and draw us into the deeper realms of Mind. When pursued with sincerity, it touches the very quest we have undertaken to know ourselves. As such, it can awaken limiting self-images more forcefully than the other meditations introduced thus far. As with all meditations, it is good to keep a notebook next to you so that you can keep track of the states of mind triggered by this exercise and the sequence of thoughts to which your mind jumps.

Penetrating Questions

Once you've gotten used to the basic meditative technique of following the breath, you can combine it with the studies introduced in chapter 14, the ones that Plato called by such names as arithmetic and geometry. To do this, you simply choose your preferred posture and start following the breath. Once you've reached a relaxed state of mind, you can turn your thoughts to one of the metaphysical issues raised by Plato. Continue the same long, deep breathing as you ponder your question. While it certainly is not necessary to use formal meditative posture or breathing techniques in order to engage in Plato's studies, doing so combines our hunger for answers with the expanding states of mind that formal meditation opens us to. This meditation may also prove to be a segue into the more structured form of contemplation that we call dialectic. Dialectic will be introduced in the next chapter.

Watching Thoughts

All of the meditations we have discussed up to now have involved directing the focus of our thoughts. This helps us discipline ourselves, and it also helps us recognize which false beliefs are hindering our efforts. Now we are going to look at a different type of meditation. We still want to keep our notebook nearby for this one as well. In this practice, we take a few long, deep breaths to relax ourselves. Then we give our thoughts free reign to roam where they please. The goal here is to watch our thoughts as though they were a movie that we are outside of.

We are watching daydreams as well as any other scattered thoughts our minds jump to, but doing so without getting sucked into those stories and participating in them. Depending on the particular nature of your thoughts, this might be an enjoyable and relaxing experience. However, it may at times be extremely unpleasant.

We have a tendency to get sucked into our daydreams, to feel the pain or joy of the story. In this practice, we are learning to observe without participating. This means that we must remain aware that the thoughts that we identify with are actually separate from us; there is something that daydreams and something else that watches the daydreams.

Working Meditation

One final type of meditation I would like to introduce is a variation that can be utilized at those times when we don't have the luxury of sitting alone for a set period of time. We live in a busy age where there are floors to be vacuumed and clothes to be folded. There are reports to be written and long walks between the car and the office.

Living in what most people call "the real world" by no means requires us to put our practice on the back burner. Ideally, our spiritual lives are not separate from our professional or social lives. Granted, you would probably spook more than a few of your colleagues if you talked at the next team meeting about being a divine essence in reincarnating forms. However, this does not mean that you must file away your quest to know yourself.

A working meditation is a practice of focusing on some activity that we are carrying out. This is simplest with activities that do not require conversation. Say you are at your office and you want to go down to the coffee shop on the first floor. This could be turned into a meditation by mentally running through your mind each activity as you are doing it. It might go something like this: *Standing up, pushing in my chair, straightening my jacket, walking to the elevator, nodding to my friend across the room, waiting for the elevator....* This deceptively simple practice helps us train our minds to remain squarely in the moment. If our focus is centered on our current actions, then we cannot be lost in a daydream or fuming about the "moron" who cut us off on the highway earlier that day. Further, focusing on each action, no matter how mundane, prevents us from running on auto-pilot. We are fully present to our actions. Over time, this carries over into all of our interactions and into all areas of our lives.

Creativity

Our society tends to value outward activity over internal contemplation. To our friends and family, the hours we devote to reading, meditating and contemplating may seem like a waste of time. I've been accused more than once of spending my days doing nothing at all! And although my husband is joking when he calls meditation "taking a nap," I don't think he is entirely convinced that I am spending my time in a particularly productive way.

However, we actually are evolving through these efforts. And as our practice takes root, we will find a natural interplay between our inward endeavors and our desire to express our new resultant way of being. We will understand with greater clarity the dynamics at work both in our immediate circles and on the world stage. We will recognize the underlying currents where others are caught up in the surface story.

One fact that becomes increasingly clear as our practice matures is that our lives are lived through our minds. The more ordered our inner world is, the more effective we have the potential to be in the world at large. This does not mean that tragedy never befalls the wise person, but rather that this person will carry life's burdens with as much grace and wisdom as is possible. Conversely, the person whose inner world is disorganized will suffer regardless of having wealth, fame, physical beauty and so on. Grimes explains:

> "Most of us think that feelings determine our lives, but the reality is that we live our lives through our *minds*. We resolve our conflicts only through our minds, and we eventually understand the unity of life through our minds. This helps us resolve our feelings, and eventually leads us to a deeper understanding of the mystery of our existence. The way to this understanding is the ancient path of philosophy."[5]

When we combine meditation and energy-movement practices such as kundalini yoga and Tai Chi with our core practices such as reading and contemplating, we are likely to find ourselves going through great internal changes. We will start to see the world through our evolving outlook. This may get us reconsidering political issues (such as the government's role in our lives), social issues (such as civil

---

[5] Grimes, *The Pocket Pierre*, pp. 94~95

liberties), or our relationship with Mother Earth. We may rethink our ideas about romance or friendship or what it means to be a good neighbor. Our explorations of long-standing self-images will undoubtedly bring us to recognize nuances to our relationships with our friends and relatives that had passed unnoticed before.

Integration and creativity are healthy elements in our lives. This is the bringing together of action and thought that Plato captured in his ideal of the *philosopher-king*. On the journey towards that ideal, we should expect to go through periods in which we pull away from society and turn inward, but then other periods in which we feel the need to be in the world. Both are genuine elements of growth, and so it is important to honor that inner wisdom when it tells us that it is time to change gears. That means pulling inward even if our friends think we're acting weird or boring. That also means turning outward even if that doesn't fit our image of the life of a philosopher.

It helps to have people around us we can exchange ideas with, or we can start an online blog or connect through social media with others who share our interests. Creative expression in other forms is also important—for example, through sports or music or art. It is healthy, and indeed vital, to make time for such activities. These needn't be diversions from our spiritual practice, compartmentalized moments when we put our insights aside and slip into an old mask. It is healthier to instead treat these activities as the integration of new energy patterns and ways of thinking. Getting our thoughts out and expressing our unique perspective makes room for new growth. You don't have to have any great talent; you can keep a journal or take up a new hobby such as gardening or building model planes.

*   *   *

It is understandable why the techniques introduced in this chapter might raise a few eyebrows among those readers who are more academically focused. What does any of this have to do with living as a Platonist? We are used to thinking of Platonism as an academic study, and perhaps as a platform into theorizing. However, those who give these meditative techniques a sincere try will discover that over time, they enhance our efforts in all areas of practice. Those who are serious about moving beyond the mental challenge the Platonic canon offers will undoubtedly discover at some point that these techniques are instrumental to taking the leap into direct experience.

Chapter 19 : Dialectic: Getting Our Feet Wet

"To rob us of discourse would be to rob us of philosophy."

Plato[1]

Contemplation

If pressed to define *contemplation,* most people would probably say something along the lines of thinking deeply about some topic. Platonists sometimes use contemplation in this colloquial way as well. In its highest sense, though, contemplation can be seen as the activity of Mind at all levels of the unfolding of reality.[2] Contemplation is described metaphysically as *ousia,* the intellect of each realm reverting to its own summit or essential nature [hyparxis]. Intellect thus knows itself and its own causes because it contains within itself the reason-principles of those causes.[3] The result of this reversion is for the contemplator to quietly abide in itself and simultaneously, to create its subsequent. Plotinus explains this using the soul as an example:

> "The intellectual soul of the world contemplates indeed a sublime spectacle, and that which she thus contemplates, because it rises higher than soul, generates that which is posterior to itself, and thus contemplation begets contemplation..."[4]

Although there is certainly a great deal that can be explored in terms of how contemplation functions at each realm of reality, in this chapter I want to get away from metaphysics and focus instead on the role of contemplation in our philosophical practices. In this context, I will define contemplation as one-pointed absorption into the object of the soul's focus. The most common Greek words for *contemplation* are *theoria* and *theaomai,* and their cognates.[5] These words mean *to look or gaze at,* and can also be used in the more honorific sense of *to behold.* Our goal when we contemplate, the same as we saw at the opening of this chapter in regards to Nature or Intellect or any other realm, is *ousia.* What this means is that rather than our contemplations focusing us on some topic outside of ourselves, we are turning inward to know the psychical causes we contain.

---

[1] *Sophist,* 260a, trans. F. M. Cornford
[2] For more on this, see Plotinus, Ennead III:viii
[3] This notion will be explored in greater detail in Chapter 20
[4] Ennead III:viii:5
[5] I thank Tim Addey for his help with the Greek in this section.

Theasthai, a cognate of *theaomai,* means *to behold* and is the root for the English word *theater.* The audience in a theater is beholding the activity on the stage as one whole, with the ideal being that they are absorbed into the story and become part of that whole. We as an audience become part of the whole not through the activity of watching the drama that is outside of ourselves, but by turning inward and relating our own thoughts and emotions to what is playing out before us. It is that shared human experience that makes theater a kind of contemplation.

In the case of theater, of course, the benefit of the contemplation depends on the show we are watching. We may gain insights that further our aspirations to understand ourselves and the reality we are a part of. We may also, however, be connecting on the level of false beliefs with the various fears and pleasures they give rise to, thus hindering rational thought as we are swept up by the drama and emotions on stage. In the contemplations we engage in through Platonism, in contrast, it is through rational thought that we reach a contemplative state.

Platonism is fundamentally a contemplative practice. What this means is that our goal is not merely to think about certain abstract concepts, but to actually become one with the Reality that the terminology names. Our concentration is on the Realities beyond the names. We might, for example, contemplate what Justice is, or what Bound is, or even what Contemplation is. Whatever question we are tackling, our aim is complete absorption, and so contemplation at its highest maturation culminates in peak experiences.

> "[B]y how much the more it [the soul] becomes reason [*logos*] by so much the more silent…and contemplation constituted in a habit of this kind, intrinsically reposes, from a perfect assurance of possessing. And by how much the more certain the assurance, by so much quieter the contemplation; which indeed rather reduces the soul into one, and on this account that which knows, as far as it knows, (for we are now treating the subject seriously) passes into one with the thing known…"[6]

We are doing far more than merely ruminating on a given topic when we contemplate. We are unifying and strengthening the soul's energy. Dialectic provides the structure of choice for our contemplations, so let's turn our attention now to dialectic.

---

[6] Ennead III:viii:6, parentheses included but brackets added

Why We Need Dialectic

Energy-focused techniques such as yoga and meditating on the breath are vital ingredients to the success of our contemplations. In fact, they benefit all areas of our practice. However, it is our contemplations themselves that truly awaken our understanding. Our efforts to build and purify energy are meant to enhance and support our contemplations—they don't replace them. And of course contemplation also functions to build and purify energy in its own right. Our path, ultimately, is to use the mind to know Reality itself. We are not building energy with the hopes that wisdom will somehow come to us. Rather, this is an active path of seeking answers within ourselves, discovering the light that is our essence.

With the recent explosion of spiritual books and online courses, it is not hard to find spiritual teachers who talk about our essence being spiritual energy. However, few go into the details of the metaphysics behind their teachings. For many people, this is enough. They just want to learn the conclusions those teachers have reached and then move on to application. Those of us who hunger for understanding, though, are left unsatisfied by this approach.

One value of studying metaphysics is that we gain a degree of understanding of these conclusions and, once our practice blossoms, we also gain the wisdom to navigate the nuances of which teachings reflect truth and beauty, and which are faulty. Platonism recognizes that the process of gaining the understanding of why certain conclusions must be true is in itself an exercise that deepens our connection to the Intelligible. As we advance, we get a clearer sense of the kinship between ourselves as spiritual beings and ourselves as social beings operating on the physical plane. This means that we are increasingly able to function in the world with the understanding of what we truly are and how this physical realm fits into all that *is*.

Plato recognized that in order to maximize the benefits of our contemplations, we need a systematic method by which to advance. The state of mind that we seek demands that we look under every rock and that we leave no assumptions unquestioned. The studies that Plato calls by such names as arithmetic and geometry[7] are the preparation for the crowning practice of the Platonic system: dialectic.

---

[7] There are five studies in total, discussed in *Republic* from 521d, and they were introduced in chapter 14.

These earlier studies can bring you to a higher degree of *understanding*, but *knowing* requires challenging our assumptions dialectically.[8] Dialectic will be discussed further in Chapter 25, as it is mainly a technique for the later stages of practice. However, we can familiarize ourselves with it by using it as a logical reasoning tool early on. Dialectic is a precise method of investigation. Plato writes that "no other method can attempt to comprehend, in any orderly way, what each particular being is."[9]

In the early years of our practice we still hold many assumptions about Reality that color our understanding of our readings and discussions. Of course, some of us also bring to our practice one or more powerful experiences which we have not yet fully come to understand. Such an experience is often what draws a person to the study of metaphysics in the first place. In these situations as well, we must be careful not to jump to conclusions. On-line bookstores offer book after book written by mystics who purport to know what it means to have experiences such as out-of-body and near-death. These authors tell us what must be true about the nature of Reality in light of the existence of these kinds of experiences.

The problem is that, while there is a great deal of overlap in their conclusions, there are discrepancies in their conclusions as well. Don't be afraid to be skeptical; questioning conclusions and explanations of experiences (your own as well as other people's accounts) is not the same as denying the experiences ever happened. We simply need to acknowledge that we still hold assumptions, even after a powerful experience, and that we carry these assumptions into our analyses.

As we saw in the section on interpretation, our initial efforts to read about and discuss metaphysics are hindered by assumptions and pre-conceived notions, many of which we don't even realize we are holding. They can easily be overlooked because they seem fundamental, and so we think they are "obviously true." The concepts that we study and contemplate, although they point us toward Reality, are not the same as Reality itself. The power of dialectic is that it forces us to apply rigid precision to our investigations. This slices away our layers of assumptions, gradually taking us beyond words and revealing truth.

---

[8] See *Republic,* 531d~e and 533b~c
[9] *Ibid.,* 533b

Of course, Platonists aren't the only students of spirituality who use logic. Where we do stand out, though, is in our insistence that our reasoning is bringing us to something real in itself. Truth is not just a concept to us, and we do not treat thoughts as mere abstractions. Conventional mindsets treat the physical world as what is real and thought, in all of its forms, as something less than real. However, to a Platonist, the Intelligible absolute Realities are the only true objects of reality, and that reality is weakened with each subsequent unfolding of later realms. Therefore, the ultimate goal of dialectic is to lead us back from concepts such as justice to the absolute Realities, such as Justice itself.

Another area where Plato's methods stand out is in the focus on the assumptions of the argument, rather than on the conclusions. Plato recognized that our reasoning is only as good as the assumptions it is built on. The atheist, the fundamentalist, and the mystic all reason—they reach different conclusions, in large part, because their starting points differ.

The fundamentalist who insists that we must accept the historical Jesus of Nazareth as our savior reaches different conclusions than the mystic who relates to Jesus as symbolical, for example, of the immanent aspect of the Divine as it flows providentially through the realms of being. Accepting this divine providential goodness into our hearts leads our reasoning to a different notion of what salvation is than that reached by the reasoning of the Christian fundamentalist.

The atheist, of course, rejects the whole debate and declares that any notion of salvation is a pipe dream. We should stop wasting our time on idle fantasy and instead focus on finding happiness here on earth. All of these arguments can—and have—been cogently put forward by supporters both intelligent and well-read. Debates only allow us to put our currently held beliefs into words; they do not cut through the confusion or get us beyond opinions.

The only way to wade through the myriad of options is to treat our conclusions as hypotheses. We can then explore what conditions would have to exist in order for a particular conclusion to be true. The next step is to look for the assumptions in *that* reasoning and keep working backwards. In this way, we inch our way beyond belief into a reasoned understanding. Eventually, of course, we aim to open ourselves to direct knowing of things in themselves, and then to an understanding of that knowledge.

How to Use Dialectic

Plato's system of dialectic can seem daunting at first. We are going to start out with a simplified version to familiarize ourselves with this way of approaching our contemplations of metaphysics. Later, in Chapter 25, we will dive more deeply into this important aspect of Plato's teachings.

Plato describes his basic approach in the *Phaedrus:*

> "Is it not, therefore, necessary to think respecting the nature of everything, in the first place, whether that is simple or multiform about which we are desirous, both that we ourselves should be artists, and that we should be able to render others so? And, in the next place, if it is simple, ought we not to investigate its power, with respect to producing anything naturally, or being naturally passive? And if it possesses many species, having numbered these, ought we not to speculate in each, as in one, its natural power of becoming active and passive?"[10]

There is a lot in this quote, and we will unpack it as we go on. At the heart of it all, though, Plato is looking at the nature of some object of inquiry, and how that object functions—how it acts and how it is acted upon. Thinking in this precise way tends to feel awkward when we first try it. I remember the first time my son discovered a calculator. He was maybe four or five years old. He looked the calculator over carefully and ran his fingers over the keys. Then he hit a few buttons to see what would happen, and he laughed with glee to see numbers flash across the screen. He had many questions: What is this? What does it do?

Questions of what it is and how it functions were jumbled together. This feels very natural to most of us. His questions were probably the same sorts of questions most of us would ask when discovering some new gadget. We would never think to ask, for example, what this thing is that calculates numbers. Defining what a thing is by stating its function is fine with objects such as calculators and thermometers; it becomes a problem, though, when we engage in the language of metaphysics and need to be more precise.

---

[10] 270d

In our dialectical searches, our aim is to hone our questioning to this higher level of precision as we explore what must follow if some metaphysical object of inquiry exists. For example, we might choose to focus on providence, or soul, or *ousia*. If our object of inquiry is providence, we would ask ourselves, "What must follow if providence exists?" If our object of inquiry is *ousia,* we ask ourselves, "What must follow if *ousia* exists?" Plato uses the example of *soul* in the *Phaedrus,* and offers us this advice:

> "(We) ought first, with all possible accuracy, to describe, and cause the soul to perceive whether she is naturally one and similar, or multiform according to the form of body: for this is what we call evincing its nature."[11]

Plato, then, is starting by naming and defining his object of inquiry. Don't worry if you are not able to define it precisely. When we are new to the study of metaphysics, there probably aren't many statements we would feel confident making—and that's no problem. Dialectical explorations are exercises we return to again and again.

It is a lofty undertaking to tackle the issue of whether our souls are truly a manyness of separate entities, or if soul is actually one. This is the kind of question most of us have turned to philosophy with the hope of answering. Starting with this question, then, is something akin to putting the cart before the horse. I would recommend taking a step back from this and asking: "If soul is simple, what follows?" or "If soul is multiform, what follows?" In these cases, the first task would be to define what soul would have to be in order for our particular hypothesis to be true.

This format (If x is y, what follows?) is a more common approach early in dialectic exercises, as there is more to work with than the bare-bone exploration of things-in-themselves. As we will see in Chapter 25, there are stages to our dialectical searches, and exploring things-in-themselves is a later stage. Early on, we are still developing our working vocabulary of metaphysical terms. The "If x is y" format, then, is a way of tackling our questions about those terms.

Once we've described what our object of inquiry would have to be in order for the hypothesis to hold, we can go on to Plato's second step:

---

[11] 271a

"But, in the second place, he ought to show what it is naturally capable of either acting or suffering."[12]

Here, Plato is asking us to consider how our object of inquiry functions. If soul is simple, for example, how does it act upon body? And how can body or anything else act upon it? This will undoubtedly raise a number of questions, and this is good—so long as you hold onto the confusion and the sense of wonder. We will carry those questions with us as we read, and so this will hone our studies and considerations. When this happens, dialectic becomes meaningful. Before this, it can feel academic and stiff. With the wrong attitude, dialectic is little more than a cerebral exercise, like doing homework for a class you have no interest in.

The search becomes meaningful when it is our own ruminations that fuel the responses. We don't need to come up with the "perfect answer" for each question, only the best answers we are currently able to provide. The intention here is to uncover our assumptions and expectations. This form of questioning is a method of exploring our confusion. Dialectic is not a one-time exercise; we must come back and polish it again and again like a fine gem.

In fact, some of dialectic's greatest benefits come not from the answers themselves, but from the uncertainty we experience while trying to generate answers. If you attempt to generate your own list of answers (and I encourage you to do so!), you will likely find that there is at least one statement that you are tempted to include but are not sure is correct. That is how dialectic highlights our confusion.

As we move along in this way, we will find that deeply-held false beliefs get stirred in the process. When our systematic questioning reveals these hidden beliefs, many of them will disturb us. We need to be prepared for this so that we can recognize what is happening and address the issue appropriately. In this way, we can keep our studies from getting sidetracked.

Pitfalls and Stumbling Blocks

As you are reading this, you can probably imagine some of the pitfalls that lie in wait for the stumbling practitioner. Digging to the very root of our belief systems is even more difficult than it sounds,

---

[12] 271a

and it sounds very hard! It is easy to fall into rationalizations which we might think are dialectic, but actually have the negative effect of distorting our practice and derailing our growth. This occurs when we recognize some false beliefs we were taught in childhood about the just, the good, and the beautiful but do not yet see the correct alternative.

Images of what is just, beautiful, and good have been thrust on us since we were very young. They molded us at a time when we were too innocent to realize what was happening. Plato tells us: "We have certain dogmas from our childhood concerning things just and beautiful, in which we have been nourished as by parents, obeying and honouring them."[13] When we, as adults, recognize falsehood in these images, it is common—and indeed, natural—to feel angry and to rebel.

Imagine meeting someone who is in such a state, and this person challenges you to define what justice is, or goodness or beauty.[14] If the person argues down everything you had been taught but hadn't yet questioned, you might be left to conclude that this angry person might have an accurate view of Reality after all. We are bombarded with chop-logic from all sides. We've all heard it before: *There is no justice in the world. It's a dog-eat-dog world; you've got to look out for Number One. It's fine to have ideals, but you've got to be practical.*

False assumptions fuel not only the cynical conclusions such as in the above examples, but also the rose-colored ones, such as: *It's a sign! God wants me to have this new car!* Following whims, however, is not the same as honoring intuition. Another one I hear often is, *Whatever is meant to be will be.* This implies that our lives are fated and so we needn't take any action to alter life's current trajectory. Of course, inaction is also a choice, and making that choice affects our future just as surely as choosing to change would.

You are already perfect just the way you are is one of my favorites. As a way to build a person's self-esteem and ability to forgive themselves for past mistakes, this teaching can be helpful. The problem is that it transfers the goodness of our divine essence to our manifestations in human form. As humans, we are a complex blend of not only the divine beauty that is our essence, but also ignorance that distracts us from the reality of our true nature. Think about it: if the Buddha,

---

[13] *Republic,* 538c
[14] Cf. *Ibid.,* 538a~539a

Socrates, Jesus, or any other teacher believed that we as people were already perfect just the way we currently were, then what would be the point of their teachings? What benefit could we hope to gain from a spiritual practice if we were already perfect without one? And what does it even mean to become perfect? We will find that whatever we think perfection to be is actually only an image.[15]

Of course, we *are* perfect in the sense that we are exactly what all the forces in our lives up to this moment have shaped us to be (including, perhaps, the choice to forego self-reflection because we think we are already perfect). In that sense, we are exactly where we are meant to be. However, this statement is very different from concluding that where we are is our final destination or that recognizing that our souls are beautiful is enough to declare that the goal of knowing ourselves has been reached.

Rationalizations are powerful, and so without better reasoning of our own, it is easy to get sucked into them. These faulty arguments are built on various false assumptions about the nature of Reality, including the assumption that we cannot know anything about it.

At this stage in our practice we accept that there is much we are unsure of about the nature of Reality. Therefore, faulty rationalizations can be built around virtually any conclusion. This allows for a lot of cleverness and creativity. Here is a short sampling of some of the arguments I've heard over the years. You undoubtedly can add to this list:

Salt and pepper shakers

This theory suggests that creation is something analogous to a person sprinkling salt and pepper from shakers. In this analogy, God is like the person and the physical realm is like the salt and pepper sprinkling down. God is responsible for the unfolding of the universe, but He[16] stays out of earthly affairs. That is, providence is not functioning in the world.

---

[15] I address this issue in Chapter 27.

[16] This term is colloquial. Since what we mean by God in this example is comparable to the mythological image of Zeus who is the immediate cause of the physical realm, God is Intellect and encompasses the whole of existence. Therefore, even though both the Judeo-Christian religions and Greek mythology use a male image for this function of God, the debate over male vs. female pronouns is moot; God is actually beyond all physical

God has pets

We are only here for God's amusement. He picks someone up now and then the way a person might enjoy holding a pet guinea pig, but then He puts that someone back down. Wars and famines are all just forms of entertainment for this god, a cruel form of fun perhaps no different than cock fights or cutting a worm in half to watch the two parts both wiggle away.

God is like a cattle rancher

Cattle ranchers provide their cows with fresh grass to graze under the warm sun. They provide shelter and safety—until the day the cows are led to the slaughterhouse. God, in an analogous way, only cares for us because it serves His ulterior motives.

The best defense against clever chop-logic is to learn to live with uncertainty. We tend to accept faulty logic because we don't have a better answer. We think, "I don't have a logical answer, but this person does. If I can't come up with anything better, then this reasoning must be right." This is a mistake. A false argument can be logical even though it is built on false assumptions. The physicist and Platonic philosopher Dr. John H Spencer reminds us: "We all need to slow down and take a long, hard look at our own assumptions....If we want to discover truth, we have to be prepared to question our own assumptions and abandon them when we realize that they are false."[17]

Logic only tells us, for example, that "If A is true, then B must follow." It never tells us what is true and what is false. Logic alone is not enough to know truth. If challenged by such an argument, the best response just might be, "I don't know, but I'll get back to you after I've uncovered the false assumptions that I've been carrying around since childhood!"

Now it is time to get to work. Nothing zaps the magic out of chop-logic quite like dialectic. In each of the examples above, *God* is a personification of the nature of Reality. We can ask ourselves what nature of Reality is being painted in any given scenario. Then, our

---

dichotomies. *It* has a connotation in English of being less in worth or dignity, and so is also problematic. I've therefore chosen to follow convention for lack of a better alternative.

[17] Spencer, *The Eternal Law*, p. 10.

goal would be to see what follows from assuming that nature to be true.

This takes us back to our basic "If x is y" format. In other words, If God is selfish, what follows? If the nature of Reality is arbitrary, what follows?

Just as we saw with our example of *soul,* a dialectical treatment would break our inquiry down by first forcing us to consider what would have to be true about the nature of Reality in order for our chosen hypothesis to be true. Then we would consider how that nature functions, both how it acts and how it is acted upon.

The deeper our understanding, the easier it will be to see the flaws. Early on, we will be tempted to acknowledge that we don't know the nature of Reality, so we can't dismiss many of these scenarios. That is valid, but we must keep in mind that if we lack the knowledge to declare them wrong, then we also lack the knowledge to declare them right. It is at this point that we need to find the courage to hold onto our questions.

What we are ultimately reaching for is more than simply our opinion about which scenario *sounds* best. We have to resist being draw into charismatic arguments that are logical and clever but are built on a foundation that is metaphysically unsound. Finding answers will require more than one discussion; after all, the quest to know the nature of Reality is the very spiritual journey we have embarked on.[18] This is the question we will spend our lives examining and refining.

In Plato's dialogue the *Meno,* the title character suggests that the concerns of philosophers are nonsense since we can never know the essence of anything beyond what we already do. Socrates' reply is a classic one:

> "I would not contend very strenuously for the truth of my argument in other respects; but that in thinking it our duty to seek after the knowledge of things we are at present ignorant of, we should become better men, more manly, and less idle, than if we suppose it not possible for us to find out, nor our duty to inquire into, what we know not; this I would, if I was able, strongly, both by word and deed, maintain."[19]

---

[18] The quest to *know thyself* is ultimately the same journey, for the essence of the individual will ultimately be discovered to be no different from essence itself.

[19] 86b~c

Chapter 20: Extended Contemplations

"[I]t is better for my lyre to be unharmonized and dissonant, and the choir of which I might be the leader...than that I, being one, should be dissonant and contradict myself."

Plato[1]

All of our reading ultimately is an extended contemplation of Reality itself and the condition for its existence—namely, the One or the Good. What I've presented thus far in terms of metaphysics is an overview of the basic Platonic vision of Reality. However, passively reading a book is not sufficient to make this vision our own. To reach the transformational level, we must each see the truth of it for ourselves. That means going deeply into the ideas and wrestling with any points of contention we currently hold. Our goal while reading accounts of metaphysics is to internalize, not merely memorize. Therefore, stopping to contemplate is an important aspect of our reading. Of course, early on we are contemplating in the colloquial sense of the word; becoming one with the object of our attention, and so truly contemplating in the highest sense of that word, is the goal we are aiming for. Chapter 14 introduced a number of contemplations. After you've worked with them for a while and gained some familiarity with metaphysics, you will be ready to take those contemplations to the next level.

To demonstrate this, I'd like to return to the notion of reality unfolding through realms. Each realm can be understood triadically as Being, Life, and Intellect. The Intelligible realm, for example, which when experienced is recognized to be Reality itself, can be understood using this triadic relationship of Being, Life, and Intellect. These three aspects are inseparable. Once you grasp this conceptually, perhaps you feel this is enough and you are ready to move on.

However, this is a complex issue that requires jumping beyond language and linear thinking. It is important to take frequent breaks from the reading to think about what you've just read. You need to *know* it as a thing-in-itself, as an absolute Reality. During times of contemplation, you may wish to sit in a traditional meditation pose

---

[1] Socrates in the *Gorgias,* 482c

(cross-legged or *sayza* style). However, a good contemplation can be just as effective while walking, sitting in a chair, or lying down.

What we are aiming to do is to venture beyond words and to know this triad that is, in turn, made up of three triads, as illustrated in the diagram below.

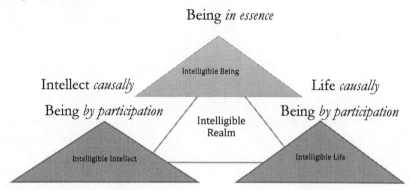

In metaphysics, terms are said to participate in their causes and to cause their subsequents. For example, Life participates Being because it is subsequent. In turn, it is the cause of Intellect. Because the three terms of the triad exist together in each triad, we can say that the terms exist "causally" in their causes and exist "by participation" in their subsequents.

Proclus captures this in proposition 103 of his *Elements of Theology*. We can look at this dynamic in detail here and use it as a launch pad into an extended meditation. The entire proposition is included in its entirety at the end of this section. Turning back to the diagram above, we see that in the highest expression of this triad, Being is the unified summit that holds Life and Intellect causally, and so tightly that there are no divisions or separations between them. In the second expression of this triad, Being is in Life by participation and Life contains Intellect causally. These three terms—Being, Life, and Intellect—are still undivided at this stage, but the whole is proceeding away from unity; think of a stretched rubber band. Finally, in the third expression of this triad, both Being and Life are in Intellect by participation. The three terms have now completed their procession into differentiation.

Can you grasp it? It's a real challenge to conceive that which is beyond physical form. It may take a few tries, but with patience and sincere determination, something will come of your efforts. Your image may be symbolized with shapes or a diagram. This is fine initially, but we are aiming to go beyond that to a non-visual understanding. Once you get hold of some conceptual understanding, indistinct though it may be, you are ready for the next step.

Now try to meld the three together, for the separation into a triad is only a verbal convenience. Whatever your understanding of Intellect, merge it with your understanding of Life. Let this conglomeration melt into your understanding of unified Being. Remember, these three moments exist outside of time. They are eternal, and their activity never pauses.

However vague your apprehension might be, it is helpful to sit with it for a few minutes. It may be hard to hold at first, but with practice this can be done. Holding it in silence has a way of triggering insights and questions that would not likely spring up otherwise. If you sincerely attempt this exercise, you will come to see that contemplation allows for an understanding that moves us beyond language. Even if your initial attempt lasted only a few seconds, it would be hard to describe what you discerned in that contemplation, wouldn't it? Whatever it was, it was so much richer than words on a page.

We initially learn in pieces, and it is through contemplation that we put the pieces together. Understanding requires grasping both the pieces and the unification of them, and understanding can be deepened further by exploring the implications that follow from the very different view of Reality that emerges from these efforts. Don't worry about putting the pieces together correctly the first time. It is common to spend years modifying and polishing our comprehensions, removing errors and adding what didn't make sense before, all in preparation for that moment when we jump beyond concepts to true knowing.

Let's continue building this model, learning it in pieces. Depending on the particular aspect of metaphysics we are exploring, we may discuss the triad as Being—Life—Intellect, or we may talk of abiding—proceeding—reverting. Another way of talking about this triad is unified—differentiating—differentiated. These are not three different triads. We are using these triads to highlight different qualities or functions of the same realm of Reality.

- **Being abides** in itself, holding Life and Intellect causally in its bonds, and so it is **unified**.

- **Life** is motion and **proceeds** from itself. Because it is always in the process of proceeding, its differentiation is never complete. It is always **differentiating**.

- **Intellect** is already **differentiated** and so, through **reversion**, it can see its various parts and know itself as a differentiated whole.

Reversion itself, however, is not a process of one part turning to look at another part; the whole turns and looks at the whole. It is a dynamic Being that turns intellectually on itself for ever greater depths of insight into itself. While the summit of each triad is generally denoted by the Greek word *ousia*, *ousia* or essence is also this dynamic quality of the triad as a whole.

Being - abides - unified

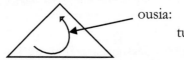

ousia: the dynamics of Being turning intellectually on itself

Intellect - reverts -
differentiated

Life - proceeds -
differentiating

The moments of the triad are not truly separate; it is only for our convenience that we talk about them in this way. Reasoning is the act of understanding the whole by way of its parts. Intellect, on the other hand, sees the whole simply as a whole. The intention of extended meditations such as the one in this chapter is to reason our way to a higher mode of cognition. The dynamic circular activity of Intellect, for example, is not separate from the stillness of Being abiding in itself. "Thought and being are the same," as Parmenides tells us.[2] These triads, strictly speaking, do not exist as triads *per se*. Yet, in another sense, they are absolutely true.

This is a contemplation. Following the words and grasping the concepts requires in itself a great effort, but this is not enough to develop the kind of understanding that transforms us. We need that moment of intuition, that lightning bolt that slashes through our confusion and compels us to exclaim, "Ah! Now I get it!"

---

[2] Wheelwright (ed.), *The Presocratics*, p. 98.

Logic alone will not allow us to see, for example, *in what way* triads are not true or *in what way* they are true. More importantly, logic alone will not convey to us the meaningfulness of this study. Our educated, practical side will ask, *Who cares? What does this have to do with me?* When you look around you, do you notice any triads of Being—Life— Intellect floating about?

But wait. You can see yourself, can't you (a few body parts at least)? Are you an intellectual being that has vitality? *Something* about you is, right? Whatever that *something* is that thinks and plans, it has the dynamic ability to revert intellectually on itself for deeper insights into its own essence. This *something*—whether you call it divine essence or soul or by some other name—has various affections (desire, pride, etc.) yet is a whole. And the moment of insight requires unified focus; it does not come when you are torn between two or more thoughts. The whole turns and looks at the whole, and the result is that it understands itself at an ever greater depth. Why, this would mean that the insightful *a-ha* moment is in itself an example of *ousia*, an experience of Reality to some degree.

We can see the triad of Being—Life—Intellect by looking at ourselves as souls. As Being, our essence has a vitality and intellect that are part of its essence. As Life, we can say the soul exists and intellects vitally. As Intellect, the soul exists and moves intellectually. It therefore has this triadic quality that we had contemplated in relation to Reality. Does it abide in itself? Yes, and the more proficient we get at silent meditation,[3] the more aware we become of this great stillness. Our essence proceeds, too. When we turn inward, we become aware of movement. Without procession, there could be no reversion. There has to be a moving away before there can be a return. And indeed, we are all very good at turning our attention outward. It's the turning inward that takes practice. In time, though, we grow more skillful at reversion.

We've all had *a-ha* moments on a lesser scale. For example, you have to write an essay but you have no idea how to begin. You ponder how to organize your thoughts. Suddenly the answer hits you. A-ha! This, too, is a form of reversion. You may recall from the discussion of reversion that there are two results of reversion. That discussion focused on divine Intellect. One result is the deeper insight into its essence; the other is the unfolding of the subsequent realm of reality. An analogous relationship occurs at the level of soul. The

---

[3] This will be introduced in Chapter 29.

example of writing an essay is an intuitive moment, a turning inward that results in an outward creation. Yet this intuitive moment also brings an inward change relative to the depth of the insight. Ideally, that writing assignment is educational in nature, not just busywork.

The type of reversion that we are all aiming for in our practice is a more profound degree of reversion. We are in search of the nature of our essence. That level of insight manifests inwardly as wisdom and manifests outwardly in our ability to function in the world with spiritual maturity and a healthy state of mind.

If these triads are descriptions of Reality, and if our essence is no different than Reality, then triads absolutely do have something to do with us. These are not dry, abstract concepts that are far removed from our lives. It takes time, though, to internalize these studies and recognize ourselves in them. The study of metaphysics is about far more than gathering new pieces of information to add to our collection of data. This study, when properly undertaken, is transformational.

Proclus, *Elements of Theology*, Proposition 103[4]

All things are in all, but appropriately in each.

For in being there is life and intellect; and in life, being and intellection; and in intellect being and life. But in intellect indeed, all things subsist intellectually, in life vitally, and in being, all things are truly beings. For since everything subsists either according to cause, or according to hyparxis, or according to participation; and in the first, the rest are according to cause; in the second, the first is according to participation, but the third, according to cause; and in the third, the natures prior to it are according to participation;—this being the case, life and intellect have a prior or causal subsistence in being. Since however, each thing is characterized according to hyparxis, and neither according to cause (for cause pertains to other things, *i.e.* to effects) nor according to participation (for a thing derives that elsewhere of which it participates,)—hence in being there is truly life and intellection, essential life and essential intellect. And in life, there is being indeed according to participation, but intellection according to cause. Each of these however, subsist there vitally. For the hyparxis is according to life. And in intellect, life and essence subsist according to participation, and each of these subsists there intellectually. For knowledge is the essence and the life of intellect.

---

[4] Translation by Thomas Taylor

Knowing

Introduction

The top of the steep ascent to the mouth of Plato's proverbial cave is the pinnacle of understanding. Once here, we are at the doorway into knowing. It is common to pass through this doorway without any mind-blowing experience to mark its occurrence. It will most likely reveal itself in more subtle ways, such as through dreams or through a heightened connection with intuition.

In fact, if you have been waiting for a bolt of lightning to race up your spine to mark your wisdom with internal fireworks, the insight that you have crossed that abyss may be hard to accept at first. You don't *feel* any different—but gradually it sinks in. Your life has been stable and happy for so long that a bit of reflection is required in order to recall the emotional rollercoaster that used to mark your sense of normal. When did it all come together?

You can't put your finger on the precise moment, but students new to the practice have been turning to you with their questions in increasing numbers. You amaze even yourself at your ability to recognize the root of their confusion and to advise them appropriately. Your past studies have come to life. You see providence, justice, and beauty at play in the world around you. Yes, something has definitely changed. Realizing this, you feel elated—and you have every right to. You've worked hard. Finally, you've arrived!

Or have you? Here is where the danger lies. You've passed through the doorway into knowing. Technically, that makes you a knower. For some, when they reach this juncture, they want to jump into the role of teacher and share their insights with the world. Certainly, at this point, they have gained some insights that could benefit others.

However, knowing—much like understanding—admits of degrees. Yes, from the perspective of your earlier journey you have evolved and grown, but the end of one leg of the journey marks the start of another. It is not uncommon for students who excelled at the practices of understanding to hit a plateau at this point and go no further. They cross the chasm that separates understanding and knowing, but they remain in the mouth of Plato's proverbial cave and never fully enter the upper world.

Plato uses the Greek word *dianoia* to indicate the type of understanding that has been gained at this pivotal stage in our journey. The understanding of direct experience is a different kind of understanding from that of concepts. Once we climb to the upper world of Plato's cave allegory, we are faced with the daunting task of surveying all that can be known. It is here that our practice really begins. It is in this sense that Plato calls everything prior to this "the introduction."[1] The methods presented in the *Understanding* section are all methods to educate the soul and purify ourselves of false beliefs in preparation for this later stage of practice.

In our metaphysics, the objects of knowledge in Plato's upper world are called Intelligibles or what I've been referring to as absolute Realities. We can only explore this realm by participating in the realm of Intellect. Teaching our souls the habit of turning our focus upward is therefore a central component of our practice. All of the aspects of our studies in the first section were to that end.

Once we make that connection with Intellect, our practice takes a turn. Yet we will quickly discover that despite the many changes that have come to our lives and our practice, one thing remains the same: we still must see through what is false in order to accept what is true. This leg of our journey continues the process of clearing away whatever hinders our vision of that which is knowable.

The practices in the first section of this book are ones we will continue to use throughout our lives. However, with our initial cleansing behind us we are ready to embark on our true journey. The remaining chapters will focus on how to do two things: (1) gain a firmer foothold in the realm of Intellect, and (2) survey the Intelligibles. When this leg of our practice ripens, we more fully identify with the Intelligible realm rather than only looking into it as an object. Even this realization is not the culmination of our journey. Dialectic will aid us in our understanding of the nature of Reality and our contemplations of *its* cause.

Gaining *dianoetic* understanding, then, is not the end of the road, the ripening of the fruit. Many questions still remain. And the long sought after peak experience of knowing "the sun himself"[2] in the upper world still lingers out of reach. If this description fits you, then take heart. Congratulations are in order; you've worked hard to get this far. Looking back at who you were at the start of this journey, you've earned the right to feel a sense of accomplishment. You've entered a doorway, but a long and winding road is stretched before you. You'll have to put forward greater courage and effort from this point forward. Here is where the real practice begins. You've blossomed into a flower; now it is time to bear fruit.

---

[1] *Republic*, 531e
[2] *Ibid.*, 516a

Chapter 21: What is Wisdom?

"[W]hen this true lover of learning approaches, and is mingled with it, having generated intellect and truth, he will then have true knowledge, and truly live and be nourished…"

Plato[1]

Seeing the Sun Himself

Here we are some two-thirds of the way through a book about a wisdom tradition, and we've yet to discuss what the wise state of mind actually is. We commonly call any person *wise* who gives helpful advice, but for Platonists this word has a more precise meaning, tied to the more precise meaning of *knowledge* as described in the divided line in Book 6 of the *Republic*.

There are many misconceptions about wisdom, and I feel I need to walk a tightrope of sorts in this chapter in order to address as many of these errors as is reasonably possible. On the one hand, wisdom needs to be lifted up from its colloquial uses that confer the title of *wise* onto anyone who gives advice about financial matters, love matters and so on. Yet we also need to dispel the superhuman myths attached to notions of enlightenment, realization, awakening, and similar terminology.

So what is wisdom? Does this state of mind require what mystics describe as *enlightenment experiences?* And what does it mean to say that wisdom is a state of mind? What sort of state of mind is it? Is it all-or-nothing, or does it have gradations? Is there an end point, a point of completion?

This is one of those issues on which dissension seeps in among Platonists. We all agree that descriptions of and references to mystical experiences can be found in the writings of Plotinus and various other Platonists who followed him. Disagreements hinge over the question of whether such experiences can be found in Plato's works, as well. On one side of the issue are those who argue that discursive reason is the height of human wisdom for Plato. Other Platonists, however, whether they are personally open to mysticism or not, recognize Plato

---

[1] *Republic*, 490b

guiding us to insights that reach far beyond the conclusions of discursive thinking.

Plato tied philosophy to the religious mystery schools that were flourishing throughout the Greek world during his lifetime. Various references can be found scattered throughout his dialogues. The clearest example is arguably in the *Phaedo,* where Socrates tells his friends:

> "And those who instituted the mysteries for us appear to have been by no means contemptible persons, but to have really signified formerly, in an obscure manner, that whoever descended into Hades uninitiated, and without being a partaker of the mysteries, should be plunged into mire; but that whoever arrived there, purified and initiated, should dwell with the gods. For, as it is said by those who write about the mysteries, *The thyrsus-bearers numerous are seen, But few the Bacchuses have always been.*"[2]

The thyrsus-bearers are a reference to the Titans, who according to mythology tempted their half-brother Dionysius down to the material world in part by replacing his scepter with a thyrsus. Thyrsus-bearers, then, are those who are not who they appear to be. As the story has it, Hera was jealous that Zeus had impregnated yet another mortal woman. She despised their son, Dionysius, and so devised a plan to have her children, the Titans, kill him. Once they lured Dionysius away from his father and captured him, they brutally ripped his body apart. However, Athena found his heart still intact, and used it to bring him back to life. He was reborn a full god and took his place on Mount Olympus. The Bacchuses in Socrates' quote above refers to those devout mystics who were followers of the god Dionysius. Socrates continues this statement by counting himself among these mystics:

> "These few are, in my opinion, no other than those who philosophize rightly; and that I may be ranked in the number of these, I shall leave nothing unattempted, but exert myself in all possible ways."[3]

---

[2] 69c~d, italics included
[3] 69d

We too, as students of Platonism, endeavor to philosophize rightly and leave no part of our practice unattempted. The chapters that make up the *Knowing* section of this book will introduce practices to ripen our states of mind. First, though, let's take a few pages to look more closely at the state of mind we are cultivating and the experiences that may (or may not) accompany it.

Talk of a wisdom tradition triggers in many people thoughts of enlightenment in the form of a one-time burst of spiritual energy, popularly associated with the notion of a *kundalini*[4] energy release. While such peak experiences certainly can occur in the course of our practice, this is not what we are aiming for in Platonism. We are focusing instead on a consistent increase in familiarity and understanding of the Intelligible. This might make Platonism seem less exciting than some other systems, but the effects of this sober and mature approach are more meaningful and lasting.

When the ex-prisoner in Plato's allegory of the cave finally steps out into the upper world, he does not experience a burst of energy up the spine and then gain wisdom in a flash. Rather, he gradually adjusts to his new surroundings:

> "And first of all, he would most easily perceive shadows,
> afterwards the images of men and of other things in water, and
> after that the things themselves."[5]

We've seen that reaching the direct knowledge of things themselves is one of the main goals of dialectic. We also saw, though, that our efforts with dialectic must be an on-going process that evolves over time. We use names, definitions and concepts in our dialectical explorations, but with the intention of eventually reaching beyond all three. Plato explains in a private correspondence:

> "There are three things belonging to each of those particulars
> through which science [knowledge/*episteme*] is necessarily

---

[4] This term was introduced in Chapter 17. It is a Sanskrit word generally associated with spiritual energy that is said to lie dormant at the base of the spine in the unenlightened. Sometimes this word is used to refer to the obstacles to the rising of energy, but more commonly, *kundalini* is used in reference to the energy itself. A *kundalini* energy release is colloquially understood as the sensation of *kundalini* energy rising up the spinal column, usually associated with peak experiences.

[5] *Republic*, 516a

produced. But the fourth is science [knowledge/*episteme*] itself. And it is requisite to establish as the fifth that which is known and true. One of these is the name of the thing; the second is the definition; the third the resemblance; the fourth science [knowledge/*episteme*]....[U]nless among these someone after a manner receives that fourth, he will never perfectly participate the science [knowledge/*episteme*] about the fifth."[6]

What Plato refers to here as the fifth will be discussed in Chapter 24. Our focus right now is on the fourth thing in this quote, namely the knowledge that is beyond names, definitions and concepts. To see Plato's meaning more clearly, let's use one of the absolute Realities as an example: Justice. The word *justice* is its name. We can take time to work out a definition and even hold an image of justice in our minds. However, this image is malleable and open to dispute. It will always fall short of knowing Justice itself. The concepts in our minds are only images, resemblances that fall short of true knowledge.

Plato tells us:

"But after agitating together the several names and reasons, and sensible perceptions of these things, confuting in a benevolent manner, and employing questions and answers without envy, then, striving as much as is possible to human power, wisdom [*phronesis*] and intellect [*nous*] about each of these will scarcely at length shine forth."[7]

We've seen the word *phronesis* in a number of contexts, as the eye of the soul that turns from the world of becoming to the world of being. What Plato is alluding to here is reaching a state of mind beyond conceptual thinking to a grasping in the soul of things themselves. This is stage 3 of the journey outlined in Chapter 3. We are crossing now into the stages of wisdom.

Wisdom is a state of mind; indeed it can be seen as a range of states of mind that admit of infinite degrees of maturity. We enter the range of wise states of mind when we take our first step out of Plato's proverbial cave. The upper world is, of course, analogous to the Intelligible realm. We access the Intelligible realm via the Intellectual triad. As the extremity, or last position, of the Intelligible realms,

---

[6] *Seventh Epistle*, 342a~e, brackets added
[7] *Ibid.*, 344b, brackets added

Intellect is our entryway into the Intelligible. This, you might recall, is one of our definitions of the Greek word *nous.*

Plotinus, too, recognized *nous* as a realm we can participate in, but not possess directly. Here, he beautifully contrasts it with the senses:

> "And with respect to sense, indeed, it seems that we always grant it to be ours; for we are always sentient; but this is dubious with respect to intellect, because we do not always use it and because it is separate. But it is separate because it does not verge to us, but we rather looking on high, tend to it. Sense, however, is our messenger, but intellect our king."[8]

We've all participated in *nous* at some point in our lives. Our most poignant moments of creativity touch this realm, whether through sports, music, the arts, or even business. However, these moments in themselves are not the same as stepping out into the upper world. In these instances, our focus is on, and our state of mind is still rooted in, the physical plane. It would be helpful to recall here that preparing for knowledge—described throughout the *Understanding* section of this book—is not about opening one's eyes, but rather about turning the eye of the soul upward.[9]

Therefore, it is not participation in *nous* that in itself marks the wise state of mind. Our attention must be focused upward, our desire fixed on knowing our cause. The significance of Plato's ex-prisoner stepping out of the cave is that it is in the upper world that he can see the objects of Truth, the absolute Realities. When we get our first glimpse of the absolute Realities, however faint that vision may be, we can be said to have our first taste of knowledge. However, how wise could we be without understanding or relating to those Realities?

Our initial entry into these realms is usually subtle. It often passes unnoticed, because it doesn't fit our expectations. We were expecting internal fireworks. Instead, we find ourselves stumbling and groping because we don't know how to relate to this unfamiliar mode of cognition. And so it is through the struggle to understand these objects in the Intelligible realm that we adjust to the brightness of that region and also venture further into it.

We make these adjustments through a gradual shifting of focus away from our earthly attachments. In the *Phaedo,* Socrates lists a

---

[8] Ennead V:iii:3

[9] *Republic,* 519a~b. Quoted in Chapter 15.

number of separations we must make—not only from physical pleasures (such as eating, drinking and love-making) and bodily adornments (such as fashionable clothes and jewelry) but also from sensory perceptions and even identification with the body itself.[10] This shifting of our attention pulls our emphasis little by little away from bodily concerns of vanity and pleasure, and directs our focus to the eternal world of being. "[T]he lovers of learning therefore, I say, know that philosophy, receiving their soul in this condition, endeavours gently to exhort it, and dissolve its bonds..."[11]

He calls this gradual shifting of focus a "purification."[12] We've seen that methods of purification consist of efforts to clear away ignorance both about ourselves and about reality. We challenge our notions of the way things are on multiple levels. This process strengthens and unifies our energy, opening us to insights and spiritual growth. Once the soul is sufficiently purified,

> "it departs to that which is pure, eternal, and immortal, and which possesses a sameness of subsistence: and, as being allied to such a nature, it perpetually becomes united with it, when it subsists alone by itself....And this passion of the soul is denominated wisdom."[13]

The soul that has been sufficiently purified will, over time, grow more allied to a truly healthy state of mind. It is not enough to have an experience that brings sudden insights; we must live with those insights and let their implications reverberate through us. This is the sober and mature state of mind we call wisdom.

What Plato is pointing to here is an ongoing process that deepens over time as we grow more courageous and our aspiration takes a firmer hold. As we advance further, we open ourselves to the peak of stage 3 of our spiritual journey, which Plato describes in the *Republic* in this way: "And last of all, he will be able, I think, to perceive and

---

[10] See *Phaedo*, 64c~65d. Incidentally, one of the ways Dionysius was lured away from his father was by being presented with a mirror, thereby drawing him to the physical form.

[11] *Ibid.*,83a

[12] *Ibid.*, 67c

[13] *Ibid.*, 79d

contemplate the sun himself, not in water, nor resemblances of him, in a foreign seat, but himself by himself, in his own proper region."[14]

After our look at contemplation in the last section you undoubtedly recognize this description to be of a peak experience and not merely conceptual reasoning about the most majestic terms in Platonic metaphysics. There is further evidence yet that conceptualizing is not what Plato deemed to be the highest form of knowledge. The sun himself is a reference to the unified intelligible, or what Plato in the *Symposium* simply called "Beauty."[15] The *Republic* presents our ex-prisoner contemplating Beauty neither "in water, nor resemblances of him in a foreign seat..." In other words, we are going beyond reflections of Beauty, such as those we find in our physical realm or even intangible beauty such as the beauty of mathematical and scientific laws.

We are also going beyond resemblances in a foreign seat. The Greek word here for *resemblances* is *fantasmata,* from which we get the English word *fantasy*. *Fantasmata,* though, encompass more than daydreaming and story-telling. This is the faculty of mind that forms images, including visualizations. It is an element of conceptual thinking. Plato, however, is telling us that we must perceive "the sun himself" not as an image in our heads—in a foreign seat—but himself by himself.

Plotinus explains this in his characteristically poetical style:

"[B]y what collected intuition can we perceive a nature exalted above intellect itself? We answer, that this can only be accomplished by something resident in our souls as much as possible similar to the first; for we possess in our inmost recesses something of this exalted nature; or rather, there is not anything endued with a power of participating this first god in which he does not abide."[16]

As we have already seen, our contemplations are not focusing us on some object beyond ourselves but rather are executed through reversion to what Plotinus called in the above quote "our inmost recesses." This is, from the human perspective, the true significance

---

[14] 516a
[15] See from 210c
[16] Ennead III:viii:9

of Proclus' *proposition 103:* "All things are in all, but appropriately in each." As souls, we contain our causes psychically. Proclus explains this in his *Theology of Plato:*

> "When however, she [the soul] proceeds into her interior recesses, and into the adytum as it were of the soul, she perceives with her eyes closed the genus of the gods, and the unities of beings. For all things are in us psychically, and through this we are naturally capable of knowing all things, by exciting the powers and the images of wholes which we contain."[17]

We have an understandable tendency when pondering metaphysics to let localization slip into our calculus. Doing so while reading this quote of Proclus' would compel us to separate this cause that we contain from the intelligible itself. I'm anticipating now the possible interpretation that the psychical causes we encounter are something separate from the intelligible itself.

This notion would multiply the already crowded metaphysical map exponentially. By this reasoning, not only would there be an intelligible realm, but also a separate intelligible that exists causally in each realm that follows. And so on for every other realm, multiplying their existences throughout the metaphysical map. This convoluted image hardly makes sense, though. The assumption of localization has complicated matters. What Proclus' *proposition 103* is describing is closer to what Plotinus stated in the quote just above Proclus', namely that "there is not anything endued with a power of participating this first god in which he does not abide."

Taking spatial locality out of our metaphysical considerations also calls into question our assumptions that the soul—whose essence is beyond time and space—is somehow *in* the body. At the very least, we have to rethink what it means to be ensouled. We can no longer leave unquestioned our conventional image of soul literally being *in* our bodies. "[S]elfhood has nothing to do with spatial position," Plotinus explains.[18] Plotinus compares the relationship of body to soul to that of air to light. In this analogy, air is like body and light is like soul.

---

[17] *The Theology of Plato*, bk. 1, ch. 3.

[18] Ennead IV:iii:11, trans. Stephen MacKenna and B. S. Page

"Shall we therefore say that when the soul is present with the body, it is present in the same manner as light is with the air?...And being present through the whole, [the light] is mingled with no part of it. It is also itself permanent, but the air flows by it. And when the air becomes situated out of that in which there is light, it departs possessing nothing luminous; but as long as it is under the light, it is illuminated. Hence, here also, it may be rightly said that air is in light, rather than light in air."[19]

However, this is not meant to suggest that soul is one and the individuality of souls is an illusion. The multiplicity of souls having their own proper mode of reality can be seen in Plato's dialogues, such as the mythological description of the forming of individual souls in the *Timaeus*.[20] Plotinus also describes a monadic Soul which proceeds into multiplicity so that "the universe may be complete."[21]

Rather than talking about the soul being in the body, however, it would perhaps be more accurate to state that there is a center of identity to a body. Shifting our center of identity away from the body to the causes contained in the soul is the ultimate form of separation from the body that we can obtain while alive, and in the *Phaedo*, Socrates calls this, along with the other forms of separation discussed above, a kind of death. He proclaims that those "who are conversant with philosophy in a proper manner, seem to have concealed from others that the whole of their study is nothing else than to die and be dead."[22] Socrates describes this study of how to die and be dead as:

"separating the soul from the body in the most eminent degree, and in accustoming it to call together and collect itself essentially on all sides from the body and to dwell as much as possible, both now and hereafter, alone by itself, becoming by this means liberated from the body as from detaining bonds..."[23]

Notice that Socrates talks of "accustoming it to call together and collect itself." He does not say that we must collect the soul together,

---

[19] Ennead IV:iii:22

[20] 41d~43a

[21] Ennead IV:viii:1, trans. Stephen MacKenna and B. S. Page.

[22] 64a

[23] *Ibid.*, 67c

as if we are the subject and soul is the object that we act upon. Had he done so, he would have been advocating the common assumption that identifies who we are with the body and treats the soul as a possession that is literally contained inside the body. Rather, he states that it is the soul that collects itself together. This is a skill, Socrates tells us, that we as soul must learn. We are pulling our identity away from the body. This doesn't mean that we stop identifying with our bodies all together. It is more of a recognition that what we are in essence is beyond the body; we use the body as an instrument with which to function on the physical plane.

Also key to that phrase is the notion of the soul "accustoming" itself. It is learning a habit. Developing a habit implies a gradual process and, in the case of nurturing the health of the soul, it requires a steady, sober approach. We gradually gain this state of mind through all the practices outlined in this book. While there certainly have been people who experienced powerful peak experiences that were triggered suddenly and perhaps even unexpectedly by drugs or physical accidents, having such an experience is not the same as achieving psychical health.

Much as physical health requires effort and maintenance, psychical health does not happen overnight and it is not a one-time occurrence. It matures by molding for ourselves a lifestyle that promotes and encourages a healthy state of mind. What Plato is telling us, through the character of Socrates, is that we must adjust to functioning at a higher degree of unity so as to nurture a commensurate state of mind. We see here that Socrates' notion of separating from the body includes, but goes beyond, a peak experience that touches Reality itself. It also includes adjusting our relationship to human affairs, valuing our connection to Mind over such pursuits as physical pleasure and social status. We must rethink what is truly good and meaningful, and let other concerns fall away.

The person who can do this might enjoy a vision of "the sun himself." This separation is a peak experience and enhances that state of mind called wisdom, but it is important to understand that having such an experience is not in itself what it means to be wise. Wise states of mind are marked by a melting away of our adherence to the belief that our individuality is ultimate Reality. This is true not only of the peak experience described in the *Phaedo* but of all the separations from the body listed in that dialogue.

Wise States of Mind

Platonism recognizes the Soul realm as having a mode of reality, as does our physical universe. However, these realms are not ultimate reality. As such, experiences that reach more unified realms necessarily carry with them a commensurate shift in perspective away from the individual toward the One Self, or the One that underlies all that *is*.

To be clear, the One Self transcends experience. As such, it cannot be known. However, we can recognize Reality itself as the *presence of the One Self*, like light emitted from the sun or the fragrance that flows from a flower. It is from this more unified point of view that an experience unfolds.

Such an experience is certainly meaningful, but even more significant is the state of mind that has the experience. What do we become in that moment? We certainly are not the man or woman who listens to rock-and-roll or who likes extra-crunchy peanut butter, or the person who needs to pick up the dry cleaning after work. In that experience of Reality itself, we've risen to the causes we contain in our souls. There was a shift in identity, and it is important to recognize that this shift occurred through reversion. Reflecting on that memory and recognizing our essence is to know Reality and to know ourselves to be that.

This is where the distinction in English translations between *the One itself* and *the One Self* becomes significant.[24] The term *the One itself* focuses us on the word *One*. It is easy to fall into the habit of thinking about the One in theoretical, objective terms, which lends to it feeling separate from and unconnected to us. In contrast, the term *the One Self* focuses us on the term *Self*. When our practice takes us to its highest reaches and we begin asking ourselves what we became in that peak experience, we will find ourselves in a quandary. The very question—what did I become in that experience?—implies the experiencer identifying with the experience itself. We are stretching the very definition of the word *experience*.

Anyone who knows this experience (with our new caveat now added to this word), knows that it carries with it no sense of

---

[24] Introduced in Chapter 8.

separation or "otherness." It is because we can identify with the One Self and feel its presence that we can know that we are *that*. This is where the search to know the nature of reality and the search to *know thyself* intersect.

There are two requirements to developing a wise state of mind, and both admit of degrees:

(1) The direct encounter with Reality

(2) Understanding what "you" are in that encounter

Developing our state of mind, then, requires both continuing our purification of ignorance and also sharpening our understanding of absolute Realities. Purification may very well lead to more profound peaks and experiences. However, it is understanding rather than seeking deeper experiences that will feed our soul's maturation.

To clarify this point, consider the difference between a **description** and an **explanation**. Imagine you traveled to a distant land with a culture and customs very different from your own. People's actions and the tools they use might be so foreign that you can't even guess what they are doing. You could certainly describe what you were witnessing, but if you couldn't speak the language and had nobody to explain to you what was going on, you would only be able to surmise what they were doing based on preconceived notions and past experiences. Some of your shots might hit the bull's eye, but most would miss—and how would you know which was which? Description alone is not enough; we need understanding as well. We need to be able to explain Reality, and that is where metaphysics comes in.

A growing number of us have had at least one powerful peak experience. Without subjecting our conclusions to dialectical analyses, these experiences are interpreted through the teachings and beliefs we currently hold. Following such an experience, insights naturally flow. Even here, though, there is room for interpretation. This goes a long way toward explaining why there is a great diversity in teachings from system to system, yet a core that is highly compatible.

It is also worth noting that while the purest state itself never changes, our beliefs and expectations hinder and mold experiences of it to varying degrees. Therefore, some people have nibbled only a taste of Reality, while others have drunk in a full cup. Because even the shallowest of peak experiences is powerful in comparison to our usual states of mind, one could be mistaken for "the big one" and the insights that follow confused for truth unhindered by interpretation.

On the other side of the fence are those who have studied wisdom literature and so have gained a conceptual understanding of Reality. Yet without direct experience, misunderstandings are unavoidable. No matter how well intellectuals can discuss wisdom teachings, no matter how long those people have studied, true wisdom still eludes them. Being able to talk at length about this system or that one might sound impressive, but it does not equate to being wise. Nor does being able to read wisdom literature in its native Sanskrit or Chinese or Greek. All words, regardless of the language, are just signposts pointing to truth. The person who understands only the words has not yet touched the Reality that the words are pointing to. The understanding of direct experience is a different kind of understanding from that of concepts.

Chapter 22: Living With Wisdom

"[W]e are not to admit the merely living, but living well, to be a thing of the greatest consequence."

Plato[1]

Beyond the Familiar

Over the years, I've met people who long for peak experiences, but are blocked by fears. All of us on this spiritual path must confront this issue in one form or another. This is an inevitable element of accustoming ourselves to a yet-unfamiliar mode of cognition. I've received warnings that strengthening spiritual energy could be dangerous—even deadly. Lay practitioners such as myself should not make such an attempt, the fearful have warned me. While the mainstream popularity of spiritual practice is a positive trend overall, one negative side effect has been the misconception that peak experiences are only for a special few.

It is understandable that someone writing a book for mass consumption would want to include warnings. People from many different backgrounds pick up the same book, and some may misuse it. Hence the warnings that spiritual energy is powerful and not to be taken lightly. That message has been picked up loud and clear. It is repeated frequently, even by people who have never personally had a peak experience. I suspect this is because, like anything else we don't understand, we fear it.

I find this most unfortunate. Wisdom is every human being's birthright. Granted, I see people in the news and even in my own town who, I'm sorry to say, seem unlikely to claim that birthright this time around (although it's not impossible). Still, sincere readers of a book such as this one may yet discover that wisdom is nothing to fear. It needn't be only for someone else. It is for you—in this lifetime.

Fearing spiritual energy is tied to a fear of the realm of Mind. People with this fear imagine the divine realms to be something dangerous—perhaps even sinister. Plato, however, recognized that fortitude is what allows us to hold fast to the conviction that God is

---

[1] *Crito*, 48b

good in Reality.[2] If existence presupposes unity, and whatever unites is good,[3] then God must be purely good. The Platonic system recognizes no evil entity such as the devil. God is the cause of good things, not all things.[4] Selfish and hurtful behavior play an inevitable role in our physical realm, but the culprit is ignorance, not an evil supernatural entity.[5]

People who grew up with a belief in evil—especially the belief that evil exists in our own souls—naturally dread what they might encounter when they step away from conventional states of mind. Even those who have already tasted wisdom could be frightened out of proceeding further. They anticipate danger if they venture any farther from the familiar.

Quite possibly, one of the most well-read accounts of the effects of raising *kundalini* energy is the autobiography of an Indian man named Gopi Krishna. He was a working-class man who, in 1937, experienced a powerful *kundalini* rising. However, he initially had little understanding of what occurred or the changes that would result from that experience.[6] He had not worked through any of his false beliefs or self-images, and so he was flooded with unhealthy states of mind that needed to be sorted through.[7] He also had not studied metaphysics or built up a balanced practice of energy movement.

---

[2] *Republic*, 429c~430b. The conclusion at 430b reads: "Such a power which is a perpetual preservation of right and lawful opinion, about things which are to be feared or not, I call and define as fortitude..." The beliefs being referred to were discussed at 379b~383c. In summary, the beliefs are (1) God is good in Reality and never causes harm and (2) God is unchanging and never deceives. As with all beliefs, these are intended to be treated as hypotheses rather than embraced blindly. As our understanding grows as to why these conclusions must be true, our fortitude to push forward strengthens as well. Ultimately, we seek to go beyond understanding this goodness to knowing this goodness firsthand.

[3] See *The Elements of Theology*, prop. 13. (Discussed in detail in Chapter 8.)

[4] *Republic*, 379c

[5] See *Ibid.*, 382b~c

[6] His autobiography *Living with Kundalini* (See the bibliography, p. 371).

[7] Many passages in his autobiography point to this. For example, Krishna writes: "I now had no doubts that the experience was real and that the sun had nothing to do with the internal luster that I saw. But, why did I feel uneasy and depressed? Instead of feeling exceedingly happy at my luck and blessing my stars, why had despondency overtaken me?" *Living with Kundalini*, p. 6.

He endured great physical suffering for a period of time when energy was initially cleansing and strengthening. Yet he concluded that looking back, the state of mind he had gained made it all worthwhile.[8] His conclusion has inspired many, but the price he had paid to reach that conclusion has contributed to much of the fear and misunderstanding that surrounds mystic practices.

Imagine you wanted to build up your upper body muscles. Now imagine that to do this, you started lifting the maximum amount of weight you could every day, and that this was your sole practice. No warm-ups, no gradual building up of weights, no aerobic exercise. Also, you didn't read up on physiology or dietary science. You made no changes to your eating or sleeping habits. Your weight-lifting routine targeted only the muscles you wished to build up and no others. How long do you think it would take before you sustained serious injury? Probably not long. Yet it would be foolish to conclude that the problem was that large muscles are dangerous and most people should avoid cultivating them.

However, something analogous to this has been a common reaction to Gopi Krishna's story. According to his autobiography, he meditated every day for two hours. He would focus each time on the top of his head, visualizing the Hindu image of a thousand-petaled lotus. This was his sole practice. When his energy awakened, he had no understanding of what was happening, nor did he have a background in any metaphysical system. The suffering that ensued for him has led some to conclude that seeking wisdom is too risky for the average person. A more sensible conclusion would be that his meditation practice ought to have been part of a well-rounded spiritual program.

The potential harm in raising spiritual energy is most prominent in people who have some fantasy about being enlightened and believe that enlightenment is an experience. They therefore engage in various practices and techniques to build energy, but do not respect the commensurate state of mind that ought to accompany this heightened

---

[8] See for example p. 293: "I had drunk the cup of suffering to the dregs to come upon a resplendent, never-ending source of unutterable joy and peace lying hidden in my interior, waiting for a favorable opportunity to reveal itself, affording me in one instant a deeper insight into the essence of things than a whole life devoted to study could do."

energy. They leave in place their false beliefs about themselves as individuals and as spiritual beings. There must be a balance in which heightened energy feeds our learning and, in turn, our learning feeds the cleansing and heightening of our energy. People engaged in a well-rounded spiritual system that values gradual growth towards wisdom needn't fear repeating the tumultuous journey taken by Gopi Krishna.

A Useful Exercise

There are many misconceptions about wisdom, and these fuel not only the fear surrounding it, but also the various errors in practice that lead students astray. The fantasies that experience-seekers hold of wisdom are very much like the dreams many people hold of winning the lottery. Many a daydream has undoubtedly been built around being the exact same person you are now, only rich. Perhaps you see yourself living in a mansion with multiple swimming pools, or going to lavish parties and rubbing shoulders with celebrities and power players. Do you think of wisdom in the same way? Do you imagine that it will bring you knowledge and psychic gifts without otherwise changing you?

If so, think again. Wisdom is not something that happens to us or that we stumble into. There is no magic lightning bolt from the gods that marks us as special or chosen. Rather, we are gaining knowledge of the nature of Reality and integrating that knowledge into our lives. Wisdom is an evolution that we must embrace and allow ourselves to grow into. We are in the midst of a way of life, one that opens us to a new way of being and a new way of relating to the world around us.

The word *enlightenment* carries with it images of supernatural powers, far more so than does the more mundane notion of *wisdom*. However, these two words can be used synonymously once the myths surrounding both *enlightenment* and *wisdom* have been dispelled. To better understand what these states of mind we call wisdom or enlightenment actually are, let's first take a look at what we *think* they are. Here is a useful exercise: visualize what it might be like to be enlightened. See yourself functioning as a wise sage, or visualize your idea of the quintessential enlightened being. Take a few minutes. Once you've got the image, make a list of whatever attributes naturally arose during your visualization. There is room for variation here, so don't worry what other people's lists might look like.

Here are some examples. You might imagine that with enlightenment, you will gain psychic gifts. You will be able to sense trouble before it happens and so always avoid it. You will never make a wrong decision again. Further, because you will be able to read people's spiritual energy, you will know when you are being lied to and so nobody will ever be able to deceive you.

Of course, you will also have infinite compassion, and so you will not harbor so much as a single negative thought towards those who had tried to hurt you. Forgiveness will be second-nature, because not even the seed of anger can exist in the heart that knows only love. Your love for humanity will pour into a greater love for all living things and for Mother Earth herself. Your presence will inspire birds to sing and flowers to bloom.

Or perhaps you picture the sage as always happy, always surrounded by joy and never sorrow. Those unavoidable events in life that sadden ordinary people, such as death and illness, are somehow seen only as beautiful through eyes that are wise. Therefore, they cause no grief. Emotional pain is non-existent in the life of one who is wise.

Another common assumption is that wisdom brings with it complete knowledge of everything. The wise person supposedly is never without an answer, and manifests the perfect words for every situation. This person can aptly strike down every doubt and objection that is presented and then, in a flash, change gears and speak with such eloquence about the beauty of the Divine that even the most unrepentant skeptics feel choked with emotion.

This person, of course, would also have answered all of those aching questions that anyone reading a book of this sort certainly wrestles with: Why are we here? What is the purpose of my life? What will happen to me after death? Why do bad things happen to good people? No mystery remains unresolved.

Health and vigor is another benefit many assume of enlightenment. Enlightenment will supposedly cure any disease. It will ensure its benefactors youthfulness and agility well into their eighties or even beyond. No creaky knees or feeble eyesight for the enlightened one; only the energy and limberness of a teenager—with a libido to match!

Certainly, wisdom does bring us some degree of these benefits, such as a greater awareness of psychic energy and a clearer sense of the whole into which the physical realm fits. While our list of questions will never be extinguished, we do gain many insights which give our lives a greater sense of purpose and direction. Further, wisdom allows us to see our existence from a wider perspective, and so our reactions to various events in our lives will reflect this change. We will understand tragedy from a broader point of view, as well as enjoy more frequent moments of pithy insights and poetic utterances. Some health conditions may improve or be cured, but not necessarily. We must be careful not to assign to wisdom our fantasies about who we'd like to be. Wisdom is not a panacea.

Actually, these conjectures about wisdom can be used as examples of the way our current state of mind interferes with our ability to see clearly. Let's take two of these examples: having all the answers and remaining youthful and healthy. These are examples of wishes we hold because they counter negative self-images and our deepest fears. Having all the answers, for example, is a common fantasy in reaction to the fear of looking foolish in public. Remaining youthful and healthy counters, among other things, our dread at growing old and facing our inevitable death. Our expectations about wisdom actually reflect little to nothing about wisdom itself, and everything about our current states of mind.

Negative assumptions about wisdom also are reflections of our own states of mind. These include the image of the sage as cold and lacking emotions. Another negative image is that of being disheveled and indifferent to all matters of society. The stereotype is of someone who is socially awkward or even embarrassing to be with in public. These images would be most off-putting to someone who valued being popular, or at least fitting in.

Living Wisely

If wisdom does not function in any of these ways, then how does it function? In Plato's dialogue the *Laws*, he compares living wisely to the able navigation of a ship:

> "[D]ivinity, and, together with divinity, fortune and opportunity, govern all human affairs. But a third of a milder nature must be admitted,—I mean, that art ought to follow these. For I am of opinion, that it would make a great

difference, during a storm, whether you possessed the pilot's art, or not."[9]

The skilled captain of a ship can circumvent some storms that less experienced captains may get caught in. However, no captain can always avoid every storm all the time. Even the most capable of captains will find some cloudbursts unavoidable. Hence Plato's acknowledgement that "together with divinity, fortune and opportunity, govern all human affairs." However, Plato recognized that we are not merely leaves blowing in the wind, incapable of directing our course. Which captain is more likely to come out of danger unscathed: the one with strong navigation skills or the one who is less skilled? And so it is that the skilled navigator seems to be luckier.

Such is the captain's art. Being knowledgeable about the sea does not imply that the captain is knowledgeable about anything else. Nor does it mean that storms will never shake his or her boat, or that the captain will be in complete control at every moment. Skilled navigators are not super-humans; these people just seem to be luckier than others. They get caught in fewer storms and find the gentlest, quickest way out of the ones they do get caught in.

Wise states of mind are aptly compared to this. The knowledge that is the mark of wisdom is the knowledge of our essence and the nature of Reality. Knowing this and looking to this knowledge as a pattern to guide our lives is what it means to live wisely. In the *Republic,* Plato describes philosophers who know Reality as "looking up to the truest paradigm, and always referring themselves thither, and contemplating it in the most accurate manner possible to establish on earth just maxims of the beautiful and just and good..."[10]

A wise state of mind will not bring answers to *every* question, nor will it make us great speakers or the life of the party. It will not guarantee us physical health or longevity of life. It carries with it no promises that grief or hard times will never touch us again. Psychic abilities may come and go, but this differs from person to person. And while compassion certainly is a mark of wise states of mind, anger and other emotions that are often unhealthy can still rear their ugly heads when the "right" buttons are pushed.

---

[9] 709b~c

[10] 484d

Some people who have crossed into the range of wise states of mind resist the word *enlightenment*. They associate that word with loftier images then what they would comfortably assign to themselves. They recognize their insights, yet they haven't gone through that grand transformation depicted in the various erroneous images of the enlightened man or woman. Actually, I intentionally slipped an error into that earlier exercise. Many people assume—and I had made this mistake myself early in my practice—that once you have a peak experience you can now call yourself an enlightened person.

We've already put some big dents into this theory. There is one more point we need to clarify. While we talk loosely of this person or that one being enlightened or wise, it would be more accurate to say that there are only enlightened or wise states of mind. When you are in that state of mind, you are in it. When you are out of it, you are out of it. Indeed, we must recall that the faculties of the mind summarized in the divided line can exist simultaneously in the same soul. Belief still functions in a soul that has touched Truth. Even false beliefs that have not yet been worked through can function.

This is a large part of the reason I have stressed throughout this book that Platonism is a way of life. A life of wisdom is a choice that we not only aim for early in our practice but also one that we continue to cultivate for the remainder of our days. We must hold onto the insights we have gained and integrate them into our lives. Otherwise, we risk slipping back into old habits and ways of being. Again, wisdom is not something that happens to us; it is something we must embrace and choose again and again.

The day-to-day life of living wisely may not be as exciting or glamorous as some people fantasize it to be. We don't all write bestselling books and become world-famous teachers. Nor does entering this range of states of mind mean that we will shave our heads, wear religious garb and become enigmatic gurus. Among those of us who continue the philosophic life, it is not unusual for us to work in the same job, to live in the same house, and to shop at the same stores. In fact, to the casual observer, there will probably be nothing different about us at all. We will just seem luckier somehow—or perhaps more boring! We will lack the drama in our lives that others less skilled at navigation find unavoidable or even attractive.

At this point, some of you might be wondering what the point is of developing wisdom. After all, it takes a lot of work. People spend years immersed in such practices as studying, reflecting, and meditating. It is easy to understand doing this for the goal of gaining psychic gifts or other impressive abilities. However, what is the point if we will still be "ordinary" people? Is it really worth the effort just to gain a heightened state of mind?

In this modern age, book stores and online shops are chock-full of books about the secrets of living wisely. Teachers from all walks of life tell us how to live in conformity with divine law, without us having to do the work that they did. Isn't that enough, some of you might be wondering? We can believe in a divine intelligence that is the essence of all, and we can live in line with teachings about wisdom. Why do we need to know this state of mind for ourselves?

Imagine you had a friend who struggled with depression. Perhaps you would advise her to seek professional help, or you would recommend some method to release her negative thoughts and feelings. These would be reasonable responses; we all wish our friends to enjoy happy and healthy lives. Now suppose that her reply went something like this: *Will this healthier state of mind mean that I will get a more prestigious job? Will I live in a mansion? Will I look younger? Will I be famous or more respected? No? Then I don't see the point. Maybe if I just hang out with people who are not depressed I'll get a sense of how to live as though I were happy. I think that's enough; I don't need to work harder than that.*

You'd probably conclude that it was her depression talking. Nobody who was thinking clearly would *choose* to stay in an unhealthy state of mind simply because it didn't bring changes that were irrelevant to the issue at hand. The healthy state of mind you'd encourage your friend to seek has value in itself. Whatever other benefits may follow would be the icing on the cake, but being healthy and happy *is* the cake. Nobody who was thinking clearly would conclude that living *as though* you were happy was just as good as truly being happy. This hypothetical woman seems too wacky to be realistic. Yet, when it comes to wise states of mind, we too often reach the same conclusion as this imaginary friend did.

Wisdom is a healthy state of mind. This may seem like little compared to what you had imagined it to be, but it most certainly is not. Wisdom is not just any state of mind; it is a state of psychical health in which we have direct insights into the nature of Reality. Of course, our insights deepen as we continue our studies.

People in this state of mind know true beauty, justice, and goodness. We know these to be the nature of Reality and the model for the entire cosmos that flows from the root of all Being. And although we cannot prove this knowledge to other people, we absolutely know that we know, and that this state surpasses belief and even conceptual understanding.

In one sense, we can belittle the value of this and point out that this is *the only thing* that is confirmed by understanding peak experiences. Put a bunch of people with wise states of mind in the same room, and they surely will disagree about politics and social issues, and even some areas of spiritual doctrine. Yet this *one thing* that touching Reality teaches us is everything that is worthwhile. It will allow us the means to navigate from moment to moment, recognizing the beauty in our physical world and discerning what is truly meaningful from each event in our lives.

Returning to the Cave

At the end of Plato's cave allegory, he has his ex-prisoner leave the upper world of knowledge and return to the cave.[11] Why not stay in that glorious upper world? Because returning to the cave is part of the process of moving beyond experience to the understanding of experience. It is through the struggle of bringing knowledge to our everyday world—of recognizing reflections of the absolute in our world of multiplicity—that we move beyond experience and awaken to the deepest levels of spiritual maturity. This is stage 4 of our journey.

As glorious as peak experiences can be, they are not enough to deem us wise. We must hold onto that memory; we must feel it and live it on a daily basis. As our energy grows stronger, we learn to eventually maintain our participation in *nous* even while functioning in the physical world, and this memory is an important tool towards that aim. Yet, this goal also introduces a challenge. How does that knowledge change the way we view our relationships and the roles we play in society?

---

[11] *Republic,* 520b~d

When we know our essence as no different from that of Essence itself, when this is our experience and not merely a conceptual belief, it can be difficult to reconcile that with the roles and limitations we face in our physical bodies. We understand that this physical realm is real, yet we also know that it is not ultimate reality. There is a sense in which all the roles we play are fictions. As reincarnating essences, we played entirely different roles in past lives, and in future lives we will change roles again. So how can the person at stage 4 go back to playing the roles of spouse, parent, employee, and so on?

Imagine that an adult wants to assess the states of mind of a group of small children. She passes around finger puppets and gives the kids an imaginary setting to get them started. Then she sits back and watches them play. Of course, the specifics of the story as it unfolds will not be significant; those details will fall away as soon as the experiment ends and the kids take the puppets off their fingers.

However, the way they played out their roles would speak volumes about their states of mind. Would they be considerate of other characters in the story? Would they be manipulative? Mean? Understanding? If the game went on long enough, they would learn from their interactions with one another. Depending on the dynamics of the group, the lessons might be positive (such as the value of friendship) or they might be negative (such as concluding that honest people get the short end of the stick). Those lessons may very well stay with them long after the finger puppet experiment ends.

In an analogous way, our incarnations (and the roles we play in each one) are like this finger puppet scenario. The importance of the way we play our roles is not necessarily in the surface story, but in the ways in which we interact as divine essences. Do we touch people's lives in ways that encourage beauty and goodness, or in ways that spread distrust and pain? From the perspective of soul, a good life is not measured by money or social status. These things fall away with the death of our bodily vehicle. What we take with us is our learnings, both the wisdom and the ignorance.[12]

Much of the wisdom and advice that we read about from other traditions comes from this stage of insight. The intention of this book is to inspire and encourage you to turn the eye of your soul upwards

---

[12] Compare to Plato's myth at the end of *Republic*, from 614b.

and ultimately discover this wisdom for yourself, so I won't focus on such insights themselves here. Application, after all, focuses us squarely in the physical realm.

However, there is a proper time in our journey for such a focus, and the value on the insights this brings is high. When the ex-prisoner in Plato's allegory returns to the cave, he must learn how to function in accordance with this higher vision of justice, beauty, and goodness. It is here that the melding of insight and action—the *philosopher-king*—blossoms, maturing into compassion and wise judgment. Anyone who has tried to live wisely knows that it is not easy. There are a myriad of subtle nuances to wade through, and no definitive book of rules to follow. We must make judgments throughout the day, which means we must trust ourselves to find the right answer when we look inward. We must carry with us an image of what we beheld in our highest, purest encounter with Reality.

Plato presented Socrates as the ideal model of a wise man. His Socrates took his role as a servant of God quite seriously, weighing it to be of greater importance than physical survival.[13] His understanding of the nature of Reality informed the way he saw his roles as a husband, a father, and a friend. The example of Socrates stands as a reminder that touching unified Reality is not the end of the road. A great deal of courage is required to allow for the growth and spiritual maturity that could potentially follow such an experience. Wise states of mind are hard to achieve, but not out of reach. They are our birthright, and seeking them is both healthy and good. For those with the strength and humility to keep pushing forward even after a peak experience, the beautiful rewards of the love of wisdom[14] are finally ready to fully blossom.

---

[13] Consider, for example, this excerpt from Socrates' speech at his trial where he was ultimately sentenced to death, *Apology*, 37e: "Perhaps however someone will say, Can you not Socrates, live in exile silently and quietly? But it is the most difficult of all things to persuade some among you, that this cannot take place. For if I say that in so doing I should disobey Divinity, and that on this account it is impossible for me to live a life of leisure and quiet, you would not believe me, in consequence of supposing that I spoke ironically."

[14] Etymologically, the word *philosophy* means "the love of wisdom."

Chapter 23: Metaphysics Revisited

"[T]here is in general no doctrine more ridiculous in the eyes of the general public than this, nor on the other hand any more wonderful and inspiring to those naturally gifted."

Plato[1]

A Second Look at the First Cause

As our state of mind matures, it is inevitable that we will revisit metaphysics multiple times, each time fine-tuning our understanding. This is a normal and healthy process. We've seen a great amount of detail just in the summaries that I have scattered throughout this book, and much of it can be confusing. There is always room to test our vision and further our insights.

Before moving on, then, let's revisit our basic outline of Platonic metaphysics. The First Cause of all is called the One itself in reference to the unity that is the condition for all existence. The One Self is an alternative translation of the One itself. Selfhood stresses our connection with the One, that we are *that*. This First Cause is also called the Good itself, in reference to the providential goodness that is the basis for all existence and that permeates through all the realms of being. The Good itself is also a reference to the desire that awakens in us to return to our source.

Following this, two terms—the bound and the infinite—indicate the super-essential dyad that immediately flows from the One. The bound denotes that which binds all into a unity, and the infinite is its infinite power. Although they are a dyad, this dyad is collectively a oneness.

Also undifferentiated from the One come the many onenesses. These are the gods. The gods are real and they point us to divine providential functions that are real, yet they are not taken literally as mythological personifications. Each god correlates to a henad, or super-essential oneness, in the metaphysical map. These henads are distinct from one another and yet, like the dyad, they are collectively a oneness. Beyond this oneness, of course, the One itself is pure; it is without divisions or aspects.

---

[1] *Second Letter,* 314a, trans. L. A. Post

At this stage in our studies, we are ready to fine-tune our understanding of the First Cause. Even though the First Cause is actually beyond any name we might give it, metaphysics gives a different name to the unnamable each time a different train of exploration is being followed. We have already seen a number of different names. Now is a good time to bring them all together and summarize them:

- **The Ineffable:** stresses that which is beyond all description and discourse.

- **The One itself:** stresses the unity we nurture through its contemplation, and the unity that allows anything that exists to be.

- **The Good itself:** stresses the providential goodness that is inherent in the unfolding of the cosmos, and the goodness that we each strive for in our desire to know our essence.

- **First Cause or Principle:** points to that which is the condition for all existence, even though this condition is itself beyond existence and therefore cannot technically be said to exist. Yet, as the condition for all existence, it also cannot be said *not* to exist. It is completely transcendent and exempt from all that *is*.

- **The Bound:** this is generally placed after the One in metaphysical structures. In another sense, though, it is the Truly One in that it is what makes each thing bound into what it is.

- **The Infinite:** the infinite power of the bound. Like Bonnie and Clyde or Tom and Jerry, the bound and the infinite are a pair that are never separated. We don't think of one without the other. Together, they are the One as First Cause, as the infinite power of the One that overflows into existence.

- **The One Self:** this name has not been justly treated in English translations, but is an indelible part of the Greek tradition. This is what we might call the personalized aspect of the One. It stresses our sameness with the One, our connection to it and our lack of separation from the underlying fabric on which all existence unfolds.

There are no words that accurately describe or name the First Cause. Our understanding of it comes not through words themselves, for words can only point us in the right direction. We must keep in mind that words limit us to negations, metaphors, and similes. I've heard the First Cause likened to a movie screen; if the screen were torn or had any marks on it, this would interfere with the movie being projected onto it. The screen must be completely unblemished. Also, it is significant that the screen remains unchanged by the movie currently being projected. Whether the movie is a comedy or a horror film, the screen remains the same.

Next on the metaphysical chain is the root of Being. The most common name for this is perhaps the One-Being. It is Being that is one and the One that *is*. All the realms of being flow from this source.

The higher realms of being are more unified than the lower realms, and the more unified they are, the more potent they are. As realms unfold, differentiation is increasingly introduced, diffusing the realm's potency proportionately.[2] Being unfolds from the unified Intelligible realm to the realm of Intellect, and then ultimately to the realm of materiality. Each realm of reality can be understood triadically not only as being, but also as life and as intellect. Much of the writings of the later Platonists focus on better understanding the dynamics and implications of this triadic relationship.

Our picture of reality is far from complete, but we have enough structure in place now to give our discussion a working framework. My hope is that it will also function as a roadmap for those of you who choose to jump into the writings of the ancient Greek philosophers on your own—a roadmap onto which a great amount of detail is yet to be added.

This initial layer of study is essential not only because it exposes us to a different view of reality, but also because working through the intricate details of these texts challenges us on multiple levels. We are forced to look at any obstacle that hinders our ability to read just what is on the page without overlooking anything or adding to what is written. We also must confront false beliefs that convince us we cannot comprehend anything so obtuse. Some of us may struggle with the notion that having a high IQ or thriving in academic surroundings is not by itself sufficient to excel in this undertaking. Everything that we had thought we knew about the nature of reality is now open to scrutiny.

Early in our studies, we learn the metaphysical schemes laid out by the giants in this lineage. As we gain proficiency in our initial studies

---

[2] Cf. *The Elements of Theology*, props. 61, 62 and 126.

and start putting them together—moving from stage 1 to stage 2^3—
we begin to appreciate the differences from one thinker to the next. I
don't want to downplay the importance of this avenue of thought. It
is not only the scholarly but also the mystical student of Platonism
who will benefit from considering, for example, how Plotinus differed
from the later Platonists and whether these differences can be
reconciled,[4] or to what degree Damascius truly diverged from Proclus.
The insights that result from such explorations are rich fields for
contemplation, and they also have the potential to reveal our own
areas of confusion.

A potential problem comes when we get so caught up in the
theoretical aspect of identifying these distinctions that we forget the
higher purpose behind all of these writings. The bond that all of these
great thinkers share, I believe, is that they had beheld Reality directly,
and they brought intelligibility to that experience by putting it into
words to the degree that such a task is possible. All of the writings in
the Platonic canon are like fingers pointing to truth. To some degree,
there were differences in that vision. Yet at the same time, there was
tremendous agreement. At the highest reaches of our studies, we
must let the divisions created by words fall away; only then do we
have any chance of seeing the truth they point to. Differences jump
out at us fairly early on. It is only when we gain vision for ourselves
that we can appreciate the similarities—the different approaches that
writers took to raise language beyond its boundaries and point to the
one Reality.

Stumbling Blocks

I will now turn the discussion toward five areas that are particularly
difficult stumbling blocks for the advancing student. The
metaphysical points presented here (and throughout the whole book)
are not included with the expectation that readers will embrace them

---

[3] I'm referring here to the stages of our journey as outlined in Chapter 3.

[4] Consider, for example, Plotinus' view on the descent of the soul: Ennead
4:8:8: "[T]he whole of our soul also does not enter into body, but something
belonging to it always abides in the intelligible, and something different
from this in the sensible world…" This contrasts with Proclus' *Elements of
Theology*, proposition 211: "Every partial soul descending into generation
descends wholly; nor does one part of it remain on high, and another part
descend."

as gospel. In fact, I would be disappointed if that were the result. Growth comes through reading and pondering for ourselves, working through our unique difficulties and seeing through our assumptions. Our insights must be our own. I expect that the cursory summary I present here will spark more questions than it answers. This is good—if we have the courage to hold onto our confusion and use it as a launch pad.

The metaphysics of the Platonic tradition challenges our conventional notions of Reality. I am reminded of an old Tibetan proverb: *You cannot discover new oceans unless you are willing to lose sight of the shore.* We can gain a fair grasp of metaphysics without losing sight of the proverbial shore, but eventually the time comes when we must lift anchor and sail away. The points presented in this chapter are in anticipation of some of the difficulties that the student faces who dares to penetrate these metaphysical teachings beyond an intellectual understanding.

Distinctions without divisions

Learning to read without interpretation is a lifelong practice. Once we cross the threshold from conceptually understanding to directly seeing, this practice takes on a new form. At this point, a student has mastered the basic metaphysical hierarchy and can discuss it with some degree of proficiency. This is undoubtedly enough to get high marks in a university class. However, our goal is loftier than that. We want to truly know Reality, not merely be able to talk about it. We have a vision of it, but that vision is still hazy. We need to fine-tune our understanding—to bring our vision into sharper focus.

One key to achieving this is to challenge the limitations that language invariably imposes on our vision of Reality. Direct seeing takes us beyond words. Although words are central to our path into understanding, we must eventually leave them behind.

One way to do this is by remembering that every term in our metaphysical system points to Reality and, as such, has a necessary function. Those readers who have familiarity with other mystic systems have probably noticed some differences as to which aspects of Reality are emphasized in the Platonic tradition. In general, where there are names, there is awareness and clarity. That which remains unnamed remains unexplored.

Students of Platonic metaphysics, then, have to question each term in the system. Why do we have multiple names for that which is unnamable? Why is Being said to be triadic? Why not a dyad or a tetrad? Sharpening our vision requires seeing what each term adds to our understanding and why additional terms beyond these are not necessary. Each term can be understood as a finger pointing to a divine function. We must look to the unity and beauty they point to rather than stubbornly clinging to the divisions as if they were real. Damascius tells us:

> "We employ the terminology of things that are subject to differentiation either as single predicates or as complex predicates, intending to indicate something about that which is entirely free from differentiations, whose name and conception we are unable to articulate, owing to the great divisiveness of our own thought. For we must gather all of our conceptions into one metaconception, the summit of all thinking, if we would get hold of any trace of that transcendently co-aggregate nature."[5]

The divisions greatly benefit us in our studies, but eventually our mental maps must be adjusted in order to enter a higher, more unified vision. These maps can become a crutch if we hold onto them too firmly. This will be easier to see if we take a step back and look at the understanding we have gained thus far. Do any of our discussions about metaphysics help us better understand who we are or the whole of which we are a part? How does the hierarchical structure we have studied help us fulfill that loftiest of quests to *know thyself*?

Initially, we know ourselves only as physical beings. We can experience ourselves in this physical realm via our senses and our thoughts as they function in this realm. However, what we each call *myself* is more accurately *the experience of myself*. There is something beyond the experiences that this realm offers, something that the physical senses cannot touch. To the degree that we recognize this, we can consider ourselves to be intuitive. To deepen these higher experiences, we must unify and raise our energy and our thoughts to the realm of Intellect. The better we are able to understand and access the Intellectual realm, the better acquainted we become with ourselves as divine essence, or *ousia*.

---

[5] *Problems and Solutions Concerning First Principles,* p. 326

As we go deeper into our exploration of essences, we eventually come to Essence itself. Here we finally know the oneness of Reality and know that our own essence is ultimately no different from that of Essence itself. This is the experience Plato called Beauty in the *Symposium;* the one he described as seeing the sun himself in the *Republic.*

Yet once again we have been brought to a border. Just as we had reached the limit of the lower realms with our sensual experience of ourselves, here too we have reached the limit of the Intelligible realm. We have touched the unity of Reality itself, but we still do not know the One Self that is beyond experience. The oneness that we touched would more accurately be called *the experience of unity*, in much the same way we called our knowledge of ourselves as physical beings, *the experience of myself.*

Analogous to that earlier experience, something about this *one* or this One Self is beyond the experiences the Intelligible realm offers, something Mind cannot touch. Whatever is beyond experience has no attributes, no distinguishing marks. However, going back to the start of this example, we see that all the terms we've used—from *the experience of myself* to *the One*—cannot entirely be separated. The divisions we make do not indicate actual pieces that we can separate one from another.

And yet, it would be equally foolish to simply throw metaphysics away. We don't want to make the mistake of concluding that there is no difference *at all* between the One and the realms of being, or among the various realms. We saw this with the example above. There is something beyond what the senses can touch, something beyond even what Mind can touch. This points us towards differences that are actual and significant.

Some students of philosophy veer towards the tendency to treat metaphysical terms as mere concepts that have no reality. Yet that is an error the Platonist can never make. These terms not only point to realities, but to the only true Realities. One of the great conflicts our practice presents us with is the need to reconcile the differences within our metaphysical map with the lack of separation among these Realities. Attempting to do so challenges the very limits of linear thinking.

To See or Not to See

Some assumptions are so fundamental to our way of thinking that we hit a wall when it comes time to question them. The notion that perceptions originate in the body and are brain functions falls into this category. We even call these perceptions our *physical senses.* An ample number of scientific studies have shown particular brain activity associated with visual, aural, or other sensory stimuli. How could anyone in this modern age deny that perceptions originate anywhere else than in the body?

However, questioning this assumption is precisely what any student wishing to go beyond conceptual insights will have to do. We must at least leave open the possibility that the physical activity that can be scientifically documented is not the origin of the perception, but is rather a physical correlate to psychical activity. In other words, perhaps perceptions are psychical and are experienced *via* the body but are not *in* the body. This is precisely the view that Plato maintained.

Plato's idea that perceptions are in the soul and the soul uses the body as an instrument may seem at first like a quaint antiquity to be forgiven due to his lack of modern scientific knowledge. With further reflection, though, we recognize that it is a critical element in the understanding of the nature of soul. In addition to assigning to soul the ability to perceive, Plato also credits soul with desires, hopes, fears, pride, and, of course, wisdom and ignorance.[6] It is the soul that primarily defines what we are as humans; the body is only a means for the soul to function in the physical realm for a certain period of time. In the *Laws,* Plato writes: "[T]he soul is in every respect different from the body;…in the present life, it causes each of us to be that which each of us is; but…body follows each of us like an image…"[7] Once the body wears out, as all physical things do, the soul journeys forward, perhaps settling into another physical vessel.[8]

Plato sprinkles this view throughout his dialogues. Consider, for example, the *Phaedrus:*

"Every soul is immortal: for that which is perpetually moved is eternal. But that which moves another and is moved by

---

[6] On the tripartite soul, see *Republic,* from 436b.

[7] 959a, trans. A. E. Taylor

[8] See for example, Plato's myth of Er, a warrior who witnessed the afterlife and then returned to tell the tale, *Republic,* from 614b.

another, when it has a cessation of motion, has also a cessation of life. Hence that alone which moves itself, because it does not desert itself, never ceases to be moved....Since then it appears that a self-motive nature is immortal, he who asserts that this is the very essence and definition of soul, will have no occasion to blush. For every body to which motion externally accedes, is inanimate. But that to which motion is inherent from itself, is animated; as if this was the very nature of soul."[9]

This view was hardly new to the Greek world when Plato put it forward. A more ancient example is Xenophanes, a Greek philosopher who lived in the sixth century BC. He declared: "It is the whole that sees, the whole that thinks, the whole that hears."[10] This whole is the Intelligible. If we as souls are of the same essence as the essence of the whole, then it follows that soul, too, sees and thinks and hears.

This view carried into the writings of the later Platonists, as well. For example, Plotinus writes: "Since the animated body is illuminated by the soul, a different part of the body differently participates of it; and the power fitted to effect a certain work is denominated according to the aptitude of the organ to the work. Thus the power in the eyes is denominated visive, in the ears acoustic..."and so on through all of the senses. Plotinus extends this reasoning to the brain, to bodily organs and to every aspect of our bodies.[11]

Anyone serious about penetrating the philosophy of the Platonists, even those who had never before questioned the modern view that sensual perceptions originate in the body, will have to address this conclusion at some point. Indeed, how can anyone fully embrace a path of using the mind to know Reality without acknowledging the intellectual nature of soul? If soul were void of perceptions and thoughts, it could hardly be called intellectual.

Time and Space

Turning the eye of the soul upward to contemplate things in themselves forces us to consider realms beyond time and space. It is easy to fall into the trap of separating ourselves from these endeavors,

---

[9] 245c~e
[10] Wheelwright (ed.), *The Presocratics,* p. 32.
[11] Ennead IV:iii:23

to think of the Intelligible as something other than ourselves. When we do this, our contemplations take on a greater theoretical and abstract quality. We compartmentalize our studies from our everyday lives. After all, what would we be if we were to remove time and space from our self-images? It is mind-boggling even to attempt it, but attempt it we must.

Recall that the creation of the physical realm marks the creation of both space and time. The physical realm is perpetual; it exists throughout all time. There could not be a physical realm prior to the creation of time, nor could there be one after a hypothetical ending of time. Likewise, we can see that time cannot exist without the physical realm. The passing of time is a kind of movement; without the physical realm, there would be nothing to move in the ways that require time. The two must therefore have come into existence together.

Yet we focus our studies on realms prior to the physical. Time and space have a tendency to creep into our contemplations of the Intelligible. At the realm of Soul, we have a foot in both worlds, so to speak. On the physical plane, soul moves through time and is subject to change. With the proper nurturing, we grow wise and flourish. In unfavorable circumstances, the opposite occurs. This moldable aspect of the soul is the level of soul which most of us find easiest to identify with. However, it is only the soul's activity that is in time. The soul's essence is divine, and that means that ultimately the soul is unchanging, for nothing can be added to or taken away from it in essence, and it is beyond time and space.

Just as we see that the physical realm is real but not ultimate reality, so too, must we acknowledge that time and space—being part of the physical realm—have a mode of existence that is real, yet they are not ultimate reality. While it is true that we function separately—you as the reader and I as the author of this book are two separate people—we see that if our essence is beyond the physical realm, then our essence is also beyond time and space. Separation is not our ultimate reality. We are not separate, and we are able to experience higher realms where connection is obvious. The implications of this are far-reaching, and they make for some powerful dialectical contemplations.

Providence vs. Grace

Grace is a concept that many people hold dear to their hearts. Those of us raised amidst one of the Biblical traditions learned that grace is God's means of reaching out to humans in what would otherwise be a cold world devoid of hope and love. Grace is God's way of showing His love for His flesh-and-blood children.

This image presents us with an analogy in which God is like the father and we are like His children. The term that links both sides of this analogy would be love, and so grace is equated with love. As God's children, we show our love by honoring and obeying our father. As father, God shows his love through grace.

By this view, devoting one's life to God is comprised of efforts to live in line with Biblical commandments, much as being obedient children means to follow our parents' rules. This analogy is in no way meant to belittle Biblical paths. Ideally, our parents know what is best for us and always have our best interests at heart. Analogously, following God is wise in that only God truly knows what is best, and God will never lead us astray. There is plenty of room for growth in systems that follow this reasoning, and much to admire about those who have the fortitude to devote their lives to the pursuit of love and compassion in the world.

Of course, grace must be an integral part of every mystic system, right? How could any spiritual system not include grace? As perplexing as it may seem on the surface, there is no room for this notion of grace in the Platonic system. The problem is that inherent in Biblical notions of this father-child relationship is an element incompatible with the divine law of providence. The implication here is that humanity and divinity are split apart, and the dichotomy this creates successfully eliminates any hope humans might have of reaching the Divine on our own. Some even view such efforts as heretical—a vain desire to build a tower of Babel.[12] Hence the need for grace.

Depending on each particular religious system, Biblical views of humanity render us small or helpless or even inherently sinful. This colors the relationship we forge with God, rendering grace a necessary factor; the only way to bridge the distance between our

---

[12] Genesis 11: 1~9.

lowly selves and the Almighty is through His compassion and love for us. All of these views share the belief that the Divine is not intelligible to us nor can we carry in our souls a perfect model of Truth.[13] Simply put, we cannot embrace the warm and fuzzy side of this teaching of grace without also accepting the distance and powerlessness that it implies. According to this view, being a good person means following the rules. Beyond that, it is God's whim to pick us up—or not.

This stands in stark contrast to our insights into providence. The law of providence, you may recall, states that reality is a hierarchy of being we each participate in to the degree that we are able. God as First Principle is called the Good as a means of denoting the providential goodness that emanates through the gods to all the realms of being.

Yet our upward journey is guided by providence as surely as the downward unfolding is. It is because of the order and goodness inherent in the very being of the cosmos that the return is possible. This return is achieved through our efforts to bring unity to our souls and thereby participate more fully in divine intelligence. In fact, our entire practice has been one of turning our focus upward and of purifying ourselves of false beliefs, so as to participate more fully in the higher reaches of the divine realms. Living in line with divine law, then, is a natural result of our purification and unification efforts. It is not in itself the means of practice.[14]

There is a common notion that God shows his love by forgiving us of our errors, and that we in turn can behave in a god-like manner by forgiving others. *To err is human; to forgive, divine.* Letting go of anger is of course a healthy thing to do, but it is not in itself an act of grace. If it were true that mistakes could be erased with the words "I forgive you," then learning would not be a factor in becoming a better person. Of course, being forgiven feels good, but it's a mistake to think that the wrong has been erased if the person you hurt is not angry. From that erroneous perspective, it seems that the ideal is to do wrong and get away with it.

From the perspective of being divine essences that reincarnate, however, no fate could be worse.[15] False beliefs that we have not seen

---

13 Cf. *Republic,* 484c~d

14 See Chapter 2 for more on this.

15 Cf. *Gorgias,* 480c~d and 527b

through in our current incarnation will be carried with us into the next. The price for wisdom is recognizing and seeing through our own ignorance. There are no shortcuts, no opportunity to be let off the hook without learning.

Living spiritually involves honoring that part of us which is divine, and living in line, to the best of our ability, with that higher aspect of what it means to be human. This requires humility. After all, we can't grow wiser without acknowledging that there is room for growth. In the *Gorgias*, Plato writes:

> "But among so many arguments, while others are confuted this alone remains unmoved, *viz.* that we ought more than anything to endeavor not to appear to be good, but to be so in reality, both in private and public. Likewise, that if anyone is in any respect vicious, he should be punished; and that this is the next good to the being just, *viz.* to become just, and to suffer through chastisement the punishment of guilt."[16]

When we hurt others, it is not enough to say "I'm sorry." Being responsible means more than letting the buck stop with you. The word *responsible* can be seen as being made up of two words: *respond* and *able*. It means being able to respond better the next time we find ourselves in a comparable situation, and that requires understanding why we acted hurtfully in the first place—what belief we were acting on and how we came to hold that false belief.

Socrates tells us: "since the soul appears to be immortal, no other flight from evils, and no other safety remains for it, than in becoming the best and wisest possible."[17] Learning and letting go of what is false are the costs of spiritual growth. Anything else is not a lifting up. Salvation without wisdom and growth is no salvation at all. This is not to say that Platonists don't recognize love in the divine order of the cosmos. Love is eternally shining down from above in the form of providence, and love likewise is what draws us to the Intelligible and to goodness here on Earth in all of its manifestations.

---

[16] 527b~c. Plato approaches this topic from a different angle in *Republic*. At 337d, Socrates is asked by a pugnacious interlocutor what punishment he deserves if he turns out to be wrong. Socrates replies: "What else but what is proper for the ignorant to suffer? And it is proper for them to learn somewhat from a wise man…."

[17] *Phaedo*, 107d.

Therefore, grace can be understood in this structure as the inclusion of providence in the unfolding of the cosmos. It is providence itself—the divine order of and goodness inherent in the cosmos—that is God's gift and an expression of His love to all of creation. Were there an actual dichotomy between the Divine and the earthly, and were we not able to participate in divine goodness to a degree commensurate with our growth, then we truly would be helpless and at the mercy of a whimsical god.

Déjà Vu All Over Again

Reincarnation is one of those staples of most mystic systems that Western societies are loath to embrace. Plato referred to the soul's changing of bodies in many of his dialogues, and other philosophers in this tradition accepted this doctrine as well. To modern Platonists, though, reincarnation can be a difficult notion to accept even as a valid hypothesis. We have grown up in societies that wholeheartedly reject this idea.

The social implications of how reincarnation would ripple through our justice system and politics are powerful—from our penal codes to our reactions to famines and human rights issues. Such a discussion stretches well beyond the scope of this book. From the more personal perspective of our spiritual practice and way of life, the implications are equally far-reaching. This issue touches the very question of why we are here.

Reincarnation is consistent with the conclusion that we are here to learn. We need to learn both the true beauty that is our essence and also how to manifest the beauty of the soul here in the physical world. What we don't learn in our current lifetime, we have the potential to learn in the next. We take our past learning with us, both the wisdom and the ignorance, and this influences our next incarnation. We continue our education in each lifetime. Regardless of our social standing, we always have exactly the circumstances we need in order to learn.

Being that we have lived thousands of lifetimes, we likely have experienced a myriad of social situations. In some lifetimes we were rich, in others we were poor. We might have been born into royalty in one lifetime and slavery in the next. We have been born into various races and nationalities, have been both male and female, have been physically vigorous in some lifetimes but sickly in others.

Each set of circumstances offers its own unique challenges and also its own unique lessons. Yet, whatever we endure on the physical plane, our essence is always divine. The significance of this is that while we cannot always control our physical circumstances, we as souls can always thrive and grow if we face whatever life offers us with openness and integrity.

Plato often offered such hypotheses in the form of myths. He ended the *Republic*, for example, with the story of a warrior named Er who died in battle and traveled to the netherworld, only to be told that he would be returning to life and was to function as a messenger. His task was to observe what happens to souls after death and to report his findings to humanity. According to the myth, he saw souls gather in a meadow. There, it was decided which would go up to the heavens and which down to Tartarus, and for how long. For the Greeks, both Tartarus and the heavens (often referred to in mythology as the Elysian Fields or the Isle of the Blessed) are parts of Hades. Neither is a permanent afterworld but rather all of Hades refers to the state the unembodied soul either suffers or enjoys between incarnations, depending on the choices that soul made in its previous lifetime.

Er also witnessed other souls returning to the meadow after their allotted time away. Once back, they gathered together and chose what their next incarnation would be. Each soul was drawn to what it most valued and repelled by what it most feared. Some chased power or wealth, only to discover after it was too late that they would suffer terribly in the chosen life.

The worst choices were made not by those coming from Tartarus, but from those returning from the heavens. He wrote of such a fated man:

> "For he did not accuse himself, as the author of his misfortunes, but fortune and destiny, and everything instead of himself. He added, that he was one of those who came from heaven, who had in his former life lived in a regulated republic, and had been virtuous by custom without philosophy."[18]

Plato is highlighting here that following rules simply because we were taught to or because we fear punishment is not the same as

---

[18] *Republic*, 619c~d

knowing what is truly good. Only the soul that has foresight and understanding can wade through all the various images of goodness and find the life that is truly happy, regardless of social measures such as wealth and status.

It is only the soul that has gained wisdom that can:

> "understand what good or evil is created by beauty when mixed with poverty, or riches, and with this or the other habit of soul…so as to be able from all these things to compute, and, having an eye to the nature of the soul, to comprehend both the worse and the better life which shall lead it to become more just, and to dismiss every other consideration."[19]

In other words, the good life is the one that will lead us to a life of philosophy and psychical health, regardless of social power and creature comforts.

In the dialogue the *Gorgias,* Plato presents another myth, this one focusing on the procedure of judging souls when they first arrive at the meadow in the afterlife. He says they are judged naked, stripped of their physical attributes and social status. The judges don't care if the soul standing before them had been a king or a pauper, popular or unpopular, rich or poor, a physical beauty or an ugly duckling. They care only about the condition of the soul. Socrates tells us that "all things are conspicuous in the soul after it is divested of body, as well whatever it possesses from nature, as those passions which the man acquired in his soul, from his various pursuits."[20] Even if the person had been highly influential in life, unhealthiness of soul will show if it is present.

> "[The judge sees] that all things in it are distorted through falsehood and arrogance, and that nothing is right, in consequence of its having been educated without truth. He likewise sees that such a soul through power, luxury, and intemperate conduct is full of inelegance and baseness. On seeing however a soul in this condition, he directly sends it into custody with disgrace…"[21]

---

[19] *Ibid.,* 618d
[20] *Gorgias,* 524d
[21] *Ibid.,* 525a

According to this myth, we are not judged by our charitable good deeds or by how many people think us good and likable; we are judged only by our condition of soul. Of course, the person who was truly charitable and kind will have this mark in the soul and not only outwardly. The one who cared more about reputation and public standing will expose a very different condition of soul when stripped naked of the body.

According to this hypothesis, then, our goal in this lifetime is to bring our souls to as healthy a condition as possible. This is done by ridding ourselves of falsehood and by recalling the truth that is our essence. When we know goodness, beauty and truth, we will not be swayed by false images of them. Socrates ends his account by concluding: "[I] consider how I may appear before my judge, with my soul in the most healthy condition. Wherefore, bidding farewell to the honours of the multitude, and looking to truth, I will endeavor to live in reality in the best manner I am able, and when I die to die so."[22]

Platonism recognizes a difference between acting out fate on the one hand and, on the other, participating in providence. We bring a certain disposition and state of mind to each lifetime. When placed in the circumstances we found ourselves in at birth, a certain course unfolds. We have free will, but our choices will likely fit within the parameters determined by those who influence us, our beliefs, and our mindset. Most of us move along through life in this manner, fated as it were to a certain lifestyle while, hopefully, picking up a few lessons along the way.

However, we always have the power to jump outside of our conditioning. We can choose to turn and look at this very dynamic of which we are a part, this divine intellect that plays itself out through the unfolding of the cosmos. Instead of running through a maze like rats, we can stand back and look at the maze itself to understand the whole of which we are a part. Plato presented this mythologically as the reign of Cronus, Intellect. He contrasted it with the age of Zeus, who rules over the mundane realm where fate plays itself out.[23]

When we finally choose to know our essence and its source, we are no longer limiting ourselves to our physical existence and the laws of

---

[22] *Ibid.*, 526d~e

[23] See *Politicus*, 269a~274e. Also, Proclus discusses this myth in *Theology of Plato*, bk. 5, ch. 9.

fate tied to it. We are instead rising to the level of intellect and so opening ourselves to greater participation in the laws of providence: the divine goodness we each participate in to the degree we are able. Plato called such a life the life of philosophy, and through the character of Socrates he presented it as the destiny of us all.

Chapter 24: Participation, Part 2—
The Problem of One and Many

"[C]ontinuing to be the self-same [One], it co-exists with that which proceeds as a certain characteristic…"

Damascius[1]

The Quandary

The process of integrating the divisions we have made often hinges on working through apparent paradoxes, which are an inevitable byproduct of reducing divine functions to a name and a description. For example, *one* and *many* raise a lot of questions. Namely, how does *many* proceed from *one*?

In one sense, this is really just another way of posing the questions raised by the notion of participation. How does unified Reality become the many absolute Realities that we commonly call Ideas or Forms? How do these absolute Realities, each a one, proceed into the multiplicity of the physical world around us? For example, how does absolute Beauty give itself to each of the many things we recognize as beautiful?

Socrates raises the challenge in the dialogue *Philebus:*

"Whether we should suppose every such monad to be dispersed and spread abroad amongst an infinity of things generated or produced, and thus, from being one, to become many; or whether we should suppose it to remain entire, itself by itself, separate and apart from that multitude. But, of all suppositions, this might appear the most impossible, that one and the same thing should be in a single one, and in many, at the same time."[2]

Seeing through this apparent paradox was recognized as a major challenge by all the great thinkers in this tradition, as Plotinus acknowledges:

"For now indeed the soul perceives the necessity of the existence of these things. It desires, however, to understand this

---

[1] *Problems and Solutions Concerning First Principles,* p. 123

[2] 15b

which is so much spoken of by the wise men of antiquity, *viz.* how from *The One* being such as we have said it is, each thing has its subsistence, whether it be multitude, or the duad, or number; and why The One did not abide in itself, but so great a multitude flowed from it..."[3]

Much like being trapped in quicksand, we find that we sink deeper into this quandary the more we struggle to get out of it. Damascius captures this dilemma beautifully in his notes on Plato's *Philebus:*

"Why does this question of one and many cause us such perplexity? Because, when they coincide, we do not understand how opposites can go together. Yet there would be more reason for perplexity, if the many existed without unity; for they would so completely disintegrate as to be non-existent. On the other hand, the one without the many will be sterile as it were, or isolated; in fact, it will merely be a minimal quantity, as current opinion believes it to be."[4]

The Way Out

Plato tackled the one-many problem both from the perspective of creation itself and from the questions surrounding participation. We will look at the *Philebus* shortly to consider the mystery of creation. As for the problems of participation, Plato took those on most directly perhaps in the *Parmenides*. He raised a number of dilemmas associated with this issue, many of which were summarized in Chapter 12. The most pressing challenge quite possibly came in the form of the Third Man Argument. To briefly summarize, that argument suggests that the Idea itself is one of the things collected among participants, and therefore we always have to look beyond the Idea for an earlier cause. It points to an infinite expanse of causes without ever reaching a first cause. Plato recognized that this argument demonstrates a lack of understanding of divine functions. He pointed to the way out in this exchange between Parmenides and his gifted student, the young Socrates:

---

[3] Ennead V:i:6.
[4] Damascius, *Lectures on the Philebus*, p. 24.

" 'Perhaps, O Parmenides, each of these forms is nothing more than an intellectual conception, which ought not to subsist anywhere but in the soul...'

That Parmenides said, 'What then? Is each of these conceptions one, but at the same time a conception of nothing?'

That Socrates said, 'This is impossible.'

'It is a conception, therefore, of something?'

'Certainly.'

'Of being or of non-being?'

'Of being.' "[5]

We may be tempted to use this line of thinking to generate creative arguments, such as suggesting that there is an Idea for purple elephants because they exist as a figment of my imagination. If they exist in my mind, then they have being (or so this reasoning goes). However, we must remember that in the parlance of Platonism, *being* refers only to intelligible Realities. That which exists in our material world and as thoughts in our imaginations are in the realm of *becoming*, or *generation*. Parmenides, then, is leading Socrates to the conclusion that Ideas are intelligible and so they transcend the infinite regress of the Third Man Argument.

As we touched on back in Chapter 12, the entire dialectical exercise that is the heart of the *Parmenides* can be seen as a response to Socrates' questions and confusion around the issue of participation. Parmenides explores the One at each hypostasis, starting from the transcendent One itself. He then explores how the One functions as an immanent cause that enters into the procession of unfolding realms of reality. The absolute Realities, in turn, imitate this pattern, starting as transcendent henads and flowing through all the realms until reaching the realm of matter. In matter, we find only a passive receiver of reason-principles.

Proclus carried on this basic vision, but more openly unfolded the metaphysics behind it. He called this transcendent cause the imparticipable principle. In describing the vertical progression from first principles down to our material world, he showed that each chain

---

[5] *Parmenides*, 132b

of causality must start with a monad that is the exempt principle cause of that chain.[6] The terms *imparticipable* and *unparticipated* are used to indicate that these causes are outside of their respective chain.

There is an unparticipated monad for each of the realms, as well as for each of the absolute Realities. As causes, they are beyond that which they are the cause of, much as the One itself is beyond all that *is* precisely because it is the cause of all that *is*. The unparticipated monad of Justice, for example, transcends the proliferation of justice at each realm, the unparticipated monad of Soul transcends its whole chain of self-motive subsequents. The One-Being is the unparticipated monad of Being, and as such transcends the realms of Being. In fact, all of the unparticipated monads have their hyparxis beyond Being. As such, we cannot directly experience or know them in the way we can know that which *is*.

These causes transcend their subsequents and so are unparticipated in relation to them. However, they are still dependent on the One itself as their cause. This point is, admittedly, confusing. In relation to the One they are caused and so in that sense they are said to be monads that participate the One. Yet, in relation to their chain of subsequents, they are gods that transcend the chain by being its cause. In this sense, they are unparticipated. "*Qua* caused," Proclus explains, "it is a participant, not an unparticipated principle; *qua* unparticipated, it is a cause of the participated and not itself a participant."[7]

After the imparticipable principle comes the participable cause. Here you have that which is most fully that which it is a cause of: Justice that is most truly justice, Soul that is most truly soul, and so on. It is the participable monad of Being that is the object of peak experiences, for that is Being that is most truly being; that is Reality itself. These participable causes comprise the realm of Forms or Ideas, what I have been referring to as absolute Realities.

---

[6] See *The Elements of Theology*, props. 23 and 24:

> Prop. 23: "Every imparticipable gives subsistence from itself to things which are participated. And all participated hypostases are extended to imparticipable hyparxes."

> Prop. 24: "Everything which participates is inferior to that which is participated; and that which is participated is inferior to that which is imparticipable."

[7] *Ibid.*, prop. 99.

The term *participable* implies that these monads give something of themselves to their participants. The cause in and of itself is never changed, yet it is affected by its participants in the sense of manifesting differently at each realm or level of its unfolding. "Every God, from that order from which he began to unfold himself into light, proceeds through all secondary natures, always indeed multiplying and dividing the communications of himself, but preserving the peculiarity of his own hypostasis."[8]

The third in rank is the participant, which receives the power of the cause to the degree it is able to. This power flows down through unity, through vitality, through intellect and so on all the way down to the bodily form. Proclus explains:

> "all things are suspended from the Gods. And different natures are illuminated by different Gods; every divine series extending as far as to the last of things. And some things indeed are suspended from the Gods immediately, but others through a greater or less number of media. But all things are full of Gods. And whatever anything naturally possesses, it derives from the Gods."[9]

Proclus ties a bow on this image of the vertical progression of unfolding reality by clarifying that the flow is continuous; there are no gaps between grades.[10] With this, we have a concise theory that allows us to conceptually see the flow of reality from the imparticipable principle to the participated monad and through all the grades of participants. We put the Third Man Argument to rest by recognizing that the imparticipable monad transcends the procession of participants and therefore cannot be added to the group of things that share that Form or Idea, while each Form or Idea as a participated monad gives its quality to its participants without itself being changed or affected.

The vertical progression is, of course, coupled with the vertical return as discussed in previous chapters. The Third Man Argument treats the Ideas as abstract concepts rather than as absolute Realities that unfold and return to their cause. This vertical progression and

---

[8] *Ibid.,* prop. 125
[9] *Ibid.,* prop. 145
[10] *Ibid.,* prop. 147

return as Proclus describes it gives us, in contrast, a more mature understanding of unfolding reality. "The imparticipable must always precede the participated. This is Plato's doctrine in the theory of Ideas, and it is for this reason that he says that a character as it is in itself is prior to its existence in something else."[11]

Still, though, our picture is not yet complete. We need to add to this image that this is the vertical unfolding of realms only. It is easy to get caught up in the complexities of this schema and lose sight of the profundity added by what we might call the horizontal breadth of each realm. Although Proclus is perhaps best known for his metaphysical descriptions of the vertical progression, he also went to great lengths to paint with words the beauty and majesty of each realm as a whole world.

The imparticipable principles, for example, are not atomized entities separate from one another—Justice here and Beauty there. Rather, all is in all at each realm in a way appropriate to each realm. Even here in our realm of materiality, we would be hard pressed to completely separate justice from beauty even though we can distinguish one from the other. This is even more so in the divine realms, which are unified to a degree beyond any example we can point to in the physical world. On this point Proclus writes:

> "Consequently, we must not suppose that the Ideas are altogether unmixed and without community with one another, nor must we say, on the other hand, that each one is all of them....We must say that each of them is precisely what it is and preserves its specific nature undefiled, but also partakes of the others without confusion, not by becoming one of them, but by participating in the specific nature of that other and sharing its own nature with it."[12]

This interflowing unity of the absolute Realities exists at each realm at a power proper to that realm. Damascius shared a similar vision, described succinctly in this passage about the first three realms [referred to here as substance (or being), life, and intellect]:

> "Therefore, substance is a perfectly complete world that gathers all things in the undifferentiated, and intellect is a perfectly

---

[11] *Proclus' Commentary on Plato's Parmenides*, sec. 1242, p. 580.

[12] *Ibid.*, sec. 754, p. 125.

complete world subsisting in the differentiated aspect of its nature, and life is a perfectly complete world that gives birth to all things in the aspect of the middle term that is subject to differentiation."[13]

It is when we put the horizontal breadth of each realm together with the vertical progression that we start to grasp the complexity of the absolute Realities unfolding through subsequent worlds of diminishing power and with a commensurate degree of increasing differentiation. As Proclus puts it in his explication of Plato's *Parmenides:* "In all the preceding discussion he [Plato] understood 'participation' in the sense of the organization into unity of the things that come after Being itself."[14] This more holistic image allows us to finally start to understand *participation* as this receiving of essence and power from prior realms.

The Mystery Deepens

It is easy to feel that now we understand this whole issue of participation. But do we? We need to take a step back and look again at the fundamentals of this issue, for we will never fully grasp what *participation* means—and therefore what Plato, with a little help from Proclus, is really pointing us towards—without looking more deeply at what is actually being signified by the terms *one* and *many*. Consider this passage from Plato's *Philebus:* "[T]hose beings said to be forever derive their essence from one and many; and therefore have in themselves bound and infinity connatural to them."[15]

Plato is stating, in other words, that the One-Being—the transcendent fountain from which all existents flow—is the result of the blending of the finite and the infinite: "God, we said, has exhibited *the infinite,* and also *the bound* of beings…Let us take these for two of the species of things; and for a third let us take that, which is composed of those two mixed together."[16] This now gives us three classes: the infinite, the bound and the mixed.

---

[13] *Problems and Solutions Concerning First Principles,* p. 269.

[14] *Proclus' Commentary on Plato's Parmenides,* sec. 1242, p. 580.

[15] 16d.

[16] 23d, italics included

A fourth class is added, namely "Of that commixture, the combination of the former two, consider the cause: and besides those three species, set me down this cause for a fourth."[17] This fourth class is initially credited to *sophia* and *nous*, or wisdom and mind, respectively.[18] Later in the dialogue, Socrates clarifies that this cause of the combination goes beyond our usual understanding of wisdom and mind to the Good or the One.[19] Indeed, what could be the cause of the super-essential dyad of the bound and the infinite uniting except the First Cause of all, which is ultimately the cause of all unity? And so Plato tells us in this passage that the bound and the infinite are somehow mixed because of the One and the result, mysteriously perhaps, is the fountain of Being. If we have any hope of making sense of this, we need to better understand what is meant by the terms used to name these classes.

Damascius calls the bound the *one-all* because it is "the One before all things…"[20] He recognizes the infinite also as being one, since it is neither divided nor a unified many. He called it the *all-one* and describes it as "simply many, so that it is all things, yet all things neither as divided nor as Unified, for it is all things not as participating in, but as being itself manyness."[21]

In our struggles to understand the *Philebus*, we tend to make the error of reducing the four classes to a simple math equation, as if we could simply add together the One, the bound and the infinite and then One-Being will result. Or we envision something along the lines of two ingredients being combined in a cauldron, with the One as the spoon that mixes them. Damascius warns us that we must go beyond such imagery:

> "the principles [i.e., the bound and the infinite] are both one and many, not in terms of an inherent quality, nor number, nor in terms of quantity, nor a quantitative nature, nor because of the principle of quality nor any qualified nature, but by being beyond all and every such conception….Perhaps it would have

---

[17] *Ibid.*

[18] 30c

[19] 64e~65a

[20] *Problems and Solutions Concerning First Principles*, p. 186

[21] *Ibid.*

been better, if this too were allowable, not to render the two as two monads, but to make the two principles a dyadic one, just as one might think of the one of the dyad. But not even this method can actually reach those principles…"[22]

Damascius' suggestion to avoid separating the bound and the infinite is reminiscent of what Proclus wrote in his *Theology of Plato*. He presents the bound as what we might call the truly one, and the infinite as its infinite power:

"nor in reality is that which is the first The One; for, as has been frequently said, it is better than The One. Where therefore is that which is most properly and entirely one? Hence there is a certain one prior to being, which gives subsistence to being, and is primarily the cause of it….If however this one is the cause of being, and constitutes it, there will be a power in it generative of being."[23]

We have to keep in mind here that the One is pure; it has no parts. Further, the bound and the infinite are said to be undifferentiated from it. Damascius reminds us that we should not think of the bound and the infinite as either one or two, because they are prior to number.[24] In other words, they are not separate from the One, even

---

[22] *Ibid.*, p. 188, brackets added. On the notion of both terms being both one and many, see also p. 180: "The first of the two principles was itself all things, but in the sense of what tended to have more of the form of limit; the second was likewise all things, but in the sense of what tended to be more unlimited." On p. 193, he explains that it is "not the case that either of the two principles is divided such that each is a principle of one of the elements, that is, one as the principle of the limit, and the other as the principle of the unlimited. Rather, each of the two is the principle of all things, one is the principle of all things as differentiated and many and indefinite, or however [one likes to express it], and the other is the principle of all things as unified, and as ones, and as informed by limit." Brackets included in text. *The limit* is an alternative translation for *the bound; the unlimited* is an alternative translation for *the infinite*.

[23] *The Theology of Plato*, bk. 3, ch. 3. Compare to Damascius, who presents the finite, the infinite, and being as three aspects of the same father, following the Chaldean triad of father, power, intellect. *Problems and Solutions Concerning First Principles*, p. 400: "Thus the father is one, and the indefinite power of the one is many, and the intellect of the father is all things."

[24] See *Problems and Solutions Concerning First Principles*, p. 187.

though we give them different names. As the cause of the One-Being, the One itself can be said to extend into the bound and the infinite, although it does so without any activity on its part. Yet as that which is ineffable, the One itself is that for the sake of which the bound and the infinite function as a cause.[25] It is not that the One itself actually mixes the bound and the infinite, for the One itself does not *do* anything. Rather, it is the bound's and the infinite's desire to return to the goodness of their cause that results in their uniting into the first Being.

Now we are brought back to our original puzzle, the one Plato had presented to us in the *Philebus*. The mystery of how the many come from one has deepened. Now we are looking at the truly one and the infinite power of one, mixed by their desire for the One itself, and the result is the *not-one* or *the mixed*. When we consider the conditions for this *not-one's* existence we are forced to concede that whatever this *not-one* is, it is strange to imagine it being completely different from *one*. Bread, for example, is not flour, but it has the taste of flour; it is not butter, but it has the taste of butter. Likewise, One-Being is not the One, and indeed the One is completely incommensurate and transcendent, yet in another sense it has what we might call the "taste" of the One. Recognizing this points us to the true mystery of the unfolding of Being and of all that in any way exists.

---

[25] See *Philebus* from 53b. Socrates concludes at 54c that: "Now that, for the sake of which is always generated whatever is generated for some end, must be in the rank of things which are good…"

Chapter 25: Dialectic Revisited: Diving In

"But I think you do not give dialectic to any other than one who philosophizes purely and justly."

Plato[1]

Those readers who have been doing the actual work outlined thus far have probably developed a fairly detailed metaphysical map of reality by this stage, and are able to discuss philosophy with some degree of proficiency. Perhaps you've even had some experiences that point to your having at least glimpsed the Intelligible realm, the upper world of Plato's allegory of the cave. This is a happy period for most of us, marked by a sense of accomplishment.

Go ahead and pat yourself on the back if you feel the urge to do so, but then it's time to get back to work. We've purified our energy enough to participate in Intellect, but more purification is still necessary. The highest reaches of the Intelligible have yet to open to us, and false assumptions about Reality still function as obstacles.

The way to move forward is to raise our own questions, to find our own unique problems and confusion. No question will grab us quite like our own. Early on, it is helpful to follow a teacher's lead. Teachers have far-reaching insights and so can prod us with inquiries we hadn't even considered. In this second leg of our journey, though, we are ready to venture off on our own to some degree, although a teacher's input is always invaluable.

Reading, meditations and dialectical contemplations are all ways to uncover our own confusion and raise our own questions. We will therefore take the practices already discussed and adapt them to this later leg of our journey. Let's start off with a more in-depth look at what dialectic is, one that builds on the simplified version of dialectic presented earlier, and see how to incorporate it into our practice.

Dialectic

The copestone and quite possibly the most famous component of Plato's spiritual system is his dialectic. It consists of a precise method of questioning ourselves so as to reveal the assumptions of our arguments. To most people today, mentions of Plato's dialectic

---

[1] *Sophist,* 253e

conjure up images of Socrates playing verbal acrobatics with pompous intellectuals. However, dialectic has a loftier goal than that.

Chapter 19 introduced dialectic as an exploration of the nature of some object of inquiry, and that object's function. We are going to see a more formal structure of questions in this chapter. Plato perhaps presents his methodology most concisely through the characterization of the great philosopher Parmenides. In the dialogue bearing his name, Parmenides explains that a thorough inquiry requires considering not just what a thing is, but also how its functioning affects itself and others:

> "[C]oncerning everything which is supposed either to be or not to be, or influenced in any manner by any other passion [experience/interaction], it is necessary to consider the consequences both to itself and to each individual of other things, which you may select for this purpose, and towards many, and towards all things in a similar manner; and again, how other things are related to themselves, and to another which you establish, whether you consider that which is the subject of your hypothesis as having a subsistence or as not subsisting; if, being perfectly exercised, you design through proper media to perceive the truth."[2]

As we did back in Chapter 19, we start by choosing the subject we want to focus on. We previously used *soul* as our example. Other possibilities include any of the five genera of Being: motion, rest, sameness[3], difference, and being. We could also choose an absolute Reality such as Beauty or Justice, or even stretch beyond the metaphysical Realities to ponder the super-essentials or the One itself. For any hypothesis beginning with "If X exists...,"[4] we can break down the quote above into four categories.

We want to look at X:

> ➢ In regards to itself
> ➢ In regards to others

---

[2] *Parmenides*, 136b~c, brackets added.

[3] *Self*, as you may recall from Chapter 14, is another possible translation of *sameness*. Here, of course, we would be using the term *self* at a level commensurate with the five genera of being, not as the *One Self*.

[4] Of course, when X is the One itself, we use the word *exist* loosely

Then we want to look at other things that interact with X (We choose the parameters. If we are exploring soul, for example, "others" might be body):

> ➤ In regards to themselves (in light of X functioning as it does)
> ➤ In regards to X

The Four Activities of Dialectic

We are going to expand these four categories into a series of 24 (yes, 24!) questions, but let's take a step back before doing that. For many students new to contemplating metaphysics in this way, the formal list of questions makes dialectic seem rather stiff. It helps to think of this format as a way of giving structure and accuracy to four activities we are engaging in when we ponder the formal dialectic questions. These four activities are not discussed all together in any of Plato's dialogues, but they were credited to him at least at the revised Platonic Academy.[5] Proclus, who admittedly is not known for his accessible approach to metaphysics, actually does shine some light on dialectic by focusing on these four activities.

He writes of dialectic that it:

"places the mind at the outset in the region of thought where it is most at home, looking at truth itself, "sitting on a sacred pedestal" [*Phaedrus*, 254b] which Socrates says unfolds before the mind the whole intelligible world, making its way from Form to Form until it reaches the very first Form of all, sometimes using analysis, sometimes definition, now demonstrating, now dividing, both moving downwards from above and upwards from below until, having examined in every way the whole nature of the intelligible, it climbs aloft to that which is beyond all being."[6]

---

[5] See Damascius, *Lectures on the Philebus*. References to these four activities are scattered throughout. One particularly clear example is on p. 26, where Damascius writes among other references: "Socrates' subject is primarily the methods of division and analysis, but ultimately the whole of dialectic, of which the four methods are parts."

[6] *Proclus' Commentary on Plato's Parmenides*, sec. 653, p. 43, brackets included. Discussion of these four activities is scattered throughout this writing. See especially pp. 334~340.

It is tempting to try matching these four activities—dividing, defining, demonstrating, and analyzing—to the four basic categories on the previous page. While there is some correlation, we will find that they do not directly correspond, one activity to each category. Rather, these four activities describe the overall process that we are going through as we tackle the full series of questions. With this in mind, let's look at each activity individually. We will then put these activities together with our 24 questions to get the full picture of how to use dialectic.

Dividing: Our initial division is simply the act of choosing our topic of inquiry. That decision separates it off from everything else. As we go on, we will continue making divisions—Soul is incorporeal not physical, for example. It is life-giving, not inanimate. And so on. Plato demonstrates the use of division in the dialogue the *Politicus* [aka the *Statesman*] and, a bit more tongue-in-cheek, in the dialogue the *Sophist.*

Defining: Closely tied to dividing is the notion of defining that which has been separated off. Defining necessarily involves both sameness and difference. If there were no difference, there would be no basis on which to divide what is being defined from everything else. Yet, if there were no sameness, there would have been no initial connection prior to division. There can be no division without sameness.

To see a simple example of this, imagine we are defining *cat*. We may start with a rudimentary definition that a cat is an animal that meows. The inclusion of the word *animal* is recognition that cats share a sameness with dogs, rabbits and other such species, as well as a difference from everything else, from chairs to amoebas. The first division, then, was in separating cats from everything else. The second division was separating animals from non-animals.

At the same time, noting that *this* animal meows shows that we recognize some way in which cats are different from other animals. Our initial definition, then, recognized both sameness, in that cats are animals, and difference, in that cats are different from animals that moo or bark or are silent like rabbits. And so we continue dividing and defining in this way, recognizing both sameness and difference as we go. As we run through these steps subsequent times, we can expand our definition to include such features as *mammal, feline, small* and *house pet*. These terms also, of course, express both sameness and difference from other things.

Demonstrating: In our dialectical explorations, we are focusing not on cats but on absolute Realities such as Providence or Soul, or we are looking even above these to their cause. Therefore, we have to see how these divine names unfold throughout the realms of reality. To put that another way, once we define our object of inquiry, we are ready to consider how it functions. We look at our divine object of inquiry in relation to others, such as soul in relation to bodies. We also look at how the others function with one another in light of the object of inquiry functioning as it does. For example, how do bodies function in light of soul functioning as it does?

Proclus tells us that "definition is the beginning of demonstration."[7] The significance of this statement is that we should not cut corners or skip steps. Of course, we can—and should—run through these exercises multiple times, continually refining them. Still, the quality of our contemplation at each stage builds on the previous stages. We must make the right divisions in order to properly define, and the better our definitions, the better our demonstrations. Proclus wrote: "Definition is a more august and sovereign art than Demonstration, and Division in turn than Definition. Division gives to Definition its first principles, but not vice versa."[8] Therefore, getting the early stages right is key, as everything else falls into place after that. This is one of the ways in which dialectic forces us to question our assumptions.

Analyzing: We are now ready to complete the circle by bringing everything we have thought about back to our original divine object of inquiry. Whereas demonstrating pulled us down into the lower realms, analyzing returns us to the cause. Proclus beautifully describes the role of analysis in returning us to causes, to that which is simple and universal:

> "Analysis also should be included among these arts. For it serves as complement to Demonstration, inasmuch as it leads us to analyse effects into their causes; and to Definition, inasmuch as it proceeds from the composite to the more

---

[7] *Proclus' Commentary on Plato's Parmenides*, sec. 980, p. 335.

[8] *Ibid.*, sec. 982, p. 336

simple; and to Division, inasmuch as it proceeds from the particular to the universal..."[9]

Forming Our Questions

Now that we have some idea of what it is we are trying to do with dialectic, let's return to the four categories we saw at the start of this section. We want to make them more user-friendly by generating questions out of these categories:

If X exists:

1: **What can we say about X in regards to itself?** What is it? What is its nature? What is it in essence? What, for example, is Soul? Dividing and defining largely function here.

2: **What can we say about X in regards to others?** In other words, how does X function? What does it do? What is its good? Now we are getting into demonstration. We are thinking about what effects X gives in its unfolding. For example, what can we say about Soul in regards to bodies? What effects does Soul give to bodies in its extension into the physical realm?

3: **What can we say about the others in regards to themselves?** Again, this centers us in demonstration. This time, our focus is on the implications of X functioning as it does. How do the others interact with one another because X is functioning? For example, how do we as bodies interact with one another because Soul is functioning as it does?

4: **What can we say about the others in regards to X?** To continue with our example, we would ask what we can say about bodies in regards to Soul. This question is most closely tied to analysis. By considering how the others interact with X, we are taking all of the effects we generated in questions 2 and 3 and returning them to their cause. We are seeing here the implications of all we have worked out. If absurdities result, then we know we must have made an error in one or more of the earlier stages. To the degree we are not satisfied with our conclusions, we must go back to the start and

---

[9] *Ibid.*

repeat the process. Each time, though, we have hopefully gained some insights that we can build on.

This is not so different from what we saw back in Chapter 19. In fact, the activities of dividing, defining, demonstrating and analyzing are very much what we are always trying to do whenever we contemplate anything. With dialectic, we are simply making our contemplations more systematic and precise. Our goal is to define the object of inquiry and then to explore all of its interactions. Therefore, we are considering how the object of inquiry functions and the implications of that.

Building Our Structure

With these basic four questions, we are ready to build on this structure. For each of these four questions, we want to consider three things:

    A. What is true

    B. What is not true

    C. What is partly true and partly not true

This will extend the list of questions to 12, if we take A, B and C above as each a separate question. We then do the same for the hypothesis beginning "If X does not exist or is not functioning..." Therefore, the formal list of questions that comprise all the considerations of the dialectic will total 24.[10]

Admittedly, this method is cumbersome in the beginning. It takes practice to get the knack of it. Once we do get used to this pattern of questioning, though, it becomes second nature to think about metaphysics in terms of essence, function and implications.

To help us get started, Proclus offers a few examples. He took the hypothesis beginning "If soul exists" and wrote out responses to all 24 questions.[11] It is a lengthy piece, but well worth studying in whole. For our purposes, I have summarized the first 12 of his responses (addressing the question "if soul exists, what follows?") so as to clarify

---

[10] The complete list of 24 questions can also be found in *Proclus' Commentary of Plato's Parmenides*, sec. 1002, p. 352.

[11] See *ibid.*, secs. 104~6, pp. 354~6. For "the others," Proclus contrasted soul with body.

the methodology. I have organized his responses to correspond with the four categories in which I have presented the questions.

What can we say about soul in relation to itself? What is soul? (Dividing/Defining)

  1. **What is *true* about soul in relation to itself?**

   - Essential life; soul is the source of life in the physical realm

   - Self-motive; soul moves itself rather than being moved from an outside force

  2. **What is *not true* about soul in relation to itself?**

   - Moved from outside itself

   - Total ignorance of itself

  3. **What is *partly true and partly not true* about soul in relation to itself?**

   - Eternal existence: soul is immortal yet it is subject to change through time;

   - Indivisibility: soul is one, yet we experience soul as separate or individual

What can we say about soul in regards to body? How does soul function? (Demonstration)

  4. **What is *true* about soul in relation to body?**

   - Soul is productive of life to bodies because it is the principle/source of life

   - Soul initiates motion in those bodies it rules over

  5. **What is *not true* about soul in relation to body?**

   - Having no interaction

   - Being the cause of changelessness

  6. **What is *partly true and partly not true* about soul in relation to body?**

   - Soul being present to bodies: present by providence, yet separate in essence

What can we say about bodies in regards to themselves, in light of soul functioning as it does? What are the implications of soul functioning as it does? (Demonstration)

7. **What is *true* about bodies in relation to themselves?**

- Sympathetic affection: it is because of soul that we have compassion for one another and feel connection to one another.

8. **What is *not true* about bodies in relation to themselves?**

- Lack of sensation: it is by the presence of soul that bodies experience sensation

9. **What is *partly true and partly not true* about bodies in relation to themselves?**

- Bodies move themselves: it is actually soul that is motive, yet in another sense we can say that because of soul, bodies move themselves

What can we say about bodies in regards to soul? Here we are taking the effects we generated in (2) and (3) above and returning them to their cause, soul. (Analysis)

10. **What is *true* about bodies in relation to soul?**

- Bodies are preserved through soul and dependent on soul.

11. **What is *not true* about bodies in relation to soul?**

- Filled with lifelessness

12. **What is *partly true and partly not true* about bodies in relation to soul?**

- Participation: body participates in soul as a passive receiver of psychical reason-principles, yet as a passive receiver of natural and other reason-principles, it does not participate in soul.

This collectively gives us a brief run-through of the first half of a dialectic exploration, examining what follows if soul exists. It is the result of Proclus going through a series of divisions as he honed his definition. From that foundation, he went on to demonstration and analysis. As we do this on our own, we aim to tighten our definition over time and to correct any earlier errors. When we have the best definition we are currently able to form, we continue the list of questions to explore soul's functioning and the implications that follow.

After that, we would use the hypothesis "If soul does not exist or is not functioning" for questions 13~24. By looking at the possibility of soul *not* functioning, we can better see how preposterous that possibility is. This can trigger meaningful insights as well. To demonstrate this, let's look at some of the responses Proclus offered to the hypothesis "If soul does not exist or is not functioning:"

13. **What is *true* about soul in relation to itself?**
   If soul did not exist or were not functioning, non-existence, lifelessness, and mindlessness would follow. This is because soul possesses being, life and intellect.

14. **What is *not true* about soul in relation to itself?**
   None of the powers we attribute to soul would be true of it: such as self-preservation and self-motion.

15. **What is *partly true and partly not true* about soul in relation to itself?**
   Being an object of knowledge: if it did not exist, how could it be an object of knowledge? Yet, if it did not exist, it could not have the nature of being unknowable.

One thing that probably jumped out at you right away while reading these examples is that a person who did not already have some insights into soul could not have generated these lists. What's worse, a person filled with false beliefs about soul might have generated very different responses to each question. You might be wondering, therefore, what benefit dialectic holds for those of us who fall short of Proclus' experience and vision.

Actually, though, it is in our shortcomings and our confusion that we see dialectic's benefits. Our early attempts at dialectic tend to be academic-like efforts to follow the steps and to recall various things we've read. Once we've learned the basics of this metaphysical system, though, we are able to add logical reasoning to the mix. Where an earlier dialectical exploration highlighted false assumptions that had slipped into our responses, our continued reading will challenge those assumptions. As time goes on and our studies continue, questions jump out, nagging us and pulling us deeper in, until our explorations in due course evolve into true contemplations.

Our questions and dialectical explorations also shape our approach to reading. Early in our practice, we read books from cover to cover to get the overall image the author has painted.[12] When we are new to metaphysics, or to the Platonic presentation of metaphysics, it makes sense to employ that practice we learned in Chapter 5 of reading just what is on the page. We want to clear our thoughts of as many assumptions as we possibly can.

Later on, though, we will have developed some suppositions that we want to test and open up further. We still follow the basic practice of reading just what is on the page, but now we are guided by some aspect of our inquiry that is especially puzzling. Different questions press us at different times, and this means that we are likely to notice things that we might not have were it not for those nagging questions in the backs of our minds. For example, perhaps thinking about how bodies are affected by soul in the sample dialectical exploration above illuminated doubts about what exactly it means to say that body "participates" in soul, or that soul "participates" in Intellect.

If I had questions about participation in my mind while reading, say, Proclus' *Elements of Theology*, they would bring attention not only to those propositions that deal with participation directly,[13] but also to a proposition such as 98: "Every separate cause is at one and the same time everywhere and nowhere." Proclus goes on to demonstrate that as transcendent entities, causes are nowhere, yet as imminent entities they are everywhere. The argument is interesting in and of itself, but when combined with questions about participation, a new

---

[12] The works cited throughout this book are all examples of this. Most of Plato's dialogues are tightly knit units with a distinct introduction and conclusion. Plotinus' *Enneads* are beautiful images packaged in pure poetry. Proclus' *Elements of Theology* presents the One prior to Being and then systematically unfolds all the realms of Being from the Intelligible down to the soul. He does it in far greater detail in his *Theology of Plato*, reaching down to the physical realm. Damascius, too, takes on a systematic exploration in his *Problems and Solutions Concerning First Principles*. The inquiry guiding that entire work is how the One ever split into many. All of these books are in the bibliography.

[13] Namely, props. 21~24 and 65~69. Discussions about participation can also be found throughout his *Commentary on Plato's Parmenides*.

line of inquiry is opened. How are our notions of participation affected by eliminating the physical limitations of spatial locality? In other words, when we consider that a cause such as Soul exists both everywhere and nowhere, how does this change our understanding of what it means for ensouled bodies to participate in Soul?

Exploring Our Own Questions

As we read and contemplate metaphysics, we will find ourselves ruminating on various puzzles. Any one of these puzzles can be an ideal launch pad for a dialectic inquiry. In fact, the way we frame the issue will itself highlight at least some of the assumptions that we are bringing to the table. As an example, I'll present one of the puzzles that I had struggled with myself, which formed out of a contemplation on a peak experience. I have never before—or since—come across another person who posed this problem in exactly this way, although I imagine there are many out there who have. Still, the question was not influenced by anyone else; it was a product of my own state of mind.

I will call this *the merging versus recognition question*. I had used this question to explore my assumptions about peak experiences. Many teachers, both within and outside of the Platonic tradition, have offered hints and glimpses of such experiences. Often, it is described as a merging of sorts, such as in this passage from Damascius: "It is true that we encounter the One as knowable from afar, and when we have become one with it, then we transcend our own ability to know the One and we are resolved into being the One, that is, into the unknowable instead of the knowable."[14]

Other times, the experience is described as more of a recognition, in which we instantly know that we are *that*, and that thinking that we were ever anything else was just an illusion. As Plotinus writes: "As the One does not contain any difference, it is always present and we are present to it when we no longer contain difference."[15]

We can try to join the two by arguing that first we merge and then we recognize that the differences were only illusions. The problem is, these two models are to some degree irreconcilable. Recognition implies sameness of two or more things, with only perception having

---

[14] *Problems and Solutions Concerning First Principles*, p. 126
[15] Ennead VI:ix:8, trans. Elmer O'Brien

given the appearance of separation. Script writers commonly use recognition as a technique in television and movies, such as when a protagonist dreams of being heroic, only to discover by the end of the story that he or she was courageous all along and just hadn't realized it. Merging, on the other hand, implies an actual separation that becomes extinguished. The merging of two corporations is one example. The question then becomes: which model is better? And if we want to save both models, how can there be a merging where there is no true difference?

In some cases of merging, it is the thing itself that differs. A cocktail, for example, is a merging of different liquids into a single concoction. In other cases, the difference is one of location. Think of grease floating on the top of a liquid surface. Two grease patches can be merged together, creating one large patch. In both of these examples, the merging created something new, a combination of its parts. In the first case, a new drink emerged that is different from any of the single ingredients. In the second, the substance was the same but the size changed.

Since we are journeying beyond the physical realm, however, the only type of separation possible would be some sort of difference in the things themselves, either in their essence or in their power. To explore this dialectically, we might pose the question: "What follows if our souls are inherently different than Essence itself?" Another approach would be to ask: "What follows if our souls can grow in power?" In either of these cases, we would accept that assumption about soul and then ask our questions: What is true, not true, and partly true about soul? What is true, not true, and partly true about the way it functions? We'd go through the whole list of 24 questions in this way.

Other starting points are possible as well; I offered just two examples here. We pick the one that grabs us. Applying our earlier list of 24 questions would compel us to contemplate in detail what it would mean for soul to merge into Essence itself. Keeping our "if" scenario in mind, we explore what must be true, not true, and partly true for soul. We can explore Essence, too, in this way. This, of course, would challenge our images of soul and of Essence itself.

The same level of scrutiny could also be applied to the question of recognition. What follows if our souls' separation from Essence itself is purely an illusion? As in the previous cases, we'd be forced to consider what the implications are of our hypothetical scenario. Doing so would reveal the limitations in our understanding. Those pesky details we hadn't worked out cannot be skipped over. Our understanding would fall short, and questions would emerge. This is ultimately the way to take the contemplations called arithmetic, geometry, astronomy, and harmony[16] to the next level. The issue presented here of merging versus recognition is only an example; dialectic can be applied to any metaphysical question that grabs you.

The Limitations of Linear Thinking

To put it simply, we need to move beyond our linear reasoning. As long as we remain in our usual conventional mode of thought, we will struggle with every possibility we tackle. Let's leave the question of merging or recognition, and look at another example that allows us to see clearly the limitations of linear thinking. At the end of the *Republic*, Plato puts forth the idea that we, as divine and immortal beings, leave each lifetime with our learning intact.[17] The conclusions that we drew about the way things are, whether accurate or not, color our choices for the next incarnation.

If this is true, then we have a serious logistical problem. If every lifetime is influenced by previous ones, then there must always be previous ones; there cannot be a first that did not emerge from a prior lifetime. Try to wrap your thoughts around the notion of there being no first incarnation. No matter how far back you reach, you must imagine a still earlier lifetime that influenced that one. Go ahead and try this exercise. Are you visualizing time stretching backwards? It doesn't make any sense to our logical, linear thought processes.

Yet it is equally ridiculous to imagine that the soul *can* be traced back to a first lifetime. If the soul is immortal, then how can it have a starting point? What was it doing before it started using a physical body as its vehicle, and why didn't it keep on that way? This line of reasoning proves just as futile as the previous one.

It is these sorts of puzzles that turn some people away from mysticism. They quickly conclude that it is all nonsense, because none of the conclusions make sense on the surface. If you are still reading this book, though, then you probably at least intuit that there is a way

---

[16] These were introduced back in Chapter 14.

[17] See the myth of the warrior Er, from 614b

out. Here's a question that Grimes likes to ask his students when we are tackling our own personal riddles: How do you know that you have answered any question sufficiently? In other words, When is an answer "good enough?"

There are two mistakes that we as students commonly make in the quest to find answers. One is to settle for something that merely satisfies our logical reasoning—whether that means finding a way out of a dilemma or, as in the above example of reincarnation, concluding that no solution exists. We reach a conceptual answer and then think that we are done. When we make this mistake, our curiosity wanes. In the *Understanding* section of this book, we learned to resist this urge and to hold onto our questions instead.

Holding onto our questions gets us past that first pitfall of grabbing an answer too quickly, but it also makes us susceptible to a different mistake: some of us then flip to the opposite extreme of never seeking answers. We conclude that our wisdom is found in this very act of holding onto our questions. However, wisdom is not in the questions *per se*; it is the reward for having the courage to push beyond logical arguments and touch Reality directly, and then to explore that experience.

Such is the ultimate role of dialectic. The bantering that Socrates was famous for is an example of dialectic at the earliest stages of spiritual practice. Before anyone would possibly devote their lives to searching for truth, they must first recognize that they don't already know truth. Plato viewed the philosopher as one who purges souls. In the *Sophist*, he explains this aspect of philosophy in this way:

> "[T]hese mental purifiers think that the soul can derive no advantage from disciplines accommodated to its nature, till he who is confuted is ashamed of his error, and, the impediments of disciplines being expelled, *viz.* false opinions, he becomes pure, and alone thinks that he knows the things which he does know, and not more than he knows."[18]

Dialectic can accompany us through every stage of our spiritual development. As our spiritual practice gets underway, dialectic provides us some guidance and direction as we wrestle to understand concepts that challenge our conventional views of Reality. Those of us who stick with this practice eventually develop a solid theoretical understanding of Reality, but then we need to stir the pot some more

---

[18] 230c~d

to find where assumptions are still hiding within our reasoning process.

Following this, dialectic is our main tool to explore the objects of knowledge in the upper world of Plato's cave allegory. It is here that we venture beyond the assumptions that limit our understanding. Plato recognized that words can give us a working definition of our object of inquiry, but cannot bring us to truly know it. Back in Chapter 7, we opened our discussion on metaphysics with the recognition that in order to know any particular thing, we must look to its cause. Such is ultimately the goal of dialectic. We move beyond conceptual understanding to truly beholding things-in-themselves, "able to disregard the eyes and other senses and go on to being itself in company with truth."[19]

Plato tells us in the *Republic* that the philosopher using dialectic "does not desist till he apprehends by thought itself the nature of the good in itself...."[20] Therefore, this highest function of dialectic is a deep contemplation that peaks in silence. Proclus seconds Plato's view of dialectic: "But obviously if the dialectician is reasoning with himself...he employs the highest form of dialectic, that which reveals the truth in its purity."[21] Of course, truth in its purity is beyond words.

Coming down from this peak, dialectic is again our companion:

"[A]fter attaining to that again taking hold of the first dependencies from it, so to proceed downward to the conclusion, making no use whatever of any object of sense but only of pure ideas moving on through ideas to ideas and ending in ideas."[22]

It is in this function that Plato bestowed on dialectic the title of being the copestone of his system. Platonism has the potential to be far more than is commonly recognized in modern universities; it is a profound spiritual system rooted in the knowledge that we can only know Mind through the mind.

---

[19] *Republic,* 537d

[20] *Ibid.,* 532b

[21] *Proclus' Commentary on Plato's Parmenides,* sec. 655, p. 45

[22] *Republic,* 511b~c. *Ideas* here refers to absolute Realities, not to discursive concepts.

Chapter 26: Reading as Extended Contemplation

"It is characteristic of those who are being led upwards first to reject, then to suspect the truth, and then to grasp at it and move always onward."

Proclus[1]

The writings of great mystics such as Proclus, Plato, and Plotinus are not meant to be read only once and then filed away. These are works that we must return to time and again. We see something new with each reading, and we can even gauge our progress to some degree by how much more we recognize with subsequent read-throughs.

These books serve as our close companions on the road to *dianoetic* understanding. They should accompany us on the journey beyond, as well. However, the dynamics of this new relationship have to change. Our goal before was to understand the basic metaphysical structure as presented by a particular philosopher. Now our goal is to reach beyond words and behold true vision. We are now adjusting our eyes to the brightness of the upper world. With a new goal, we need a new approach.

Any of the great works in this tradition can be read as an extended contemplation. We got a taste of this with Proclus' proposition 103 in Chapter 20. Now imagine doing the same with his entire *Elements of Theology,* starting with proposition 1 and carrying it straight through to the last proposition, number 211. To do this, we would look for how the propositions connect together. Many of them function in clusters, either consecutively or more spread out; other propositions could easily stand alone as a contemplation.

After thoroughly reading a proposition or cluster of propositions, try closing the book and putting the meaning in your own words. Once you can do that, you are ready to open the propositions up. What difficulties or questions arise when you try to put the pieces together? If you are early in the book, you might consider what the early propositions anticipate. For middle and late propositions, do you see how they build on everything that came before?

This same approach can be taken with longer writings, such as Plotinus' *Enneads* and even Proclus' *Theology of Plato.* This method

---

[1] *Proclus' Commentary on Plato's Parmenides,* sec. 758, p. 127

requires going slowly through the text, stopping frequently to contemplate. A tome such as those of the loquacious Proclus could easily take a year or more to explore in this way.

Reading Plato and his successors as extended contemplations is the closest we come to testing our own vision against theirs. Perhaps the most straightforward example of this is Damascius' *Problems and Solutions Concerning First Principles*. As the final headmaster of the revived Platonic Academy, he undoubtedly was confronted with well-read students who needed that final push beyond words. I suggest this because such is precisely what this central work of his is designed to do. True to the title of the work, Damascius raises problems that would be confounding to a student who had a good conceptual grasp of the metaphysical structures of Proclus and Iamblichus, but who lacked direct vision of Reality itself. Then he runs through the various difficulties that arise from one erroneous solution or another. Once Damascius purges the reader of these errors, he launches into his solution, demonstrating the clarity that emerges when false assumptions have been cleared away.

This basic pattern is followed throughout the whole book, building gradually until a conception of Reality is unveiled as accurately as words can capture. This organization, then, challenges the reader's interpretations of Damascius' most significant predecessors. The effort required to reap the rewards of this text go far beyond merely reading the words. The book is an extended contemplation; it requires frequently stopping to contemplate the images that Damascius paints with words.

Consider, for example, this passage about the One:

> "[I]t will be all things before all things, not in an imperfect state that is in potential, nor yet causally as not yet all things, but rather all things according to their undifferentiated subsistence, which is not the Unified before all things, but rather the super-Unified before all things, being all things by means of its own unity such as they are and the way that they are as they arise in differentiation. The One is all things in the most authentic way. For differentiation is what obscures that which is differentiated from the One, because of the very nature of differentiation."[2]

---

[2] *Problems and Solutions Concerning First Principles*, p. 123.

What would it take to *see* the reality that Damascius describes in that beautiful passage? The entire unfolding of the cosmos is contained in a few sentences, but the person with no vision beyond the *dianoetic* would struggle to recognize it. We have to contemplate, and to sit with the words and the images they inspire. We need to exercise the fortitude to let those images evolve within us and carry us to a state of mind beyond images. Only in this way can they transform us. Otherwise, this passage is merely an interesting idea that we came across in a book one day.

Plotinus is another philosopher whose writings are fertile ground for contemplations. His poetic style can be uplifting and inspiring. Beyond that, he includes contemplative exercises throughout his works:

> "For that which is investigated is soul; and what it investigates should be known by it, in order that it may in the first place learn whether it has the power of investigating things of this kind; and also whether it has such an eye as is able to see them, and whether they are properly objects of its enquiry. For if they are foreign to its nature, why should it investigate them? But if they are allied to it, it is expedient and possible to discover them."[3]

He also encourages his readers to seek peak experiences for ourselves, not merely to read about them:

> "[T]he soul has then another life. The soul also proceeding to, and having now arrived at the desired end, and participating of deity, will know that the supplier of true life is then present. She will likewise then require nothing farther; for on the contrary, it will be requisite to lay aside other things, to stop in this alone, and to become this alone, amputating everything else with which she is surrounded. Hence, it is necessary to hasten our departure from hence, and to be indignant that we are bound in one part of our nature, in order that with the whole of our

---

[3] Ennead V:i:1.

[true] selves, we may fold ourselves about divinity, and have no part void of contact with him."[4]

Some may read this as nothing more than a description. Plotinus is recounting what for them is an experience that is uplifting to ponder, but exists only in theory. The student with a strong aspiration to know this experience firsthand, however, recognizes that Plotinus is offering us some direction. He is describing the attitude that we must cultivate, the hunger that we must nurture, and the task that lies before us. Reading such passages is interesting, but taking on their challenge will change our lives.

---

[4] *Ibid.,* VI:ix:9, brackets included in text.

Chapter 27: Images of the Beautiful, the Just and the Good

"[E]verything that deceives appears to cast a spell upon the mind."

Plato[1]

Integrating Our Growth

Plato makes it clear in his *Republic* that mingling with Intelligibles is as difficult a task as it is a worthy one. Our entry into the upper world of his cave allegory is not the end of the road, a victory that marks the cessation of our struggles. Rather, we are venturing into a whole new leg of our journey, replete with both its own difficulties and also its own insights into who or what we truly are. He writes of his ex-prisoner emerging into the sunlight:

> "But he would require, I think, to be accustomed to it some time, if he were to perceive things above. And, first of all, he would most easily perceive shadows, afterwards the images of men and of other things in water, and after that the things themselves. And, with reference to these, he would more easily see the things in the heavens, and the heavens themselves, by looking in the night to the light of the stars, and the moon, than by day looking on the sun, and the light of the sun."[2]

Once in the upper world, we find ourselves stumbling along and groping our way through the blinding brightness. Largely, this effort is in the form of activities such as reading, discussing and dialectic contemplations. However, we will discover at this later stage, much as we did in our earlier stages, that we must reconcile our insights into our true essence with the beliefs we still hold of ourselves as social beings. The practices described throughout this book are intended not only to rattle our assumptions about Reality itself, but also to challenge our assumptions about ourselves and our societies.

Exploring self-images is often overlooked as being too mundane for the lofty goals of a sincere spiritual quest, but it is, in fact, essential. Integrating the knowledge of the Beautiful, the Just, and the

---

[1] *Republic*, 413c, trans. Paul Shorey
[2] *Ibid.*, 516a-b, trans. Thomas Taylor

Good ³ into our lives requires re-examining how their images have shaped us. Anyone who has reached this stage undoubtedly knows the difficulty it poses. Changing inwardly and holding those insights in our souls is quite an achievement in itself; living outwardly as this more authentic version of ourselves is another hurdle all together.

Our families, friends, and co-workers may be slow to accept the changes. More significantly, we ourselves need a period of adjustment in order to figure out how to relate to ourselves and to the world. We have to re-examine our self-images and throw away those images that are no longer compatible with the way we now understand reality to be.

Some of those old images, unhealthy though they may be, have a powerful hold on us. We identify with them strongly and do not initially know how to live without them. Yet until we clear those false beliefs away, they have the potential to wreak havoc in our lives even after a peak experience, blocking and distorting the vision that is coming into view as we adjust to a new level of brightness.

Chapter 3 presented an outline of six stages through which our spiritual practice unfolds. Looking at our growth in broad strokes, we can see this general pattern marking our progress. However, it may only be in retrospect that we can pinpoint these stages. The day-to-day experience of going up the steep ascent to the mouth of the cave and the arduous process of examining the objects of knowledge in the upper world continually force us to return to purification, even at later stages of our practice. We also come to appreciate that the process of deepening our knowing implies that belief, understanding, and knowing function side-by-side in the same soul; confusion in some areas can remain even though clear vision has emerged in other areas.

In practice, we repeat the process of examining the objects of knowledge in the upper world multiple times. It is a mistake to think that once out of the cave, we quickly soak in the scenery and then we are left only with the task of subjecting that vision to dialectical analysis. The process of making an exact account of Reality and of the One smacks us against assumptions that we haven't yet cleared away.

---

³ Plato states in *Republic* at 520c that those going back down into the cave "have perceived the truth concerning things beautiful, and just and good."

Working through these assumptions, in turn, opens us to a more profound and inclusive vision of Reality.[4]

There is a common image that after a peak experience, a person instantly becomes a sage and loses all interest in bodily experiences. Those who still fear death or display pride are accused of being hypocrites or frauds. In truth, we can be "the real thing" while still having self-images and other false beliefs to work through. A powerful peak experience leaves us with the conviction that we are indeed divine essences beyond time and space, but our old identification with our bodies and the physical realm does not simply disappear. A whole new level of insight must follow such an experience before we can grow into this new identity, and what that new identity will be is something that we cannot fathom beforehand.

Plato wrote in regards to dialectic: "For in learning these objects it is necessary to learn at the same time both what is false and what is true of the whole of Existence..."[5] He was referring specifically to the objects of knowledge in the upper world of his cave allegory, the absolute Realities of the Intelligible realm. However, knowing both what is false and what is true implies studying not only these objects of Mind, but also recognizing their images in our daily lives. This means cutting through not only false metaphysical theories but also those images in our souls that make these erroneous theories seem attractive.

In regards to our peak experiences, we may embrace wrong conclusions about the nature of Reality, or even deny our experiences once the immediacy of the experience has passed. In regards to our self-images, we need to discover the false beliefs at their root. Much as dialectic ultimately brings us to look for causes in order to know Reality, so too we must look for the causes of our false self-images. Wherever understanding falls short, we run the risk of rejecting truth and embracing images.

You can probably guess from your study of metaphysics that eventually we all must face the false belief that separation is our

---

[4] Many mystic systems recognize degrees of enlightenment. Zen Buddhism, for example, utilizes a 10-level system depicted in drawings that have come to be known as the Oxherding Pictures. See Kapleau, *The Three Pillars of Zen*, pp. 332-345.

[5] Epistle VII, 344b

326 Discovering the Beauty of Wisdom

ultimate reality. We will all eventually have to question our identification with our physical bodies and, beyond that, even our identity as a soul individual and separated from Mind. You may assume that if we jump to working on these issues, we can sidestep dealing with the more mundane varieties of false beliefs.

This is a reasonable assumption from a theoretical perspective. As we advance, though, we discover that one of two things happens. One possibility is that we explore false beliefs whenever we recognize them, uprooting them along the way, either fully or at least enough to advance. This is the process I've been advocating throughout this book.

Another possibility is that we build enough spiritual energy to bypass our blocks. This is a common pattern in systems that focus strongly on meditation, chanting, and other methods of energy building. Platonists can do this, too, pushing distractive thoughts aside and exerting will power to stay on course. While certainly there have been wise teachers in both the Platonic and in other traditions who followed this path, the reality is that very few of us are able to. The best case scenario for most of us would be to achieve a state of mind in which a number of our false beliefs are not yet uprooted, but they are temporarily not functioning in us.

Without a doubt, this state of mind allows for a high degree of insight and growth. However, these insights do not necessarily render our false beliefs powerless. Even if we behold a peak experience, we will eventually come down from the high of that experience, and our false beliefs will be waiting for us. Wisdom, after all, is a state of mind, not an experience. Our studies must continue long after a peak experience. Bypassing blocks does not mean that we will never have to deal with them; they will function again. Therefore, we will continue to interpret through those false images of ourselves, regardless of how wise we are otherwise. This is why even some highly respected teachers have been known to have volatile lives.

Building energy to bypass dealing with unhealthy states of mind overlooks the fact that these states of mind are the very thing that puts a limit on our insights in the first place. As we clear more blocks away, we open ourselves to increasingly profound states of mind. However, as we saw with the example from my own life in Chapter 16, we may sabotage our own growth if the person we are growing into is in conflict with the self-image we currently hold.

Detour, Dead-end or Direct Route?

There is one criticism that paying attention to false beliefs can conceivably be open to: we can potentially get trapped in such a focus, never pushing toward that peak opening because we always have more false beliefs to explore. This is a valid concern, but when it occurs it is an error of the practitioner's, not of the awareness itself.

Any element of practice, from meditation to dialectic, can be misused if approached in the wrong spirit. Perhaps some of us have studied wisdom literature, but with the prideful aim of impressing others. Then there are some who revel in meditation, but apply unexamined beliefs to it that keep them trapped in a dichotomy that separates those higher states of mind from their earthly, "normal" states. Dialectic attempts that deteriorate into rationalizations and chop-logic (discussed in Chapter 19) offer another example of a meaningful technique being misused.

To some degree, misuse of techniques is inevitable, whatever the techniques are. A great deal of trial and error is involved, and we learn much about ourselves and about the nature of Reality by muddling through this process. We also learn a great deal about our beliefs by seeing which false assumptions compelled us to misuse a particular technique in the first place.

In regards to focusing too much on false beliefs, I would argue that this error itself is rooted in false belief. There are a number of false beliefs that could possibly underlie this. For example, there are many fears that could hold us back from mature growth, even while we are working towards it as a goal. We might sabotage our own efforts out of fear of the darkness we suspect to find if we dig any farther into our own hearts, fear of the unknown, or fear of letting go of our old identity. These fears will be discussed in more detail later in this chapter.

Whatever our reasons, we may at some point in our journey find ourselves looking for a way to back off from our goal while still going through the motions sufficiently to give ourselves the illusion that we haven't quit. Getting muddled in our own personal psychological issues could be an ideal tool by which to do this. In all fairness, though, a person looking for such a diversion will find it somewhere else if not here. The benefit of being aware of our own states of mind is that when we are ready to be honest about sabotaging ourselves, we can turn our misuse of the technique on itself to explore why we got off track in the first place.

The Self or a Self-image?

Another objection I've heard is the idea that this attention to false beliefs undervalues our uniqueness and individuality. This is a criticism that has come up multiple times throughout my practice. One example that comes to mind is a man I used to work with who told me that he embraces his idiosyncrasies because they are what define his personality. He interpreted my interest in uprooting false beliefs as a desire to change into someone else. He accused me of being insecure and not liking myself.

His point of view is not at all surprising in a culture that values individuality as highly as our Western cultures do. It is a rare person who has never wished to be unique and to stand out from the pack. We all want to be noticed and appreciated by those around us, and it is often assumed that showing the world our fun, witty and outgoing side is the key to getting this appreciation. And so we value sharing our opinions with anyone who will listen—and sometimes even with people who won't! We celebrate the personality through reality TV shows and social media, where too often the wise insight is eclipsed by the clever put-down and the witty retort.

This brings me back to my former colleague who thought uprooting false beliefs was masochistic and that I didn't love myself. In reality, the opposite is true; it was out of my intuitive sense of my own goodness and worth that my desire took root to know truth and, in the process, to clear away whatever is false. The point is not to tear down who we are, only who we have been convinced to *think* that we are. Granted, it can be hard to recognize the difference early in our practice, but that distinction becomes more pronounced the further we advance.

Through Platonism, we both contemplate the nature of Reality itself and also explore our own states of mind. These two avenues allow us to break out of the false dichotomy I too often hear from those around me, a dichotomy that bulks all of our various mannerisms together and sets them up as something either to repress or to embrace. On one hand is the belief that we are a bundle of idiosyncrasies and imperfections that we ought to hate, repress and deny. On the other extreme is the belief that we should embrace all of our mannerisms and identify with them; that these are all true aspects of who we are and therefore integrating them into our self-identity is an act of self-love.

Both of these views are false. Platonism helps us recognize that beliefs and reactions born of ignorance are not who we are; they are what holds us back from discovering who we are. The personality is something different. It doesn't diminish with insights into truth, and in fact becomes more apparent once some of the images we had been embracing fall away. Distinguishing one from the other is virtually impossible if we focus only on our behavior and on social images of which attitudes are favorable. However, we shine a great deal of light on ourselves when we focus instead on our states of mind.

We needn't fear losing our personalities as wisdom matures. Great differences still exist among the personalities of teachers. We are each a unique expression of divine goodness. We each have different temperaments and dispositions. Some people are outgoing, whereas others are more reserved. Some of us are more action-oriented while others are more thought-oriented. There is no one right way to be.

After touching Truth, we each must find our own best way to live our insights. Every teacher I have ever met has a certain charisma that sprouts not from mannerisms or idiosyncrasies but as a natural radiation of the self. Many of the attitudes and behaviors that my former co-worker identified as being his true self I recognize as self-images that block him from knowing the true self. Exploring and questioning our false beliefs, then, is a practice of self-discovery in the highest sense possible. We are not denying who we are; we are *discovering* who we are.

The Need to Be "Perfect"

Tied in with the question of personality is yet another concern. A third criticism the study of false beliefs opens itself to is that it could potentially feed a person's unhealthy desire to seek perfection. We saw a number of false images of wisdom in Chapter 22. These are images we may hold because we don't want to ever be wrong or to have any qualities we deem negative. We'd like to have the perfect reaction to every situation.

However, the desire to be "perfect" is in itself a false image. This is a complex issue. I'll focus on two areas in particular where the desire to be perfect shows itself. One is the desire to have the perfect personality. The other is never to be caught off guard or to feel anger, jealousy and so on.

In regards to personality, it helps to keep in mind that there are many personality types, and most of us have a range of tendencies depending on our mood. We can be chatty or reserved, spontaneous or long-range planners. Perhaps we are athletic or perhaps bookish. We might be a little of all of the above. How one person responds to a given situation may not be how another person would. There is not one right response.

Nor can we be all things to all people. What the easy-going person deems a wise response might raise the eyebrows of a more serious-minded person, and vice versa. Even among the wisest of people, differences of temperament exist. Whatever we deem "perfection" to be is actually just an image of perfection that is built on assumptions. It is a series of images that can each be opened up and explored. Diving into such an exploration is far more beneficial to us than validating and accepting those voices in our heads unquestioned. We will likely discover that at the root of the desire to be "perfect" are social and familial images, as well as our various fears of inadequacy.

As a child, my personality seemed to be the exact opposite of what my family and society expected of a girl. Rather than enjoying social interaction, I found it draining after a while. I've always had a penchant for logic, and tended to see the world through cause and effect rather than through emotions. Of course I do experience emotions, I've just never been the type to show my emotions as openly as the other girls around me did. As a result, I was called cold more than once. Well intentioned people had all kinds of advice for me, and it took me years to figure out that little of it served me well.

Developing awareness of our states of mind is valuable to our lives, yet doing so requires bringing along a commensurate level of good judgment and compassion towards ourselves. We must be able to judge what is a false belief versus what is a difference in temperament or personality. For this reason, in our explorations of self-images, I advocate focusing only on states of mind that block us from reaching a meaningful goal, such as those that arise in the course of spiritual practice. We know there is a false belief to explore when our one-pointed focus gets hijacked by our "monkey minds" that swing us from thought to thought, when we find ourselves looking for diversions or when we get frustrated, restless, moody and so on. This holds true for all of us, regardless of our personalities.

Our study of states of mind never starts from a desire to develop a certain personality trait, such as becoming more outgoing. Our goal is never to mold ourselves into anybody's image of perfection. In fact, we will more likely find ourselves unraveling those images instead. When we take our cues from our states of mind, we do not know what personality will emerge from under our conditioning. We may discover that we really are that more outgoing person after all. Alternatively, we might discover that our natural ways are more reserved. The conditioning we will throw off, then, is the false belief that there is something inferior about being reserved. This conclusion is a healthy one, too. Either way, the person we incrementally are growing into is a vibrant, authentic reflection of divine goodness.

This brings us to the second area where the image of perfection plays itself out. Beyond all of the personal and social images that we embrace is a pure essence that is divine and good. Our goal is to discover that inherent goodness to the degree we are able to and to bring that goodness into our lives and into the world at large.

What we are actually doing is growing into a more authentic version of ourselves. That means developing the virtues of wisdom, justice, fortitude and temperance as fully as we can. This is often expressed in Platonic literature as becoming as godlike as is humanly possible. However, this lofty language should not be interpreted to mean that the Platonist is above human emotion or can never have a bad day, can never be moody or annoyed or feel restless. We must be cautious not to let ourselves fall into the fantasy of becoming some quintessential model of perfection that others admire, or believe that if we ever stumble, then we are not "the real thing."

Philosophy is greatly misunderstood in our Western societies. The image of the all-wise sage who has all the answers is what most people think of when they imagine what it means to be involved in any sort of philosophic practice. As a result, there is a tendency for the people around us who are not philosophers to hold us to a very high standard, and perhaps some of us hold ourselves to that very high standard as well. However, that standard is unrealistic. As we've already seen, wisdom describes a state of mind, and it is a state that we are likely to go into and out of. It is a rare person who has advanced to the point of staying in that healthy state of mind all day every day.

It is okay to be a student and it is okay to be imperfect. You are allowed to sometimes feel nervous, angry or have hurt feelings. You don't have to have the unwavering wisdom or fortitude that Plato displayed of Socrates in order to be "the real thing." The virtues deepen and mature as we advance. It might help to keep in mind that Plato showed us only a glimpse of Socrates when he was young, so we don't know which states of mind he battled in his youth. And even later in life, for all of his wisdom, Socrates may very well may have had his bad days, too.

The proper way to study states of mind, then, is to uproot beliefs that block us from advancing in the other areas of our practice. Our focus should always be on our goal to know the nature of Reality, and to know ourselves as no different in essence from that nature. Once a particular block has been sufficiently explored, we get back on course.

We may notice other red flags in our interactions with others or in our states of mind, but if they don't hinder our practice then we can put them on the back burner or explore them at our leisure. We needn't become consumed by concerns that we still see within ourselves some vanity or pride or feelings of insecurity. And we never want to get sucked into a comparison game with another person. The student whose aspiration is strong will never let exploring false beliefs become an end in and of itself. It always points us toward something more profound. Plotinus wrote: "The similitude, indeed, to good men, is an assimilation of one image to another, each being derived from the same thing; but a similitude to God, is an assimilation as to a paradigm."[6]

Potential Impediments

Here are three other issues to consider as your spiritual practice ripens:

False Image or the Real Me?

Even after the initial layers of blocks have been cleared away, we will still find ourselves hitting against fears and doubts. In fact, for

---

[6] Ennead I:ii:7

some of us (depending on our unique web of beliefs), fears and doubts may actually intensify at the deeper layers. One fear that we are likely to face at some point on our journey is the fear that we will never be able to trust ourselves to drop our guard. Let's look a little deeper at why this fear is pervasive, and why it is ultimately unfounded.

Once we gain the experience of unraveling a few of our false beliefs, we are better able to appreciate that these beliefs are never reflections of our true essence. They are learned behavior, and anything learned can be unlearned. The face we show the world is a combination of various behaviors influenced by social and familial beliefs, and the rays of truth that manage to shine through. As we clear away more false images, the balance shifts such that gradually we become more accurate reflections of Truth.

However, as we peel away unhealthy states of mind, we are all bound to wonder at some point whether the qualities we deem to be negative are actually rooted in false beliefs, or if they are glimpses of our true selves. When we reach our deeper layers of belief, we touch attitudes that we may fear are too fundamental to be learned behavior. By this time, we have come to recognize the social masks we'd formed over the years, and we have gotten at least a glimpse at which beliefs the masks are reflecting, but most of us still have some degree of doubt that pure goodness lies underneath. We suspect that our unhealthy qualities are who we really are, which is largely why we created the masks in the first place.

Think of the classic onion analogy. The layers of belief that we peeled away initially were beliefs built on top of layers of belief. The deeper we go, the more closely we identify with the beliefs we uncover. Eventually we reach a fundamental level of beliefs. In this respect, our practice can seem more challenging the further we go.

Fortunately for us, there is also an aspect in which it gets easier. Clearing away what is false helps us strengthen and unify our souls, and so we grow more courageous each time we see through a false belief and cast its destructive force out of our lives. We come to see for ourselves that these self-images do not define us. By the time we hit this deeper level of beliefs, we more easily recognize that the states of mind we are grappling with are images and not the true self.

We have seen that formal dialectic focuses on what a thing is and how it functions. Confusing the two, or not being clear about the distinction between essence and function, is responsible for many of our errors and false assumptions about the nature of Reality. We can find the same dynamic play out regarding our self-images as well. When we describe ourselves as shy, chatty, mean, insecure, and so on, we think we are defining our own natures. We think this is what we are. However, we are actually describing how some self-image is functioning. Recognizing this error opens us to the question of how that image got there in the first place, and so points us toward the underlying false belief. We are getting closer to distinguishing the true self from our various self-images.

Fearing the Unknown

Another reason we fear being inherently bad is simply that we are reaching depths unfamiliar to us. It is natural to fear the unknown. When faced with something new, many of us have the tendency to expect the worst. Perhaps our rationale is that we can never be disappointed this way. However, we can never reach more profound degrees of insight this way, either. Our practice will be expanded by our ability to grow courageous in the recognition that the nature of Reality is good and never evil.[7] The more clearly we can see this, the further we will allow ourselves to grow. False beliefs that counter this insight—that of supernatural evil forces or a supernatural evil nature such as the devil—will create a ceiling that we must bust through in order to keep growing.

Another fear of venturing into the unknown is that of falling into nothingness. As our practice ripens, we increasingly reach states of mind that go beyond anything we've ever before put words on. Having the language of metaphysics at our disposal not only brings intelligibility to our highest experiences, but it also brings comfort. There is comfort in being able to expand our range of what we think of as normal human experiences. We learn to embrace experiences and states of mind that, in conventional circles of society, are met with skepticism and confusion.

But what happens when we rise beyond the positive affirmations—beauty, stillness, infinite, etc.—into the *via negativa*—neither existing

---

[7] See *Republic*, 379b~380c

nor not existing, neither still nor in motion, and so on? We saw Damascius' description of this in the last chapter:

> "It is true that we encounter the One as knowable from afar, and when we have become one with it, then we transcend our own ability to know the One and we are resolved into being the One, that is, into the unknowable instead of the knowable."[8]

Our reasoning tells us that whatever has the ineffable power to be the cause of all that *is* cannot be a pure nothingness. Further, to declare that whatever is beyond the One-Being is nothingness implies that we know what nothingness is, or what it means to be nothing. In practice, we will discover that metaphysics is a loyal ally while we are building the fortitude to keep pushing forward. However, even the *via negativa* has its limitations. Describing the One as neither still nor in motion tells me no more about the One than describing music as neither round nor square tells me what music is. Ultimately, it will be our own steadfast refusal to quit, our courageous willingness to dip our toes into the pool of the unfamiliar, that will eventually get us over this hurdle.

Embracing Ourselves

Letting go of long-held beliefs can be a struggle. The other side of that challenge is to embrace the new sense of self that emerges when old images are dropped. This has the potential, at times, to be a wonderful discovery or a painful process. Knowledge always carries with it both freedom and responsibility, both of which are healthy and ultimately to be embraced. However, depending on our particular web of beliefs, we may have to work through some blocks in order to reach that goal.

We all like the idea of dropping negative images—the role of the awkward one, the clumsy one, the one with anger issues, or the underachiever, to name a few. Once the beliefs at the foundation of such images have been successfully worked through, we are changed. We wouldn't be able to go back to those old images even if we wanted to.

Yet this doesn't imply that we instantly accept the new, healthier "me" that results. It may take time for our self-image to catch up to

---

[8] *Problems and Solutions Concerning First Principles,* p. 126

these changes. We had fallen into the habit of seeing ourselves certain ways and of expecting the people around us to interact with us in certain ways. An adjustment will have to run through all of our relationships—including our relationship with ourselves. This is a natural and healthy process; our growth needs time to be incorporated into our lives.

Connected to this is the challenge of recognizing our own growth. The common stereotype is that someone has a few insights and then takes on a title such as guru and starts a spiritual school to pontificate their newfound wisdom. As tends to be true of stereotypes, there are undoubtedly some people who fit this image, but most of us do not.

The more common pattern, perhaps, is for people to downplay their insights and cling to the role of the student. Of course, false beliefs are at the root of this error. The precise make-up of this belief structure will differ from person to person. Whatever our particular blocks are that compel us to deny our own vision, they tend to keep their hooks in us long after we have passed the threshold into knowing.

Platonists in particular may find that these beliefs actually served us well early in our practice. The early stages involve recognizing that we do not know, thus clearing the way for insights. Indeed, many of Plato's dialogues feature Socrates embarrassing some pompous intellectual who has mistaken himself for a knower. Because modesty often serves us well early in our practice, it tends to pass unquestioned until these later stages.

There are two ways in which ignorance manifests. Thinking that we know something that we don't is only one of them. The second way is to think that we don't know something that we do. As we advance, we are likely to experience this second form of ignorance firsthand. We may feel as though we are caught in a balancing act between modesty and arrogance. However, this is a dichotomy we can transcend. In time, we learn to embrace our insights without pridefulness or competition with others. Our most basic rule of thumb is always to be honest with ourselves about what we know and what we don't. Exercising that level of integrity will in turn open us to deeper insights into that larger question of who or what we really are.

Chapter 28: Interacting with Mind

"[E]ach of us is an Intellectual Kosmos, linked to this world by what is lowest in us, but, by what is the highest, to the Divine Intellect…"

Plotinus[1]

Personalized Wisdom

We've seen that we are bound to hit blocks as we struggle to advance on the later legs of our journey, just as we had in our early years of spiritual practice. Fortunately, even those of us who are working without a teacher are never truly alone; divine Mind communicates with us. Learning to recognize its modes of communication is paramount to reaping the benefits of this personalized wisdom.

One of the greatest benefits of exploring our own states of mind is that doing so enters us into an interactive relationship with Mind. We learn how Mind functions in our lives as we follow what seems at times like a breadcrumb trail. Mind actually speaks to us loudly and clearly, but few of us are proficient in its language.

We will, however, gain that competency as our practice blossoms. As our outlook on life matures, we gradually come to see how past events have shaped us and how the beliefs we had embraced in childhood have played out in our lives. We can also explore other modes of communication; namely, dreams, daydreams, and seemingly random thoughts. Together, these studies help us develop a mature understanding of ourselves as intellectual, divine essences operating on the physical plane.

When we pay attention to the themes of our dreams, daydreams, and inner dialogues, it becomes obvious to us that these private thoughts are indelibly tied to our web of self-images. Plato asks of the chained prisoners in his cave allegory: "And what if the opposite part of this prison had an echo, when any of those who passed along [the bearers carrying objects on their heads and walking on the high wall behind the prisoners] spoke, do you imagine they would reckon that whatever spoken was anything else than the passing shadow?"[2]

---

[1] Ennead III:iv:3, trans. MacKenna, Stephen and B. S. Page
[2] See Chapter 3 for a fuller discussion of the cave allegory. Quote from *Republic*, 515b. Brackets added. I changed the word *spake* to *spoke* and *spoken* in conformity to modern English.

Our inner dialogue is very much like a distorted version of these voices. We accept it as true, but it is nothing more than the hollow echoes of the influential people whose words, behaviors, and actions played a vital role in shaping our views of ourselves and of the world. We take these echoes to be the opinions of others, but they are really our own beliefs about ourselves. These private critics and judges exert over us the power of belief, countering our efforts to grow beyond the limits within which they bind us. It is our unquestioning acceptance of them as truth that gives them their force. Noticing them for what they are, then, is the first step in tearing them down.

Therefore, keeping a journal of our inner dialogues is an effective way to recognize the central role beliefs play in our interpretations of the world. We have a tendency to conform our experiences to fit our beliefs. We see things as we expect to see them and we overlook what we need to notice. This is in large part what makes recognizing and uprooting false beliefs so difficult. We can still gain a fairly mature grasp of metaphysics without picking apart this network of beliefs, and even some degree of direct vision. The further we progress, though, the more obvious our limitations will become to us.

Keeping a journal can also help us to better appreciate the divine intelligibility that flows through our lives. Whether we are looking at our random thoughts, our daydreams, or even our nighttime dreams, Mind is always communicating with us, always pointing us towards truth or showing us what we need to see through. We can (and should!) struggle with the question of whether this higher level of intelligibility is an aspect of ourselves that stretches beyond our current identification, or if it is somehow separate. I'll leave that question for you to explore on your own. One thing that is clear is that the experience of this divine gift renders its existence undeniable.

As our spiritual practice progresses, we grow to better appreciate the role this divine intelligibility plays in our lives. We can strengthen that connection and in this way, deepen our understanding of who or what we are. Considering contact with divine Mind may seem an odd excursion from our otherwise sober treatment of metaphysics. However, such interaction is actually interwoven into the very foundation and essence of our cosmos, and this is a fundamental element of our metaphysics. It is the natural result of a metaphysical structure that recognizes (1) goodness as the foundation of all existence and (2) existence unfolding through multiple realms. If goodness is always present with existence as it unfolds, then it follows that goodness, too, flows through each unfolding realm of reality.

As discussed at various places throughout this book, this divine goodness is called providence and it is carried by the gods throughout all of reality. It is the law of providence that we each participate in this divine goodness to the degree that we are able. Evidence of this law operating in our own lives can be found by exploring our private thoughts, be they elaborate daydreams or scattered bits of memories. What may seem haphazard and irrational on the surface gradually reveals its inherent intelligibility and meaningfulness. We've also seen this with seemingly random thoughts, which parallel the voices bouncing off the wall of Plato's cave of ignorance.

Dreams

There has long been controversy around the question of the value of dreams. Throughout human history, various cultures have viewed dreams as prophetic. In the Greek tradition, Homer used dreams in both his *Iliad* and his *Odyssey* as a means for the gods to communicate with humans. While there is no formal method of dream analysis in the Platonic tradition, including such a practice is perfectly in line with our metaphysics and our understanding of the role of providence in our lives.[3]

Our nighttime dreams play an important role in our development. They point us towards what we have ignored in our waking world, that which is vital for us to see in order to understand the beliefs currently blocking us. The mystic Synesios of Cyrene wrote that "it is to the minds given to philosophy that dreams especially come, to

---

[3] For a more in-depth look at incorporating dream exploration into spiritual practice, see *Philosophical Midwifery*, listed in the bibliography. My treatment of dream analysis is based on the methods of Dr. Pierre Grimes. It is important to note that what I am focusing on here is only one kind of dream. For most of us, it is the most common kind. Lucid dreams also tend to fall into this category. In Chapter 29, I will refer to an instructional dream that helped me turn off discursive voices while meditating. Other types of dreams include prophetic ones that predict some future event. We can also enter powerful peak experiences while in a dream state.

enlighten them in their difficulties and researches, so as to bring them during sleep the solutions which escape them when awake."[4]

I have found the mastery with which my dreams complement and support my waking thoughts and experiences to be nothing short of astonishing. After years of analyzing my own dreams, I have come to recognize that dreams must be crafted with a degree of intelligibility that reaches beyond that of our everyday states of mind. After all, our dreams show us what we have overlooked or failed to recognize the significance of. This requires a judgment in determining which information ought to get re-examined. Merely pointing to a theoretical storage of subconscious memories is insufficient to explain this intelligibility. Our dreams show us *what* we need to see *when* we need to see it.

Plato also considered at least some dreams, if not all, to be of divine origin. Consider this exchange in the *Sophist:*

"We know that we and all the other animals... are one and all the very offspring and creations of God, do we not?

Yes.

And corresponding to each and all of these, there are images, not the things themselves, which are also made by superhuman skill.

What are they?

The appearances in dreams..."[5]

Some dreams are straight-forward. Others are more like riddles. Even to students with years of experience opening up dreams, dreams still come along that we struggle to make heads or tails of. Those of you who wish to give dream analysis a try will find that it helps to nurture a playful attitude toward this pursuit. Our dreams function as personalized oracles. They are lovingly crafted for our own private viewing, and we are blessed with one or more of these gifts every

[4] Saint Synesios, *On Dreams*, p. 26. Synesios of Cyrene was a Platonist who, according to the biographic details listed in this book, was born around 370 CE and died around 413 CE. In the later years of his life he became a Christian and was eventually canonized as St. Synesios by the Roman Catholic Church.
[5] 266b, trans. Harold North Fowler

night. They point us towards the false beliefs that we still need to address in order for our growth to continue.

The first challenge in recognizing wisdom in our dreams is to remember the gift that we have been given. After all, you have to have the gift before you can unwrap it. We often only remember the dream we were immersed in at the time we wake up, or perhaps we can recall snippets of a few different dreams. Of course, the more we recall the better, but even a small fragment is a glimpse into our state of mind. Also, paying attention to our dreams has a way of triggering better recall over time. With diligence, it won't be long before we start remembering whole dreams.

I keep a voice recorder next to my bed and then transcribe the dream into a journal later. I have found this helpful, as writing takes me longer and so I risk forgetting later parts of the dream. Also, speaking is easier than writing on those groggy days. However, this method does not fit everybody's situation. Transcribing can be time-consuming, and describing the dream out loud may be a problem for those who need to be considerate of a light sleeper in the room.

However you choose to record your dream, there are a few things to keep in mind. First, it is important to record as many details as we can, even those that seem insignificant or don't make sense. We don't want to do any editing. Connected to this, it is important to recount the dream as soon as possible after waking up. The details that flitter away first tend to be those that challenge our interpretations.[6] Thirdly, some dreams employ bizarre imagery and so are hard to put into words. Still, we must try. The significance of this imagery will, hopefully, unfold with our analysis. One last point, which I learned the hard way, is that it is a good idea either to write double-spaced or to leave wide margins. This allows us to go back and add details that we recall later.

To go deeply into the dream, we need to leave the story behind. This is the only way to dig to the true message of the dream. With experience, we learn not to identify with the events of our dreams. In my dream analyses, I refer to myself in the dream as *my dream-self*. That looked and sounded like me in that dream scenario, but I was never really there. I never did those things or had those interactions. A

---

[6] You might find it interesting to compare this concept to the practice of memorization in Chapter 6. The same principle is behind both.

providential message was sent to me in the form of symbolic imagery. The meaning is in the states of mind and the beliefs that they point to. It is in these ways that the dream's imagery is absolutely personal, and recognizing the significance that those states of mind and those beliefs have played in our lives is a meaningful and powerful lesson.

In this way, dream analysis has some parallels to our spiritual practice as a whole. This physical realm, also, can be said to be an image of sorts. It is not an image in the way that our dreams are images, yet it is also not real in the way that Reality itself is real. It is the challenge of our practice to figure out what is meaningful about our lives, without getting caught up in the shadow-show on the wall of the proverbial cave.

We are not these bodies that carry out various roles in our families, societies, and companies. Yet there *is* something real about us; something that shows itself in our thoughts, feelings, and states of mind. We at least sense that our interactions are meaningful, even if our roles ultimately are not. In a similar vein, we need to recognize that the true significance of our dreams is not in the surface story, but in the thoughts, feelings, and states of mind that function through that story. Just as our spiritual practice teaches us to break our identification with our bodies, so too dream analysis teaches us to break our identification with our dream-self.

Once we've recorded and transcribed the dream, what we want to do is go back over it, focusing on words and states of mind. What do these states of mind feel like? Describe them. When in our past did we experience these same states of mind? A recent event will likely spring to mind, as this would explain the timing of the dream. From here, we work backwards as far into our childhood as we can. What role has this state of mind played in our lives?

Our dreams tend to focus on those states of mind that we knew were there, but whose significance eluded us. We ignored them or pushed them aside as something tangential to our nobler goals. We were working on other areas before, so that was fine. When such a state of mind is featured in a dream, though, this signals the need to turn our attention to what had been on the back burner. Dream work is useful at all stages of our practice, but it becomes an invaluable tool at these later stages when we have gained some degree of vision and want to bring it into greater focus. It is now that the states of mind we could ignore before need to be addressed.

Daydreams

Everyone loves a good daydream now and then, and daydreams can serve beneficial purposes. They allow us to try on a new way of being from the safety of our own thoughts. This test run might give us the courage to implement changes in our everyday lives. Many of us also look back on less pleasant periods in our lives and see that daydreams were the escape that helped us get through the pain and confusion.

Even more advanced students find that the occasional daydream remains one of life's lingering guilty pleasures. But are they really something to feel guilty about? Daydreams are harmless, aren't they? Certainly, we can gain a high degree of spiritual maturity without giving up daydreams.

Unfortunately for those of you wanting to save your coveted daydreams, there will come a point where a crossroads is reached. You will have to choose: your daydreams or your highest goal. You needn't feel guilty about daydreaming, but you will eventually need to pull your daydreams off their hallowed pedestals and see them for what they really are.

When we daydream, we are often trading self-images that we deem negative for ones that we deem positive. The poor person fantasizes about life as a billionaire, the unpopular high-school student dreams of being homecoming king or queen. This is all harmless enough if our goals are of the ordinary variety. In fact, such daydreams can help us drop a debilitating image, such as an insecurity, and this often leads to meaningful growth. The fruits of those efforts are found in securing goals such as starting our own business or taking that adventurous trip we had long dreamed of taking.

To students seeking wisdom, however, this level of growth, meaningful though it may be, is not enough. Images surround social success as surely as they surround its opposite. Our aim ultimately is to see through *all* images, because whether those images are deemed positive or negative, they are all rooted in belief.

Think back to high school. One kid is popular, and this gives him a burst of inner strength and confidence. Another is unpopular, and her insecurities are intensified by her perceived daily social rejection. Our conventional notions tell us that of course the popular kid is better off; he is confident where the other kid is insecure. To a Platonist, however, both of these hypothetical high school students are in the same predicament. These two states of mind are dancing around the same belief-images regarding popularity. Popularity is no more a basis for confidence than the lack of it is a justification for self-deprecation. Gaining confidence from an arbitrary, false image is only an *image* of health; it is not the real thing. Ultimately, it is empty.

Our fantasies—whether they be about wealth, popularity, social power, or having super-human abilities—all dance around the same beliefs that hinder our vision in our lives outside of our fantasy world. What's more, those beliefs shape our goals, such as seeking wisdom because we think it is an experience that will make us all-knowing or impervious to heartache.[7]

Paying attention to our daydreams, then, can point us toward a recognition of which self-images are coloring our interpretation of our studies and of the conclusions we are reaching. To the student early in the spiritual journey, this is largely an interesting and fun psychological exercise. To more advanced students, attention to daydreams takes on a greater urgency.

One additional factor in understanding the significance of our daydreams is the question of what we were doing at the moment we drifted into one. Daydreams are the manifestation of a block, and as we have seen, blocks affect us when our studies smack us against a self-image that is not compatible with the insights we are reaching. Daydreams snatch us away from what is uncomfortable and allow us instead to wallow in the familiar, whether it's a pleasant fantasy of being famous and admired, or a negative self-image we strongly identify with, such as daydreams involving being ridiculed or put down.

Exploring our daydreams, nighttime dreams and inner dialogue are all meaningful endeavors. When combined with the more formal aspects of Platonism, these various ways of studying our states of mind hold the potential to get us over those subtle hindrances that the study of metaphysics alone would not likely reveal. Equally important, this practice could play a vital role in quieting mental chatter, and thus ushering in more profound contemplative states.

---

[7] This ties to Chapter 22, where we saw that our assumptions about wisdom tell us about our current state of mind, not the wise state of mind.

Chapter 29: Silence

"And her announcement, being identically true concerning both the Other and the Same, is borne through the self-moved without speech or sound…"

Plato[1]

The Role of Silence

Those of you who have been doing the actual work outlined in the previous chapters have likely already touched the realm of Mind through your studies, contemplations, and meditations. Now it is time to cultivate a more intentional relationship with Mind, one you can enter often and at will. With the proper preparation, silence is the pathway into this realm. As such, it holds an honored place in this tradition. Plotinus wrote that the soul receives "a certain reason, what is it else but silent reason?"[2] Upon resting in the Intelligible, the soul "acts quietly, and being full requires nothing farther… "[3] He goes on to explain that "[t]he worthy soul becomes reason itself, and what it is in itself it demonstrates to others; but with respect to itself it is sight; for it is now collected into one, and perfectly quiet, not only so far as pertains to externals, but with reference to itself, and is all things within itself."[4]

Dialectic helps prepare the soul for vision and it is an essential tool in the process of understanding that vision, but the vision itself is beyond words:

> "In that, however, which is perfectly simple, there is nothing discursive; but it is sufficient to come into contact with it intellectually. That, however, which comes into contact with it, when it is in contact is neither able to say anything, nor has leisure to speak; but afterwards [when it falls off from contact] reasons about it."[5]

---

[1] *Timaeus*, 37b, trans. R. G. Bury

[2] Ennead III:Viii:6

[3] *Ibid.*

[4] *Ibid.*

[5] Ennead V:iii:17, brackets included

Even Plato, who treated dialectic as the copestone of his system and insisted that "no other discipline can with propriety be raised higher than this"[6] acknowledged that the vision itself is wordless. He wrote in a personal correspondence:

> "I never have written, nor ever shall write, about them [the Intelligible objects]. For a thing of this kind cannot be expressed by words like other disciplines, but by long familiarity, and living in conjunction with the thing itself, a light as it were leaping from a fire will on a sudden be enkindled in the soul, and there itself nourish itself."[7]

In the *Symposium*, Plato depicts Socrates falling into a contemplative state on his way to a dinner party. "Socrates had withdrawn himself into the porch of some neighboring house, and was there standing…"[8] When the host of the dinner party wants to call Socrates inside, a friend of Socrates' objects to this. "As he [Socrates] goes along he will sometimes stop, said he, without regarding where, and stand still awhile."[9] Towards the end of the dialogue, we learn that Socrates once stood in meditation for an entire night.[10] True to his word, though, Plato never wrote about what vision Socrates encountered in those states. We can only image the heights to which Socrates reached.

Perhaps Damascius had a lofty vision of this sort in mind when he wrote: "And what will turn out to be the limit of discourse, except silence…"[11] He reminds his readers numerous times that words hit a wall that can only be penetrated in silence. For example: "Intellect[12] alone can apprehend the forms, and we do not yet possess intellect, if we are too content with engaging in dialectic."[13] Those who wish to proceed to that highest of experiences must venture beyond language.

---

6 *Republic*, 534e

7 Epistle VII, 341c~d, brackets added

8 175a

9 175b

10 220c~d

11 *Problems and Solutions Concerning First Principles*, p. 81

12 Here he is referring to divine Mind, not to our colloquial understanding of our individual intellects.

13 *Ibid.*, p. 73

The methods that had aided us thus far must be abandoned for this leg of our journey:

"[W]e purify ourselves for the reception of unfamiliar concepts, and so we ascend by means of analogy and by negations, deprecating the things of our world by comparison to that and being led to this away from what is less valuable, the things of our world, toward what is more valuable. Such, in fact, has been our constant method *up to now*. And it is perhaps the case that the absolutely Ineffable is that about which we cannot even posit its ineffability."[14]

Even Proclus, who was arguably the most precise logician in the Platonic canon, placed great value on silence. In his *Theology of Plato*, he offers this contemplative prayer:

"And let all things extend us with a tranquil power to communion with the ineffable. Let us also, standing there, having transcended the intelligible (if we contain anything of this kind,) and with nearly closed eyes adoring as it were the rising sun, since it is not lawful for any being whatever intently to behold him—let us survey the sun whence the light of the intelligible Gods proceeds…and again from this divine tranquility descending into intellect, and from intellect, employing the reasonings of the soul…"[15]

Here we see Proclus also acknowledging a form of silence that transcends dialectic. He reminds us, however, that dialectic is what meets us on the descent and aids our downward journey through "employing the reasonings of the soul." He goes on in his prayer to clarify this final point further: "And again, after these things descending into a reasoning process from an intellectual hymn, and employing the irreprehensible knowledge of dialectic, let us…survey the manner in which the first God is exempt from the whole of things. And let our descent be as far as to this."[16]

His *Commentary on Plato's Parmenides* reiterates this role of silence:

"[A]ll dialectical activity ought to be eliminated. These dialectical operations are the preparation for the strain towards

[14] *Ibid.* pp. 73~4, italics added
[15] *The Theology of Plato*, p. 166, parentheses included
[16] *Ibid.*, p. 167

the One, but are not themselves the strain. Or rather, not only must it be eliminated, but the strain as well. Finally, when it has completed its course, the soul may rightly abide with the One. Having become single and alone in itself, it will choose only the simply One."[17]

After vision, we use dialectic to help us make an exact account of the One and what we were during that encounter. However, the vision itself is not reached by formulating the perfect, most comprehensive answer. Vision requires pushing beyond all verbal answers.

The reason for this long introduction to silence is to stress the importance of the role silence plays in our practice. People drawn to intellectual systems such as Platonism tend to rely heavily on a penchant for logical reasoning. We enjoy the challenges introduced to us by the main philosophers in this system, and we eagerly jump into debates or contemplations about them. We are uplifted by the insights these conjure up.

However, our areas of strength always contain our pitfalls. In the case of those of us with an analytical bend, turning it all off and reverting into silence pulls us out of our comfort zone. I suspect this is a big part of the reason why too many students reach a high level of understanding but then hit a plateau. We may find ourselves looking for a diversion, or we may find that our silence is interrupted by dialectical explorations and imaginary debates.[18] These are examples of ways we pull ourselves back into the roles we are most comfortable playing. The "knower's mask" is powerful; it is difficult to let go of.

I recommend aiming to sit in silence for just five minutes a day to start, and then gradually stretching the time, even if it is in one-minute increments. The urge to continue that internal dialogue will be strong at times, but it helps to remind yourself that it is only for five minutes. You'll still have the other 23 hours and 55 minutes of the day to analyze and to talk to yourself.

---

[17] p. 603

[18] Any technique, no matter how effective when used correctly, can be abused and become a distraction. Even connecting to the realm of Mind can be used as a distraction. I've had conversations with my *daemon* that ended with me being told to shut up already!

If you do this every day, you will be amazed at how much more productive your dialectic explorations become. Silent meditation allows us to tap into the higher reaches of our minds; insights spring out. It often happens hours or even days later, but there is no doubt that the periods of silence are an underlying factor. I've had periods in which I was very good about spending time in silent meditation every day, and then other periods in which I fell out of the habit. A clear pattern developed: my explorations were more insightful and productive when silent meditation was my daily habit. And ultimately, it is silent meditation that ushers in peak experiences.

Learning how to turn off the discursive thoughts that are our usual companions is one of the key areas that separates mystic Platonists from our strictly academic counterparts. In fact, I would argue that silence is the bottleneck that *all* spiritual systems have to pass through. Our entire practice up to now, with all of its various methods to purify ourselves and our vision of Reality, is to bring us to this point of transcending our physical existence.

Talking Our Way into Silence

The common image of Platonism is that it involves a lot of talking. Indeed, talking with a teacher or with other students is a crucial element of many people's practice. However, there's a time and a place for everything, as the saying goes. There's a time to talk and a time to, well, shut up. In a sense, the vast majority of the talk is really just preparation for diving into silence—and much of the remainder of the talk is our efforts to understand what we encountered in that silence.

Let's look at some techniques that can ease our transition into silence. It is a good idea to make note of difficulties that arise, but to address them later. For these techniques to be effective, you must be committed to sitting in silence for at least the pre-determined period of time with no distractions. If you allow yourself to chase after other thoughts, you will find the flow of thoughts to be never-ending.

As Easy as Flying a Kite

Sitting in silence does not mean that we stop thinking. Our intention is to stop the flow of discursive voices. It is not necessary to also turn off the visual images that dance before our mind's eye. Of course, visualizations without discursive commentary means that we are not analyzing the images at the time we "see" them.

Visualizations can provide us something to focus on, and this eases the initial discomfort of not talking to ourselves. The most effective visualization I have ever used to turn off discursive voices came to me in a dream. It came at a time when I was struggling with my efforts to sit in silence. Either I would become restless, or I would fall asleep. It was obvious to me that I had hit a block and a false belief was the main culprit, but I also suspected that my technique was not correct. I was wrestling with the voices in my head rather than doing anything that felt productive.

This was a markedly frustrating period, as I understood in theory that I needed to learn this skill. As I drifted off to sleep one night after yet another failed attempt, I wondered what I should do differently. I dreamt that night that I was alone in a large field. It was a sunny, warm day with a light breeze. I was flying a kite. I never got a good look at the pattern on the kite. It was just an indiscernible diamond shape in the distance. My eyes were focused on the kite, but the dream pulled my attention to my hands. I was holding the reel and string with both hands at a level just above my waist. As I watched the kite bouncing gently in the wind, I moved my hands accordingly to adjust the string. A little to the right, then a tad to the left. Always side to side; never up or down. In this dream, I was not controlling where the kite went, but rather I was actively following it and maintaining its steadiness. The words *steady, balance,* and *harmony* were repeating in my mind's ear as I woke from the dream.

It did not take long to recognize the gift I had been given. That morning, I used the imagery from the dream to have what I would call my first successful silent meditation. I continued using this technique for many months, until eventually I did not need it anymore.

Let's break this down into steps to take a closer look at why this imagery is particularly effective:

● Once you are in a comfortable meditation posture and ready to begin visualizing, see yourself in a bright, sunny green field. Feel the breeze against your skin and the warmth of the sun. Let yourself become relaxed; this is the ideal state of mind from which to begin.

- Now see yourself flying a kite. It does not matter what your kite looks like, or even if you are able to make out its precise shape or color scheme. What is important is that you imagine yourself looking up at it. Keep your eyelids closed during this visualization, but let your eyeballs turn upward as though you could really see that kite. Your eyes are now turned toward an energy point at the top of your head. This directs the flow of your spiritual energy upward.

- Although your eyes are turned upward, your attention is on your hands. In the visualization, they are somewhere between the waist and the navel. This is another important energy point. In Japanese Zen, it is called the *hara*[19] and is considered to be "a wellspring of vital psychic energies."[20] Consistent focus on the *hara* is said to encourage mental equilibrium and strengthen our will power.

- Now you are watching the kite, directing spiritual energy upward, but you are also aware of your hands at the level of your *hara*. As the kite bobs slightly to the right or the left, you imagine moving the string as appropriate. Of course, your hands are not really moving; your attention is rather on your hands in the visualization, which means you feel the movement in the *hara*.

- It is not necessary to control the breath in this meditation. Just breathe naturally. When you feel inner dialogue pushing to burst into your thoughts, you can hold it off by your focus on the kite. Extend the silence until the kite sways one more time, and then once more, and then once more, for as long as you are able to stretch it. When chatter does break through, gently bring your focus back to the bobbing of the kite in the wind. With practice, silence becomes easier to maintain.

Some of you may prefer to experiment with other visualizations of your own, such as surfing or hang gliding. There is no harm in experimenting. However, you will be hard-pressed to find other imagery that directs the flow of energy in through the *hara* and up and

---

[19] *Hara* is the Japanese word for *belly*, but it's significance in this context extends beyond the physical.

[20] Kapleau, *The Three Pillars of Zen*, pp. 15~6

out through the top of the head, while also maintaining this same balance of control and letting go.

Seeing yourself as the kite, for example, or a leaf blowing in the wind, is too passive and so you will probably fall asleep. More importantly, such imagery does not capture our proper relationship with the realm of Mind. Our aim is to enter an interactive relationship with Mind, not merely to be carried away by it. Trusting our intuition and respecting the wisdom of Mind does not mean that we relinquish our free will. We must actively choose to enter and honor this relationship. Living wisely means choosing to honor what is good and beautiful and in accordance with Truth. Wisdom is a choice—it isn't something that passively happens to us. And once we make this choice, it is a choice we must make again and again, every moment of our lives.

On the other hand, visualizing yourself doing something active, such as skiing, gives yourself far more control. However, this lends itself to a different problem. Here there is no letting go. The ideal relationship is to trust and respect wisdom, and to let it be our guide while we still are active participants. We look to Truth as a pattern we hold in the soul, and that pattern guides us in all our activities. Truth in a certain sense is like a breeze that blows through us, and by recognizing its movement we adjust to match it accordingly. This requires an openness and spontaneity that a person demanding constant control is not able to muster.

Once you become comfortable with this imagery and can sit in silence for extended periods, you can let the kite imagery go. Continue to turn your eyes upward, though, and feel the flow of energy in through the *hara* and out the top of the head. Also, the balance that you found that had allowed you to follow the kite without being passive is an important skill, one that ought to mark all of your meditative and contemplative efforts from this stage on.

Following the Breath

Those who are not comfortable utilizing imagery such as that described above may find that the meditation of following the breath, introduced back in Chapter 18, can be an effective bridge into silence. We can take that meditation a step further by imagining energy being sucked into the *hara* with each inhalation and then moving up the spine and out the top of the head with each exhalation.

As a practice for sitting in silence, we can trick ourselves into holding discursive thoughts at bay by first carrying the silence just up until the exhalation, then stretching it to the next inhalation, then the next exhalation, and so on. Five minutes can feel like an eternity, but keeping silent just until the next exhalation is much easier. When discursive thoughts do break through, simply acknowledge them and gently bring your attention back to the breath. The balance of passive and active participation achieved with the kite meditation applies here as well.

Working Meditation

Eventually, silent meditation needs to be extended beyond formal sitting times. It is not the actual act of sitting in formal meditation that awakens higher states of mind, but rather the key is in our penetrating focus. We want our meditative focus to evolve into a state of contemplative oneness. Once we gain some proficiency with silent meditation, the next step is to carry silence with us all day long, wherever we go. As we strengthen our energy and also quiet the voices triggered by self-images, this becomes easier to do.

A nice transition from formal sitting is to start with activities you do alone. When I'm by myself—walking, riding the subway, cooking—I try to focus on the activity I'm engaged in without any discursive thoughts. Following the breath as described above is a helpful way to keep mental commentary at bay. It is a difficult practice to maintain for large stretches of time, but when successful it results in truly peaceful and beautiful states of mind.

As beautiful as these states of mind are, they can be deepened even further. Maintaining silence is powerful when combined with dialectic. To do this, we penetrate our question and hold it in the silence. Early on, such efforts function more to surface our false beliefs and limiting self-images. Once our practice ripens, though, its true rewards manifest.

Any question that grabs you can be effective. Two of my favorites are, *What is the One?* and *What is the Self?* Whereas we use logic and reasoning to grapple with these questions in other areas of study, here we are giving ourselves time to sit with the question and let it silently fold inward. Our dialectic efforts feed our silence, and in turn our silence feeds our dialectic efforts.

We can still carry on our other formal practices, but now we are ready to stop compartmentalizing. As a silent contemplation, our question never leaves us. Whatever our outward activity—vacuuming the floor, walking the dog—the question is ever-present, burning within us. When the quest for truth ripens beyond a theoretical curiosity, we can no longer devote certain hours to it and then file it away during family time or get-togethers with friends. The search must become all-consuming.

In a very important sense, silent contemplation is nothing more than carrying dialectic to its natural end. All dialectic work—and every insight—culminates in silence. It requires reaching the boundaries of language and then taking that leap beyond. Proclus ends his *Commentary on Plato's Parmenides* with this very point:

> "But after going through all the negations, one ought to set aside this dialectical method also, being troublesome and introducing the notion of the things denied with which the One can have no neighborhood. For the intellect cannot have a pure vision when it is obstructed intelligising the things that come after it...nor in general is it possible to have perfect vision with deliberation."[21]

The question, *What is the One?* draws us upwards, fueling our desire to merge with the First Cause of all. The question, *What is the Self?* draws us inwards, in search of the recognition that seeing the sun himself "in his own proper region"[22] is an act of reversion. We, in essence, are no different from that.

Which question we choose depends on which question appeals to us more. What does it mean—really—to *know thyself* or to know the One? Is it something beyond us? Is it something within us? If it is outside of us, then what is our connection to it? But if it is found within, then where do we search? Can it be found in our heart, or our head, or perhaps our left big toe? On one level, this search seems to make no sense at all, yet surely *knowing thyself* is something more profound than tracing back our biological ancestry or engaging in

---

[21] p. 602
[22] *Republic,* 516b

practices to overcome insecurities. As meaningful as such efforts can be, our current goal is even grander.

Is it enough to turn inward and feel a warm, soothing tingle? Is the Self happy, or confident, or at peace with the world? These states of mind are outgrowths of touching the Self, yet they are not the Self. Does the Self remain focused on the moment? Does it follow the ebb and flow of life? Does the Self extend patience and compassion to all living things? These are ways of being that come naturally to those who are wise, yet the Self itself has no attributes, no distinguishing marks whatsoever. It does not smile or hug or laugh. We cannot even say that it is good or compassionate because it is beyond all descriptions. It is even beyond existence itself.

The name *the Self* is another name for the One, the Ineffable that is beyond all names. The Self or the One is not in the moment, or in anything at all, because it is beyond the dichotomy of being in time and place or not being in time and place. Whether we penetrate inward or upward, we seem to find nothingness; yet the Self is not nothing. The One is not nothing. After all, it is the cause of all the goodness and beauty in the entire cosmos. And so we are left with our elusive question: What is the One? What is the Self? This is the silent contemplation that we carry with us throughout the day and night.

First the Bad News…

It is an unfortunate fact in medical science that we often feel worse before we feel better. Such is also the case when healing the soul. Like medications for physical ailments, silent meditation and contemplation have some side effects that we must be aware of. These practices are more intense than the preparatory meditations introduced in Chapter 18. Even short sittings have the ability to open energy blocks and awaken limiting self-images that had been lying dormant.

For this reason, I recommend giving yourself at least a year of initial cleansing before taking on this stage of practice. Many people like to skip ahead when reading spiritual books, but there is a reason this practice is outlined near the end. All of the exercises introduced previously give us the foundation we need to handle whatever states of mind emerge from the silence. Some people gently enter into this stage. For others, it is tumultuous. It takes a stable and courageous character to recognize unhealthy states of mind for what they are and to subject them to analysis, rather than validating them and letting them control us.

Unhealthy states of mind, whether in the form of insecurities or fears or restlessness, are residue from an earlier way of being, self-images picked up in childhood. They are not who we truly are. Rooting out those false images is part of the process we must go through to behold the Reality that is our essence and the essence of all that *is*.

Now the Good News...

Before mastering this practice, we tend to think of silence as nothing more than the absence of sound. Most of us treat this absence as a hardship that we must struggle to endure. We try to hold the sound of our thoughts at bay, exerting our will and treating this exercise as a form of repression. This is the error I had been making before the dream about flying a kite pointed me in the right direction.

We must come to recognize silence as a fullness rather than as an emptiness. It is only when we are in the doorway that we are straining to hold sound away. As we proceed further, silence sucks us in. We discover that it is a *thing* in its own right (not just the lack of something else). It has movement and texture; we become enveloped in its vitality and intelligibility. This is generally felt only faintly at first, but it will strengthen over time. It is here that we can ask questions and feel the answers. In metaphysics, this is called the realm of Intellect or Mind. With practice, we can enter this state of mind as often as we want, whenever we want. Our aim eventually is never to detach from Mind.

Deepening our Connection with Mind

At this stage of our practice, we have cleansed ignorance enough to recognize noticeable improvements in our states of mind, and our understanding has matured considerably. Our continued reading and contemplating contribute to this goal. Understanding and experience go hand in hand in the cultivating of wisdom; a peak experience without the commensurate degree of purification and understanding is a hollow achievement.

Alongside these established methods, meditation will also play a role. Silent meditation trains us to deepen our connection to Mind. We are now treading far beyond where academia dares to venture. We are ready to forge a relationship with our *daemon*.

What is a *daemon*, anyway? The word *daemon* is a transliteration of a Greek word that means *a lesser god*, or *a guiding spirit*. Socrates often talked of hearing one, most famously perhaps in the *Apology of Socrates:* "[A] certain divine and daemoniacal voice is present with me, which also Melitus in his accusation derided. This voice attended me from a child..."[23] This "voice" offers guidance and wisdom. In the *Timaeus,* Plato suggests that the *daemon* equates with the highest functioning of the wisdom-loving aspect of our souls: "Divinity assigned this to each of us as a daemon; and...it resides in the very summit of the body, elevating us from earth to an alliance with the heavens..."[24]

Initially, it doesn't matter if you believe that there actually are spiritual guides within the realm of Mind called *daemons,* or if you think of them as a personification of Mind itself. Perhaps you hold some other theory, such as that of having a "higher self." There is no need to decide right away which hypothesis is best, or if none of them are right.

What is important is being open-minded enough to venture into this experiment. The first step is to reach a place of profound silence. The practices described earlier in this chapter can help you to build to this level of proficiency. Once you feel enveloped in silence, you are ready to ask a question. It might be a question about a perplexing area of metaphysics, or perhaps related to a block you are having trouble opening up. Whatever question you choose, make it a meaningful and sincere one. Then stay in that silence, "watching" and feeling its texture. Wait for the answer to gradually form.

Some people take to this practice more quickly than others. Please don't despair if you do not succeed in the first few tries. If you are sincere and determined in your endeavor, you are bound to get results eventually. Patience is a virtue here; the answer can't be forced or rushed. In my own experience, I've found that my efforts improved

---

[23] 31d

[24] 90a. The three aspects of the soul—the wisdom-loving part (*logos*), the high-spirited part (*thumos*), and the desiring part (*epithumia*)—were introduced in Chapter 4.

once I learned to enjoy being immersed in silence. Answers to my dilemmas are always appreciated, but the experience itself is equally (if not more) important.

You want to keep in mind here that the answers may form in words in your mind, but they may also come to you as images. It is good to pay attention to any thoughts that pop up, never forgetting that there are no truly random thoughts. Within those images might be your answer, or there may be clues to the false belief that is blocking you from reaching the answer. A great openness is required of you in order to forge this relationship.

One technique I have used is to write down my question before turning inward. Then, when I felt the answer forming, I would pick up my pen and write whatever came to mind without any editing. Those who are more comfortable speaking than writing may find similar results by using a voice recorder in the same way. It was this practice I was embarking on when I hit the block introduced back in Chapter 16, that of seeing myself as the perpetual student. The answers I found myself writing were beyond anything I ever expected.

A variation of this which I highly recommend is to write only the answer. Writing the question opens us to the error of creating a false dichotomy between ourselves as questioners and the wisdom that flows in the answer. This was the error I had made. Writing the question reinforces our identification with a lower state of mind. We must trust that the wisdom of the answer is also coming from ourselves.

Whether writing or speaking, let the answer flow without holding anything back or trying to inject the answer you would like or expect into your response. This is crucial to the success of this method. Therefore, I don't recommend that you share your answers with anyone else, at least not until you have gained a certain degree of proficiency with this technique. We are all more likely to self-edit if we imagine our friends and loved ones reading our answers.

It is wrong to think of our *daemons* or of Mind as a resource to be tapped. There is no servant ready to satisfy our every whim, and the maxim that the customer is always right does not apply here. We are more like explorers venturing into a foreign land. Mind/our *daemon* speaks to us in its own native tongue, and it is our responsibility and our task to learn that language. It is now time to immerse ourselves in what perhaps feels like a foreign culture. We can find lifelong rewards in this yet-unfamiliar land, but we must work hard to do our part.

We will quickly discover that interpretation colors our understanding of the realm of Mind as surely as it does our understanding of this physical realm. When wisdom comes to us in words, there is room to read between the lines. When it comes as a feeling or a vague sense, we fill in the blanks with our expectations and our beliefs about the nature of Reality. Therefore, it is important that we never abandon our reading, contemplations, or dialectical explorations. All of the various areas of our practice aid one another.

Learning this language is a continuation of our purification and education. Becoming a friend to our *daemon,* we become a friend to ourselves.[25] The more our practice deepens, the better we can appreciate that Platonism is a way of life. Our higher communications will help us in our efforts to clear away what is false and further unify our energy. In this way, they open us to peak experiences and insights into truth. In turn, the quality of the wisdom we access grows with us as we mature spiritually. The insights we gain to our metaphysical and other questions feed and deepen this healthy state of mind.

Connecting with Mind is an important milestone in our growth. As we gain familiarity with the realm of Mind, we are also fostering continued growth into the fullest flowering of Mind: an encounter with Reality itself. Yet our ventures into the realm of Mind are more than a step toward this further goal, and they will continue long after a peak experience. Our connection to Mind is the reward of a life lived courageously. This return to Mind is the natural passageway for anyone on the quest to *know thyself.*

Our connection to Mind is a return to our roots. We gradually come to realize that this foreign land is more familiar to us than the bizarre societies in which we were raised and in which we currently live. What may seem at first like a sojourn abroad is more accurately a return home. Learning, after all, is nothing more than remembering.[26] Remembering the realm of Mind brings us closer to remembering ourselves. Plotinus tells us:

---

[25] Cf. W.H.D. Rouse's translation of *Republic,* 443e: "[H]e must have…set all in order, and become a friend to himself."

[26] See *Meno,* 81c~d. This tenet of Platonism was introduced in Chapter 5.

"God is not external to anyone, but is present with all things, though they are ignorant that he is so. For they fly from him, or rather from themselves. They are unable, therefore, to apprehend that from which they fly. And having destroyed themselves, they are incapable of seeking after another. For neither will a child, when through insanity he becomes out of himself, recognize his father. But he who knows himself, will also know from whence he was derived."[27]

---

[27] Ennead VI:ix:7.

Chapter 30: A Final Word on the Wordless

"But everything good is beautiful…"

Plato[1]

Finding Meaning

A spiritual journey could potentially culminate with a connection to the realm of Mind, as described in the last chapter. Philosophers in the Platonic tradition, however, challenge us to make an account not only of what was encountered in the upper world of Plato's cave allegory, but also the cause of the Intelligible and that for the sake of which it exists.[2]

All things desire the Good and exist for its sake, but the Good itself desires nothing. Why would it? For to desire something implies a lack, yet the Good is beyond all things and therefore needs nothing and desires nothing. "For other natures indeed possess an energy *about*, and for the sake of, The Good, but The Good Itself is not indigent of anything, and on this account nothing is present with it besides itself."[3] This higher contemplation peaks as the fifth stage of the spiritual journey, although certainly we ponder the First Cause at every stage.

Anything that exists must have a cause, and so Existence itself must surely have a cause as well. Anyone who has been blessed with a direct experience of Reality, though, can appreciate the resistance this argument meets. The Intelligible is felt with such immediacy and power that anyone immersed in it knows beyond a doubt that nothing—no thing—can be beyond it. It is the apex of all.

This apex is vital, it is intelligible, it truly *is*, its truth and presence are unquestionable, it is Beauty itself. It is Reality itself as a unified whole, not in a seed form or as a mere potentiality. It is the paradigm whose likeness unfolds through all the realms of being. All of this can be discerned from the experience of Reality or deduced afterwards.

---

[1] *Timaeus*, 87c

[2] See *Philebus* from 53b. Socrates concludes at 54d that: "Now that, for the sake of which is always generated whatever is generated for some end, must be in the rank of things which are good…"

[3] Ennead III:viii:11

Yet, if it is all this, then it is a unified manyness; not truly one. But our reasoning tells us that for a union to exist, there must be the source of union prior to it.[4] And so we are forced to acknowledge that although this union is the zenith of existence itself, there is that beyond it which is prior to existence and is its cause. Being prior to existence, it itself does not exist. Yet it is nonexistent *not* in the sense of being less than existence, but in the sense of being greater than it.

This cause is referred to by many names, although it actually is beyond any of them. It is the One which gives union to all and so allows existent things to exist. It is the Good which is the desire of all and the source of providential goodness flowing to all to a degree commensurate to their being and their ability to receive. Some simply call it Ineffable, but all recognize it to be the *why* behind the mechanics of the entire cosmos. For to say that Being unfolds into subsequent realms or that learning is the method of return still leaves us without any insight into why this great cosmos exists. Are we no different than the itsy-bitsy spider, climbing up only to get washed down again with each incarnation?

The mechanics of the *how* do not give us the *why*, which is needed to find meaning. It is only by knowing the Good for which all causes unfold and for which all activity is aimed that this greatest of wonders of which we are a part begins to make sense.

> "But when you behold, behold him totally; and when you energize with intellect concerning him, whatever you retain in your memory of his nature, be careful to understand it as the good. For he is the cause of a wise and intellectual life: since he is that power itself, from which life and intellect is produced; and he is the author of essence and being, because he is the one itself. And he is perfectly simple, and the first, because he is the principle of all."[5]

---

[4] This was discussed in Chapter 8. See also *The Elements of Theology*, prop. 3: "*All that becomes one does so by participation of unity [the One]*. For what becomes one is itself not-one, but is one inasmuch as it is affected by participation of unity [the One]: since, if things which are not in themselves one should become one, they surely do so by coming together and by communication in each other, and so are subjected to the presence of unity [the One] without being unity [the One] unqualified." Brackets added.

[5] Ennead V:v:10

Just as all the realms of being exist for the sake of the Good itself, so too all human endeavors are undertaken with an eye on what is understood to be good. What we see as good, we deem to be beautiful. Plato recognizes here not only physical beauty, but also the beauty of theories and, of course, divine beauty. He wrote in the *Timaeus:* "But everything good is beautiful..."[6] This connection between what we see as good and what we see as beautiful is true across the board, even for those goals that we recognize to be harmful to ourselves or others, or goals that we judge to be immoral or foolish. If we proceed anyway, there must be some benefit we surmise, some image of beauty we desire.

Whatever we see as good and beautiful, we love. Plato calls love "desire of things good, and...longing after happiness."[7] This holds true for charitable acts and acts of greed alike. It applies to both the faithful spouse and the adulterous one. All of our actions are guided by what we deem good in the sense of capturing some image of what we see as beautiful and so being beneficial to securing our happiness. "Love, then, in fine" Plato tells us, "is the desire of having good in perpetual possession."[8]

Love binds all the realms of being—from the Intelligible to our physical realm of becoming—into one,[9] and it powers all of our actions. And indeed, the power of love and its connection to the good and beautiful compels Socrates, who is perhaps most famous for his claims of knowing nothing, to declare that love is the one thing he does know about.[10]

Knowing love at its deepest levels means knowing wisdom. Our higher impulses towards goodness conceive pregnancy in the soul rather than in the body. "For those there are who are more prolific in their souls than in their bodies; and are full of the seeds of such an

---

[6] 87c

[7] *Symposium,* 205d

[8] *Ibid.,* 206a

[9] See *Ibid.,* 203a

[10] *Ibid.,* 198d. Although Socrates makes this claim, love is actually not the only thing he ever claimed to know. In the *Theatetus,* for example, he talks about knowing the art of philosophical midwifery. See also the *Meno,* 98b, where he declares that he knows the difference between right opinion and understanding.

offspring as it peculiarly belongs to the human soul to conceive and to generate. And what offspring is this, but wisdom and every other virtue?"[11] In its highest expression, love draws us to the most dazzling beauty of all, Beauty itself:

> "Suddenly he will discover, bursting into view, a beauty astonishingly admirable…it subsists alone with itself, and possesses an essence eternally uniform. All other forms which are beauteous participate of this; but in such a manner they participate, that by their generation or destruction this suffers no diminution, receives no addition, nor undergoes any kind of alteration."[12]

We can potentially spend years integrating knowledge of the Intelligible. Yet our journey stretches on, for we have yet to turn to that for the sake of which Reality itself exists. Stage 5 of Plato's spiritual journey is to rise to the Good. Plato tells us that philosophers who have reached this stage "are obliged, inclining the ray of their soul, to look towards that which imparts light to all things, and, when they have viewed *the good itself*, to use it as a paradigm…during the remainder of their life."[13]

While the Good itself is beyond existence and therefore beyond experience, we can experience the Good that *is*. This is also known as the One that *is*. Throughout this book, I have been calling this the One-Being.[14] This fusing of knower and known stretches to its very limits our notions of what an experience is. We therefore must use the word *experience* loosely, and readily acknowledge that it is all but impossible to fathom what we are loosely referring to until we ourselves know this fusion. Nevertheless, fathoming it is important to

---

[11] *Ibid.*, 209a

[12] *Ibid.*, 210e~211b, italics included.

[13] *Republic*, 540a

[14] This distinction between unified Being as the peak of stage 3 and the One-Being as stage 5 was carried on after Plato. A number of quotes from Plotinus appear throughout this chapter. Proclus, also, emphasized this distinction. Here is a quote from his *Commentary on Plato's Parmenides*, sec. 969, p. 316: "Parmenides was raising the hypothesis about the Forms from the sense-world up to the very peak of the intelligible world, in which are found the Forms in their primal manifestation and the unitary aspect of numbers which is deified by light from the Good, from which the ascent to the One-Being and the 'hearth' of real beings is easy for him."

try. Plotinus uses the example of the centers of two different circles overlapping. There is no longer any separation between the two points, and so they become the same:

"The man who obtains the vision becomes, as it were, another being. He ceases to be himself, retains nothing of himself. Absorbed in the beyond he is one with it, like a center coincident with another center."[15]

Our contemplations lead us to this highest of visions when we look beyond the Intelligible itself to its source. Plotinus writes:

"For he who desires to know intelligible essence, then only perceives what is above sense, when he possesses no image of a sensible object; so he who desires to contemplate a nature superior to intelligible essence, will enjoy the ineffable vision, if he neglects everything intelligible, while merged in the most profound and delightful of all contemplations…"[16]

And the insight that we nurture from this "ineffable vision" is the power of the Good, not only in the physical realm but throughout all the realms of being. All of our actions, spiritual or otherwise, are guided by love for what we deem good and so see as beautiful. The more accurate our understanding of what is truly good, the healthier our choices. When we recognize that goodness is what guides everything in the universe, we see the need for all creation, from the unfolding of Being, to procreation, to our human endeavors to manifest our insights through art and business. We see why love drives all of us in our search for union and return, whether on the physical plane or a return to Self.

A Beam of Light

Love in the Intelligible realms can be described as the gods also acting on what they see as good, and this goodness shines through our cosmos as providence. Providence, then, is the manifestation of the will of the gods.[17] In an analogous way, we too act on what we see

---

[15] Ennead VI:ix:10, trans. Elmer O'Brien

[16] Ennead V:v:6

[17] Consider this line from *Commentaries of Proclus on the Timaeus of Plato* I, 371, 8: "For providence indeed, is suspended from will, but will from goodness." Proclus here is setting up a triad with goodness at the hyparxis, will as the power of the triad, and providence at the extremity.

as good, and acting on the love that powers our endeavors we call free will. Again, this holds true even if we recognize our actions to be immoral or illegal; we engage in "bad" behavior because we think doing so will benefit us in some way.

Think of a beam of light shining from a flashlight (see diagram below). If the flashlight represents the Good, then the light closest to it is like the unified, potent Intelligible.[18] It never veers from the Good and so its will never veers, either. The farthest reaches of the beam, however, are weaker and more differentiated. This analogy is imperfect because unlike the beam of light from a flashlight, being does not spread out in its unfolding as if it were a physical thing that exists in space. Still, this imagery can be useful to us.

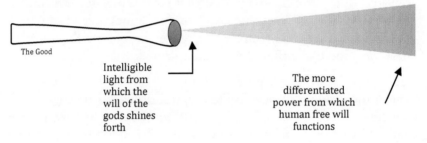

The Good

Intelligible light from which the will of the gods shines forth

The more differentiated power from which human free will functions

The farthest reaches of the beam are where most of us function, pursuing our images of goodness—appearances of goodness on the wall of the cave—rather than knowing the Good itself. Therefore, our will is only sometimes powered by what is truly good and oftentimes misses the mark. We call this exercising free will. It is in this sense that Socrates maintains that nobody does wrong voluntarily.[19]

Those who interpret a spiritual life as a giving up of free will don't recognize the connection between Mind as it functions in the Intelligible and how we function as intellectual beings in our everyday conventional ways of thinking. As the flashlight analogy demonstrates, it is the same beam functioning at different degrees of unity and potency. Plotinus tells us:

---

[18] Compare *Ibid.*, p. 292: "unified truth…is the light proceeding from *the good…*"

[19] This is the theme of the dialogue *Lesser Hippias*. See also the discussion in the *Laws* at 860~2. The story in the *Phaedrus* of the chariots of the gods and their contrast with the chariots of human souls is also relevant here.

"[S]omeone becomes himself intellect, when dismissing other things pertaining to himself, he beholds intellect through intellect, and by it also surveys himself, just as intellect likewise beholds itself."[20]

It is difficult to reconcile free will with the oft-repeated conclusion of mystics that our thoughts are not truly our own. We are understandably repelled by this apparent attack on our individuality, and as students we struggle with it terribly. This perhaps shows itself most prominently in our work with our own states of mind. The more we notice the hand of providence in our dreams and our private thoughts, the more we wonder where the intrusion ends. If our dreams are divine gifts, then there is a sense in which they are not our own. Even our mental wanderings throughout the day that seem to be intensely personal reveal themselves to be tinged with providence. Where do we draw the line?

There seems an inherent contradiction between identifying with divine Mind on the one hand and exercising free will on the other. However, with the recognition that the Good is the motivation behind all action at all metaphysical levels of the cosmos, such a reconciliation is possible. The more we recognize ourselves as Mind, the better we appreciate that beyond our temporal and individual existence is a unified mode of being that is outside of time. In other words, the beam of light in this analogy is not only analogous to some distant metaphysical reality that we call Mind; it is analogous to each of us as well. We are not separate from Mind or from providence. The line we are trying to draw between our own thoughts and those that are divine gifts is an artificial one, for we will find ourselves on both sides of the line wherever we draw it.

Therefore, ultimate freedom is not found in chasing every whim without knowledge of whether or not doing so is truly beneficial. Freedom is found in freeing ourselves of the ignorance that binds us to a life of confusion and mediocrity. It is found in making ourselves sacred and as godlike as is humanly possible.[21] Doing so puts our will

---

[20] Ennead V:iii:4

[21] Making ourselves sacred was discussed in Chapter 2. Plato makes many references to this notion of becoming godlike throughout his works. There is one example in the footnote to this discussion in Chapter 2. Another is *Theatetus,* 176a: "Divinity is never in any respect unjust, but is most just. And there is not anything more similar to him, than a man when he becomes most just."

to a commensurate degree in line with the will of the gods. Carrying in our souls a vision of the Good and aligning our lives to that is the ultimate expression of freedom, justice, and wisdom. With this insight, we come to fully appreciate and embrace why the Platonists view *good* and *bad* in terms of what is healthy or unhealthy for the soul.

Healthy States of Mind

And now our journey has come full circle. We sought to find a methodology to guide us toward the state of mind of one who would naturally desire what is good.[22] We found that instead of thinking of good in the conventional sense of ethical or moral behavior, Platonism focuses on a healthy condition of the soul, which manifests as the healthy state of mind that Plato calls virtue. A person whose soul is healthy would naturally wish to preserve beauty and unity in the world, and would see no value in hurting others. This person would naturally behave ethically and morally without coercion or strain.

By recognizing the virtues collectively, and each individually, as a state of mind, Plato is able to go the next step by declaring that the person with a healthy state of mind is the one who is truly happy. "I consider temperance as a certain mighty good; and I am persuaded, that if you possess it, you are *blessed*."[23] He ends the dialogue *Charmides* by having Socrates advise the title character to examine himself in search of temperance. "I shall advise you to consider yourself happy in proportion to the degree of temperance which you possess."[24]

Plato fleshes out this connection even more strikingly in the *Republic*:

> "[S]hall we boldly say concerning all the pleasures, both respecting the avaricious and the ambitious part, that such of them as are obedient to science [knowledge/*episteme*] and reason, and, in conjunction with these, pursue and obtain the pleasures of which the wise part of the soul is the leader, shall obtain the truest pleasures, as far as it is possible for them to

---

[22] See Chapter 2.

[23] *Charmides*, 175e

[24] *Ibid.*, 176a

attain to true pleasure, and in as much as they follow truth, pleasures which are properly their own; if indeed what is best for everyone be most properly his own?...When then the whole soul is obedient to the philosophic part, and there is no sedition in it, then every part in other respects performs its proper business, and is just, and also reaps its own pleasures, and such as are the best, and as far as is possible the most true."[25]

We have discovered that such a state of mind is not only possible to attain, but is our birthright and human destiny. The truly spiritual life is not forged by imposing a list of ideal behaviors or commandments onto ourselves, but by seeking to *know thyself* and thus discovering that divine goodness is not separate from the self of our search.

Once we reach this state of mind, the effort of maintaining this healthy state and living with wisdom as our guide turns every minute of every day into a personal adventure that opens us to lessons we hadn't even imagined. Our practice becomes one of discovering all the various ways that the mystery of being alive is indelibly tied to the vision of Truth we beheld when we recognized the very essence of our being. We tackle this in part by returning to our reading and to our various forms of contemplation, but also by integrating our insights into our daily interactions in the world. Reality is around us and throughout us. It is from here that the significance of *knowing thyself* is just starting to unfold.

Socrates lived a life of selfless service to his fellow Athenians. He found joy in questioning others and challenging them to grow, and he felt friendship towards both those who appreciated him and those who did not. This state of mind naturally develops as we grow into the recognition of our rightful place in the whole. While our identity as an individual remains, that identity, at the same time, gradually widens to more fully encompass our connection to the great unfolding of Being. We are each a unique expression of divine goodness.

It is this shift that marks the start of our progression into stage 6 of our journey, that of becoming a guide to others. It is a continuation of the blossoming of a healthy state of mind. We discover that a

---

[25] *Republic,* 586d~e, brackets added

curious student and a wise teacher can exist together in the same soul, without contradiction and without conceit. With each new insight, new questions emerge; with each step we take, a new beginning reveals itself.

Bibliography

Publications from the Prometheus Trust catalogues:

Addey, Tim, *The Unfolding Wings: The Way of Perfection in the Platonic Tradition*, 2003.

Aristotle, *Works of Aristotle volume 6: On the Soul* (Trans. Thomas Taylor), 2003.

Damascius, *Lectures on the Philebus* (Trans. L. G. Westerink), 2010.

Plato (trans. 1804) *The Works of Plato in Five Volumes* (Trans. Thomas Taylor), 1995~6.

Plotinus (trans. 1817). *Collected Writings of Plotinus* (Trans. Thomas Taylor), 2000.

Proclus (trans. 1816). *The Elements of Theology* (Trans. Thomas Taylor), 1994.

----- (trans. 1816). *The Theology of Plato* (Trans. Thomas Taylor), 1995.

Taylor, Thomas, *Theoretic Arithmetic of the Pythagoreans*, 2006 (originally published 1816).

Additional publications of translated works:

Balboa, Juan F. (Trans.), *Parmenides Plato and Parmenides Poem*. Self-published: Lulu.com, 2017.

Damascius, *Problems and Solutions Concerning First Principles* (Trans. Sara Ahbel-Rappe). New York, NY: Oxford University Press, 2010.

Edwards, Mark (Trans.) *Neoplatonic Saints: The Lives of Plotinus and Proclus by their Students*. Liverpool, UK: Liverpool University Press, 2000.

Euclid, *Elements* (Trans. Thomas L. Heath) Ann Arbor, MI: Sheridan Books, Inc., 2007.

Homer, *The Iliad* (Trans. Robert Fitzgerald). New York, NY: Oxford University Press, 1974.

King James Study Bible, Liberty University, 1988.

Proclus (trans. 1810) *Commentaries of Proclus on the Timaeus of Plato* (Trans. Thomas Taylor). Stuminster, Prometheus Trust, 1998.

Plato, *Plato: The Collected Dialogues* (Edith Hamilton and Huntington Cairns, editors), NJ: Princeton University Press, 1989.

Plato, *Great Dialogues of Plato* (Trans. W.H.D. Rouse). New York: Signet Classic, 1999.

Plato, *Loeb Classical Library*, Cambridge, MA: Harvard University Press.

Plotinus, *The Essential Plotinus* (Trans. Elmer O'Brien). Indianapolis, Indiana: Hackett Publishing Company, Inc., 1964.

----- (trans. 1930) *The Six Enneads* (Trans. Stephen MacKenna and B. S. Page). See 1990 reprint New York, Larson Publications.

Proclus, *Proclus' Commentary on Plato's Parmenides* (Trans. G. R. Morrow & J. M. Dillon). Princeton, NJ: Princeton University Press, 1987.

-----,*The Elements of Theology* (Trans. E. R. Dodds). Oxford: Oxford University Press, 1963.

Saint Synesios, *On Dreams* (Trans. Isaac Myer). Washington, D.C.: Self-published, 1888. Available on Internet Archive from the collections of Harvard University.

Wheelwright, Philip (Editor), *The Presocratics*. Upper Saddle River, NJ: Prentice-Hall, Inc., 1997.

Xenophon, *Conversations of Socrates* (Trans. Hugh Tredennick and Robin Waterfield). London, UK: Penguin Classics, 1990.

Other Publications:

Audi, Robert (editor) *The Cambridge Dictionary of Philosophy, Second Edition*. Cambridge, UK: Cambridge University Press, 1999.

Avalon, Arthur, *The Serpent Power*. New York, NY: Dover Publications, Inc., 1958.

Benson, Hugh H., *A Companion to Plato*. West Sussex, UK: Blackwell Publishing Ltd., 2009.

Desikachar, T.K.V., *The Heart of Yoga*. Rochester, VT: Inner Traditions International, 1999.

Emerson, Ralph Waldo, *The Essential Writings of Ralph Waldo Emerson*. New York, NY: Random House, Inc., 2000.

Grimes, Pierre, *Unblocking: Removing Blocks to Understanding*. Costa Mesa, CA: Self-published, 2014.

-----, *Is It All Relative?*. Costa Mesa, CA: Hyparxis Press, 1995.

-----, *The Way of the Logos Volume I: The Demonstration*. Lulu.com, 2011.

-----, *The Way of the Logos Volume II: The Reflection*. Lulu.com, 2011.

Grimes, Pierre, and Regina Uliana, *Philosophical Midwifery: A New Paradigm for Understanding Human Problems with its Validation.* Costa Mesa, CA: Hyparxis Press, 1998.

Grimes, Pierre with Cathy Wilson, *The Pocket Pierre.* Costa Mesa, CA: Self-published, 2012.

Kapleau, Philip, *The Three Pillars of Zen.* New York, NY: Anchor Books, 2000.

Krishna, Gopi, *Living with Kundalini.* Boston, MA: Shambhala Publications, Inc., 1993.

Lindberg, David, *The Beginnings of Western Science.* Chicago, IL: University of Chicago Press, 2007.

Matt, Daniel C., *The Essential Kabbalah: The Heart of Jewish Mysticism.* Edison, NJ: Castle Books, 1997.

Nails, Debra, *The People of Plato: A Prosopography of Plato and Other Socratics.* Indianapolis, IN: Hackett Publishing, 2002.

Spencer, John H, *The Eternal Law.* Vancouver, BC: Param Media Publishing, 2012.

Telushkin, Joseph, Rabbi, *Biblical Literacy.* New York, NY: Harper Collins, 1997.

Uzdavinys, Algis, *Orpheus and the Roots of Platonism.* London: The Matheson Trust, 2011.

Whittaker, Thomas, *The Neoplatonists: A Study in the History of Hellenism.* Cambridge, UK: Cambridge University Press, 1928.

Wilber, Ken (editor), *Quantum Questions.* Boston, MA: Shambhala Publications, Inc. , 2001.

Wright, Didley, *The Eleusinian Mysteries and Rites.* Kessinger Publishing, LLC., 2010.

Yates, Frances, *Giordano Bruno and the Hermetic Tradition.* Oxon, UK: Routledge Classics., 2002.